# FIELD GUIDE

TO

## NEWFOUNDLAND & LABRADOR

THE ISLAND OF NEWFOUNDLAND

### MICHAEL A. J. COLLINS & DEREK H. C. WILTON

# FIELD GUIDE

# TO

## NEWFOUNDLAND & LABRADOR

### THE ISLAND OF NEWFOUNDLAND

MICHAEL A. J. COLLINS
& DEREK H. C. WILTON

BREAKWATER
BOOKS LIMITED
www.breakwaterbooks.com
P O Box 2188 · St. John's · NL · Canada · A1C 6E6

CERTIFIED CANADIAN PUBLISHER

LIBRARY AND ARCHIVES CANADA CATALOGUING IN PUBLICATION
Field guide to Newfoundland & Labrador : the island of Newfoundland/ [compiled and edited by] Michael A. J. Collins & Derek H. C. Wilton.
    Other titles: Field guide to Newfoundland and Labrador
Collins, Michael (Michael A. J.), editor | Wilton, Derek H. C., 1954- editor
    Includes bibliographical references and index.
Canadiana (print) 20250277948 | Canadiana (ebook) 20250277956
ISBN 9781550813562 (softcover) | ISBN 9781778530838 (EPUB)
LCSH: Newfoundland and Labrador—Guidebooks. | LCGFT: Guidebooks.
LCC FC2157 .F54 2026 | DDC 917.1804/5—dc23

PRODUCTION Beth Oberholtzer, Oberholtzer Design Inc.

THE PUBLISHER GRATEFULLY ACKNOWLEDGES THE SUPPORT OF
The Canada Council for the Arts
The Government of Canada through the Department of Heritage, and
The Government of Newfoundland and Labrador through the Department of Tourism, Culture, Arts and Recreation

Canada Council for the Arts    Conseil des Arts du Canada    Canadä    Newfoundland Labrador

PRINTED AND BOUND IN CANADA.

Breakwater Books is commited to choosing papers and materials for our books that help to protect our environment. To this end, this book is made of certified and other controlled material.

MIX
Paper | Supporting responsible forestry
FSC® C103567

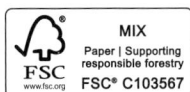

# CONTENTS

**6 INTRODUCTION**
Island of Newfoundland
Habitats
Climate

**48 FUNGI**

**68 LICHENS**

**82 PLANTS**
Mosses and Liverworts
Ferns
Fern Allies
Conifers
Broad-Leaved Trees
Wildflowers

**150 ANIMALS**
Insects
Amphibians
Reptiles
Birds
Terrestrial Mammals

**214 MARINE LIFE**
Marine Plants
Seashore Invertebrates
Marine Vertebrates
 (Phylum Chordata)
Fishes
Marine Mammals

**276 FOSSILS**

**284 ROCKS AND MINERALS**

**310 WINTER**
Tracking Animals
Winter Gulls
Icebergs

**328 NIGHT SKY**

**338 SITES OF NATURAL INTEREST**

**348 APPENDICES**
Acknowledgements
Contributors
Useful References
Photo and Illustration Credits
Index

Welcome to the island of Newfoundland in the North Atlantic Ocean off the east coast of Canada and the piece of continental North America closest to Europe. Kalaallit Nunaat (Greenland) is part of the North American tectonic plate, and is closer to Europe, but it is separated from the rest of North America by the Labrador Sea. Newfoundland, on the other hand, is as close as 15 km from mainland Canada across the Strait of Belle Isle; almost close enough to see on a fine day. Whether you are a resident or a visitor you should find this guide singularly valuable in identifying plants, animals, fungi, rocks, fossils, icebergs, and stellar constellations that you might come across on your travels.

As a province of Canada, Newfoundland and Labrador (405,720 km²) consists of the island of Newfoundland (111,390 km²) and the coast of Labrador (294,330 km²). The population is 545,579 (est. 2025), with ca. 518,924 people living on the island for a population density of ca. 4.66 per km².

Following the Seven Years' War, the British Crown granted the 'Coast of Labrador' to the Newfoundland Governor in 1763 to administer the Newfoundland-based migratory fishery. They reversed their decision in 1774 and granted all of Labrador to Québec. In 1809, they re-granted the 'Coast of Labrador' to Newfoundland, but with a southern boundary along the 52nd parallel north from Blanc Sablon.

Subsequent disputes between Newfoundland and Canada as to the size of the Labrador coast (i.e., was it just a thin coastal strip) and whether the interior belonged to Québec were brought to the British Privy Council for adjudication in the early 20th century. In 1927 the Privy Council announced its decision, proclaiming that the 'Coast of Labrador' belonged to Newfoundland and that it covered the region from the shoreline inland to the Height of Land (i.e., to the continental divide where the headwaters of rivers that flow to the Labrador Sea arise). They kept the southern boundary along the 52nd parallel north of Blanc Sablon to the Romaine River.

After flirting with Confederation since 1869, Newfoundland finally joined Canada in 1949. On December 6, 2001, the province was renamed Newfoundland and Labrador through amendment to the Constitution of Canada at the request of the Government of Newfoundland to recognize the geographic and social duality of the province. This Field Guide only deals with the island of Newfoundland in the Province of Newfoundland and Labrador.

Newfoundland has three airports—located in St. John's, Gander, and Deer Lake—with regularly scheduled flights to the US, Mexico, the Caribbean, and Europe from St. John's and Gander. Marine Atlantic operates ferries between North Sydney, NS, and both Port aux Basques (year-round) and Argentia (seasonal). Labrador Marine operates a ferry service between Blanc Sablon, QC, at the terminus of the Trans Labrador Highway, and St. Barbe on the Great Northern Peninsula; this ferry service can be interrupted in the winter due to ice conditions. The Trans Canada Highway (TCH) runs for 900 km between Port aux Basques and St. John's. Most towns in Newfoundland are connected by road networks to the TCH. There are isolated communities and islands that are serviced by the provincial ferry service.

The island of Newfoundland is, in many ways, a unique place. Here you will find a true natural paradise quite unlike anywhere else in North America. Where else can you observe some of the largest seabird colonies in the world, view majestic icebergs as they travel down from their birthplace in Greenland, and see whales and dolphins close up? Add the sight of a wild caribou herd a two-hour drive from the major urban centre, and moose, the largest member of the deer family, almost anywhere on the island. In winter, the capital, St. John's, hosts a variety of seabirds, many from northern Europe, making it the only place on the North American continent where one can see these birds.

Although many other locales boast fossil beds, the island is one of a few places on the planet where you can see not one, but several horizons with ancient soft-bodied fossils. These fossil beds are exceptional in that they provide a glimpse of what life on the Earth was like at an early stage of evolution when living things were experimenting with a variety of body forms, many of which no longer exist.

Here you can stand on different ancient continents at the same time! Geologists have shown that the island consists of geological environments with three quite different origins. The west coast rocks were originally part of the primordial North American continent (Laurentia), whereas the east coast rocks (Avalonia) were of British Isles and Northwest African origin. The rocks in the centre of the island are exposed ocean floor that separated the North American and Avalonia plates.

Even though the island is relatively southern as regards latitude, it lies at the northern boundary for many southern species. But because it is bathed by the cold waters of the Labrador Current, it is also at the southernmost limit for more northern plants and animals that would not otherwise occur this far south.

Because of the vast expanse of wetlands on the island, it is home to a variety of insectivorous plants (sundews, bladderworts, butterworts, and pitcher plants) and those most sought after of wildflowers, the orchids. Due to its more northerly aspect and limey bedrock, the Great Northern Peninsula hosts ecological reserves protecting a number of rare sub-Arctic plants not found anywhere else in North America.

If you are a lichen or mushroom enthusiast, you should certainly be at home, as it is assumed that there are around one thousand different species of lichen, as well as several thousand different species of fungi, living on the island. As this guide will demonstrate, there is a tremendous amount of nature to view here and keeping oneself occupied should not be a problem!

But in the end, this guide can only provide a glimpse of the species that live here due to the island's staggering biodiversity. For example, there are only around 120 species of fungi and lichens described herein.

Please note that in the fields of biology and botany, names, ranging from species to common, can change with new data and more research. We have attempted to keep up with existing taxonomic nomenclature at the time of publication, but science moves on and there may be some incorrect labels in the immediate work, and there will surely be more in time. There may also be some favourite plants or animals missing from the guide; their absence results from a variety of reasons, for instance, lupins, though widely dispersed across the island are considered 'garden escapes' and thus are not part of the natural landscape (yet!).

This guide has been in preparation for a number of years and almost all of the material herein dates to before 2023. A new generation of researchers has arisen since we embarked on this project and we look forward to their discoveries.

This work is designed to be a field guide that visitors to and residents of the island can use to identify—and hopefully better understand—the current animals and plants and ancient flora and fauna of the island; the incredible bedrock geology beneath it; the stars above it; the sometimes vexatious, but never dull, climate and weather; and finally, the majestic icebergs that visit this magical island that we call home.

We hope that you enjoy the guide, that it meets with your satisfaction, and that you will use it to explore our magnificent outdoors. Hopefully we'll see some of you in the 'field'. Remember Tolkien's words 'All that wander are not lost'—we'd like to think that they are exploring natural Newfoundland.

Michael Collins
Derek Wilton
St. John's, January 2026

## THE ISLAND OF NEWFOUNDLAND

Newfoundland, affectionately referred to as 'The Rock' by residents, is just that, a large island of rock projecting into the North Atlantic Ocean just off the east coast of mainland Canada, bathed by the cold waters of the Labrador Current from the north, and by the warm waters of the Gulf Stream from the south. The island, the sixteenth largest in the world, is, geologically speaking, partly North American, partly North African and British Isles, and partly ancient ocean volcanic in origin. The underlying bedrock, in turn, influences soil development and the plants in different areas.

Between two million and twelve thousand years ago, the island was buried under ice sheets, some over 1 km thick. As the glaciers moved slowly across the island, they carved the landscape, smoothing it and pushing much of the surface sediment into the waters of the North Atlantic. These ice sheets also annihilated plant and animal life on the island. There is, however, evidence that some parts of the island remained ice-free during these ice ages. These ice-free areas would include some higher elevation points (nunataks), such as in the Long Range Mountains, and coastal areas (coastal refugia) where some hardy plants and invertebrates may have survived glaciation of the island.

When the glaciers melted some ten thousand years ago, the island emerged as a lifeless bastion of rock and glacial sediment deposits, devoid of any significant animal or plant life. The retreating glaciers also left behind deep fjords, especially on the west and south coasts,

*Granite boulder in till, East Coast Trail, Port Kirwin*

*Groove carved by glacial meltwater, Brigus South*

an undulating landscape, and boulders (so-called erratics) of various sizes dumped by the melting ice. With landscape emergence, pioneer species began the slow process of recolonization. The melting glaciers left behind fine to coarse gravels, silts in seepages, and alluvial outwash deposits along rivers, streams, and ponds. These areas were colonized by pioneer rooted plants whose seeds were blown in by the wind or deposited by birds. Spore-producing plants (mosses, ferns, fern allies) colonized the plentiful wet/moist substrates.

Along with this natural plant recolonization, animal life returned, beginning probably with insects and spiders, which could fly or float through the air from southerly 'lively' locations. Birds could also have easily visited or recolonized the island from the adjacent mainland, perhaps bringing with them their own contributions to the plant and invertebrate animal populations. Bird visitors would have voided seeds in their droppings—the remains of berries eaten else-where—or dropped seeds, which had clung to their bodies during flight from away. Their feet, too, would have brought with them

*Great Horned Owl*

both seeds and smaller organisms (and/or their eggs) from contact with soil or mud on the mainland.

While the types of birds observed on the island today do not differ that much from those in adjacent parts of the mainland (southern Labrador, Québec north shore, Cape Breton Island) the same cannot be said for freshwater fish, amphibians, reptiles, and mammals. With glaciers melting, the island was separated from the mainland due to sea-level rise. The only animals that migrated from the North American mainland had, therefore, to fly across the sea, swim through the salt ocean, or cross winter sea ice like that which still forms between the island and Labrador. Consequently, the island has no native amphibians nor reptiles, and only fourteen extant native mammal species (as well as the now extinct Newfoundland wolf). The mammals that did manage to cross over from the mainland were bats (flew); beaver, otter, and muskrat (swam); and caribou, wolf, fox, hare, vole, and bear (more recently, coyote) that probably crossed on ice. All native terrestrial mammals are active through winter, so there are no true hibernators (the black bear goes into a deep sleep but can wake up during the winter and become active for short periods of time).

*Red Fox*

Freshwater fish with no tolerance for salt water (e.g., pike, perch, cyprinids) do not exist on the island, so those few fish species that did manage to make the crossing can survive periods of exposure to salt water. These fish include salmon, brook trout, char, sticklebacks, eel, and killifish. Several introduced fish (e.g., rainbow trout, brown trout) can also survive in salt water.

Such an environment with a reduced number of species is typical of offshore islands colonized from adjacent mainland(s). Some Newfoundland species that have been isolated from their mainland counterparts for thousands of years have evolved into separate subspecies (e.g., muskrat, pine marten). Beginning in the late 1800s, several mammal species were also deliberately introduced for economic or other reasons, and some possibly arrived without invitation. Assorted amphibians have also been introduced, with no official approval.

Flying over the province today reveals a topographic panorama that includes dense stands of coniferous forests, sprinkled with smaller stands of deciduous trees, interspersed with large expanses of wetlands of various types, many ponds and rivers, barrens (open, treeless areas), and, of course, bare rock together with lichens. Water, whether in the form of ponds, bogs, or rivers, is a dominant aspect of the terrain. These different areas do not have permanent fixed boundaries as each can undergo changes in environment and vegetation through time. The landscape, therefore, is subject to continuous change and examples of environmental succession are to be seen everywhere.

The climate of the island is predominantly maritime-influenced boreal, with mild winters and short, warm summers, although conditions vary tremendously throughout the island. The most easterly portions, the Avalon and Burin peninsulas, are the mildest, whereas the Great Northern Peninsula is the coldest. The climate of the central and western regions tends to be more extreme than the eastern regions, with longer, warmer summers, and colder, snowier winters. It is no accident that one of Eastern Canada's major ski resorts is in western Newfoundland at Marble Mountain.

The somewhat milder winter conditions in the eastern parts of the island can all too frequently lead to a climatic condition that has serious repercussions for both plant and animal life, as well as

*Coniferous forest in winter*

the human population; so-called 'freezing rain', or as it is known locally, 'glitter'. Such events can last for several days at a time with the accumulated weight of ice being enough to snap off tree branches, topple power lines, and break telephone wires.

Fog is also a common occurrence in coastal areas. The Avalon Peninsula is one of the foggiest areas in Canada.

The average daily wind speed in the St. John's area is over 20 km/hour. Together with freezing rain, this so severely limits the growth of trees such as beech, oak, cedar, and sugar maple, that they are absent from the island, other than as introduced examples in some communities. Wind strength is also a major factor in coastal areas and in elevated exposed locations, stunting tree growth and leading to a situation in which there are large expanses of dwarf trees (mostly spruce and balsam fir) known locally as 'tuckamore'.

Newfoundland soils are very shallow, highly acidic, and generally poor in nutrients, particularly nitrogen and phosphorus, all of which cause poor tree growth. Tree height rarely exceeds 10 m on the more exposed peninsulas, and 20 m in the interior. Several local species are well adapted to such environments, especially insectivorous plants, such as the pitcher plant, which have evolved a wide range of solutions for living in nutrient-poor environments. Many plants have symbiotic associations with fungi (mycorrhizas) that break down organic material in soil and transfer the inorganic minerals into plant roots. Several mushrooms that one can encounter in the forests are the above-ground varieties of these mycorrhizas.

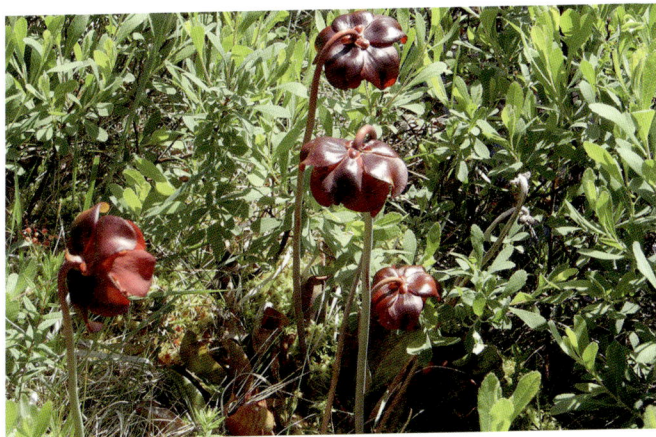

*Pitcher Plants, the provincial flower, Coastal Ridge Trail, Salvage*

# HABITATS

## ■ COASTAL AND OFFSHORE WATERS

The coastline of Newfoundland is over 4000 km long, indented by innumerable bays and inlets. Much of this coastline features sheer rocky cliffs with little underlying seashore. Although unsuitable for most forms of life, these vertical surfaces are ideal nesting sites for seabirds. The more precarious the foothold, it seems, the more likely it will harbour colonies of seabirds. The island and its smaller offshore satellite islands are home to a great variety of marine bird life, and some of the colonies are among the largest in the world. Auks, murres, gannets, gulls, and puffins, among others, number in the hundreds of thousands. Their nesting sites are not only ideal due to proximity to good fishing areas, but are also safe from land predators, as well as predatory seabirds.

One of the most fascinating offshore islands is Funk Island off the northeast coast. A visit today would reveal thousands of nesting gannets and murres, but the most interesting aspect of Funk Island is from the past rather than the present. Up until the early 1800s, Funk Island was home to the great auk, a large black and white, flightless bird, which became extinct in 1844 off Iceland. These large birds, the original 'penguins', were easy to capture and herd onto boats as supplies of fresh meat for Europeans on their way to North America after weeks at sea. (The now familiar Southern Hemisphere penguins were named after the great auk, which was very familiar to northern mariners). Subsequent 'harvesters' boiled their bodies down to render oil for use in lamps, and their feathers were used to adorn European clothing. Their large eggs were also highly prized as delicacies. The continual harvesting of these birds and eggs soon ensured that they would suffer the same fate as the dodo and passenger pigeon, and by the early 1800s, what had been the site of the largest great auk colonies in the world became a graveyard for yet another species over-exploited by greedy humans.

The waters around Newfoundland host dozens of fish species, as well as whales, dolphins, and porpoises during the summer months. While most can only be seen from a boat, some of the larger whales, particularly humpbacks, feed close enough to shore that a pair of binoculars is all that is necessary for a good view. Pods of small pilot

*Codroy coastal (sea stacks)*

whales can also be viewed close inshore, whereas the larger minkes and fin whales can be observed not too far offshore. A ride on one of the island's ferries is a good way to observe whales and their smaller relatives, the dolphins and porpoises. On occasion, it is even possible to spot the great carnivore of the seas, the killer whale or orca.

A more exciting way of coming closer to these giants of the deep is to take a ride on a local whale tour boat, with the hope of not just seeing whales, but perhaps the spectacular sight of a breaching humpback. It seems that whales enjoy putting on a display for the tour boats! Whale watching is not just restricted to the summer, as many whales stay in Newfoundland waters during the whole year. Several seal species also call these waters home. Grey seals and harbour seals are readily visible in the summer. In the winter, if ice conditions allow, it can be possible to view hundreds of harp seals giving birth to their young on the ice pans.

### ■ THE SEASHORE

Most of the shoreline around the island is rocky, so most common seashore residents are the same as those in similar seashores of northern Europe. The tidal range is relatively small (ca. 1 m) around most of the island, so a well-developed shore zonation isn't present as in say, southern England or northern France. Even with a small tidal variation, however, it is possible to distinguish definite zones on the shore.

The splash zone above the high-water mark is a harsh dry environment, home only to microscopic algae clinging to the rocks and hundreds of small rough periwinkles that feed on the algae. The upper shore zone, which is only covered by water around high tide, is characterized by fronds of bladder wrack relying on their air bladders to keep vertical when covered at high tide. The other prominent animal in this zone is the common barnacle permanently attached to the rocks, filter feeding in the tide water.

In the mid-shore zone, bladder wrack yields to the distinctive knotted wrack. Three types of periwinkles can be found here, with the common, or edible, being the most abundant and largest. Dense colonies of small, edible blue mussels grow here as well, anchored to the rocks by their byssal threads, together with the predatory dogwhelks that feed on them. The whelks usually have greyish shells, but they can also be brown, orange, or yellow, depending on their food.

Organisms become much more numerous moving into the lower shore zone, where the flat leaf-like winged kelp (*Alaria esculenta*) shows. The smaller brown bootlace seaweed (*Chorda filum*) also occurs here. Several green algae live in this area, including slimy green sheets of sea lettuce, *Ulva lactuca*, the hollow intestine-like *Ulva intestinalis*, and the tufted *Cladophora rupestris*. Red algae appear in large numbers here as well, including Irish moss, *Chondrus crispus*. An unusual red seaweed, the hard chalky coralline weed, *Corallina officinalis*, also inhabits this area.

*Blue Mussels*

*Rocky shore of Burnt Cape*

There is a wide inventory of animal life present in this zone as well. Common periwinkles graze on algae, and dogwhelks feed on blue mussels. Other molluscs include little chink shells and the unusual coat-of-mail-shelled chiton. The exquisitely patterned tortoiseshell limpets are also common in this area firmly clamped to the rocks. The beautiful, but deadly to planktonic animals, sea anemones are typically present in rock pools, and locally on unsubmerged rocks as shapeless blobs of jelly, quite different from the imposing flower-like shapes they assume when fully immersed in water. The dahlia anemone may also be present here. Several types of echinoderms populate this zone as well, the most numerous being the green sea urchins that browse on seaweed. The Northern sea star or minute daisy brittle star may also become stranded by the retreating tide.

The sub-littoral zone, below the low-water mark, is hidden from shore observers for the most part, and unless one is a diver, its plants and animals can only be glimpsed from a distance. The dominant seaweed is the winged kelp (*Alaria esculenta*), although in more exposed locations it is replaced by the aptly named colander weed (*Agarum clathratum*). Rock surfaces in this zone are pink as if covered by lichens, but in reality, the colour is due to the coral-like encrusting seaweeds *Lithothamnion glaciale* and *Corallina officinalis*.

Sea urchins (locally known as 'whore's eggs') are common in this zone, which is also home to the American lobster and rock crabs. A variety of fish may also swim through these shallow waters, including the slippery, eel-like butterfish or rock gunnel, cunners, and the ugly-looking, large-headed longhorn sculpin.

Although rocky shores predominate around the island, shingle (or stony) beaches are also common, particularly in bays and coves. Shingle beaches are not good environments for animals or plants as the continuous wave movement of pebbles militates against them becoming anchored. These beaches, however, become the focus of attention in mid-June to July when thousands of small fish called capelin throw themselves onto the stones at high tides to lay their eggs. This is a time for local people to gather the fish for food, or fertilizer, without having to use nets or fishing rods. Many larger fish, as well as marine mammals and seabirds, use this opportunity to feed on the capelin.

Sandy shores, while not as common as rocky and shingly ones, are present in a number of places, most notably on the west side of the Great Northern Peninsula. At first glance sandy shores look relatively lifeless, other than for eel grass in shallow water, but this is only because many of the animals spend much of their time buried in the sand when the tide is out. A common resident on this type of shore is the sand dollar, a flattened version of the sea urchin. Its flat shape is well adapted for burrowing through sand. Several molluscs also inhabit the sand, including the razor clam. Moon snails typically reveal their presence by furrows left in the sand when moving along the surface. Many of these sandy locations are relatively unvisited and offer the traveller the chance of uninterrupted rest and sunbathing, and if hardy enough, swimming.

*Cobble seashore*

### ■ FORESTS

Newfoundland forests are typical boreal forests, composed predominantly of coniferous trees with intermixed deciduous trees. Since Newfoundland is part of the circumpolar taiga biome, also termed the 'spruce-moose biome' because of its dominant tree and associated major mammal, the forests are clad in their needles all year round.

The principal trees of the modern-day Newfoundland forest are balsam fir and black spruce, the mainstays of the pulp and paper, and lumber industries. This state of affairs, however, has not always been the case. The provincial anthem *Ode to Newfoundland* contains the phrase 'pine-clad hills', and there is strong evidence that in past centuries the truly majestic white pine was a dominant tree in the island's forests. Alas, the once majestic pine stands are reduced to a few scattered remnants of their former glory, mostly due to overexploitation for lumber, particularly in boat building, and the depredations of the pine blister rust disease. A second native pine, the red pine, is a rarity on the island being better adapted to sandy soils; one protected stand near Gambo is right next to the TCH and is a welcome change from the usual fir-spruce forests.

Balsam fir is nonetheless one of our favourite trees, with its attractive shape, aromatic needles, and upright cones that lose their scales and become transformed into 'fir candles,' the central cone stalk devoid of scales. The balsam fir is the most selected (natural) Christmas tree on the island.

Black spruce, the second most common tree, is not as attractive a tree to some but thrives much better in wetter areas than does the fir. It is the dominant tree in boggy regions and in areas that have undergone succession from filled-in bogs. White spruce, a close relative, is better adapted to drier, well-drained locations such as hillsides.

*Red Pine, Gambo*

*Forests, Howley*

Tamarack, 'juniper' in local vernacular or larch as it is usually called in Europe, is better adapted to damp locations like black spruce and can be found in fairly dense stands. Unlike the other conifers, tamarack/juniper is deciduous, losing its needles in autumn. The goldish-yellow needles in the fall provide a marvelous splash of colour in areas typically dominated by the dark green needles of fir and spruce.

Several types of deciduous trees, or hardwoods, occur in the forests, particularly white birch and trembling aspen, both of which are part of the succession from bog prior to the final stage, the balsam fir/black spruce forest. Aspen and birch are widely distributed throughout the island with some large stands of white birch in the central and western regions of the island. Other deciduous trees associated with forested areas, particularly where the canopy is somewhat open, include the American and showy mountain ashes (locally called 'dogberry'); close relatives of the European mountain ash (or rowan tree), which is also found on the island, having been introduced by early settlers. Mountain maple, pincherry, and chokecherry also grow on the island. Red maple and balsam poplar are present in some parts of the island. Assorted shrubs grow in more open areas of the forests, including mountain serviceberry and sheep laurel.

Coniferous forests are dark, damp places with too little light penetration down to the forest floor to allow for much of a herb-shrub understory. Nonetheless, there is enough light to support carpets of moss, together with several ferns and even flowering plants, and large numbers of young balsam fir seedlings awaiting the chance to take over in areas when an opening in the tree canopy appears. In spring, the forest floor bursts forth in flowers with goldthread, starflower, bunchberry, and wild lily of the valley very much in evidence. In the darker areas, the yellow, bell-shaped flowers of the corn lily show through. In less shaded locations, flowers of the pink lady's slipper, an orchid, brighten up the forest floor.

By early summer the forest floor's carpet of flowers has gone, except for the bunchberries, which will continue for some time. Later summer flowers include the single wax-like flowers of the diminutive one-flowered wintergreen; they are, however, small and difficult to find. In late summer and early fall, the fungal-like ghost pipe appears. This strange plant, completely devoid of chlorophyll, is a semi-parasite on the roots of mushrooms.

In late summer and early fall a variety of mushrooms, the above-ground reproductive structures of fungal threads in the soil, make their appearance, enriching the forest floor in a bewildering variety of colours not usually present in this dark environment. At about the same time, the forest floor seems to turn red in many places as the edible red berries of the bunchberry abound. These humid, shady forests are ideal habitats for a

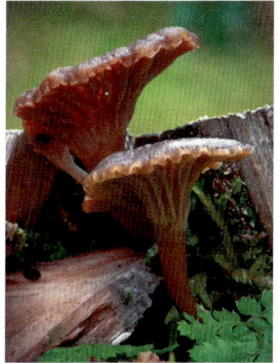

*Yellow Legs*

variety of lichens growing not only on the ground but also covering the trunks and branches of the trees. Bottlebrush shield lichen grows on tree trunks and branches, while the aptly named old man's beard hangs down from tree branches.

A variety of mammals live in these forests, though many are not restricted to the forests as they will move out into more open areas in the search for food. Among the herbivores are the majestic moose, the largest member of the deer family, the well-named snowshoe hare, and the red squirrel, the latter spending much of its time up in the trees (moose, hare, and squirrel are all introduced species). Black bear and red fox are both omnivorous, their food includes small mammals, birds, eggs, and berries. Carnivores include the wary Canada lynx, in search of its favourite prey, the snowshoe hare, ermine (or short-tailed weasel), and the diminutive, masked shrew (introduced), which

*(left) Downy Woodpecker; (right) Snowshoe Hare*

subsists on insects and other small invertebrates. Old growth forests, of which few now remain, also harbour the now rare, but recovering, pine marten.

Birds abound in these forests, with a number of owls as the main predators. The prolific cones in the boreal forest provide food sources for a variety of birds such as red crossbill, pine and evening grosbeaks, and purple finch. Other seed eaters include dark-eyed juncos, black-capped and boreal chickadees, blue and grey jays, and fox sparrows. Most of these birds are also winter residents, unlike the white-crowned and white-throated sparrows, which only reside here in summer. A number of insect eaters are common in the forests, including the Northern flicker and downy woodpecker. An older tree denuded of bark is a sure sign that one of these birds has been at work pecking off the bark in search of insect larvae.

One of the largest avian residents of the boreal forest is the ruffed grouse, which spends more time foraging on the ground than the related spruce grouse, which spends most of its time in the trees. Both of these species, although now common, were introduced to the island.

### ■ WETLANDS (BOGS, FENS, AND MARSHES)

There are various types of wetlands including marshes, fens, and bogs. The most common wetlands being bogs. Fens—wetlands where peat accumulates—are common, but there are only a few true marshes. Bogs are acidic environments where there is a surplus of precipitation over evaporation and no flowing water. Bogs cover almost one-fifth of the island's land surface.

For the nature lover, bogs are beautiful places filled with many fascinating plants. The dominant ones are the various bog mosses (*Sphagnum* species) of which there are some twenty types in Newfoundland. Each species is adapted to the specific conditions that exist in different parts of the bog. Some species live in the lower, wetter parts of the bog whilst others prefer the drier, raised hummocks. Bog mosses can absorb large amounts of water into their large, spongy

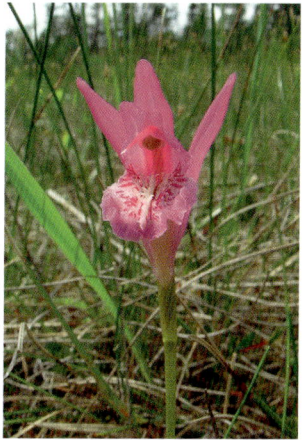
*Dragon's Mouth Orchid*

cells. In earlier times dried moss was used as packing material, an early version of polystyrene!

Mosses are the first flora colonizers in bogs but are quickly followed by a variety of shrubs including leatherleaf (the first to flower in the spring), sweet gale, Labrador tea, bog rosemary, and bog laurel, all early in the growing season.

Many bog plants supplement their nutrient intake in their nutrient-poor habitat by capturing insects and consuming (extracting nutrients from) their bodies. The most obvious insectivorous plant in bogs is the pitcher plant, Newfoundland and Labrador's provincial flower. This plant has large, hollow, pitcher-like leaves that contain water in which trapped insects are digested. It seems that the pitcher plant leaves can attract insects into the lip of the leaf. Here they suck up secretions from the leaf, which apparently narcotize the insects, leading them to fall into the digestive liquid at the bottom of the pitcher. Whilst the digestive soup spells the death knell for most insects, there are some insects that call the pitcher home for at least part of their life cycle, including some gnats and mosquitoes.

At the other end of the size scale are the various sundews, which are beautiful but deadly to insects. Sundews possess leaves covered with stalked glands which secrete a sugary solution to attract insects. This secretion acts like flypaper, trapping any unfortunate insect that alights on the leaf. The leaf then rolls up around the prey and digestive juices dissolve most of the insect's tissues with the released nutrients absorbed by the leaf. Digestion complete, the

*Coastal bog, Parsons Pond; (inset) Sweet Gale*

leaf unrolls to reveal a dead insect carcass and is now ready for its next 'meal'.

A third type of insectivorous bog plants are the various bladderworts, found in bog pools, which employ yet another method of capturing 'prey'. Bladderworts live in standing water, their stems and leaves immersed in the water. The stems are equipped with vacuum-filled bladders. When a small aquatic organism bumps into a bladder, a sensitive hair is stimulated, and the bladder door opens, sucking in the prey. The trap door closes and the prey is ingested. Being an insect in a bog is not all fun and games, it can be deadly!

Besides the various types of flowering shrubs, bogs are also home to a variety of flowering herbs. Early in the spring the dark blue petals of marsh blue violet are easily observed. In midsummer, large wild (or blue flag) iris flowers, atop their tall stems with sword-shaped leaves, add a splash of colour to the bogs, followed in late summer by the violet bog asters and yellow bog goldenrod.

The most attractive residents of bogs, though, are the orchids with their intricate and bizarre flower shapes in just about every shade of the rainbow. Among the more beautiful are grasspink (*Calopogon tuberosus*) and dragon's mouth (*Arethusa bulbosa*). A number of white orchids also occur, including white fringed orchid, bog candles, and the very tall, hooded ladies'-tresses, a fall flowering orchid.

A visit to a bog in summer quickly reveals the main inhabitants, biting insects of all kinds, including black flies and mosquitoes! While the bakeapple (which looks like an orange raspberry) is a delicacy of boglands, picking them can come at a considerable cost in lost blood! The insectivorous plants have no shortage of flying food that they share with green frogs (introduced), which are common in bogs. Bog ponds are also home to several birds including waders like the greater yellowlegs, and breeding ducks like black ducks and mallards.

Fens are usually smaller than bogs, typically occurring in poorly drained areas next to lakes or larger streams. They may also appear as small areas within forests. They receive nutrients from surrounding higher ground and so can support more plant life. Fens often resemble meadows since different types of grasses and sedges are the dominant types of vegetation. Trees are typically absent from fens, but dwarf shrubs may be present.

Marshes are rare on the island. They are the most nutrient-rich types of wetlands. They can be fen-like in appearance and are subject to seasonal flooding. They generally occur near the mouths of larger rivers and streams. Trees, including larch (tamarack/juniper) and black spruce, can grow in fens, as well as white birch and red maple.

*Fen ponds near Corner Brook*

*Bullrush marsh*

## ■ BARRENS AND TUNDRA

When fire has destroyed a forest, a process of ecological succession takes place, and gradually, over many years, a new forest is generated over the burnt area. Sometimes, however, climatic, or other, factors intervene to prevent the growth of a new forest. There are large areas in Newfoundland where forests destroyed by decades-old fires have not regenerated, becoming what are locally called 'barrens', sometimes 'blueberry barrens' because of the blueberry shrubs that fill these areas. In regions where the blueberry industry is important, prescribed fires are deliberately set to prevent forest regeneration.

The term 'barrens' tends to suggest bleak, lifeless places, when in fact, nothing could be further from the truth. In summer they are awash in colour from flowers, and in fall, they produce a wide variety of berries, of which the blueberry is undoubtedly the king. An assortment of shrubs can quickly take over barrens, including blueberry and sheep laurel, as well as the smaller partridgeberry (the cranberry of mainland North America) and dwarf juniper. Sheep laurel is an evergreen shrub that typically chokes out other plant life, quickly becoming the dominant ground cover. In between these shrubs, several tall shrubs and trees can be present, including alders, white birch, and mountain ashes.

A variety of lichens grow in more open areas, including the colourful British soldiers lichen, named for the colours of the old

*Barrens*

British military uniforms, and various types of caribou (or reindeer) lichen, light greyish clumps that can cover wide expanses in open, exposed areas. As their name suggests, they constitute a main food source for native caribou, particularly in winter. The barrens also contain several types of clubmoss, which are not actually mosses but distant relatives of ferns.

During late summer, pink flowers of sheep laurel come into prominence, followed by the magentas or purples of the tall herbaceous fireweed, the latter usually surviving well into fall. A large stand of fireweed, so typical of freshly burnt areas, is a sight to behold. The showy mass of colour that is fireweed lasts until the flowers fade to be replaced by thousands of seeds with long feathery parachutes that are borne aloft on the slightest breeze to colonize other open areas. Other late summer flowers include the light violet rough aster and the yellow-flowered bog goldenrod.

With the early fall, the explosion of ripe blue-black blueberries and dark red partridgeberries is the signal for hundreds of berry-pickers to embark on yet another harvest, turning the berries into jams, pies, and wines! Many animals, including red fox and black bear will also feast on the berries when they become available.

While few animals make a permanent home in the barrens, caribou more than any other are closely identified with this habitat. The ever-present reindeer (or caribou) lichens are a major food source for the

*Caribou*

caribou, particularly in winter when they scrape snow away with their hooves in search of this staple. Since caribou are herd animals and need large tracts of land for their survival, they are not uniformly scattered across the island but inhabit barren lands such as the Buchans Plateau, Long Range Mountains, and the Avalon Wilderness Reserve. This latter area, just south of St. John's, is home to several thousand animals. During the summer the Avalon herd migrates from inland wintering areas towards the coast in search of food; on their journey they can be encountered in the thousands. The Avalon herd exists within a short motoring distance from St. John's in a place where they seem unconcerned with cars or humans; a most unusual juxtaposition in our modern world.

Few other animals can be as readily linked to the barrens as caribou, although some spend most of their time there, including the willow ptarmigan. This northern creature prefers more open terrain, feeding on the low shrubs. Ptarmigans are well adapted to winter life when the dappled grey plumage of summer changes to white, such that the birds are well camouflaged from potential predators. Feathers grow around the talons, increasing the foot surface to act as snowshoes, and feathers also grow over the legs, acting almost like long johns.

Meadow voles inhabit these areas, feeding on the blueberry bushes, particularly during winter. Moose will also move through the barrens in search of food sources.

*Willow Ptarmigan*

## ■ LIMESTONE BARRENS

Along the western coastal fringe of the Great Northern Peninsula, the underlying bedrock is mainly limestone, hence the soil there is more alkaline with a higher calcium content than bedrock beneath other types of Newfoundland barrens. Consequently, the limestone barrens have a different flora, comprising plants not found elsewhere on the island including Arctic-alpine plants, mostly herbs.

## ■ SERPENTINE BARRENS

The west coast of the island is also home to an unusual type of barren, the so-called serpentine barren. This type of barren is extremely rare worldwide, but Newfoundland has three: the Blomidon Mountains, the Tablelands, and the White Hills (near St. Anthony). The rather unusual bedrock in these areas is serpentinite (see Rocks and Minerals), which originated in the Earth's Mantle. The soil derived from this bedrock has low calcium contents, but elevated magnesium and heavy metal concentrations, such as cobalt and nickel. These metals are extremely toxic to most plants, thus the serpentine barrens can appear to be even more 'barren' than other types of barren. There is, however, a surprising variety of plants that grow in these barrens including Lapland rosebay, shrubby cinquefoil, tamarack, as well as common juniper.

*Serpentine barren, Tablelands, Gros Morne National Park*

## ■ TUNDRA

Tundra resembles barrens, particularly limestone ones, but true tundra is only found above the tree line. One usually associates tundra with more northerly locations (e.g., northern Labrador) but so-called 'altitudinal tundra' is present at higher locations on the west coast of the island and on the tops of higher hills in the Long Range and Annieopsquotch Mountains. The tundra supports plants usually found much further north.

## ■ STREAMS, RIVERS, PONDS, AND LAKES

Water is a fact of life in Newfoundland. Wherever you look you can usually see water in lakes, ponds, streams, and/or rivers. Even the provincial capital is blessed with three separate river systems running through it, and five large ponds (or lakes). Ponds and lakes, rivers and streams are all interconnected, with ponds feeding streams and streams running into ponds. Many of the island's river systems are punctuated by ponds of various sizes, which are mostly the result of glacial erosion. Most of the rivers here are relatively short in total length, but with relatively steep inclines, rapids, and waterfalls, and they are typically very fast flowing. These fast-flowing waters with rocky or stony bottoms are cold but well oxygenated, and thus are good environments for trout and juvenile salmon as well as eel and sticklebacks, but are not good for the anchorage of tall plants.

Ponds and lakes dot the landscape, mostly with rocky margins and coniferous forests coming down to the edge, or boglands encroaching on their margins. Typically, the pond margin is an almost impenetrable jungle of low-growing shrubs, including plants such as alders, sweet gale, Labrador tea, and sheep laurel. In more sheltered, shallower locations, the pond may have emergent vegetation such as pond lilies and cattails. Most freshwater and brackish ponds harbour unseen submerged plants such as strange, primitive algae known as charophytes or stoneworts.

*Sheep Laurel*

*Humber River*

Generally, the bodies of water are relatively poor in nutrients ('oligotrophic') and do not support a large or diverse fauna and flora. The predominant fish are brook (mud) trout, and a type of landlocked Atlantic salmon (called 'ouananiche' locally), which spends its whole life cycle in a lake or pond rather than going to sea as Atlantic salmon do. The various salmonids feed on a diversity of bottom-dwelling invertebrates, smaller fish (especially sticklebacks, locally called pricklies), and flying insects, which alight on the water surface. Eels are also common in the waters on the island.

The trout population supports several primarily fish-eating carnivores, including river otter and mink (introduced), as well as the osprey, which is commonly seen throughout the island during the summer months. Watching these beautiful birds of prey hover over water before plunging down and re-emerging with a trout in their talons is an unforgettable sight! Visible even in ponds located in the middle of the capital city, St. John's.

Along the shores of many ponds, beavers and muskrat can be observed, especially at dawn and dusk. While it is not always possible to see beavers themselves, their dams and lodges are common sights throughout the island. The muskrat is also widespread, living in rush-homes, resembling beaver lodges, or on riverbanks.

A variety of waterfowl live on the ponds during the summer, with most migrating south off the island with the onset of winter. Black ducks, mallards, pintails, wigeons, loons, and Canada geese are common residents of ponds. Various sandpipers and yellowlegs are commonly seen on the shores of ponds and lakes.

*American Wigeon*

## CLIMATE

Climate is defined as the average long-term weather patterns prevailing in a region. In Atlantic Canada the ocean's influence on climate is a governing fact of life, to the extent that almost every community in Newfoundland and Labrador has a variety of sayings to express the concept of changeable weather and climate, many of which can occasionally puzzle outsiders.

Prevailing wind directions vary locally and, combined with ocean currents and local topographical effects, can produce somewhat different subclimates in adjacent areas. Regionally, mid-boreal climates prevail throughout southern Newfoundland. Northern boreal, or taiga, climates mark the Great Northern Peninsula.

The Cape Shore, along the east coast of Placentia Bay on the Avalon Peninsula, is an example of a mid-boreal climate in an exposed area. The Cape Shore is marked by relatively short, cool, and wet summers, moderately mild, wet winters (January to March), long springs, and relatively short autumns. Daily mean temperatures in Placentia are approximately -3°C in January and 17°C in July. Mean annual precipitation varies between ca. 1100 mm and 1600 mm. In coastal areas, snow represents approximately 15–25% of the precipitation. Freezing drizzle is common, with an average of 35 hours per year. Easterly and southwesterly winds alternate during the summer, and southwesterlies dominate during the winter. Fog days, with at least 1 hour of fog, average 206 per year, with a total annual sunshine of approximately 1500 hours, one of the lowest totals in Canada.

Areas that are less exposed to onshore breezes, such as Terra Nova National Park, and the communities of Gander and Grand Falls-Windsor, have mid-boreal climates marked by colder winters and warmer summers. Terra Nova has an average of 65 summer days. The frost-free period varies from 140 days over inland areas below 200 m above sea level (asl) to less than 115 days in low-lying coastal areas. Inland areas receive less precipitation (~1150 mm at Terra Nova National Park headquarters) and more snow (~300 cm). September is the rainiest month. Coastal areas receive up to 100 hours of freezing rain each year. Thunderstorms are slightly more common than on the Avalon Peninsula with an average of five per year. Snow cover persists for approximately 140 days in forested areas and for less than 100 days at exposed coastal sites. Winds are variable, blowing from all points of the compass, although west, southwest, and south winds are somewhat more common. Calm periods only account for approximately 15% of the daylight hours.

Gros Morne National Park lies near the 'fuzzy' boundary between the mid-boreal and northern boreal climate zones. At Rocky Harbour, daily mean temperatures are -9°C (February) and 15°C (July); temperatures are 2–4°C colder at higher altitudes. Mean annual precipitation on the coastal plain is 1500 mm, of which 400–450 cm falls as snow. At altitudes greater than 400 m asl, snow represents up to 70% of total precipitation, with amounts of more than 1000 cm. The mean annual duration of snow cover is 160 days in forested regions and up to 190 days in areas higher than 400 m asl. On north-facing, sheltered slopes, such as those of the northern margin of the Tablelands along the road to Trout River, snowpacks may persist until mid-July but no permanent snowpacks or glaciers exist. Isolated areas of discontinuous permafrost, representing less than 5% of the park region, occur at elevations above 500 m asl on north-facing slopes.

The combination of relatively elevated summer precipitation, relatively cool temperatures, and coastal fog limit the number of suitable sightseeing days in Gros Morne. In fact, during the summer, a succession of three consecutive days without any precipitation is rare. The prevailing winds are from the south-southwest and have a significant influence on climate and vegetation distribution. Storm winds associated with hurricanes influence both coastal erosion and vegetation.

## STORMS

The Province of Newfoundland and Labrador is noted for stormy weather. Along with true hurricanes (tropical cyclones from the Caribbean), many of the most damaging summer and early autumn events result from the interaction of northeastward-tracking hurricanes, or tropical storms, with mid-latitude storms approaching from the west, or low-pressure systems. These 'extratropical transitions' can rapidly change direction and velocity, bringing heavy rainfall.

Because of variations in hurricane track patterns and the variable interactions that form extratropical transitions, the number of summer and early autumn storms in Newfoundland is not directly linked to the total number of hurricanes that occur over the southwestern North Atlantic or Caribbean Sea in any particular year. Overall tropical storm frequency in the North Atlantic also cannot be correlated with temperature variations in Atlantic Canada.

These 'extratropical transitions' (e.g., Igor, which struck eastern Newfoundland in September 2010), can rapidly change direction and velocity, bringing heavy rainfall. Significant events between 2010 and 2024 include Igor (2010), Ophelia (2011), Leslie (2012), Matthew (2016), Dorian (2019), Larry (2021), and Fiona (2022). Igor caused at least $120 million in direct damage to eastern Newfoundland in September 2010 and took one human life. Fiona was the most intense post-tropical cyclone ever recorded to have landed in Canada, causing insured losses of > $7 million and provincial government costs of > $40 million in Newfoundland. The storm destroyed or damaged over 100 homes in the Port aux Basques region and took one human life.

Southwesterly and westerly winds associated with late autumn and early winter storms also have significant impacts on the coastlines of southern Newfoundland, leaving them typically entirely ice-free until at least February. During some years, these coastlines may remain ice-free throughout the winter. Coastlines along the Gulf of St. Lawrence and in northeastern Newfoundland generally are affected by offshore ice in winter.

Northeasterly storms are the most effective agents of erosion and property destruction in communities from St. Anthony to Cape Race that face the open Atlantic Ocean. A severe northeasterly storm surge struck the village of La Manche in January 1966, completely destroying all flakes and fishing infrastructure, all boats, the suspension bridge across the harbour, and most of the buildings, leaving only foundations; fortunately, there were no human casualties. Following this event, residents abandoned the community. The East Coast Trail passes through this abandoned community along a re-built suspension bridge. The same event caused destruction in all communities from Cappahayden north to the Battery (St. John's).

Winter storms can also be quite fierce. In November 2018, a winter storm was so intense that its wind-induced high waves crashing on the shoreline set off seismographs: it was termed the 'most intense storm' on the planet at that particular time. On January 17, 2020, a mega winter storm dropped over 90 cm of snow on ground already covered with approximately 100 cm in eastern Newfoundland. The storm was accompanied by hurricane-force winds of up to 130 km/hr and caused an eight-day state of emergency in St. John's. This highly disruptive storm was tagged 'Snowmaggedon' and to some was a harbinger of the COVID-19 pandemic declared two months later.

## SEA ICE

Sea ice, ubiquitous along the entire Labrador coast, extends southward to Cape Bonavista most years. Sea ice gradually recedes throughout the late spring, generally leaving Pistolet Bay (northern tip of Great Northern Peninsula) and the southern Strait of Belle Isle by May.

Ice extent in the Gulf of St. Lawrence and along the northeast coast of Newfoundland is influenced by climate. Warmer conditions in the southern Gulf of St. Lawrence result in part from strong southwesterly winds and lead to restricted ice cover. Southwesterly winds tend to push sea ice northeastwards along the Great Northern Peninsula, however, producing persistent ice cover north of St. Barbe, even during recent years when ice cover has been restricted or non-existent south of St. Paul's. Northerly and northeasterly winds tend to drive sea ice onshore, contributing to both the formation of ice-shove ridges and the development of pack ice along the northeast coast.

Icebergs are present throughout the year in the open Labrador Sea and drift southward along the coast (depending on the fluctuations of the Labrador Current) during the summer. All of the icebergs are produced by calving along the margins of Baffin Bay and Davis Strait, and predominantly from Greenland. An iceberg 40 m high above the water line and 100 m long (approximate volume 2,000,000 $m^3$ with a mass of approximately 10 million tonnes) will completely melt (ablate) in 24 days in 2°C water and requires only 15 days in 4°C water. Such large icebergs make up approximately 5–6% of the iceberg population at the mouth of the Strait of Belle Isle. Smaller fragments ('growlers') increase in proportion southwards as the larger icebergs disintegrate, but an average 'growler' will endure for less than 5 days in 4°C water.

Less than 10% of the icebergs that enter Labrador waters off-shore of Cape Chidley succeed in running the gauntlet to 52°N. The icebergs that reach the northeast Newfoundland coastline, thus, are rare survivors. The major factor controlling their number is the initial supply of calved ice from the glaciers in Greenland. Because a single calved chunk can break up into thousands of icebergs, increases or decreases in iceberg numbers off Twillingate or Bonavista are not directly related to changes in climate or glacial activity in Greenland.

### GLACIATION (THE ANCIENT CLIMATE)

Glacial ice covered almost all of Newfoundland and Labrador during the Quaternary Period (the past 2.6 million years of Earth history), excepting the highest mountain peaks. Glacial characteristics include both erosional features, ranging from conspicuous U-shaped valleys to millimetre-deep striations, and depositional features, defined by tremendous volumes of till. Newfoundland was glaciated several times during the Quaternary.

The most recent glaciation occurred between 20,000 and 10,000 years ago. The onset of Quaternary glaciation resulted in the formation of glaciers ranging in size from individual cirques confined to a single mountain to continent-wide complexes. One of the major Laurentide (North American) ice sheets developed over western Labrador, centred over the modern-day site of Labrador City. Although the glacial flow patterns and accumulation areas within the Laurentide

*Glacial straie (scratches) defining ice movement direction, Heart's Delight*

ice sheet changed considerably throughout its lifespan, western Labrador remained one of the centres of accumulation throughout the Quaternary glacial phases.

Newfoundland supported its own ice caps, independent of the Laurentide glaciation. Labrador ice expanded southwards across the Strait of Belle Isle but was prevented from extending south of St. Barbe and Englee on the island due to the presence of these Newfoundland-based glaciers. Thus, although rocks transported from Labrador can be found in glacial deposits from St. Louis, Cincinnati, New York City, Boston, and Prince Edward Island, no glacially transported rocks from Labrador occur on the island of Newfoundland south of the northern tip of the Great Northern Peninsula. Labrador ice coalesced with ice from Newfoundland in the Gulf of St. Lawrence.

Independent glaciers developed in several centres on the island of Newfoundland. Meanwhile the floors of the Gulf of St. Lawrence, Placentia Bay, and the Grand Banks were exposed because of lowered sea level, a direct result from much of Earth's water being incorporated in the large glaciers. During the glaciation maximum, sea level in the Gulf of St. Lawrence and the Grand Banks was as much as 100 m below the present position.

In Newfoundland, several independent glacial centres developed over the Avalon Peninsula, in central Newfoundland, the Great Northern Peninsula, and the Annieopsquotch Mountains. Ice from these centres expanded and coalesced to cover all the island, extended into the Gulf of St. Lawrence to merge with glaciers from the Maritimes and the Québec North Shore, and reached 50 km offshore in the Atlantic Ocean.

Deglaciation began approximately 15,000 years ago, and most coastal areas were free of ice by 12,000 years ago. Although remnant glaciers persisted through the Younger Dryas cold event (12,900–11,700 years ago), they did not re-advance, and final melting (ablation) of all the glaciers on the island of Newfoundland finished prior to 10,000 years ago.

Glacial landforms are common throughout Newfoundland. The most conspicuous glacial features are the streamlined landforms of eroded bedrock. These features, collectively termed 'stoss-and-lee topography', possess gentle slopes facing the direction of ice flow (stoss side), and steep slopes on the down-ice, or lee side. The features thus define the direction of glacial movement., The scale of the stoss-and-lee features varies from 'roche moutonnées', less than 100 m in length; to 'whalebacks', glacially-streamlined erosional features 100-500 m long; to the largest 'flyggbergs', which may be in excess of 2 km long. Large flyggbergs form conspicuous features on the landscape.

In central Newfoundland glacial landforms composed of sediment are characteristic. Glaciers typically deposit sediment comprising particles with sizes that range from clay to boulders, typically without any form of sorting or internal structure.

*This roche moutonnée along Roaches Line was smoothed, polished, and striated by glacial ice flowing from the gentle (right) to the blunt (left) side*

*Glacial sediment deposited 15,000 to 12,000 years ago currently undergoing active coastal erosion—Middle Cove*

Three of the more conspicuous glacial landforms are crag-and-tails, drumlins, and Rögen moraines. Crag-and-tails are composed of a bedrock crag in front of an elongate tail of sediment aligned in the direction of glacial flow. Most tails are developed on the down-ice side of the crags, pointing in the direction of glacial flow, but in some examples have the sediment plastered against the bedrock crag. Crag-and-tails vary from a few metres to tens of metres in length.

A drumlin is an elongate hill, commonly 15–25 m high and 500–1000 m long, with an oval, egg- or cigar-shaped outline, composed of sediment and associated with subglacial environments. Drumlins are generally composed entirely of sediment although some have a rock core. The long axis of a drumlin is oriented parallel to the direction of flow.

Rögen moraines are closely related to drumlins, and the two landform types may grade into one another. The best developed Rögen moraines are crescent-shaped features, up to 20 m high, with the longest axis of the crescent oriented at 90° to the direction of flow. The horns of the crescent point in the down-flow direction.

Another diagnostic glacial depositional landform is the esker. An esker is an elongated sinuous ridge or series of mounds, composed internally of stratified or semi-stratified sand and gravel (it may also have minor amounts of silt and/or clay). Eskers represent the deposits from streams that flowed under the ice (subglacially), on top of the ice (supraglacially), or through tunnels within the ice (englacially).

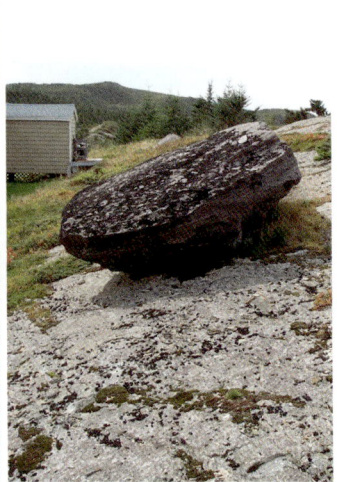

*(top) Glacial deposits commonly contain particles ranging from boulders to silt. The coarse-grained, acidic, iron-rich sediment supports the development of podzol soils and conifer forests; (bottom left) This granite erratic was transported from the Hawke Hills by glacial ice and was deposited when the ice melted—Butterpot Provincial Park; (bottom right) Glacial erratic stranded halfway up the slope of a roche mountonée—Daniel's Cove, Trinity Bay*

Most, if not all, of Newfoundland's eskers appear to have originated as subglacial streams. Individual segments of an esker may exceed 20 m in height and 20 km in length. Eskers are commonly associated with other stream features. They may be single ridges or may be aligned in a braided or reticulate pattern. Eskers served as passage routes for animals (particularly caribou) through the taiga, almost like wildlife 'highways'. Eskers are commonly used as sources of gravel and sand aggregate for road construction.

## SEA LEVEL CHANGE

On an island in the North Atlantic Ocean, sea level is the integral factor in existence. Changes in sea level are driven by a combination of local, regional, hemispheric, and global factors. Each coastal area responds differently to different combinations of these factors, and the change in sea level is not identical throughout the world or even around Newfoundland.

*The curved beds of an esker, formed by flowing water in a tunnel under glacial ice as exposed in a sand pit, Terra Nova*

Glacial ice formation required large volumes of water, most of which was removed from the oceans, causing sea level to drop by approximately 100 m along most of the Newfoundland and Labrador coast. In addition, the weight of the glacial ice depressed the land beneath it by as much as 500 m over western Labrador. As the glaciers began to melt and retreat, 14,000 years ago, the newly exposed land was still depressed, and the sea flooded in over the terrain.

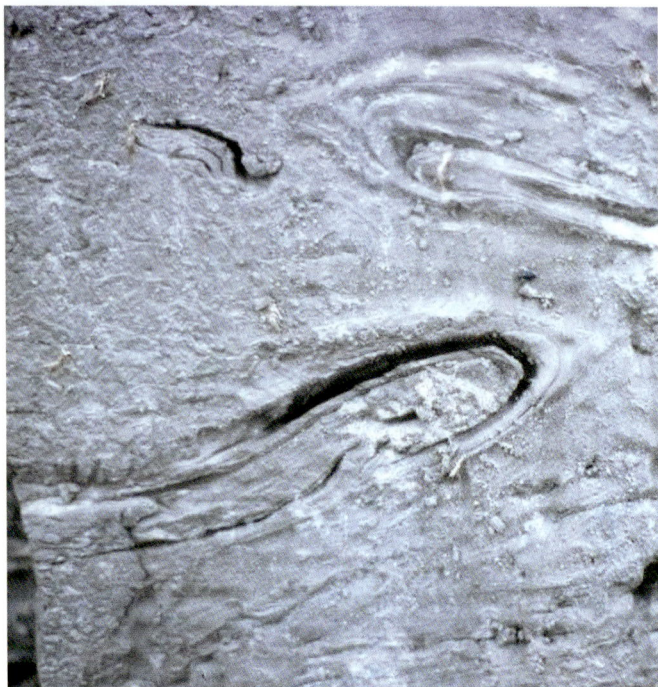

*Small drag folds preserved in this marine mud, deposited during higher sea level and now exposed 50 m above the modern shoreline*

Glacial-induced depression affected the island of Newfoundland, allowing the sea to flood coastal areas. Sea level reached 30 m above present in Terra Nova National Park, 75–100 m above present along the coastline at Gros Morne, and approximately 150 m above present on the tip of the Great Northern Peninsula. Areas where relative sea level has since fallen are indicated by abandoned ('raised') beaches.

As the land recovered with removal of the weight from glacial ice, it began to rebound, and the marine waters receded. In Newfoundland, sea level has been rising for the past 6000–3000 years. Currently, rates of sea level rise are approximately 1 mm per year at St. Anthony, 2 mm per year at Gros Morne, and 3 mm per year in southern Newfoundland.

*(top) Areas where relative sea level has fallen are indicated by abandoned ('raised') beaches. At Sandy Cove, Eastport Peninsula, the shoreline stood at the top of this gravel and sand bluff 12,000 years ago; (bottom) Terrace behind the community of Trout River indicates where sea level stood 12,000 years ago*

*Dubbed 'The Old Man' by locals, this bedrock stack was washed by the sea 12,000 years ago. Glacio-isostatic rebound elevated the land, causing relative sea level to fall, leaving the stack stranded—Trout River*

*(top) Peat deposits reveal changes in vegetation resulting from changing sea level offshore, the influence of onshore winds, and human clearance of the land for agriculture and pasture—Point La Haye; (bottom) This inundated spruce stump was carbon-14 ($^{14}$C) dated at 380 AD. Relative sea level has risen at approximately 3 mm/year since its death—Broad Cove, near Avondale*

# FUNGI

Mushrooms are the fruiting bodies of cobweb-like fibre networks, collectively called fungi, that are hidden beneath the soil or inside organic matter. Mushrooms grow in a variety of sizes, forms, and colours. The small parasol-shaped ones are likely the most familiar. They are annuals and typically have spore-bearing structures called gills or pores on the underside of a cap mounted on a stem. Equally recognizable are the shelf-like ones that grow on trees, logs, and stumps. These are called bracket fungi. Some only grow annually while others add a new layer of growth each year. Some species of mushrooms look like jelly or coral and lack most of the structures typically associated with a mushroom.

## REPRODUCTION

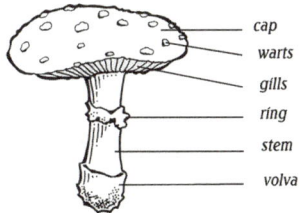

cap
warts
gills
ring
stem
volva

Fungi reproduce via microscopic-sized spores that develop on the gills and/or in the pores of mushrooms and bracket fungi. Unlike most living organisms, fungi have several sexes, but like other organisms, only certain ones can mate with certain others. Spores have cells of several sexes inside a protective coating. Spores are distributed by animals eating the mushroom or are released directly to the air currents. Spores ending up in a suitable substrate and habitat germinate, creating a single, long microscopic fibre. When two compatible fibres meet, they fuse to form a single strand called a hypha. When enough hyphae amass, a new fungus is formed. The life cycle is complete when the right environ-mental conditions stimulate fungi to produce buds that grow rapidly and emerge from the substrate as mushrooms.

## IDENTIFICATION

The 60 mushrooms chosen for this guide are considered common. We have identified almost 2000 species of fungi in the province so far, and

*< Cortinarius croceus*

it is estimated that the total number may be around 6–8000 species; thus, the majority of species are not yet known. To make matters worse, appearances are often deceiving. Different species sometimes look alike and throughout their short-lived appearances, mushrooms invariably change shape and, on occasion, colour. Unless a mushroom has distinctly visible telltale features, naming it to the species is nearly impossible without training, experience, and a microscope. Picking mushrooms for eating should **ONLY** be done in the company of someone who is an expert collector.

---

### FUNGI EDIBILITY GUIDE

**\*\* USE THIS GUIDE FOR IDENTIFICATION PURPOSES ONLY—NOT FOR FORAGING \*\***

**DEADLY:** causes fatal organ damage leading to death.

**POISONOUS:** contains harmful toxins that cause various symptoms including severe organ damage and/or death.

**EDIBLE:** suitable for eating, non-toxic.

**CHOICE EDIBLE:** highly sought after, suitable for eating, non-toxic.

---

## GILLED MUSHROOMS

**Death Angel**

*Amanita amerivirosa*

**Cap** 5–12 cm; oval to nearly flat with age; white, yellow tarnish with age; smooth when dry, slightly sticky when moist. **Gills** free; close; white. **Stem** 7–20 cm long, up to 2 cm thick; tapering slightly toward the top; white; persistent skirt-like ring near top; solid; often scaly; swollen volva. **Habits** mycorrhizal with hardwoods; solitary or in small groups. **Habitat** hardwoods and mixed forest floor. **Spore Print** white. **Season** July to Oct. **Deadly**.

*Amanita flavoconia*

**Cap** 2.5–7.5 cm; oval to convex, becoming broadly convex to flat in age; sticky when wet; bright yellow to bright orange getting paler with age; scattered pale to yellow warts that typically disappear. **Gills** free; white, sometimes with yellow edges; close. **Stem** 4–10 cm long; 0.5–1.5 cm thick; frequently with enlarged base; smooth or slightly scaly; persistent skirt-like ring; whitish to yellow with powdery yellow volval remnants at the base. **Habits** mycorrhizal; solitary or in small groups. **Habitat** conifer or mixed forest floor. **Spore Print** white. **Season** July to Oct. **Poisonous**.

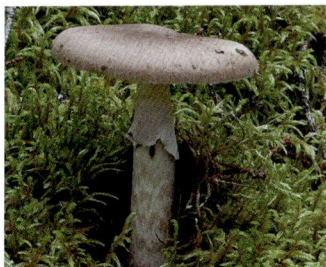

## Grey Veiled Amanita
*Amanita porphyria*

**Cap** 3–10 cm; convex, flattening with age, central bump; greyish brown to brown with scattered grey warts; smooth; slightly sticky when wet. **Gills** free; white, sometimes greyish or bruising greyish with age; close. **Stem** 5–18 cm long, 1–1.5 cm thick; more or less equal; rimmed basal bulb; stuffed to hollow; greyish ring; fibrils below the ring, smooth above. **Habits** mycorrhizal with conifers; solitary or scattered. **Habitat** hardwoods and mixed forest floor. **Spore Print** white. **Season** July to Oct. **Poisonous.**

## Tawny Grisette
*Amanita fulva*

**Cap** 4–10 cm; oval, becoming convex or nearly flat and a central bump with age; tawny brown; darker in the centre; margins lined or grooved; sticky when wet. **Gills** free; close; white. **Stem** 7–16 cm long, 0.5–1.5 cm thick; slightly tapering toward top; smooth; hollow; base has sack-like tawny volva. **Habits** mycorrhizal; solitary or in small groups. **Habitat** conifer or mixed forest floor. **Spore Print** white. **Season** July to Sept. **Poisonous.**

## American Yellow Fly Agaric
*Amanita muscaria* var. *guessowii*

**Cap** 5–25 cm; convex to flat; light yellow to deep orange; warty; sticky when wet. **Gills** free; crowded; white. **Stem** 5–18 cm long, 1–3 cm thick; white to creamy; white ring near top; slightly tapered toward top; hollow to stuffed; fibrous to cottony; ball-shaped volva. **Habits** mycorrhizal; solitary or in small groups. **Habitat** conifer or mixed forest floor. **Spore Print** white. **Season** July to Oct. **Poisonous**.

## Honey Mushroom
*Armillaria solidipes*

**Cap** 3–20 cm; convex to flat with age; dry; dark brown to reddish brown; tan to brown scales disappearing with age. **Gills** attached; whitish with pinkish hues; close. **Stem** 6–15 cm long, 2–3 cm thick; whitish, becoming nearly black; slightly tapered toward base; finely hairy; whitish ring with brownish edge; close relatives have yellowish mycelium near the base. **Habits** parasitic and saprobic; clustered; on hard and softwoods. **Habitat** hardwoods and mixed forest floor. **Spore Print** white. **Season** Sept. to Nov. **Choice Edible** intestinal upset for some people reported.

## Newfoundland Chanterelle

*Cantharellus enelensis*

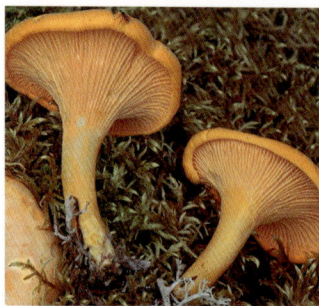

**Cap** 1.5–15 cm; convex when young becoming shallowly depressed with a wavy and irregular in-rolled margin with age; pale yellow to almost orange; tacky when wet; smooth. **Gills** cross-veined false gills running deeply down the stem; coloured like the cap sometimes with pinkish tone. **Stem** 2.5–8 cm long, 1–2 cm thick; thin and more or less equal to thick; nearly club-shaped; coloured like the cap or paler; sometimes bruises. **Habits** mycorrhizal with conifers; usually gregarious. **Habitat** forest floor. **Spore Print** pale yellow. **Season** July to Sept. **Choice Edible**.

*Cortinarius acutus*

**Cap** 2–4 cm; sharply pointed, expands but rarely flat; tan to light brown, lighter along margins, darker in the centre; lighter in colour when dry; margin with little, frilly white edge; striate. **Gills** light brown; attached. **Stem** 2–4 cm long, 0.3–0.5 cm wide; light brown. **Habits** mycorrhizal with conifers; usually small groups. **Habitat** mossy forest floor. **Spore Print** rusty brown. **Season** Aug. to Oct. **Not Edible**.

*Cortinarius collinitus*

**Cap** 2–10 cm; convex then expanding broadly conical with a low broad knob; margin incurved at first, sometimes slightly grooved; yellow brown to dark rust with age, darker at centre; viscous; drying shiny. **Gills** pale violet or clay at first, later rusty. **Stem** 5–12 cm long, 0.5–2 cm wide; apex white to bluish; colour same as cap below but covered in bluish bands; **Flesh** whitish to yellowish, sometimes tinged bluish in stem apex. **Habits** mycorrhizal with conifers; singly. **Habitat** forest floor. **Spore Print** rusty brown. **Season** Sept. to Oct. **Not Edible**.

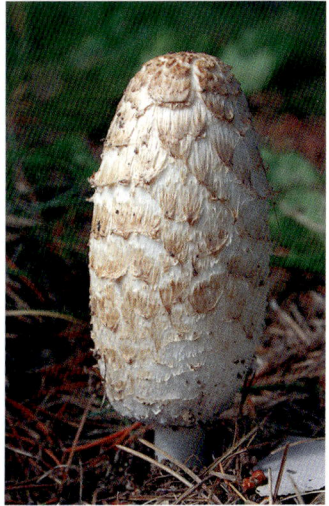

## Tippler's Bane

*Coprinopsis atramentaria*

**Cap** 3–7 cm high; ovoid, then conical with age; greyish to grey brown, black with curled split edges with age; flaky in youth, smooth in age; grooved or lined. **Gills** free; whitish, becoming pinkish grey to black when self-digesting; close or crowded. **Stem** 8–15 cm long, 6–12 mm thick; equal; hollow; smooth or finely hairy; white. **Habits** saprobic; solitary or clustered. **Habitat** woods, lawns near rotting wood. **Spore Print** black. **Season** May to Sept. **Edible**, but not in combination with alcohol within or after 24–48 hours.

## Shaggy Mane

*Coprinus comatus*

**Cap** 3–15 cm; oval to rounded-cylindrical when young, expanding to bell-shaped with a lifting margin in age; dissolves into a black 'inky goo' with age; whitish with a brownish skullcap; dry; large, shaggy scales. **Gills** free; white, becoming pinkish and then black; very crowded. **Stem** 5–20 cm long, 1–2 cm thick; frequently tapering to apex; ring may be present near bulbous base; smooth; white; easily separable from cap; hollow with single string-like fibre inside. **Habits** saprobic; solitary or clustered. **Habitat** disturbed ground, woods, lawns. **Spore Print** black. **Season** July to Nov. **Edible**.

*Collybia tuberosa*

**Cap** 2–10 mm; convex with slightly in-rolled margin becoming broadly convex to flat, central depression; whitish; dry or moist; more or less smooth; sometimes lined on the margin. **Gills** attached; close or almost distant; whitish or pale pinkish. **Stem** 1–5 cm long, about 1 mm thick; whitish to pinkish; hollow; attached to reddish-brown, appleseed-like tuber. **Habits** saprobic, decomposing dead mushrooms; very gregarious; very common. **Habitat** on remnants of dead mushrooms, in moss, on coniferous or mixed forest floor. **Spore Print** white. **Season** July to Oct. **Not Edible**.

## Yellow Legs

*Craterellus tubaeformis*

**Cap** 1–5 cm wide; convex becoming vase-shaped and perforated; dark yellowish brown to blackish brown, fading with age; wavy margin with age; smooth or somewhat roughened; sticky or waxy. **Gills** false gills, fork and cross-veined; yellowish grey, becoming brownish. **Stem** 3–8 cm long, up to 1 cm wide; more or less equal; becoming hollow; smooth; yellow to brown. **Habits** mycorrhizal; solitary, gregarious or clustered. **Habitat** moss, well decayed moss-covered conifer stumps or logs. **Spore Print** white. **Season** Aug. to Nov. **Choice Edible**.

## Banded Cort

*Cortinarius armillatus*

**Cap** 5–15 cm; convex to bell-shaped becoming broadly convex or nearly flat with age; yellow brown to reddish brown, often with a deeper, brick-red centre; sometimes fading to dull tan; dry, smooth, finely hairy becoming scaly when mature. **Gills** attached; close; pale dirty yellowish to pale cinnamon becoming rusty brown with age; whitish cortina covering when young. **Stem** 7–15 cm long, up to 2.5 cm thick; club-like; encircled by 2–4 reddish bands. **Habits** mycorrhizal with birch; singly or scattered. **Habitat** forest floor. **Spore Print** rusty brown. **Season** Aug. to Oct. **Not Edible**.

*Cortinarius camphoratus*

**Cap** 5–13 cm; initially spherical with margins turned inward, flattened with central umbo with age; pale-bluish lilac fading to tan brown with age; unpleasant smell, earthy to old rags or rotten potato. **Gills** broadly adnate and often notched; bluish purple in youth, turning brown with age; covered by noticeable pale-violet cortina when young; thick. **Stem** short, tough and bulbous at the base. **Flesh** bluish violet, browns with age. **Habits** mycorrhizal with conifers; singly or groups. **Habitat** forest floor. **Spore Print** rusty brown. **Season** Aug. to Oct. **Not Edible**

*Cortinarius traganus*

**Cap** 5–13 cm; initially spherical with margins turned inward, flattened with central umbo with age; pale lilac fading to tan brown with age; tends to crack; pleasant smell, sometimes of pears. **Gills** covered by noticeable violet cortina when young; thick, broadly adnate and often notched; brown. **Stem** short, thick, tough and thickly bulbous at the base. **Flesh** marbled brown. **Habits** mycorrhizal with conifers; singly or groups. **Habitat** forest floor. **Spore Print** rusty brown. **Season** Sept. to Oct. **Not Edible**

## The Gypsy

*Cortinarius caperatus*

**Cap** 5–15 cm; convex, becoming flatter with age; greyish brown when young becoming pale yellowish to yellowish brown with age, often with a pale margin; dry; wrinkled; fibrous, dusted with powder especially over the centre. **Gills** attached; close; pale at first, becoming brown or cinnamon brown; covered by a whitish cortina when young. **Stem** 5–13 cm long, 1–2.5 cm thick at the apex; equal or slightly swollen at the base; dry; usually rough or shaggy near the apex; pale tan; movable light coloured ring; whitish covering near the base. **Habits** mycorrhizal with conifers; solitary. **Habitat** forest floor. **Spore Print** rusty brown. **Season** June to Oct. **Choice Edible**.

*Cortinarius croceus*

**Cap** 2–8 cm; convex or nearly conical flattening with age; sometimes with a central bump; olive brown, often aging to dark brown especially over the centre; dry; silky. **Gills** attached; close or crowded; yellowish becoming cinnamon to rusty; covered by a yellowish cortina when young. **Stem** 3–7 cm long, up to 1 cm thick; dry; silky with brownish fibres; yellowish above, sometimes olive brown to reddish brown below; sometimes with a rusty ring zone. **Habits** mycorrhizal with conifers; solitary or scattered. **Habitat** forest floor. **Spore Print** rusty brown. **Season** Aug. to Oct. **Not Edible**.

*Cortinarius evernius*

**Cap** 3–9 cm; conical expanding to flat with age; purplish brown when wet, more ochre when dry, becoming pale tawny beige with age, white trim along rim. **Gills** attached; broad; violet then pale clay and finally rusty red with age. **Stem** 7–15 cm high, 1–1.5 cm thick; equal; violet; whitish band(s) near base. **Habits** mycorrhizal with conifers; singly or groups. **Habitat** forest floor. **Spore Print** rusty brown. **Season** Aug. to Oct. **Not Edible**.

*Cortinarius flexipes*

**Cap** 1–4 cm; conical, expanding with a central bump in age; dark brown especially in the centre when moist, drying light yellowish brown; covered in small white fibrous scales, usually dense along margins when young. **Gills** dark brown often with violet tinge. **Stem** brownish, some violet at top; covered with white cottony cortina that forms short-lived ring, cottony scales below ring; often slightly curved; hollow with age; smell of geranium. **Habits** mycorrhizal with hardwoods. **Habitat** forest floor. **Spore Print** rusty brown. **Season** Aug. to Oct. **Not Edible.**

*Cortinarius semisanguineus*

**Cap** 2–7 cm; becoming broadly convex, flat, or broadly bell-shaped; yellowish brown to cinnamon brown, often darker central bump; dry; silky. **Gills** attached, often pulling away from the stem in age; close; blood red, becoming cinnamon to rusty; covered by a yellowish cortina when young. **Stem** 5–10 cm long, up to 1.5 cm thick; more or less equal; dry; silky; usually pale yellowish, but often darker or reddish toward the base; often with a rusty ring zone. **Habits** mycorrhizal with conifers; groups or scattered. **Habitat** mossy forest floor. **Spore Print** rusty brown. **Season** July to Oct. **Not Edible**.

*Gymnopus dryophilus*

**Cap** 1–5 cm; convex to flat with age; incurved margin when young; dark reddish brown to brown becoming tan to orangish brown to very pale with age; smooth; greasy. **Gills** attached or free; whitish to buff or yellowish; crowded. **Stem** 1–10 cm long, 2–7 mm thick; mostly equal; dry; flexible; fibrous; smooth; whitish above, light buff to yellowish below, darker with age; hollow. **Habits** saprobic; gregarious. **Habitat** twigs or leaf litter on forest floor. **Spore Print** White to creamy or pale yellowish white. **Season** May to Nov. **Edible**.

## Witch's Hat
*Hygrocybe conica*

**Cap** 2–7 cm; sharply to broadly conical with age, sometimes convex with a conic point; reddish to scarlet orange, at times with olive to greenish tints; discolouring and bruising black; waxy; slimy when fresh, becoming dry or tacky; smooth or streaked with age. **Gills** nearly free; close; whitish, becoming yellowish orange or olive yellow; bruising black. **Stem** 6–11 cm long, 0.5–1 cm thick; coloured like the cap, white at the base; moist but not slimy; fragile; often grooved; twisted; hollow; bruising black. **Habits** alone or gregarious. **Habitat** forest floor, lawns. **Spore Print** white. **Season** May to Oct. **Not Edible**.

## False Chanterelle
*Hygrophoropsis aurantiaca*

**Cap** 2–10 cm; convex, becoming broadly convex, flat, or shallowly depressed with age; colour variable, but usually brown centre and orange margin; dry; velvety; initially in-rolled margin. **Gills** running down the stem; close or crowded; repeatedly forked; pale to bright orange. **Stem** 2–10 cm long, up to 1.5 cm thick; more or less equal; coloured like the cap; smooth or velvety. **Habits** saprobic on wood or woody debris; alone, scattered, or gregarious. **Habitat** rotted wood on forest floor. **Spore Print** white. **Season** July to Oct. **Poisonous**.

*Lactarius helvus*

**Cap** 3–18 cm; convex with in-rolled margin becoming depressed with age; light brown; dry; smooth or finely velvety becoming rough or sub-scaly with age; fenugreek (curry) smell. **Gills** attached or slightly decurrent; close; whitish becoming dirty yellowish with age. **Stem** 3–10 cm long, up to 2 cm thick; dry; smooth or very finely velvety; orangish, pinkish, or orangish brown; bleeds clear liquid when cut. **Habits** mycorrhizal with conifers; gregarious or alone. **Habitat** forest floor, sphagnum moss. **Spore Print** creamy white to pale orangish yellow. **Season** July to Oct. **Poisonous**.

*Lactarius lignyotus*

**Cap** 2–10 cm; convex with a small pointed middle, becoming flat or shallowly depressed, with the central point remaining or disappearing; nearly black when young, dark brown to brown with age; dry; finely velvety; often with a rugged or wrinkled surface. **Gills** attached; close; white turning pale with age; brownish edges; bleeds white liquid that can stain the injured tissue pink when cut. **Stem** 4–12 cm long, up to 1.5 cm thick; dry; texture and colour like the cap, except for a whitish base. **Habits** mycorrhizal with conifers. **Habitat** forest floor, rotted wood. **Spore Print** creamy yellow. **Season** Aug. to Oct. **Edible**.

*Lactarius deceptivus*

**Cap** 5–22 cm; convex, becoming funnel-shaped with age, with hole in middle; white then brownish with age; yellowish patches; smooth but becomes rough with scales; margin curled under and cottony. **Gills** attached becoming decurrent; close and occasionally forking; whitish or cream then dingy tan; bleeds milky liquid that stains gills brown. **Stem** 3–9 cm long, 1–4 cm thick; equal, or tapering to base; hollow; whitish, discolouring brownish or tan; hard; smooth or sometimes developing scales. **Habits** mycorrhizal; scattered or densely gregarious. **Habitat** forest floor. **Spore Print** white to buff. **Season** June to Oct. **Not Edible**.

*Lactarius glyciosmus*

**Cap** 2–8 cm; convex with an in-rolled margin when young, becoming shallowly depressed or flat; tan; pinkish buff but occasionally darker and browner; vague concentric zones of colour or texture; tacky; smooth; finely hairy becoming finely scaly with age; strong smell of sweet coconut. **Gills** attached or slightly decurrent; close; whitish to pinkish or yellowish; bleeds white liquid not changing colour or staining gills **Stem** 2–10 cm long, up to 1.5 cm thick; dry; smooth; coloured like the cap or paler. **Habits** mycorrhizal with birch. **Habitat** in moss on forest floor. **Spore Print** creamy white. **Season** Aug. to Oct. **Edible**.

*Lactarius hibbardae*

**Cap** 2–10 cm across; flatly convex then somewhat depressed, with a central knob; margin even or lobed; grey-tinged dark pinkish brown; hairy or scurfy; strong smell of sweet coconut. **Gills** attached to short decurrent; close to crowded; narrow; cream to pale ochre then dull pinkish cinnamon; bleeds white liquid when cut. **Stem** 2–5 cm long, 0.5–1 cm wide, becoming hollow; same colour as gills or cap, whitish towards base. **Habits** mycorrhizal with conifers. **Habitat** forest floor, in gravel, pathsides, and other disturbed soil. **Spore Print** white to cream. **Season** July to Oct. **Not Edible**.

*Lactarius thyinos*

**Cap** 3–9 cm; convex, becoming flat, with a shallow central depression, or vase-shaped; orange; thinly slimy when fresh; zoned with concentric bands, fruity smell and taste. **Gills** attached; orange; bleeds deep orange coloured liquid when cut, stains orange then red then brown. **Stem** 4–8 cm long, 1.5–2 cm thick; colour like cap; more or less equal or tapering somewhat to base; hollow, covered in shallow potholes. **Habits** mycorrhizal with conifers; growing scattered or gregarious. **Habitat** forest floor, prefers moister and richer soil. **Spore Print** whitish to pale yellow. **Season** July to Oct. **Edible**.

*Lepiota cristata*

**Cap** 1–5 cm; bell-shaped, flattening with age; dry; whitish; knobbed; smooth then covered with brown scales; centre remaining smooth and darker. **Gills** free; close; white becoming brownish with age. **Stem** 2–8 cm long, 2–5 mm thick; more or less equal; smooth; fragile white ring; whitish often turning darker towards the base. **Habits** saprobic; scattered or gregarious. **Habitat** lawns, disturbed ground, along walkways, under trees. **Spore Print** white. **Season** June to Oct. **Deadly**.

### Fairy Ring Mushroom
*Marasmius oreades*

**Cap** 2–5 cm across; bell-shaped; curled margin becoming slightly lined; broadly convex with slightly scalloped edges with age, a slight central knob; pale tan, occasionally white or reddish tan; changes colour as it dries; dry; smooth to felty. **Gills** attached; fairly distant; pale tan. **Stem** 3–8 cm long, 0.3–0.5 cm thick; equal; dry; fibrous, tough and pliant; whitish or coloured like the cap. **Habits** saprobic; forms rings. **Habitat** lawns and grassy meadows. **Spore Print** white. **Season** May to Oct. **Choice Edible**.

## Bleeding Mycena
### Mycena haematopus

**Cap** 1–3 cm across; bell-shaped or nearly convex; reddish brown at the centre, lighter towards the margin; lightly covered in fine powder when young, becoming smooth and tacky; sometimes grooved; slightly scalloped margin has a fringe of pointed, lighter-coloured scales. **Gills** attached; close; whitish, becoming greyish to purplish; often stained reddish brown. **Stem** 4–8 cm long, 1–2 mm thick; hollow; smooth but hairy towards base; bleeds a purplish red juice when crushed or broken. **Habits** saprobic; usually clustered. **Habitat** dead hardwood stumps and logs. **Spore Print** white. **Season** May to Oct. **Not Edible**.

### Lichenomphalia ericetorum

**Cap** up to 2.5 cm across; convex becoming funnel-shaped; from white, pale buff to deep brown; margin incurved, then decurved to plane, sometimes appearing scalloped in age; striate. **Gills** decurrent, widely spaced; pale yellowish. **Stem** 1–3 cm long, less than 0.5 cm wide; yellowish; finely downy. **Habits** a lichen associated with algal partners; scattered or gregarious. **Habitat** in moss, turf, or on rotten wood. **Spore Print** white to pale yellow. **Season** July to Oct. **Not Edible**.

## Angel's Wing
### Pleurocybella porrigens

**Cap** 5–10 cm; convex, petal or fan-shaped; white; smooth; margin in-rolled at first. **Gills** decurrent from point of attachment; crowded; white to cream colour. **Stem** absent to rudimentary lateral. **Habits** saprobic; solitary or clustered. **Habitat** decaying coniferous logs, stumps, and mulch. **Spore Print** white. **Season** Aug. to Oct. **Poisonous.**

## Shaggy Scalycap
### Pholiota squarrosa

**Cap** 3–12 cm; convex, becoming broadly convex or broadly bell-shaped; yellowish underneath; tawny scales; dry. **Gills** attached to the stem or beginning to run down; close; whitish to yellowish becoming greenish yellow then rusty brown with age; partial veil when young. **Stem** 4–12 cm long, 1.5 cm thick; ringed; yellowish, sometimes becoming reddish brown near the base; scaled. **Habits** saprobic, parasitic; clustered. **Habitat** base of living and dead hardwoods or conifers. **Spore Print** cinnamon brown. **Season** Aug. to Sept. **Not Edible**.

### Deer Mushroom
*Pluteus methvenii*

**Cap** 3–15 cm; convex becoming broadly convex to flat with age; pale to dark brown; smooth and glossy becoming radially streaked with fibres; sticky when wet. **Gills** free; white, becoming pink; crowded. **Stem** 5–13 cm long, up to 2.5 cm thick; more or less equal but slightly enlarged at base; white or sometimes streaked with brownish fibres. **Habits** saprobic on dead hardwood and conifer; solitary, scattered or gregarious. **Habitat** mixed forest floor. **Spore Print** pink. **Season** May to Oct. **Edible**.

*Russula paludosa*

**Cap** 2–20 cm; round to convex, becoming broadly convex then flat with a central depression; red to coppery orange, purplish with some yellow; sticky when wet; smooth. **Gills** attached; often forked at the base; close, no accessory gills; white to cream at first, becoming yellowish; bruising and discolouring slowly grey. **Stem** 4–12 cm long, 1–3 cm thick; smooth; white, variable red blush; firm when young. **Habits** mycorrhizal with conifers, growing alone, scattered, or gregarious. **Habitat** forest floor. **Spore Print** pale yellow. **Season** Aug. to Oct. **Edible, but can be readily mistaken for poisonous *Russula* varieties.**

*Russula montana*

**Cap** 3–9 cm; convex, flattening or depressed with age; bright red then fading with age; sticky when moist; skin easily peeling to show pinkish coloured flesh beneath; margin often furrowed when old; smells slightly fruity. **Gills** white, turning pale cream; attached; crowded; brittle. **Stem** 7 cm long, 2 cm thick; white; somewhat swollen towards the base; brittle. **Habits** mycorrhizal with conifers; solitary or clustered. **Habitat** forest floor. **Spore Print** white. **Season** Aug. to Oct. **Edibility unknown or presumed by some, but can be mistaken for poisonous *Russula* varieties.**

## JELLY FUNGI

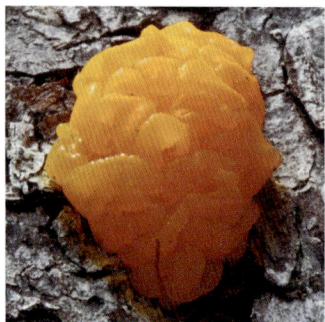

### Orange Witch's Butter
*Dacrymyces chrysospermus*

**Fruiting Body** 2–6 cm long, 1–3 cm high; gelatinous; orange to orange yellow, drying to reddish orange; spatula-shaped at first then becoming lobed or multi-lobed and convoluted with age; soft. **Gills** none. **Stem** may be present in young, otherwise none. **Habits** scattered or clustered. **Habitat** conifer logs and stumps. **Spore Print** cream to yellowish or orangish. **Season** May to Nov. or later after prolonged rain. **Not Edible**.

# SAC OR CUD FUNGI

*Byssonectria terrestris*

**Cap** 1–3 mm; begins as small cylindrical or round ball, opening to cup, then saucer shape; concave or nearly flat on top; cup edged with delicate fringe-like border; bright orange; seated on a conspicuous white mycelial or gelatinous base. **Stem** short or nonexistent. **Habits** gregarious, often in a mass. **Habitat** forest floor, often associated with moose urine and feces. **Spore Print** white. **Season** early spring, often next to melting snow. **Not Edible**.

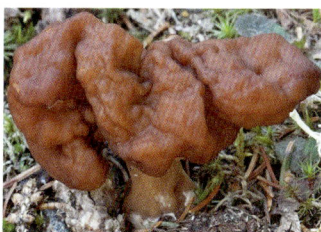

## False Morel

*Gyromitra esculenta*

**Cap** 3–12 cm; convoluted and wrinkled, resembling a brain; tan to reddish brown or nearly black; thin; brittle; chambered, not attached or loosely attached to the stem. **Stem** 3–7 cm long, 1–2 cm thick; pale or tinged like the cap; often folded; smooth to covered in fine scales; may be round in cross-section. **Habits** saprobic, possibly mycorrhizal with conifers. **Habitat** forest floor. **Spore Print** white. **Season** April to June. **Deadly**.

## Black Morel

*Morchella importuna*

**Cap** 3–9 cm; somewhat elongated and pointed; vertically arranged pits and blunt-edged ridges; ridges dark brown to black with lighter brown-grey pits; completely attached to the stem with a slight overhang; hollow. **Stem** 2–8 cm; whitish or pale tan; sometimes darkening to brown with age; smooth or with granules; sometimes tinged pinkish; variable in shape; hollow. **Habits** mycorrhizal and saprobic at different points in its life cycle; solitary or in groups. **Habitat** forest floor. **Spore Print** cream to yellowish or orangish. **Season** May to June. **Choice Edible**, **but caution with alcohol.**

## Black Elfin Saddle

*Helvella lacunosa*

**Cap** 1–10 cm; irregularly lobed and convoluted; black to various shades of grey and occasionally almost white; margin attached to the stem in several places; brittle. **Stem** 3–15 cm long, 1–3 cm thick; hollow; coloured as cap, but lighter; deeply ribbed, often with cross-ribs and holes. **Habits** saprobic; solitary to gregarious. **Habitat** forest floor, yards with hardwoods. **Spore Print** white. **Season** Aug. to Sept. **Poisonous**.

## CORAL FUNGI

*Clavulina coralloides*

**Fruiting Body** coral-like; 2–10 cm high, 3–10 cm wide; white, sometimes becoming pinkish to pale pinkish brown with age; branching near flattened tips; fairly brittle, smooth. **Habits** mycorrhizal with conifers, alone, gregarious, or in clusters. **Habitat** forest floor. **Spore Print** white. **Season** Aug. to Oct. **Edible**.

## BRACKET FUNGI

*Cerrena unicolor*

**Fruiting Body** 0.5–10 cm across, kidney-shaped to fan-shaped; concentric zones of texture and/or colour; upper surface velvety to hairy; whitish to brownish; thin; dense covering of stiff hairs; algae common on upper surface. **Underside** pores 2–3 per mm; tubes up to 4 mm deep; evenly purplish grey; maze-like, becoming tooth-like with age. **Stem** none. **Flesh** whitish with a dark line just beneath the cap surface; tough. **Habits** saprobic; crowded, often in overlapping brackets. **Habitat** dead hardwood. **Spore Print** white. **Season** annual but visible year round. **Not Edible**.

### Tinder Fungus

*Fomes fomentarius*

**Fruiting Body** up to 20 cm across; 3–25 cm wide, 2–25 cm thick; shell- to hoof-shaped with age; dull, hard, woody upper surface; grey and brownish-grey zones, blackened with age. **Underside** brownish; bruises when touched; 2–5 round pores per mm. **Stem** none. **Flesh** tube layers indistinct; dark brown with some whitish hyphae; characteristic friable marbled core at attachment point. **Habits** parasitic and saprobic; solitary or gregarious. **Habitat** fallen or standing hardwoods, mainly birch. **Spore Print** yellow. **Season** perennial; new growth layer added over growing season. **Not Edible**.

## Red-Belted Conk

*Fomitopsis mounceae*

**Fruiting Body** up to 40 cm across, 20 cm wide, 15 cm thick; convex to hoofed-shaped; white to yellow margin, red waxy belt and then brown to black where attached to its substrate; smooth but wrinkling with age. **Underside** white to cream coloured; usually bruises yellow; 3–6 round pores per mm. **Stem** absent, broadly attached. **Flesh** yellowish tan; distinct tube layers eventually fusing to form annual growth rings, tubes up to 8 mm deep. **Habits** parasitic and saprobic; solitary or gregarious. **Habitat** dead and living old conifers and hardwoods. **Season** perennial, new growth layer added over season. **Not Edible**.

*Fomitopsis ochracea*

**Fruiting Body** up to 40 cm across, 20 cm wide, 15 cm thick; convex to hoofed-shaped; ochre to light-yellow margin, non-waxy ochraceous belt and then ochraceous grey to black where attached to its substrate; smooth but wrinkling with age. **Underside** cream coloured with pinkish tinge; 3–6 round pores per mm. **Stem** absent, broadly attached. **Flesh** yellowish tan; distinct tube layers eventually fusing to form annual growth rings, tubes up to 8 mm deep. **Habits** parasitic and saprobic; solitary or gregarious. **Habitat** dead and living old conifers and hardwoods. **Season** perennial, new growth layer added over season. **Not Edible**.

## Rusty Gilled Polypore

*Gloeophyllum sepiarium*

**Fruiting Body** up to 12 cm across, 5–12 cm wide, 0.5–1 cm thick; single or fused laterally; semicircular, bracket or round if on top of log; progressive zones of texture and colour; velvety to hairy; yellow to orange on growing margins becoming yellow brown to dark brown or nearly black toward the point of attachment. **Underside** wavy, gills up to 1 cm deep; irregular; fairly close or fused; edges yellow brown becoming darker brown with age. **Stem** absent. **Habits** saprobic; alone or gregarious. **Habitat** dead conifers, hardwoods, and lumber. **Season** annual or reviving to be perennial. **Not Edible**.

*Panellus stipticus*

**Fruiting Body** 1–3 cm wide; convex with in-rolled margin, semicircular to kidney-shaped or irregular in outline; tan to pale yellowish brown, sometimes fading to off-white; dry; finely velvety to woolly; wrinkled and somewhat cracked-scaly when dry. **Underside** gills that end abruptly at the stem; close; often forked; cross-veined; pale yellowish brown. **Stem** 0.5–1 cm; lateral or off-centre; usually fuzzy-velvety with whitish, tan, or rusty-brown fuzz. **Habits** saprobic on hardwoods; usually growing in shelving clusters. **Habitat** dead hardwoods. **Spore Print** white. **Season** May to Oct., all winter during thaws. **Not Edible.**

## Birch Polypore
*Fomitopsis betulina*

**Fruiting Body** 5–25 cm across, 2–6 cm thick; kidney-shaped; broadly convex to more or less flat; growing shelf-like or hoof-like; whitish to pale brownish in age; dry; peeling smooth outer surface; rimmed margin around the underside. **Underside** white, becoming greyish brown with age; corky; 2–4 pores per mm; tubes to 1 cm long, becoming toothed with age. **Stem** absent or stubby. **Flesh** white, homogenous. **Habits** saprobic and possibly parasitic on dead and living birch; alone or gregarious. **Habitat** birch trees. **Spore Print** white. **Season** annual but persisting year round. **Edible** when small, young, and soft.

## Winter Polypore
*Lentinus brumalis*

**Fruiting Body** 1.5–10 cm; broadly convex, with a sunken central depression; yellowish brown to dark or reddish brown; margin usually in-rolled when young; dry; smooth or finely hairy. **Underside** whitish; 2–3 round pores per mm; tubes to 3 mm deep. **Stem** centred or slightly off-centre; 2.5–5 cm long, 2–5 mm wide; equal; dry; smooth or finely hairy; whitish to greyish or pale brownish; tough. **Habits** saprobic. **Habitat** dead hardwoods, particularly alders. **Spore Print** white. **Season** Nov., often overwintering. **Not Edible.**

*Trichaptum abietinum*

**Fruiting Body** 1–4 cm broad, up to 0.5 cm thick; flattened to slightly convex; light grey to pale brown, sometimes greenish from colonizing algae; margin wavy; hairy; zonate usually with a purplish margin when young; **Flesh** leathery and thin. **Underside** pored, 2–4 per mm, 1–3 mm long, randomly maze-like, circular at edge, the tissue between the pores tends to become elongated and torn into irregular spines with age; purplish when young, fading to brownish purple with age. **Habits** saprobic; overlapping tiers on dead conifer wood; annual but found year round. **Habitat** dead conifer wood. **Spore Print** white. **Season** May to Oct. **Not Edible.**

## White Cheese Polypore

*Tyromyces chioneus*

**Fruiting Body** white; plain; up to 12 cm across and 8 cm deep; convex; semicircular to kidney-shaped; white to off-white becoming yellowish to brownish with age; very finely velvety at first, becoming smooth and, in old age, developing a crusty surface that becomes wrinkled or shriveled; soft; slight fragrant odour. **Underside** pored; white, becoming yellowish in old age or when dried out. **Stem** absent. **Habits** saprobic; annual; solitary. **Habitat** dead hardwoods, especially birch. **Spore Print** white. **Season** July to Oct. **Not Edible**.

## Artist's Conk

*Ganoderma applanatum*

**Fruiting Body** 5–75 cm across, 5–15 cm wide, 2–10 cm thick; more or less fan-shaped, semicircular, or irregular; often furrowed in 'zones;' silvery grey crust, often with deposit of brown spores. **Underside** 4–6 circular pores per mm; white, staining brown with pressure or injury, becoming dirty yellowish then dingy olive brown with age. **Stem** absent. **Flesh** dark brown; tubes in layers separated by brown tissue; longitudinal white hyphae in upper layer under skin; each layer 4–12 mm deep. **Habits** saprobic and sometimes parasitic; solitary or in groups. **Habitat** birch stumps and fallen logs. **Spore Print** brown or reddish brown. **Season** perennial, new growth layer added over season. **Not Edible**.

# PUFFBALL

## Horse Fart

*Lycoperdon perlatum*

**Fruiting Body** ball or inverted pear-shaped; 2.5–7 cm wide, 3–7.5 cm high; white then brownish with age; hass-pines when young, that fall off with age leaving scars on the surface; dry; develops central perforation that releases spores with the force of rain drops and wind currents; white, fleshy interior becoming yellow olive then brown spore mass. **Habits** saprobic; alone, scattered, gregarious, or clustered. **Habitat** mixed forest floor, dead wood, along roadsides and trails. **Season** Aug. to Sept. **Edible** when white inside.

## Pear-Shaped Puffball

*Apioperdon pyriforme*

**Fruiting Body** club or pear-shaped; 1.5–4 cm wide, 2.5–5 cm high; yellowish brown darkening and becoming mottled with age; dry; smooth; develops a central hole that releases spores with the force of rain drops and wind currents; white, fleshy interior becoming yellow olive then brownish with age. **Habits** saprobic; densely clustered or scattered. **Habitat** on wood or buried wood in lawns, forest floor. **Spore Print** olive brown. **Season** Aug. to Sept. **Edible** when white inside.

# BOLETE

## Slippery Jack

*Suillus luteus*

**Cap** 5–12 cm; convex becoming broadly convex to flat with age; brown to brownish yellow, finely marbled pattern; slimy; shiny when dry; purplish-grey partial veil tissue hanging from cap margin in youth. **Underside** pores under 1 mm across; tubes 4–15 mm deep; covered with a whitish partial veil when young; pale yellow becoming olive with age. **Stem** 3–8 cm long, 1–2.5 cm thick; flaring ring, purplish grey; glandular dots above the ring; whitish becoming yellowish above ring; discolouring brown to purplish brown near the base with age. **Flesh** pale yellow; not staining. **Habits** mycorrhizal with pine; gregarious. **Habitat** forest floor. **Spore Print** brown. **Season** Sept. to Nov. **Edible**.

## Birch Bolete

*Leccinum scabrum*

**Cap** 5–15 cm; broad, convex, broadly convex in age with a decurved margin; various shades of brown with red or grey tinge; covered with fine matted fibres; wavy margin. Underside small pores; white to greyish, bruising brown. **Stem** 7–20 cm long, 2–3 cm thick; white to grey covered with brownish-black scales becoming darker towards the base; barrel-shaped when young; longitudinally ridged. **Flesh** white, firm in youth, then soft, watery, unchanging, or flushing pale pink when bruised. **Habits** mycorrhizal with birch; alone or gregarious. **Habitat** mossy forest floor. **Spore Print** brownish. **Season** July to Oct. **Edible**.

---

### FUNGI GLOSSARY

**adnate:** gills broadly attached to the stem.

**attached:** gills attached to the stem.

**bulbous:** swollen stem base.

**cortina:** partial veil—a key feature of *Cortinarius* spp.

**clustered:** growing from a single point of origin.

**decurrent:** gills growing down part of the stem.

**fibrils:** fine hairs on cap or stem.

**free:** gills not attached to the stem.

**gills:** thin, plate-like structures on the underside of mushroom cap.

**gregarious:** growing close to each other but not from a single point.

**hypha:** a single fungal fibre that forms a fungus.

**in-rolled:** turned in.

**mycelium:** a mass of single fibred hyphae.

**mycorrhizal:** growing in beneficial relationship with plants.

**parasitic:** getting food by living on or in an organism.

**pores:** tiny round or irregularly shaped holes on the underside of a mushroom cap or bracket.

**saprobic:** deriving food from decaying organic matter.

**scales:** small plate-like structures on caps and stems.

**scattered:** one here, one there.

**solitary:** a mushroom growing alone.

**spores:** microscopic single or multi-celled reproductive structures.

**spore prints:** powder from spores collected on paper or other media.

**striate:** lines or furrows running from cap centre to margins.

**substrate:** the surface on which a mushroom grows.

**umbo:** curved bump on an otherwise flat cap.

**underside** (of cap): the fertile surface where spores for reproduction are produced.

**viscous:** slimy.

**volva:** cup-like structure.

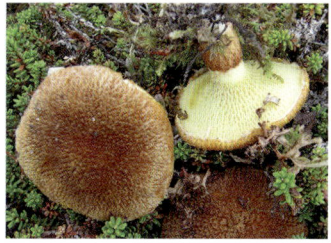

## Leccinum holopus

**Cap** 4–7 cm; convex becoming broadly convex; whitish or pale brown, becoming darker and greenish with age; usually tacky, often becoming viscid with age; finely tomentose; may become pinkish and eventually greyish when bruised. **Underside** 1–2 pores per mm; spores 2.5 cm deep; whitish, becoming pinkish to brownish; sometimes bruising yellowish to brown; depressed at the stem. **Stem** 6-14 cm long, 1-2 cm wide; coloured like cap, often green staining, sometimes bluing near the base when cut; covered in whitish scabers. **Flesh** white. **Habits** mycorrhizal with birch; alone or gregarious. **Habitat** mossy forest floor. **Spore Print** brownish. **Season** July to Oct. **Edible**.

*Suillus ampliporus* var. *cavipes*

**Cap** 3–10 cm; convex becoming broadly convex or flat, sometimes with a broad central bump; yellowish brown, reddish brown, or brown; densely hairy with whitish to brownish fibres; often with white partial veil remnants on cap margin; dry. **Underside** pores 1 mm across, angular and radially arranged; pores 5 mm deep; deep yellow or greenish yellow; not bruising. **Stem** 4–9 cm long, 0.5–1.5 cm thick; enlarging toward base; yellow and smooth toward the apex, brownish and hairy toward base; sometimes with a fragile ring; hollow. **Flesh** white to yellowish, not stained with exposure. **Habits** mycorrhizal with larch; growing alone or gregarious. **Habitat** forest floor. **Spore Print** olive brown. **Season** Sept. to Oct. **Edible**.

*Suillus clintonianus*

**Cap** 5–15 cm; convex, becoming broadly convex then flat with age; dark reddish brown to orangish brown; smooth; slimy. **Underside** 1–2 pores per mm; pores 10–15 mm deep; angular; amber yellow becoming olive yellow, turning reddish brown when bruised; attached to depressed, becoming slightly decurrent. **Stem** 4–10 cm long, 1–3 cm thick; solid, slightly club-shaped toward base; yellow to pale yellow; distinct ring; dingy in age, staining pinky brown after handling. **Flesh** thick; yellow becoming flesh pink or salmon pink when bruised. **Habits** mycorrhizal with larch; groups or dense clusters. **Habitat** forest floor. **Spore Print** olive brown. **Season** Sept. to Oct. **Edible**.

## Suillus grevillei

**Cap** 5–15 cm; convex, becoming broadly convex then flat with age; orange yellow to yellow; smooth; slimy. **Underside** 1–2 pores per mm; pores 10–15 mm deep; angular; amber yellow becoming olive yellow, turning reddish brown when bruised; attached to depressed, becoming slightly decurrent. **Stem** 4–10 cm long, 1–3 cm thick; solid, slightly club-shaped toward base; yellow to pale yellow; distinct ring; dingy in age, staining pinky brown after handling. **Flesh** thick; yellow becoming flesh pink or salmon pink when bruised. **Habits** mycorrhizal with larch; clusters. **Habitat** forest floor. **Spore Print** olive brown. **Season** Sept. to Oct. **Edible**.

The term 'lichen' is believed to have been derived from a Greek word meaning 'to lick.' This probably refers to the historic use of lichens in folk medicines or as food.

Although lichens are generally considered to be 'plants,' strictly speaking from a botanical perspective, none of the various components of a lichen actually constitutes a plant. A happy medium is to refer to lichens as 'cryptogams,' a group of plant-like organisms, including mosses and ferns, which reproduce by spores.

To the unaided eye, a lichen may appear to be a single entity but is in fact a compound organism in which a fungus, which in most cases is a cup fungus, lives together in symbiosis with an algae and/or cyanobacteria. Usually the fungus accounts for 80% or more of the entire structure of a lichen. A lichen is named after the fungus that is its major component.

A lichen does not have actual roots but instead soaks up most of its mineral nutrients from the air and rainfall by absorption directly through its cortex. Unlike vascular plants, lichens do not have a protective waxy cuticle and have little control over their water absorption or evaporation. Pollution in the atmosphere can be especially dangerous to lichens because they retain, and can accumulate, deadly amounts of airborne pollutants. This is especially true of lichens containing cyanobacteria.

The main visible components of lichens are the thallus, which is the main body and the apothecia, which is the fruiting body. Lichens are subdivided into three types: **Fruticose**, shrubby, three-dimensional; **Foliose**, flat, leaf-like lobes not firmly attached to substrate; and **Crustose**, crust-like growths that are strongly fixed on the substrate.

Lichens were probably first collected from the province in 1766 when Joseph Banks conducted nature surveys in both Newfoundland and Labrador.

The first detailed inventory of Newfoundland lichens was compiled by Finnish lichenologist Teuvo 'Ted' Ahti based on his collections

*< British Soldiers Lichen*

during one field season in 1956. Ahti suggested that we had at least 600 species. With an expanding local knowledge of lichens over the past 25 years, and through the efforts of many amateur and professional lichenologists, we now know that there are in the vicinity of one thousand species of lichens on the island. The number for Labrador is probably less, but no reliable estimate is available due to limited surveying. It is estimated that there may be up to 18,000 species of lichens on Earth. The status of lichens in Canada is monitored by the Committee on the Status of Endangered Wildlife in Canada (COSEWIC).

The most recent studies of lichens, conducted by Qalipu First Nation and Dr. Yolanda Wiersma of MUN Biology in the region known as Charlie's Place, southwestern Gander Lake, have revealed new lichens and a preponderance of bluefelt lichens. Among the new lichens are 19 previously unknown in Newfoundland and two previously unknown in Canada (*Chaenothecopsis vainioana* and *Myrionora albidula*).

This section can, but barely, scratch the surface of our lichen flora. A small but diverse group, some common species and some rare, found on trees, rocks, and soil are presented. It is hoped that this offering will allow the reader to become acquainted on a first-name basis with some of our lichens and will pique an interest in some to delve further into this fascinating field.

## ARBOREAL LICHENS (GROWING ON TREES)

### ARBOREAL FRUTICOSE SPECIES

**Witch's Hair (locally 'Molldow')**
*Alectoria sarmentosa* ssp. *sarmentosa*

Most commonly found in mature, damp, coniferous forest throughout the island. Pale, greenish yellow, pendent from conifer branches, up to 40 cm in length, with individual strands up to 2 mm diameter. Rarely has golden, cup-like **apothecia**. Has a terricolous counterpart, sub-species *vexillifera*, Prostrate Witch's Hair, which occurs on alpine heath.

**Horsehair Lichen**
*Bryoria trichodes*

Very common, usually on conifer branches and birches, throughout the island in both forest and muskeg. Ranges from pale to dark brown and usually pendent to 15 cm with narrow individual branches (to 0.4 mm). Several subspecies occur as well as a number of other *Bryoria* species that are generally similar looking.

### Punctured Ribbon Lichen
*Ramalina dilacerata*

Yellowish-green **thallus** is upright (to 3 cm) and shrubby, occurring on branches in well-lit forest edges and clearings. **Apothecia** common on branch margins and tips. Of about a half dozen *Ramalina* species occurring on the island, this species and the Frayed Ramalina (*R. roesleri*) are the most common and most widely distributed. This latter species is sorediate at its curled branch tips and does not usually have apothecia.

### Coral Lichen
*Sphaerophorus globosus*

**Thallus** greyish green to reddish brown, upright, and shrubby. Several main branches with smaller, coral-like side branches. Occasional **apothecia**, a small globe at branch tips. Can be locally common on tree bark from a number of species in mature boreal forest.

### Fishbone Beard Lichen
*Usnea filipendula*

**Thallus** pendulous, yellow green, and shrub-like, attached at a single blackened base to tree bark with several parallel main branches and numerous side branches. Branches covered in fine tendrils resembling a fish skeleton. Commonly to 20 cm long but occasionally longer. Found in mature boreal forest on a variety of tree species.

### Old Man's Beard
*Dolichousnea longissima*

**Thallus** usually a single, long, yellowish-green strand with long tendrils and resembling Christmas garland. Strands often found dangling and unattached on branches but, when attached, has a blackened base. Common in old boreal forest throughout the island on a variety of trees.

## ARBOREAL FOLIOSE SPECIES

### Powdered Honeycomb Lichen

*Hypogymnia hultenii*

**Thallus** a small, grey, circular rosette (to 2 cm), usually at junctures of small branches and usually on scrub fir and spruce at forest and bog edges. Lobes tiny (to 0.1 mm). Produces soralia bundles at tips of intact lobes. **Apothecia** rare. Black undersurface with numerous, minute, cavernous pits.

### Vole Ears

*Erioderma mollissimum*

**Thallus** brownish green to greyish with a finely hairy appearance and whitish, felt-like, upturned margin and diameter up to 8 cm. Thallus margins sprinkled with granular reproductive structures known as soredia. **Apothecia** extremely rare and not reported from island examples. This species, only recently discovered in old wet boreal forest in Newfoundland, appears extremely rare and in 2010 was assessed as Endangered by COSEWIC.

### Salted Shell Lichen

*Coccocarpia palmicola*

**Thallus** a lead-grey rosette (to 5 cm diameter), often with a 'salted' appearance from abundant, vegetative, reproductive structures (isidia) crowded on the thallus upper surface. Frequently found as an overlapping aggregation of several thalli. **Apothecia** rare and apparently not reported from Newfoundland. Considered to be primarily a tropical genus, this is the only species to occur in Canada, where it is considered to be rare. This species can be locally abundant in wet boreal forest and is considered the primary indicator species in surveys for the Boreal Felt Lichen.

### Blue Felt Lichen

*Degelia plumbea*

**Thallus** a blue-grey rosette (usually to 5 cm), but often overlapping other thalli to form large continuous patches on tree stems. Thallus frequently having a black, wooly margin (hypothallus). **Apothecia** numerous, reddish-brown to almost black discs. In southern and eastern Newfoundland, this species occurs sparingly on old-growth Yellow Birch, Trembling Aspen, and rarely White Spruce. It will also colonize mature deciduous trees of other species as evidenced by the luxuriant population on maples at Sir Robert Bond Park, Whitbourne. In 2010, it was assessed as Special Concern by COSEWIC.

## Boreal Felt Lichen
### *Erioderma pedicellatum*

**Thallus** resembling Vole Ears, except usually with abundant, small, disc-like **apothecia** (to 1.5 mm) varying in colour from pinkish to dark brown. Occurs sporadically throughout the island on mature and over-mature Balsam Fir, and rarely other trees, in wet boreal forest, with largest concentrations at Bay d'Espoir and central Avalon Peninsula. Considered highly susceptible to atmospheric pollution and forest harvest, this species is listed as Special Concern in Newfoundland by COSEWIC.

## Monk's Hood Lichen
### *Hypogymnia physodes*

**Thallus** a mineral-grey rosette of narrow (to 2 mm), hollow, occasionally branching lobes, tipped with burst or 'hooded' lobe ends containing lip-shaped reproductive structures (soralia). The undersurface is black. **Apothecia** are infrequent. This ubiquitous species is abundant throughout the island and is also found widely on heath vegetation in upland areas. This is by far the most common of the five tube lichens presently known to occur on the island.

## Lungwort
### *Lobaria pulmonaria*

**Thallus** composed of wide, leafy lobes and often is continuous over entire tree stems and branches. Usually light brownish when dry and bright green when wet. Underside tan with wooly veins. Ridged upper surface with isidia and soredia present on ridges and lobe margins. Reddish-brown, marginal, disc-like **apothecia** uncommon. This species can be locally common in old-growth forests, occurring abundantly on Yellow Birch in inland boreal forests as well as on coastal White Spruce and Balsam Fir in many coastal forests. The most common of three *Lobaria* species regularly occurring on the island. Rarely on heath.

## Textured Lungwort
### *Lobaria scrobiculata*

**Thallus** yellowish-grey to greenish-grey (to 15 cm), composed of individual ridged lobes (to 20 mm wide). Granular blue-grey soredia produced along margins and in bundles (soralia) on upper surface. Reddish-brown to dark, disc-like **apothecia** rare. An uncommon species on conifers, particularly old White Spruce in boreal forest. More commonly found on old growth Yellow Birch. Rarely on heath.

## Wrinkled Shield Lichen

*Pannaria lurida* ssp. *russellii*

**Thallus** a blue-grey, wrinkled rosette (to 5 cm), usually tightly attached to its bark substrate. Abundant **apothecia**. Red-brown discs (to 2 mm) with whitish margins. One known southwestern site, on coastal White Spruce. Discovered by Teuvo Ahti in 1956, re-discovered in 2008. Considered a high priority species for assessment by COSEWIC.

## Bottlebrush Shield Lichen

*Parmelia squarrosa*

**Thallus** of mineral-grey, flat, slightly branched lobes (to 5 mm). Usually tightly appressed to bark by root-like structures (rhizines) that are branched at right-angles (squarrose). Underside black. Upper surface often with cylindrical isidia (to 0.5 mm) and frequently with golden, disc-shaped **apothecia**. An abundant species found widely throughout the island.

## Varied Rag Lichen

*Platismatia glauca*

**Thallus** highly variable. Upper surface whitish mineral grey with black-and-white underside. Up to 15 cm broad, consisting of lobes (4 to 20 mm wide). Margins may have soredia, isidia, branching lobules, or all three. **Apothecia** rare. Extremely common and widespread on tree branches and stems of various species in boreal forest and on woody ground plants in heathlands. Likely our most abundant foliose lichen.

## Speckleberry Lichen

*Pseudocyphellaria perpetua*

**Thallus** chocolate coloured, up to 10 cm diameter. Comprising lobes (to 15 mm wide). Lobe ridges and margins covered with bright yellow soralia. Medulla (inner fungal layer) is also yellow and is exposed by making a small cut in the upper cortex (surface). A look-alike species, *P. crocata*, differs in having a white medulla. This rare species is found sporadically in Newfoundland on old-growth Yellow Birch and rarely on old conifers in both inland boreal and coastal forests.

## ARBOREAL CRUSTOSE SPECIES

### Common Script Lichen
*Graphis scripta*

This greyish-white crustose is common on smooth-barked trees and shrubs of many species. The **apothecia** of this lichen are quite distinctive and diagnostic, consisting of elongated black ridges, frequently forked, which resemble simple hieroglyphics or script.

### Heart Lichen
*Mycoblastus sanguinarius*

**Thallus** a greyish-white, granular crust over tree bark and twigs in boreal forest, particularly on both live and dead branches at forest edges. **Apothecia** dark-brown to black convex discs (to 1 mm). This lichen is readily identified by slicing into an **apothecium** with a sharp blade. The apothecial base has a layer of bright red pigment, which is evident on sectioning and from which the name is derived.

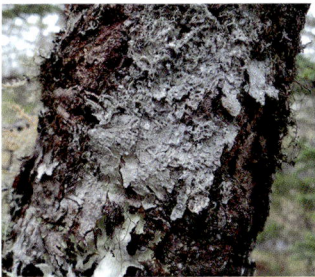

### Bitter Wart Lichen
*Lepra amara*

Greenish-grey, granular **thallus** on bark in boreal forest. Fruiting bodies are yellowish-green, warty soralia containing white soredia. Although this common Newfoundland lichen has some look-alikes, it is readily identified by the unpleasant bitter taste encountered upon licking one of its warts

## SAXICOLOUS LICHENS (GROWING ON ROCKS)

### SAXICOLOUS FRUTICOSE SPECIES

### Finger-Scale Foam Lichen
*Stereocaulon dactylophyllum*

**Thallus** an erect, grey branch (pseudopodetia) with occasional side branching and covered in coral-like projections resembling miniature fingers. Brownish, convex **apothecia** (to 2 mm) at tips of main and side branches. Found in patches, sometimes extensive, on acidic rock in open heathland.

## Concentric Ring Lichen
*Arctoparmelia centrifuga*

**Thallus** a grey-green rosette with flat, narrow individual lobes (to 2 mm). Under surface white to tan. Reddish-brown, disc-like **apothecia** common. May attain an outside diameter in excess of 30 cm although inner concentric bands may die and slough. Found throughout Newfoundland on acidic boulders in alpine heath.

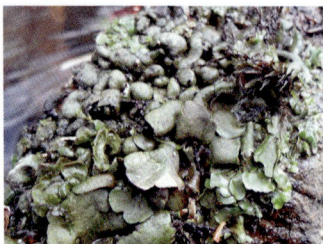

## Streamside Stippleback Lichen
*Dermatocarpon luridum*

This uncommon, grey-brown, lobed lichen, occurs on emergent rocks in streams and pond shorelines, is likely to avoid detection unless it is wet, at which time it becomes a brilliant green colour. It is able to withstand periodic inundation. Usually occurs in toonie-sized rosettes or somewhat larger patches of smaller lobes. No **apothecia** are produced, but small pores (perithecia) are evident, dotted (or stippled) over the upper cortex. Like the Common Toadskin Lichen, this is an umbilicate species with a single attachment point to its substrate. It is, however, unrelated to our other umbilicate species.

## Common Toadskin Lichen
*Lasallia papulosa*

**Thallus** a dark, greyish brown, often appearing frosted, orb with a blistered upper surface and attached to its rock substrate by a single central hold-fast. Blisters on upper surface correspond to indentations in the smooth, brownish undersurface. This distinctive lichen, along with a number of other saxicolous umbilicate foliose species (of genus *Umbilicaria*), occurs commonly in upland and alpine heath throughout the island and can be readily distinguished by its blisters and corresponding indentations.

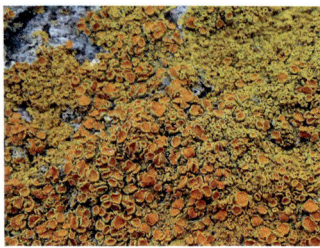

## Maritime Sunburst Lichen
*Xanthoria parietina*

**Thallus** a tightly-attached, flattened, orange-yellow rosette (occasionally grey-green) of narrow lobes (to 3 mm) usually on rock, but frequently on old lumber, concrete, and roof felt and shingles, particularly near the ocean. May occur singly or in extensive patches of over-lapping thalli. Abundant orange, disc-like **apothecia**. Often found in sites enriched by bird droppings.

## SAXICOLOUS CRUSTOSE SPECIES

### Brown Beret Lichen

*Baeomyces rufus*

Saxicolous crustose to minutely squamulose with stalked (to 2 mm) brownish apothecia. **Thallus** appears as a talcum-powder coloured crust, often with powdery soredia, occurs over wet rocks, and rarely mineral soil, usually in shady boreal forests.

### Alpine Bloodspot Lichen

*Ophioparma ventosa*

**Thallus** a thick, yellowish-white crust on acidic rock in alpine areas. **Apothecia** frequent, to 3 mm. Blood-red discs with thin, white margin. Although restricted to alpine and sub-alpine sites throughout Newfoundland, this is a striking lichen and not likely to be overlooked.

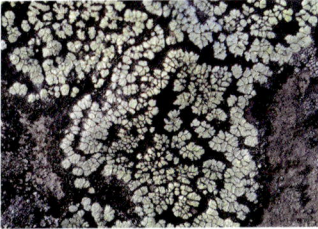

### Yellow Map Lichen

*Rhizocarpon geographicum*

**Thallus** a continuous, thin, yellowish-green, tile-like patch overlying a black background (prothallus), usually in large formations on acidic rock. Small black **apothecia** are interspersed in the black hypothallus between the minute, yellowish tiles. Common along ponds, shores and seacoasts. *R. geographicum* is the most widespread and common of four similar Map Lichen species in Newfoundland; exact species identification requires microscopy and chemical testing.

### Concentric Boulder Lichen

*Porpidia crustulata*

**Thallus** a thin, greyish-green crust over acidic stones and boulders in both shaded forest and open sites. Dark brown **apothecia** (to 1.5 mm) are arranged in concentric circles over the lichen surface. Similar to Yellow Map Lichen species (*Rhizocarpon concentricum*) and microscopic examination of spores is required to separate these look-alikes.

### Black Seaside Lichen

*Hydropunctaria maura*

**Thallus** a continuous, thick, black, minutely tile-like crust on rock in the ocean spray-zone. Surface covered in numerous, raised black bumps, which are actually spore-producing structures (perithecia). Covers extensive seashore rock throughout the island.

## SAXICOLOUS SQUAMULOUS SPECIES

### Matchstick Lichen
*Pilophorus fibula*

**Thallus** a light greenish squamulose (small leafy lobes up to 2 mm) crusty patch over boulders protruding from and alongside shaded streams. Patches can be extensive in size (up to 100 sq. cm). **Apothecia** numerous. A small (to 1 mm) black globule atop a short (to 1 mm) stalk (pseudo-podetia). Rediscovered in 2007, this extremely rare species is currently known from six southern island locations and may be under-reported.

# TERRICOLOUS LICHENS (GROWING ON SOIL)

## TERRICOLOUS FRUTICOSE SPECIES

### Iceland Lichen
*Cetraria islandica*

**Thallus** a bronzed-brown, channeled main lobe to 10 cm tall with smaller branching lobes. Very similar to the Striped Iceland Lichen (*Cetraria laevigata*), which differs in having a continuous, thin, white stripe of pseudocyphellae along lobe margins. This species has, instead, sporadic and less well-developed marginal white pseudocyphellae. An important reindeer food in Scandinavia. Both Iceland Lichens occur sporadically in upland heath and drier bogs.

### Fishnet Cladonia
*Cladonia boryi*

Yellowish to greyish, vertical **thallus** of inflated, hollow lobes (to 9 cm tall) occurring in continuous patches on thin soil, often over exposed bedrock, in heath and alpine areas and occasionally bogs. Close examination with a hand-lens reveals the sieve-like structure of older thalli, unique to this species.

### British Soldiers Lichen
*Cladonia cristatella*

Minute, yellowish, basal squamules with yellow-green to grey-green podetia (to 3 cm) topped with bright, red fruit. Common over soil and humus throughout the island. Several other red-fruit *Cladonia* occur here, but these either have podetial cups or soredia, unlike British Soldiers.

### Smooth Cladonia

*Cladonia gracilis* ssp. *gracilis*

Greenish to brown, smooth-surfaced, spike-like podetia (to 1.5 mm thick and 10 cm tall), occasionally tipped by small, closed cups, with small, brown **apothecia** on cup margins. Basal squamules usually inconspicuous. This species is usually green in shaded woodland areas but is bronzed brown in open heathland. Can be found in mosses in forest as well as on open heath. Several other subspecies of *C. gracilis* also occur in Newfoundland but are quite distinct and not likely to be confused with this subspecies. A similar, usually greenish, species, *Cladonia maxima*, occurs among forest mosses but stems are thicker (to 3 mm) and podetia are usually quite tall (to 12 cm).

### Grey Reindeer Lichen

*Cladonia rangiferina*

Greyish-white, tree-like primary podetium with frequent triple and quadruple branching. Outer podetial surface looks dull and fibrous. Height to 12 cm. Tips frequently oriented in a combed look and occasionally brown tipped. Usually found in continuous patches on heath and bogs, occasional on soil in forest clearings. The much similar Black-footed Reindeer Lichen, *Cladonia stygia*, differs in having a blackened lower podetium. Several generally similar species co-habit, but these differ in either branching pattern or stem colour. All are of considerable importance as winter caribou forage.

### Star-Tipped Reindeer Lichen

*Cladonia stellaris*

Yellowish to greenish-grey, rounded, shrub-like mounds of fine branches without a main stem. Overall widths to 4 cm and heights reaching 14 cm under optimal conditions. No browning evident at branch tips. This unmistakable species forms extensive mats in open boreal forest and heath and is our most important caribou forage lichen.

### Red-Fruited Pixie-Cup Lichen

*Cladonia pleurota*

Greyish-white podetium (to 4 cm) topped with flaring cups. Upper podetium and interior of cups covered in greyish-white, granular soredia. Red **apothecia** (and pycnidia) on cup margins. Basal squamules usually inconspicuous. Common, usually in heath and along roadsides in thin soil over bedrock. Several generally similar looking red-fruited *Cladonia* species also occur but can be separated by absence of, or differing, soredia.

## Newfoundland Reindeer Lichen

*Cladonia terrae-novae*

Pale yellowish-green, loosely shrub-like **thallus** (to 10 cm tall) with fine branches, and usual branching dichotomous (doubly-branching). Occasional browning at branch tips. This species is found primarily on coastal bogs and heaths but occurs throughout the island. Endemic to northeastern North America, it was first described in Newfoundland in 1956 by Finnish lichenologist Teuvo Ahti.

## Ladder Lichen

*Cladonia verticillata*

Greenish-brown to brown, hollow podetium (to 10 cm tall) with occasional branching and poorly formed, funnel-like cups at the tips, with in-rolled margins. Basal squamules usually inconspicuous. Minute branching evident at podetial tips and small, brown **apothecia** frequent on branch tips. Common throughout the island on humus soil and over rocks, usually in heath but also on bogs. The in-rolled margins to cups and perforations are diagnostic and give the species its common name.

## TERRICOLOUS FOLIOSE SPECIES

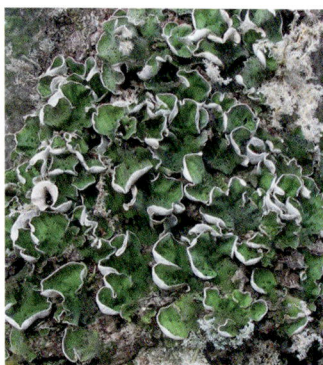

## Arctic Kidney Lichen

*Nephroma arcticum*

**Thallus** greenish-grey (dry) to green (wet), consisting of adjoining wide lobes (to 3 cm) and frequently forming continuous larger mats on moss in heath and open forest. Lower surface with tan margins, becoming darker centrally. Large (to 3 cm) kidney-shaped, reddish-brown **apothecia** on underside of lobes, which turn up to expose these discs. A striking lichen most commonly found in coastal heathland in northern Newfoundland but occurring sporadically in suitable upland heath elsewhere.

## Common Freckle Pelt

*Peltigera aphthosa*

Rarely arboreal on mossy tree bases in boreal forest. **Thallus** consisting of bright green lobes (to 50 mm) freckled with black cephalodia. Underside white at edges to black centrally with no veins. **Apothecia** common, marginal. Red-brown discs (to 15 mm) on upturned upper lobe margins.

## TERRICOLOUS CRUSTOSE SPECIES

### Pink Earth Lichen
*Dibaeis baeomyces*

**Thallus** a greenish-white or grey crust over mineral soil, often at gravel roadsides. **Apothecia** usually numerous, each a bright pink bead (to 4 mm diameter) atop a whitish stalk (to 6 mm tall), often most prominent immediately following a rainfall. Found widely throughout the island in disturbed sites.

### Fairy Puke
*Icmadophila ericetorum*

**Thallus** a greyish-green crust over humus soil and decaying wood, such as stumps. **Apothecia** abundant, pinkish discs (to 4 mm) slightly raised on inconspicuous stalks. Usually found in somewhat shaded forest sites, this species can be separated from the generally similar Pink Earth Lichen by its inconspicuous apothecial stalks, its habitat, and its usual substrate.

### Green-Pea Mushroom Lichen
*Lichenomphalia umbellifera*

**Thallus** a dark, greenish, globular crust over humus and organic soil in boreal forest. Fruiting body, a small, pale, whitish-yellow mushroom (to 4 cm high). Each individual crustose globule is composed of fungal material and contains algal cells, but these are not considered to be lichenized fungi and are consequently usually overlooked in lichenology.

### Club Mushroom Lichen
*Multiclavula vernalis*

On peat, sand, or humus. This 'lichen,' unlike most others, does not have a specialized **thallus**. The crustose thallus is a greenish layer of algal cells over the soil, and the fruiting body is a club mushroom (to 2 cm high). The usual fungal partner in lichens is a cup fungus (ascomycete). For this reason, and since no specialized thallus is formed, many experts do not recognize this and a more common relative, *Multiclavula mucida*, as lichens, preferring instead to group them with club mushrooms (basidiomycetes).

### Arctic Saucer Lichen
*Ochrolechia frigida*

Occurs frequently and extensively in alpine areas overgrowing soil and ground vegetation. **Thallus** a thick, warty, white crust, often with frost-like fruticose projections. **Apothecia** common and very prominent; bright pink discs with white marginal ring to 5 mm diameter. The striking, frost-like appearance of this species and its bright pink 'saucers' are distinctive and readily aid in its identification.

## MOSSES AND LIVERWORTS

**M**osses and liverworts are mostly small plants of damp areas that have not developed the specialized conducting tissues (xylem and phloem) of higher plants to transport water and nutrients around the plant. Unlike higher plants they do not possess true roots but instead have root-like rhizoids that attach them to the substrate. Mosses have stems and leaves, with the leaves usually arranged in spiral fashion around the stem. The leaves usually have a nerve or midrib running through the middle. Liverworts have a plant body consisting of a flattened 'thallus' or, in the case of the leafy liverworts, leaves that are divided into segments but lack a central nerve or midrib.

Both liverworts and mosses exhibit 'alternation of generations' as do the ferns and fern allies. While in the latter the 'sporophyte' generation is the most obvious generation, in mosses and liverworts the 'gametophyte' generation is the most obvious one. The green, leafy moss plants you see are the gametophyte generation that produces the eggs and sperm. The sperm can swim through a layer of water to neighbouring plants and fertilize the eggs. The fertilized egg is not released from the plant but produces a spore-bearing capsule (sporophyte generation), which releases spores into the air to be distributed elsewhere. When the spores land on suitable environments, they germinate to form new gametophytes.

Mosses and liverworts are usually very small, relatively inconspicuous plants, often growing in shaded areas where they are hidden by taller plants, and so are often overlooked. However, in Newfoundland, large areas of the island are covered by mosses, particularly bog mosses (the genus *Sphagnum*) and so here at least some mosses are very prominent.

## MOSSES

### Black Rock Moss

*Andreaea rupestris*

A small moss usually less than 15 mm tall. Typically forms dark, reddish-brown cushions that become black as they dry out. The leaves are usually less than 1 mm long and are closely pressed against each other and overlapping. Common on acidic rocks; also common and locally abundant on boulders. Generally on drier sites.

### Bug Mosses

*Buxbaumia* species

Very distinctive mosses lacking green, leafy parts. The brownish capsule, up to 5 mm long, is flattened on its upper surface and attached to a reddish to brownish seta (stem) that arises from a brown felt of filaments. The rather large capsule looks like a bug on a stick, hence the common name. Common in forests.

### Fork-Mosses (Broom Moss)

*Dicranum* species

Large mosses up to 10 cm in height and forming extensive patches. The leaves are very long (up to 15 mm) and are often characteristically and uniformly curved, resembling the shape of a scimitar. The capsules are cylindrical. Usually found in woodlands.

### Water Mosses

*Fontinalis* species

Large aquatic mosses. The shoots can be up to 20 cm in length and 1 cm wide. Greater Water Moss, *Fontinalis antipyretica*, is the most common on the island. The leaves, up to 5 mm long, lack nerves and are bluntly pointed and not toothed, and strongly folded along the keel. Commonly totally submerged in rivers and streams.

### Common Cord Moss

*Funaria hygrometrica*

An easily recognizable moss, up to 1 cm high when the capsules are present since they are borne on very long and twisted setae (like a swan's neck). Ripe capsules have a very long calyptra. The short shoots often form a dense carpet. Common in burnt-over areas.

## Staircase Moss

*Hylocomium splendens*

This bright green moss has a red stem with regular branches. The shoots can be up to 20 cm long. Annual growth arises from a bud posterior to the apex of the shoot, giving a staircase-like appearance to the plant. The stem leaves can be up to 3 mm with sharp teeth towards the tip. The branch leaves are smaller (1 mm) and also show teeth towards the tip. Capsules are generally uncommon. Usually in disturbed habitats.

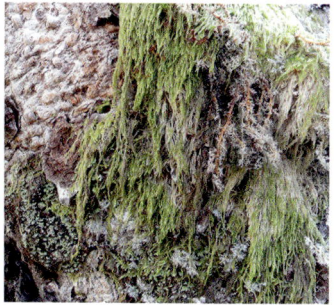

## Mouse-Tail Moss

*Isothecium myosuroides*

Shows a tree-like form with the main stem unbranched in the lower areas and heavily branched above. The stem leaves are roughly egg-shaped with a tapered tip. The branch leaves are longer and narrower, spearhead-shaped, with a sharply toothed tip. Usually found in woodlands and shaded areas, on boulders and tree trunks.

## Red-Stemmed Feather Moss

*Pleurozium schreberi*

An easily recognizable moss with its bright red stems and pinnate branches. Shoots are up to 2.5 cm long. The leaves are oval with a blunt tip. The stem and branch leaves are similar, but the branch leaves are a little smaller. Capsules are rare. Leaf shape readily distinguishes this species from *Hylocomium splendens*. A common understory forest moss.

## Haircap Mosses

*Polytrichum* species

Haircap mosses are usually readily distinguished from other mosses by the robust, upright nature of their unbranched shoots. The upright shoots can be quite tall (up to 4 cm). In spring, the male plants are quite distinctive with the upper leaves forming orange-red, star-shaped 'flowers' at their tips. The capsules are usually several centimetres tall on reddish setae (stalks). Often found on roadsides and other open habitats. Pioneers of disturbed and burnt soils.

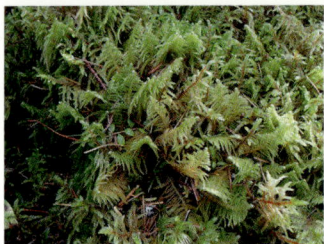

### Ostrich Plume Feather Moss

*Ptilium crista-castrensis*

The bright green, erect shoots can be up to 5 cm tall and show pinnate branching. The lower branches are of equal length, but the branches are shorter towards the tip giving the moss a feather-like appearance, hence the common name. The leaves are up to 25 mm long and taper to a long point that clearly curves to one side. The branch leaves are shorter, and the tip is more curved. Capsules are curved, 1.5–2 mm long, and horizontal to the shoot. A common forest understory moss.

### Wooly Fringe-Moss

*Racomitrium lanuginosum*

A large, quite distinctive species with shoots to several centimetres in length. It is irregularly branched with long (up to 5 mm) curved leaves that bear a conspicuous hair point with toothed edges (only visible with a hand lens). Overall, the plant has a woolly appearance and is not readily confused with other species. Capsules 1.0–1.7 mm long, smooth, and brown. A common moss of exposed rocky barrens, cliffs, and scree slopes.

### Big Shaggy-Moss

*Rhytidiadelphus triquetrus*

A very large, coarse, bushy moss forming shoots 10–20 cm long with irregularly branched red stems. The straight, pale leaves with lightly toothed edges are up to 6 mm and stick out from the stem in all directions, giving the species a rather untidy appearance, hence the common name. Capsules oblong and cylindrical. A common understory forest moss.

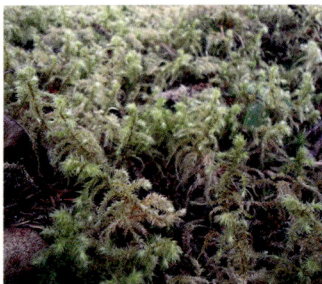

## *SPHAGNUM* SPECIES (BOG MOSSES)

There are numerous *Sphagnum* species in Newfoundland that are quite distinct from other mosses, but the individual species of bog moss are difficult to distinguish in the field. They are commonly found in wetlands where they contribute to peat bog formation, hence their common name—Bog Mosses. They differ from other mosses in how the branches are arranged in bundles on the stem. Each bundle consists of two or more branches that spread out at right angles and one or more branches that hang down along the stem. The number of each kind of branch per bundle is important in determining species. Young branches are densely crowded into a head, called a 'capitulum,' at the tip of the stems whose shape is, again, an important distinguishing character.

*Sphagnum* species bear two types of leaves: stem leaves and branch leaves. These are usually distinct and are important in identifying species at a microscopic level, which is beyond the scope of this guide.

While most bog mosses grow in open, boggy areas, green woodland peat moss, *Sphagnum girgensohnii*, is a bright green moss that grows as carpets in shady wet woodlands.

**Green Woodland Peat Moss**
*Sphagnum girgensohnii*

## SPLACHNUM SPECIES (COLLAR MOSSES)

The members of this group are quite distinctive, as their capsules have a swollen neck, or collar (hence the common name), right below the capsule. This swollen neck may be much larger than the capsule itself. These species are also unusual in their choice of habitats—animal dung in boggy areas.

**Cruet Collar Moss**

*Splachnum ampullaceum*

The most common collar moss on the island. It has an inflated collar that is much larger than the capsule itself.

**Brilliant Dung Moss (Parasol Moss)**

*Splachnum rubrum*

Very distinctive; when the red capsule opens, it becomes flattened (like a parasol) and flower-like, attracting the flies that usually visit the dung in which it grows. The spores become stuck to the flies, which carry them away to other similar habitats.

# *ULOTA* SPECIES (PINCUSHIONS)

The pincushions are aptly named since they usually form small tufts growing on trees and rocks. Two species are quite common on the island.

**Puckered Ulota**

*Ulota coarctata*

Forms small, loose, dull, green-yellowish to brown tufts, up to 1 cm tall, and has narrow leaves that are about 3 mm long and taper to a blunt point. The capsules are whitish and pear-shaped, and may have a hairy covering called a 'calyptra.' It commonly grows on trees.

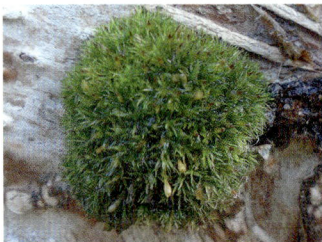

**Frizzled Pincushion**

*Ulota phyllantha*

Produces small, olive-green, pale cushions up to about 3 cm tall. The leaves are up to 4.5 mm long with a brownish nerve protruding from the tip that supports conspicuous clusters of brownish gemmae. This is the only *Ulota* that forms gemmae. Capsules are rare. It is common on rocks and trees close to the ocean.

# LIVERWORTS

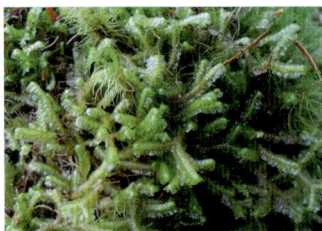

*Bazzania trilobata*

Easily recognized by its lobed leaf shape and large size. It is a bright green to brownish-green mound up to 10 cm across. The shoots are 4-6 mm across with leaves 3 mm x 3 mm pointing downwards so each leaf has a rounded back. The tips have three short teeth. An abundant component of the forest understory that can colonize logs and tree trunks.

*Frullania asagrayana*

A reddish-brown, leafy liverwort with somewhat pinnate branching up to 2 mm wide. The leaves are broadly egg-shaped with pointed lobes. The upper lobe is 1 mm wide and up to 1.5 mm long. The lower lobe is a smaller, sac-like structure that is attached to the base of the upper lobe. It is a common epiphyte on coniferous trees, frequently found growing in close association with the endangered lichen *Erioderma pedicellatum*.

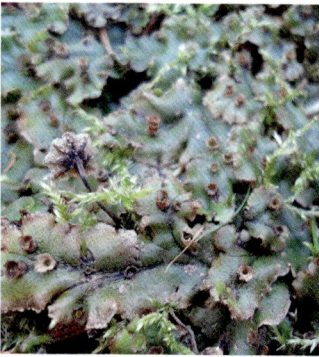

*Marchantia polymorpha*
One of the largest thallose liverworts with dichotomously branching thalli up to 2 cm wide, growing in dense mats. It is pale yellowish-green to brown. The upper surface is covered with conspicuous pores but no obvious midrib. When fertile, it bears conspicuous, parasol-like receptacles up to 2 cm in height. The thalli also bear cup-shaped structures that produce gemmae. It is very frequent in disturbed habitats such as roadsides and footpaths. It can be a serious weed of potted plants in nurseries and greenhouses.

## FERNS

Ferns are familiar plants to most people and are relatively easy to spot. However, many species are so similar in appearance that definite identification in some cases requires close examination of relatively minor details. All ferns exhibit what is termed 'alternation of generations' with two distinctly different plant bodies in their life cycle. The fern plants bear spores for reproduction and are hence called 'sporophytes' (i.e., spore bearers) with the spore-bearing areas (sori) on the underneath of fern fronds. When the spores are released and land in a suitable environment, usually damp soil, they germinate and grow into microscopic green, heart-shaped structures called 'gametophytes'. This gametophyte bears both male and female gametes. The male gametes (sperm) can swim (hence the need for water) to neighbouring gametophytes and fertilize the female gametes (eggs). The fertilized eggs can then grow into new sporophytes and the alternation of generations (sporophyte → gametophyte → sporophyte) is complete. Thus, when one sees a fern, what you are observing is the leafy sporophyte generation of a fern, so it is the sporophytes that we attempt to identify.

Fern fronds (i.e., the leaves) arise from underground stems called 'rhizomes.' Each fern frond is composed of a stalk called the 'stipe' from which arises the 'blade,' or the leafy part of the fern. The frond may be undivided or divided into smaller sections. If it is divided into smaller sections, these are called 'pinnae' (pinna, singular). A pinna may be subdivided again into smaller sections called 'pinnules.'

Pinnules themselves may also be further divided. A pinnule may have a rounded profile or be toothed. All of these features are used in the identification of the fern species, but detailed microscopic study of sori structure is typically used for critical determination. While some ferns bear spores on the back of all their fronds, many others only bear the sori on certain fronds—which are termed 'fertile'—while other fronds, though appearing to be identical, do not bear spores and are termed 'sterile'. A few ferns have specialized fertile fronds, which are quite different in appearance from the sterile fronds (e.g., cinnamon fern, ostrich fern). Sometimes the frond may have a sterile section and a fertile section (e.g., interrupted fern, royal fern).

The blade of a frond may also vary in shape with some being triangular and broadest at the base, whereas some are lanceolate (lance-shaped), with others being intermediate between the two. Note should be taken of all these characteristics to identify the actual fern species.

Included here are the most commonly encountered ferns of the over forty-five species known from the island.

## FERNS

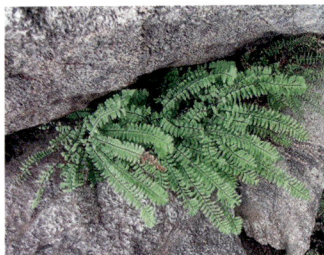

### Western Maidenhair Fern

*Adiantum aleuticum*

This delicate maidenhair fern has a thin dark stem with short-stalked pinnae, which are subdivided into roughly fan-shaped pinnules with incisions on the upper edge. **Height** to 70 cm. **Sterile and fertile fronds** are similar. **Sori** are found on the margins of the pinnules and are covered by the in-rolled edges of the pinnules. **Habitat** found in serpentine barrens.

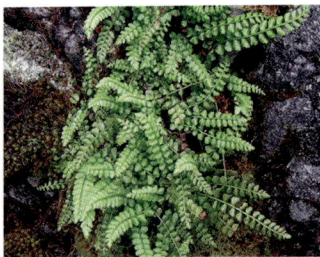

### Green Spleenwort

*Asplenium trichomanes-ramosum (Asplenium viride)*

A very small fern with rounded green pinnae, which have slight indentations. **Height** less than 15 cm. **Sterile and fertile fronds** are the same. **Sori** each pinna on the fertile fronds bears several pairs of elongate sori. **Habitat** grows in crevices of limestone rocks.

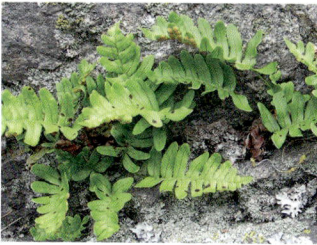

## Common Polypody
### *Polypodium virginianum*

A small fern that grows in cracks. **Height** usually less than 50 cm. **Sterile and fertile fronds** similar, the blade is leathery and roughly lanceolate, widest in the middle. The blade is deeply cut into many lobes, almost to the rachis. The stipe is shorter than the blade. **Sori** are large and round on either side of the midrib. **Habitat** cracks in cliffs, rocks, and tree stumps.

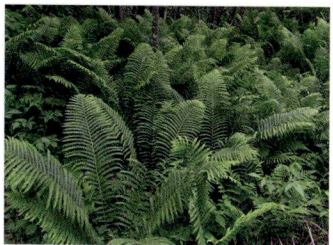

## Ostrich Fern
### *Matteuccia struthiopteris*

A very large fern. **Height** 1.5 m or taller. **Sterile fronds** widest near the tip with a rapidly pointing tip. Has numerous pairs of pinnae with each pinna cut into 20-40 pairs of lobes. **Fertile fronds** shorter than sterile fronds; initially green, then turning brown at maturity and remaining through the winter. **Sori** the fertile pinnae curl around the sori and form hard 'pea pod' type structures. **Habitat** woodlands, stream banks, and other damp areas.

## Interrupted Fern
### *Osmunda claytoniana*

A tall fern of wet areas. **Height** 1 m or taller. **Sterile fronds** lanceolate and widest in the middle. **Fertile fronds** are similar to the sterile fronds but are taller and 'interrrupted' by several pairs of widely spaced fertile pinnae midway down the rachis. These fertile pinnae are densely covered with sporangia that wither and turn brown in summer. The sterile pinnae below the interruption are usually smaller and widely spaced. The stipe of the fertile fronds is much larger than those of the sterile fronds. **Sori** none. **Habitat** damp woods and other wet areas.

## Cinnamon Fern
### *Osmunda cinnamomeum*

A large fern of damp areas. **Height** up to 1.5 m. **Sterile fronds** broadly lanceolate, narrowing gradually towards the tip. The pinnae are slender and roughly oblong. The stipe is shorter than the blade. It is easy to identify by the small wooly tufts of cinnamon coloured hairs at the junction of the pinnae and rachis (sometimes called 'hairy armpits'). **Fertile fronds** quite different from the sterile ones, being narrow with pairs of short, narrow pinnae. The naked sporangia are in clusters, green when mature, and turning cinnamon brown later. The fertile fronds die back in early summer. **Sori** none. **Habitat** damp woods and meadows.

### Royal Fern

*Osmunda regalis*

A medium sized fern of damp places. **Height** up to 1.5 m. **Sterile fronds** composed of pinnae divided into stalked ovate oblong pinnules, quite different from those of other ferns, as the pinnules are widely separated. **Fertile fronds** similar to the sterile fronds but the tips bear a cluster of branched, small pinnules bearing sporangia; green when ripe and then turning dark brown later. **Sori** none. **Habitat** stream banks, meadows, bogs, and damp woods.

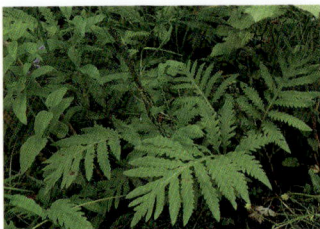

### Sensitive Fern

*Onoclea sensibilis*

A large fern of wet areas. **Height** usually less than 1 m. **Sterile fronds** triangular with twelve pairs of opposite pinnae; the margins are wavy, but not toothed. The upper pinnae are connected to the rachis by wings of leafy tissue. The stipe is usually much longer than the blade. **Fertile fronds** smaller with very narrow pinnae. **Sori** in small, hard, bead-like divisions of the fertile pinnae. **Habitat** wet areas and woodlands.

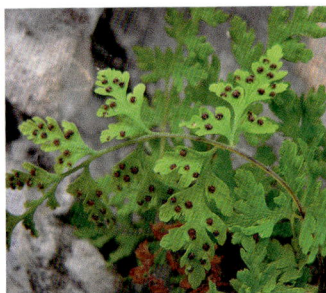

### Fragile Fern

*Cystopteris fragilis*

A very small fern of cliff faces and thin soil on rocks. **Height** up to 35 cm. **Sterile and fertile fronds** similar. The blade is lanceolate and widest just below the middle. The lower pinnae are widely spaced. The stipe is shorter than the blade. **Sori** are few and scattered on the veins. **Habitat** shady, moist areas.

### Long Beech Fern

*Phegopteris connectilis*

A small fern of wet areas. **Height** up to 30 cm. **Sterile and fertile fronds** same shape and size. The blade is triangular with a rapidly narrowing tip. The lowest pair of pinnae are angled downwards and distinctly spaced from the next pair. The stipe is long. **Sori** small and round, near the margins at the end of veins. **Habitat** wet areas, often near streams.

## Oak Fern

*Gymnocarpium dryopteris*

A small fern of shaded areas. **Height** up to 40 cm. **Sterile and fertile fronds** similar. Frond blades are broadly triangular, appearing to be three-parted with each section on a separate stalk. The stipe is slender, brittle, often dark coloured and longer than the blade. **Sori** small and few, near the margins of the pinnules. **Habitat** shaded coniferous forests.

## New York Fern

*Thelypteris noveboracensis*

A very common medium sized fern of woodlands. **Height** about 60 cm. **Sterile fronds** shorter than the fertile fronds. **Fertile fronds** larger, narrower and more upright. The blade tapers from the middle to both ends and the pinnae are almost to the ground as the stipe is very short. The pinnae are long, pointed, narrow, and lanceolate. **Sori** small, round, and few in number; near the margins. **Habitat** woodlands and stream margins.

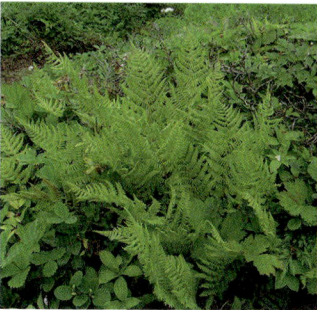

## Lady Fern

*Athyrium filix-femina*

A large fern that can grow in a wide variety of habitats. **Height** often over 1 m. **Sterile and fertile fronds** similar. The blades are broadly lanceolate and the stipe is usually shorter than the blade. The tips of the blades are lax in appearance. The pinnules have toothed margins. **Sori** often quite different from those of other ferns as they are elongated and often hooked or horseshoe-shaped. **Habitat** a wide variety of habitats, including woodlands and fields.

## Northern Holly Fern

*Polystichum lonchitis*

A small fern of rock crevices. **Height** up to 60 cm. **Sterile and fertile fronds** similar. The blades are very narrow and the pinnules have small spines. The rachis is short and covered in scales. **Sori** small and round and so dense that they touch each other. **Habitat** rock crevices, especially on limestone.

*Red spore capsules on fertile frond—
Braun's Holly Fern*

## Bracken

*Pteridium aquilinum*

A large fern of drier, open areas, unlike most ferns, which require moist habitats. **Height** up to 1.5 m. **Sterile and fertile fronds** are the same. The frond is broadly triangular and divided into three nearly equal parts. The pinnae are longer than wide. The tips of the pinnules are two to four times longer than wide. The stipe is as long as the blade. **Sori** in lines along the margins of the pinnules covered by the infolded margins. **Habitat** 'cosmopolitan' (i.e., ranges over most of Earth), forests to pastures to disturbed sites, acidic soil.

## Braun's Holly Fern

*Polystichum braunii*

Similar to Northern Holly Fern but has broader fronds and the pinnules have bristly, forward pointing spines. **Height** up to 1 m. **Sterile and fertile fronds** same size and shape. **Sori** circular. **Habitat** moist shady woods and shady alluvial deposits.

# WOOD FERNS (GENUS *DRYOPTERIS*)

The wood ferns are stereotypical ferns. They are medium to large with fertile and sterile fronds similar to each other. The fronds are divided into pinnae that are themselves further sub-divided into pinnules, which are often toothed or deeply cut. The sori are round, numerous, and covered by kidney-shaped flaps of tissue when young (indusia). Since they closely resemble one another, attention to relatively small details is necessary to successfully identify individual species. In the case of *D. campyloptera*, *D. carthusiana*, and *D. intermedia* the relative sizes of the innermost pinnules on the lowest pinnae can be used to separate the species.

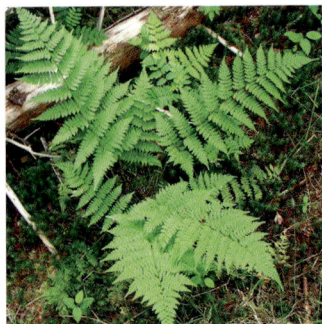

## Mountain Wood Fern

*Dryopteris campyloptera*

A medium sized fern of woodlands. **Height** up to 1 m. **Sterile and fertile fronds** similar. The blade is triangular with a long stipe. The pinnules have toothed margins. The innermost lower pinnule on the basal pinna is much longer than the innermost upper pinnule and offset (i.e., it is not opposite a pinnule on the upper side). **Sori** round and scattered over the pinnae. **Habitat** woodlands.

## A QUICK GUIDE TO THE DRYOPTERIDS

*Dryopteris filix-mas* very long, narrow pinnae subdivided into 25 or more pairs of pinnules. Blade roughly triangular.

*Dryopteris cristata* fertile fronds taller than the sterile ones, and the pinnae are twisted at right angles to the plane of the blade. Blade narrow and sides almost parallel.

*Dryopteris campyloptera* innermost pinnule on the lowest pinna longer than the neighbouring pinnules and is offset in relation to the corresponding upper pinnules on that pinna. Blade triangular.

*Dryopteris carthusiana* innermost pinnule on the lowest pinna is longer than the neighbouring ones and almost opposite the upper pinnule. Blade oval to triangular.

*Dryopteris intermedia* second innermost pinnule on lowest pinna longer than the first and third. Blade triangular.

### Spinulose Wood Fern
*Dryopteris carthusiana*

A large fern of wet areas. **Height** 1 m. **Sterile and fertile fronds** similar. The blade is oval to triangular, nearly the same width at the middle and the base of the blade. The stipe is much shorter than the blade. The pinnules have fine-toothed margins with tips that curve inwards. The lower innermost pinnules closest to the rachis on the basal pinna are twice as long as the opposite upper pinnules. **Sori** midway between the midvein and margin. **Habitat** stream banks, damp woods, and other wet areas.

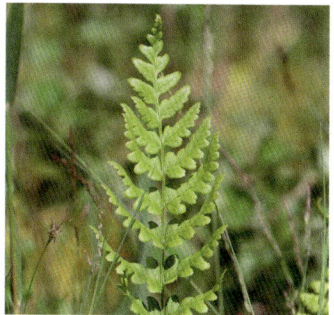

### Crested Wood Fern
*Dryopteris cristata*

A medium sized fern of wet areas. **Height** usually less than 1 m. **Sterile fronds** are shorter than the fertile fronds. **Fertile fronds** have widely spaced pinnae and are horizontally oriented (as in venetian blinds). The sides of the blade are almost parallel. The basal pinnae are triangular. The stipe is much shorter than the blade. **Sori** rounded and midway between the midvein and margin. **Habitat** wet woods and wetlands.

### Male Fern

*Dryopteris filix-mas*

A medium sized fern of wet woodlands. **Height** 1 m or more. **Sterile and fertile fronds** similar. The blade is ovate to narrowly lanceolate, widest about one-third up from the base. The pinnae are very long and narrow and there may be 25 pairs of pinnules in each pinna. The stipe is short. **Sori** large and found mid-way between the midvein and margin. **Habitat** wet woodlands.

### Evergreen Wood Fern

*Dryopteris intermedia*

A medium sized fern of woodlands. **Sterile** and **fertile fronds** similar. The blade is oval to triangular and the middle to lower pinnae are almost the same length. The innermost pinnules of the basal pinnae are shorter or of the same length as adjacent pinnules and less than twice the size of the opposite upper pinnules. The pinnule margins are toothed. The stipe is long and the rachis has glandular hairs. **Sori** small and found between the midvein and margin. **Habitat** woodlands.

## RATTLESNAKE FERNS AND MOONWORTS

Rattlesnake ferns and moonworts (genus *Botrychium*) are very different from the 'regular' ferns in that they are usually smaller (often less than 30 cm) with a divided sterile blade and a taller fertile branch (sporophore), which is also divided and bears many sporangia. Although more than six species have been reported for Newfoundland, only the two most commonly encountered are featured here.

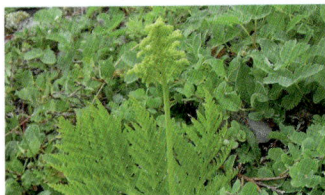

### Rattlesnake Fern

*Botrychium virginianum*

One of the largest *Botrychiums*, with a broadly triangular, much divided blade. **Height** usually less than 40 cm. **Sterile and fertile branches** fertile branch overtops the sterile branch and bears sporangia on a somewhat triangularly branched blade. **Habitat** open woodlands, and shrubby coastal and alpine thickets.

### Moonwort

*Botrychium lunaria*

A small fern. **Height** 10-25 cm. **Sterile and fertile branches** six or more pairs of roundish, fan-shaped pinnae. Sporangia are rounded and borne in clusters on the fertile branch. **Habitat** grassy fields, roadsides, meadows, and turfy slopes.

## FERN ALLIES

The group 'fern allies' includes a number of different plants not closely related to true ferns but usually included with them for the sake of convenience since they reproduce in a similar way to ferns (i.e., by spores). As with true ferns, the most obvious generation is the spore-bearing plant, the 'sporophyte,' with the spores germinating in suitable conditions to produce the usually microscopic 'gametophyte'. The latter produces male and female gametes, and fertilization results in the development of a new sporophyte generation. Unlike ferns, the spores are not produced on the undersides of fertile fronds but at the base of special leaves called 'sporophylls,' in cone-like structures called 'strobili', or in stalked cases called 'sporocarps.'

Clubmosses are small, mostly evergreen plants that are either trailing or upright. The stems are covered with many small, pointed, and unstalked leaves. The horizontal stems can either be above or below ground. The spores are borne in sporangia on strobili, which usually project above the leaves.

Firmosses, unlike the related clubmosses, do not possess strobili, but instead have evergreen sporophylls and produce 'gemmae,' or plantlets, near the top of the stem. The gemmae are released and develop into gametophytes. Firmosses, unlike clubmosses, do not possess horizontal stems.

Spikemosses are, for the most part, creeping plants that resemble the mosses and with which they can be confused, as they can grow in similar habitats. Spikemosses, however, have true vascular systems similar to those of flowering plants. Spikemosses bear their spores in strobili on the leaf bases at the ends of the fertile stems. While clubmosses produce only one type of spore, spikemosses produce two different types: microspores and megaspores. The microspores develop into male gametophytes, which produce sperm, while the megaspores develop into female gametophytes, which produce the eggs.

The familiar horsetails tend to grow in wet environments. They have erect, hollow stems, and the leaves are very small and joined together as sheaths surrounding the stem. Spore-bearing cones develop at the tips of the stems. The spores develop into gametophytes, but—unlike clubmosses and firmosses and similar to spikemosses—there are separate male and female gametophytes.

## CLUBMOSSES

### Prickly Tree-Clubmoss

*Dendrolycopodium dendroideum*

A tree-like plant with each stem having many spreading branches and needle-like leaves. The strobili are borne singly on the ends of the upper branches. Up to 30 cm in height. Found in forests and on the barrens.

### Northern Running-Pine

*Diphasiastrum complanatum*

A small, creeping, tree-like plant with wide, flattened branches at various angles. The strobili are on slender stalks in ones or twos. Found in drier forest environments.

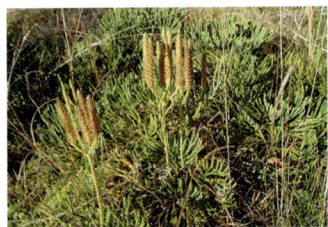

### Blue Ground Cedar

*Diphasiastrum tristachyum*

A low, erect plant that tends to grow in dense clusters, up to 35 cm tall. Fan-shaped side branches. The horizontal stem is below ground. The strobili are in threes or fours, branching off of one stalk projecting above the leaves in a candelabra-shaped arrangement. The plant is blue-green in colour. Tiny, evergreen leaves. Found in coniferous forests, open areas, and clearings.

### Running Clubmoss

*Lycopodium clavatum*

A low-growing plant of damp woods and open fields, up to 15 cm tall. The creeping stems run over the surface of the ground, putting up vertical stems at intervals; the horizontal stems are covered with leaves. The vertical stems

### Bog Clubmoss

*Lycopodiella inundata*

A small, creeping, deciduous plant up to 13 cm tall. The horizontal stems creep along the ground. There is usually only one upright stem with a single strobilus at its top. Found in bogs, lake shores, and the edges of other wet areas.

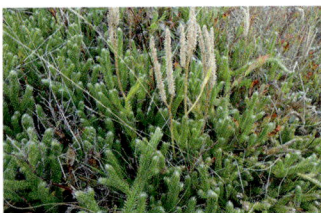

have a number of branches of differing sizes. The strobili are at the tips of long stalks with up to five strobili branching off from the main stalk.

### One-Cone Clubmoss
*Lycopodium lagopus*

A trailing evergreen clubmoss of open areas, up to 25 cm in height. Trailing stems run over the surface of the ground and are covered with leaves. The upright stems usually have several branches arising in the lower part of the stem. There is usually one strobilus at the top of an unbranched stalk bearing a few scattered leaves.

### Sharp Bristly Clubmoss
*Spinulum annotinum*

A low-growing, very prickly plant of coniferous forests with a trailing stem at or near the soil surface. Up to 15 cm in height. The upright stems branch at the base. The strobilus is at the top of the stem but is stalkless.

### Northern Interrupted Clubmoss
*Spinulum canadense*

Similar to the sharp bristly clubmoss but found in more open, exposed areas. The leaves either have very small or no teeth whereas the leaves of the previous species have very sharp pointed tips.

## FIRMOSSES

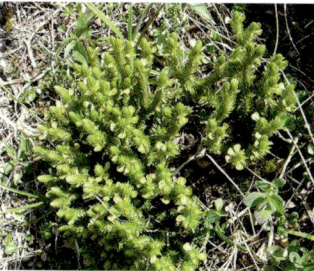

### Northern Firmoss
*Huperzia selago*

A low-growing plant of forests and damp locations, up to 13 cm in height. The upright stems are approximately at the same height, so the plant appears to be flat topped. The sporangia are in distinct zones on the upper stem. The gemmae are borne at the tips of the stem, and so the stem tips give the appearance of being very thick.

## SPIKEMOSSES

### Northern Spikemoss
*Selaginella selaginoides*

A perennial moss-like plant forming mats with prostrate sterile stems and upright fertile stems with spreading sterile leaves. Has a cylindrical strobilus at the tip of the upright stems. Up to 13 cm tall. Found on shores of lakes, bogs, streams, and on serpentine barrens.

# HORSETAILS

## Field Horsetail
*Equisetum arvense*

The common horsetail of damper areas, found in fields, woods, and waste places. The sterile stem has many branches arising from the nodes. The fertile stem is erect and unbranched, with a cone at the tip. Up to 60 cm in height. The stem sheaths have large, coloured teeth.

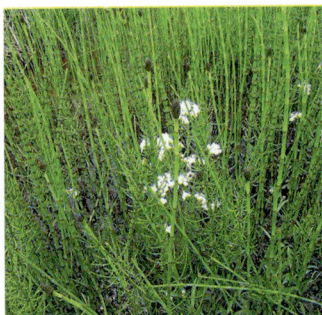

## Swamp Horsetail
*Equisetum fluviatile*

Tall horsetail of standing water such as bogs, ponds, and ditches. Up to 110 cm tall. The stems are green with black teeth. Branches only arise from the mid-stem area. The cone is at the top of the stem.

## Woodland Horsetail
*Equisetum sylvaticum*

A medium-sized horsetail, up to 65 cm tall, of damp areas such as forests, meadows, and bogs. The sterile stems have numerous braches, so the whole plant resembles a miniature tree. The fertile stems are much shorter with few branches and a cone at the tip.

## Variegated Horsetail
*Equisetum variegatum*

A medium-sized horsetail, up to 50 cm tall, of shaded areas in woodlands and on river banks and meadows. The tall, slender stems are not branched. Each bears a small, greenish cone with a pointed tip on a short stalk.

# CONIFERS

Conifers are gymnosperms or 'naked-seed' woody plants that produce their seeds on the surface of cone scales. Both male (pollen) and female (seed) cones are produced in some species on the same plants and in others on separate plants. Seed cone size and structure are frequently useful in identification. Conifers are also often known as evergreens and softwoods. Nine conifer species are native to Newfoundland: six trees and three shrubs. Trees include two spruces (*Picea* spp.), two pines (*Pinus* spp.), one fir (*Abies* sp.), and one larch (*Larix* sp.). The three low shrubs include two junipers (*Juniperus* spp.) and one yew (*Taxus* sp.). Many more conifer species have been introduced to the province for horticultural purposes or as trial forestry plantings. Several introduced species, such as Scots pine, freely seed and are becoming naturalized near urban centres. All but one of our conifers are evergreen. Only larch (*Larix laricina*) loses its leaves (needles) in late fall and produces new leaves the following spring.

The spruces and firs are commercially important for pulping and lumber as well as firewood. Cone seeds are food sources for forest birds and small mammals such as squirrels. Insects and other invertebrates associated with the trees are also important dietary sources for forest birds and small mammals. Moose typically browse heavily on balsam fir and Canada yew.

## FAMILY PINACEAE (PINE FAMILY)

### Balsam Fir
*Abies balsamea*

**Habit** a tree to 25 m, bark brownish-greyish, relatively smooth with resin blisters. **Needles** 1.5–2.5 cm long, flattened, with rounded tips, attached to twig by rounded discs leaving rounded scars when they fall. **Cones** seed cones upright, 4–10 cm long, often resinous, shattering in autumn leaving upright 'candles.' **Habitat** common tree throughout the island on well-drained sites.

### White Spruce
*Picea glauca*

**Habit** a tree to 25 m, bark rough and scaly. **Needles** angular, four-sided and sharply pointed, 1.5–2.2 cm long, pungent when crushed, attached to smooth pale-brownish twigs by short brown stub. **Cones** seed cones 3–5 cm long hanging downward at maturity, shedding seeds and falling in autumn. **Habitat** common tree throughout the island on well-drained sites.

## Black Spruce

*Picea mariana*

**Habit** a tree to 15 m, bark rough and scaly. **Needles** angular, four-sided, sharply pointed, 0.8–1.5 cm long, not very aromatic when crushed, attached to brown hairy twigs by short stubs. **Cones** seed cones 2–3 cm long, hanging downward at maturity, remaining on tree for many years. **Habitat** common throughout the island especially in wet poorly-drained sites.

## White Pine

*Pinus strobus*

**Habit** a tree to 25 m or more, old bark in scaly ridges separated by furrows. **Needles** angular, 3-sided, occurring in bundles of five, soft and flexible, 5–12 cm long. **Cones** seed cones pendulous, 8–15 cm long, shedding seeds and falling in second autumn. **Habitat** scattered in central and western spruce-fir forests, on well-drained sites.

## Red Pine

*Pinus resinosa*

**Habit** a tree to 25 m, bark scaly rusty brown, becoming furrowed into flat scaly plates with age. **Needles** half-rounded in cross section, occurring in bundles of two, firm, straight, breaking when bent, 8–15 cm long. **Cones** seed cones 4–6 cm long, old open cones remaining on tree for several years. **Habitat** uncommon, occurring only in a few dry sandy sites in central parts of the island.

## Scots Pine (Scotch Pine)

*Pinus sylvestris*

**Habit** a tree to 15 m, bark orange-brown and papery-scaly when young, becoming dark and furrowed in age. **Needles** half rounded in cross section, in bundles of two, stiff, twisted, sharp pointed, 3–7 cm long. **Cones** seed cones 4–7 cm long, taper to tip when young and point backwards along the stem, remaining on tree for several years. **Habitat** introduced but freely seeding and becoming common especially around towns and other settled areas.

## Tamarack (Larch) commonly called Juniper in Newfoundland

*Larix laricina*

**Habit** a tree to 15 m, bark grey and finely scaly. **Needles** soft and flexible, 1–2.5 cm long and borne in clusters of fifteen to sixty, turning yellow and falling in autumn, our only deciduous conifer. **Cones** seed cones are 1.5–2 cm long, purplish maturing to brown, seeds shed in autumn, old cones remaining several years. **Habitat** found throughout the island often in wet sites. (Several other larches have been planted horticulturally, but have larger cones than our native species.)

# FAMILY CUPRESSACEAE (CYPRESS FAMILY)

## Creeping Juniper

*Juniperus horizontalis*

**Habit** a prostrate shrub with creeping branches to over 1 m long, bark scaly and peeling on older branches. **Needles** leaves are scale-like and tightly overlapping on older stems in four rows, sharp tips; blue-green to grey-green on mature stems. **Cones** male and seed cones produced on separate plants, seed cones fleshy and berry-like, 6–10 mm in diameter, bluish to blue-black with a whitish bloom when mature, aromatic when crushed, young greenish and old bluish cones persist for several years. **Habitat** rocky woods, headlands and peatlands throughout the island in exposed locations.

## Common Juniper

*Juniperus communis*

**Habit** a shrub, low sprawling or spreading upright to 1 m, older branches with scaly bark. **Needles** stiff, curved, sharply pointed, 1–2 cm long, attached to stem in whorls of three. **Cones** seed cones fleshy and berry-like, 6–8 mm in diameter, bluish to bluish-black with a whitish bloom, aromatic when crushed, young green cones and older bluish cones remain for several years. **Habitat** occurs throughout the island in open exposed sites.

# FAMILY TAXACEAE (YEW FAMILY)

## Canada Yew

*Taxus canadensis*

**Habit** a shrub, sprawling or upright to 1 m tall, young bark green, becoming brown and scaly in age. **Needles** 1–2 cm long, flat, sharply pointed and are attached to twig by a green stalk. **Cones** male and female cones produced on separate plants, seed cones have a red fleshy cup surrounding the interior seed. **Habitat** occurs through-out the island as an understory shrub in moist coniferous woods.

## BROAD-LEAVED TREES

Sixteen broad-leaved trees are native to Newfoundland and comprise a minor component of our predominantly spruce-fir forests. They are also known as angiosperms (flowering plants) and hardwoods. Some—like the alders (*Alnus* spp.), cherries (*Prunus* spp.), mountain ashes (*Sorbus* spp.), maples (*Acer* spp.), and willows (*Salix* spp.)—are typically observed as bushy shrubs, but can grow to tree status in favourable sites. (Simply defined, shrubs are low, bushy, woody plants with many stems rarely reaching a height of 3 m; usually much less.) All of our willows are normally treated as shrubs; however, at least two species, the pussy willow and Bebb's willow, may attain tree status in the warm valleys of the west coast. When heavily and repeatedly moose browsed, even red maple, which is normally a tree, can exhibit a bushy state.

All of our broad-leaved trees are deciduous. That is, they shed their leaves each year prior to winter. Many broad-leaved trees found mainly in urban centres have been introduced to the island for horticultural purposes. A few of these, like some maples, poplars, and the European mountain ash have been able to moderately disperse on their own via seed production.

The birches are especially sought for firewood throughout the province. Some lesser uses include the production of fine lumber for flooring and furniture, traditional folk craft construction, sap extraction, and other minor purposes. Moose may browse heavily on winter twigs of maples, birch, dogberries, poplars, and willows. Birds utilize the buds and seeds and associated insects, especially in winter.

## FAMILY SALICACEAE (WILLOW FAMILY)

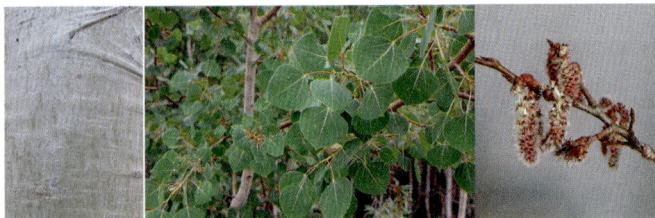

### Trembling Aspen
*Populus tremuloides*

**Habit** a medium sized tree to 25 m, young bark smooth and greenish-grey, old bark dark and furrowed. **Leaves** simple, alternate, finely toothed, hairless, with flattened leaf stalks (petioles). **Flowers** drooping catkins in early spring, male and female catkins on separate plants. **Fruit** a capsule splitting to release tiny seeds with tufts of white hairs. **Habitat** scattered stands throughout forested areas on sheltered well-drained sites.

*Balsam Poplar: (left) bark; (second from left) leaves; (second from right) male catkins; (right) female catkins*

## Balsam Poplar

*Populus balsamifera*

**Habit** a medium sized tree to 25 m, bark greyish-brown and smooth when young, dark and furrowed in age. **Leaves** simple, alternate, finely round- toothed with upper shiny surface, petiole round in cross section. **Flowers** drooping catkins in early spring, male and females on separate plants. **Fruit** a capsule with hairy-plumed seeds. **Habitat** throughout most of the island in moist rich sites.

*Willow bark: (left) young bark; (second left) old bark. Pussy Willow: (top centre) leaves; (top second right) male catkins; (top right) female catkins. Bebb's Willow: (bottom centre) leaves; (bottom right) female catkins*

## Pussy Willow & Bebb's Willow

*Salix discolor & Salix bebbiana*

**Habit** all of our native willows are normally small to medium sized shrubs, but these two species may reach small tree size, up to 6 m in warm sheltered woodlands, young bark smooth greyish-green, older bark becoming dark and furrowed. **Leaves** simple, alternate and may be slightly toothed, Pussy Willow leaves are smooth, hairless with a whitish bloom beneath, Bebb's Willow leaves are wrinkly above and hairy beneath. **Flowers** catkins, male and female on separate plants. **Fruit** a capsule producing many small tufted seeds. **Habitat** woodlands and forest edges throughout the island.

# FAMILY BETULACEAE (BIRCH FAMILY)

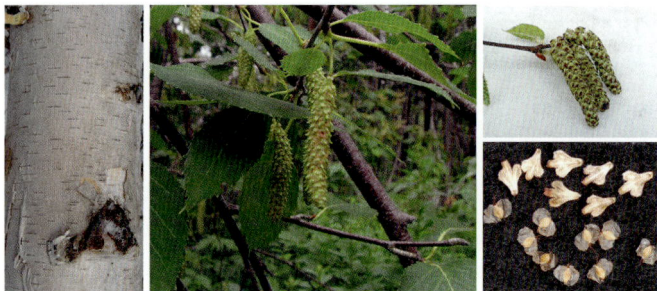

## White Birch (Paper Birch)

*Betula papyrifera*

**Habit** a medium sized tree to 25 m, young bark reddish-brown, old bark creamy-white shedding in sheets. **Leaves** simple, alternate, toothed, with fewer than 10 pairs of main veins, wedge-shaped or rounded at base of blade, surface not glandular. **Flowers** produced in spring in catkins, male and female catkins on same tree, seed catkins drooping at maturity. **Fruit** tiny winged nutlets falling when seed catkins shatter in autumn. **Habitat** common throughout the forested portions of the island on well-drained sites.

## Heartleaf Birch

*Betula cordifolia*

Similar to and often considered a variety of White Birch; can most easily be recognized by glandular leaf surfaces, heart-shaped blade bases and narrow tapering tips.

## Yellow Birch

*Betula alleghaniensis*

**Habit** a medium sized tree to 25 m, young bark reddish-brown becoming dull yellow and shredding in small papery curls, very old bark dark in furrowed plates. **Leaves** simple, alternate, toothed with larger and smaller teeth, nine or more pairs of main veins. **Flowers** male and female catkins on same tree, seed catkins erect on branches at maturity. **Fruit** winged nutlets shed in autumn. **Habitat** mostly in southern and western portions of island in rich well-drained woodlands. (Our only birch in which broken young twigs have a distinct wintergreen aroma and taste).

## Speckled Alder

*Alnus incana*

**Habit** a tall shrub or small tree to 6 m, bark smooth brown and speckled with conspicuous lenticels. **Leaves** simple, alternate, with undulating double-toothed margins, nine or more pairs of main veins, wrinkled appearance. **Flowers** male and female catkins on same plant in early spring, female catkins maturing into cone-like structures, becoming brown in autumn and may remain attached for several years. **Fruit** winged nutlets. **Habitat** moist and sheltered sites, more common in southern and southwestern portions of the island.

## Mountain Alder

*Alnus alnobetula*

**Habit** normally a bushy shrub to 3 m, occasionally small tree-like, bark brown with scattered pale lenticels less prominent than in Speckled Alder. **Leaves** simple, alternate, finely toothed, sometimes slightly undulating margins, fewer than ten pairs of main veins, wrinkly surface. **Flowers** male and female catkins on same plant, female catkins becoming brown and cone-like in autumn, remaining on stems for several years. **Fruit** a winged nutlet. **Habitat** common throughout the island in various habitats including very exposed sites.

# FAMILY ROSACEAE (ROSE FAMILY)

## Pincherry

*Prunus pensylvanica*

**Habit** a small tree to 8 m, young bark smooth shiny dark reddish-brown with conspicuous lenticels, bronze-brown to greyish in older trunks with conspicuous orange horizontal lenticels. **Leaves** simple, alternate, finely toothed, lanceolate with elongated tapering tip, a pair of rounded glands at blade base. **Flowers** white, 5-petalled, in clusters ca. earl June. **Fruit** a bright red cherry (drupe) 6-8 mm diameter in autumn. **Habitat** common throughout forested regions especially in younger successional stages.

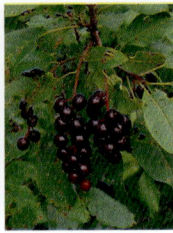

## Chokecherry

*Prunus virginiana*

**Habit** a large shrub or small tree to 6 m, bark dark greyish-brown with prominent orange lenticels becoming blackish and scaly in age. **Leaves** simple, alternate, finely toothed often broadest above the middle towards the tip, glands on petiole at base of blade. **Flowers** many 5-petalled white flowers produced in elongated clusters (racemes). **Fruit** a red to purplish-black cherry (drupe) about 8-10 mm across. **Habitat** forest edges and clearings on moist sites throughout much of the island, except the upper Great Northern Peninsula.

## Showy Mountain Ash & American Mountain Ash (Dogberry)

*Sorbus decora & Sorbus americana*

**Habit** large shrubs or small trees to 6 m, bark smooth greyish-green to greyish-brown. **Leaves** alternate and compound, each of 11–17 toothed leaflets, those of the American taper to a long pointed tip, those of the Showy taper more abruptly. **Flowers** tiny 5-petalled white flowers produced in large clusters. **Fruit** an orange to red, berry-like miniature apple (pome) 6–10 mm across. **Habitat** occur in a variety of habitats throughout the island from forests to sheltered sites.

## European Mountain Ash

*Sorbus aucuparia*

Similar to native Showy Mountain Ash and can most easily be distinguished by its densely grey hairy mature buds, whereas our native species have dark hairless or only slightly hairy buds. **Leaves** compound, 9–15 serrate leaflets. **Flowers** small 5-petalled white flowers. **Fruit** pendant clusters of orange-red drupes. **Habitat** introduced species that is spreading into natural habitats especially near habitations.

# FAMILY SAPINDACEAE (SOAPBERRY FAMILY)

*Red Maple: (top left) young bark; (top middle) summer leaves; (top right) flower; (bottom left) old bark; (bottom middle) autumn leaves; (bottom right) fruit*

## Red Maple

*Acer rubrum*

**Habit** a medium sized tree to 15 m, bark smooth grey developing grey scaly ridges with age. **Leaves** simple, alternate, double-toothed with 3–5 major lobes, often reddish when young and brilliant red/orange in autumn, upper surface smooth. **Flowers** either male or female, in separate clusters on same tree, sometimes bisexual, usually reddish-green to yellowish. **Fruit** in winged pairs. **Habitat** rich woods (hardwood forests) in central and western parts of the island.

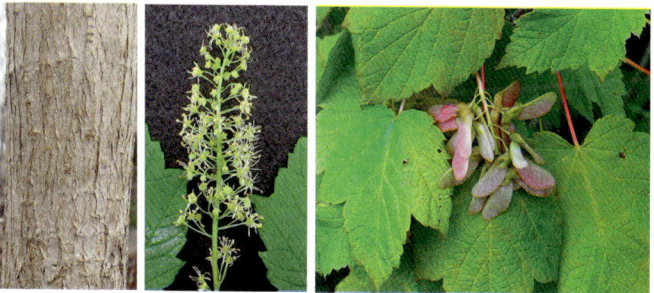

## Mountain Maple

*Acer spicatum*

**Habit** a large shrub or small tree to 6 m, bark light brownish to greyish-brown, smooth or slightly grooved. **Leaves** simple, alternate, coarsely toothed and lobed into three major lobes, sometimes five, upper surface wrinkly. **Flowers** in upright clusters, each tiny flower with 5 whitish to yellowish-green petals. **Fruit** in winged pairs. **Habitat** throughout the island in moist woodlands.

# FAMILY OLEACEAE (OLIVE FAMILY)

*Black Ash: (left) spongy bark; (middle) old bark; (top right) leaves; (bottom right) fruit*

## Black Ash

*Fraxinus nigra*

**Habit** a small tree to 10 m, often much less in Newfoundland, bark smooth light grey, sometimes becoming soft and corky, scaly in age. **Leaves** alternate and compound, of 7–11 narrow tapering and toothed leaflets. **Flowers** clusters of tiny petal-less flowers produced, either separate male and female or bisexual on the same or separate trees. **Fruit** in clusters, one-seeded flattened and winged. **Habitat** uncommon, only occurring in west-central and western parts of the island in damp and wet woodlands.

## WILDFLOWERS

The term 'wildflower' may be used to designate any plant that produces flowers, even those with inconspicuous flowers like grasses and sedges. In popular literature and general field guides, however, the term is usually restricted to herbaceous plants that have showy, colourful, and conspicuous flowers readily seen and recognized. In addition, shrubs with showy flowers are also included in this section.

All plants have their preferences for certain physical conditions, such as soil type, moisture, shading, temperature, and a variety of other factors that constitute their habitat. Some species require very specific conditions while others are more broadly tolerant. Species are organized in this section according to major habitats that occur on the island of Newfoundland. These include the following:

- FORESTS
- BARRENS AND HEATHLANDS
- PEATLANDS
- FRESHWATER WETLANDS
- SEASHORES AND SALT MARSHES
- FIELDS AND DISTURBED SITES

Representative common species are featured for each habitat. Many more can be found by the careful observer. Some species occur in several related habitats where local conditions are similar to those of their preferred environments. Habitats have been chosen in a very general, broad manner, and each may be further subdivided for detailed study by botanists. The habitats as envisioned for this guide book are characterized as follows:

### ■ FORESTS

Although we generally refer to our woodlands as 'boreal forest,' there are many forest subtypes in Newfoundland. For present purposes, forest is a tree-covered area on well-drained sites, typically spruce-fir with a sprinkling of deciduous trees and shrubs. Wildflowers will normally be found along the margins in clearings and on the forest floor where sufficient light can penetrate. Forest species tend to prefer cool, moist, and partially shaded conditions. However, in much of insular Newfoundland, hot dry spells are not common or prolonged and there is sufficient rainfall throughout the season, so a number of these species can also often be found growing in open, unforested habitats.

### ■ BARRENS AND HEATHLANDS

In Newfoundland, barrens are rocky, open areas with little good soil, typically in windswept coastal and alpine sites. Knee-high or lower shrubs of the heath family (Ericaceae) are common wildflowers in this habitat. The bedrock often determines which species can grow there. For example, the wildflower flora of limestone barrens, granite barrens, and serpentine barrens can be quite different.

### ■ PEATLANDS

Wet freshwater areas where considerable organic peat has accumulated are generally classified as bogs or fens. Bogs tend to be more acidic and nutrient-poor peatlands, hosting a particular group of wildflowers, whereas fens are more nutrient-rich and host some species not seen on typical sphagnum bogs. Nevertheless, there is some overlap of species between the two peatland types and also some overlap of species with the freshwater wetland category.

### ■ FRESHWATER WETLANDS

This category includes wildflowers of wet habitats where little or no peat has accumulated and plants grow mainly in wet mineral soil. These include stream and pond margins, marshes, wet ditches, pools, seepages, and any shallow waters where plants can successfully root and emerge. Where wetlands merge into peatlands, there is some overlap of species.

■ SEASHORES AND SALT MARSHES

From rocky and sandy seashores to mud flats and salt marshes, these wildflowers are adapted to, or tolerant of, salt water associated with either periodic flushing or from saltwater spray.

■ FIELDS AND DISTURBED SITES

Human disturbance creates conditions favourable for a group of wildflowers, many of which are introduced and have widely spread across the continent. Roadsides, fields, borrow-pits, pathways, lawns, and meadows are some of the more common examples of this habitat type. Included here are only the drier, well-drained disturbed sites and their typical common wildflowers.

## FORESTS

## FAMILY PRIMULACEAE (PRIMROSE FAMILY)

### Starflower
*Trientalis borealis*

**Habit/Leaves** a woodland herb 10–20 cm high with leaves in a whorl atop stem, leaves lanceolate short-stalked, 4–10 cm long. **Flowers** one to three star-shaped white flowers, 8–15 mm wide, each with 5–9 petals. **Fruit** a globular capsule 6–8 mm diameter. **Blooms** mid-season. **Habitat** forests, peatlands, and barrens.

## FAMILY CORNACEAE (DOGWOOD FAMILY)

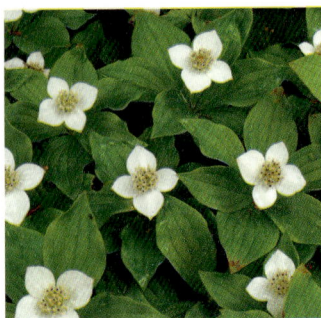

### Crackerberry (Bunchberry)
*Cornus canadensis*

**Habit/Leaves** a low sub-shrub 10–20 cm in height spreading vegetatively in colonies. **Flowers** each stem produces a cluster of tiny whitish-petalled flowers subtended by four large white leaf-like bracts, leaves oval entire, often in one major whorl of 4–6, each leaf 3–7 cm long. **Fruit** a cluster of red tasteless berry-like drupes, each 5–8 mm in diameter. **Blooms** mid-season. **Habitat** forest edges, clearings, and open barrens.

# FAMILY ERICACEAE (HEATH FAMILY)

## One-Flowered Wintergreen
*Moneses uniflora*

**Habit/Leaves** a small herb 5–10 cm high with basal finely toothed ovate leaves 1–2 cm long. **Flowers** flowering stems erect, each with a single nodding white waxy flower 10–20 mm wide. **Fruit** a 5-lobed capsule 5–8 mm wide. **Blooms** mid-season. **Habitat** shady woodlands.

## Creeping Snowberry
*Gaultheria hispidula*

**Habit/Leaves** a creeping evergreen sub-shrub to 5 cm in height with shiny oval leaves each less than 1 cm long, stems and leaf undersides have dark short stiff hairs. **Flowers** tiny white 4-petalled flowers 2–3 mm long are hidden under leaves. **Fruit** a white ovate berry 10 mm long with dark stiff hairs, and a wintergreen flavour. **Blooms** early in the season. **Habitat** shaded coniferous woodlands, clearings, and edges.

## Ghost Pipe

*Monotropa uniflora*

**Habit/Leaves** a white waxy plant 10–20 cm in height, without chlorophyll, associated with a soil fungus and coniferous trees. **Flowers** a single nodding flower 12–25 mm long produced on each stem. **Fruit** a globular capsule 5–7 mm long becoming erect and turning black at maturity. **Blooms** late season. **Habitat** dry shady coniferous woods.

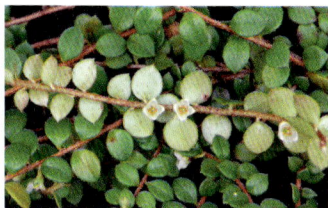

## Trailing Arbutus
*Epigaea repens*

**Habit/Leaves** a prostrate sub-shrub 5–10 cm in height with large shiny oval leathery leaves to 7 cm long. **Flowers** tubular and 5-petalled, white to pink and about 12 mm long. **Fruit** a globular capsule 6 mm diameter. **Blooms** early in the season. **Habitat** drier, open coniferous forests.

## One-Sided Wintergreen
*Orthilia secunda*

**Habit/Leaves** a 10–20 cm tall herb with long-stalked basal evergreen shiny leaves with ovate blades 2–6 cm long. **Flowers** bell-shaped 5–7 mm across, greenish-white and arranged on one side of stalk. **Fruit** a globe-shaped capsule 4–8 mm across. **Blooms** mid-season. **Habitat** shady woodlands.

# FAMILY ROSACEAE (ROSE FAMILY)

## Mountain Serviceberry (Chuckley Pear)

*Amelanchier bartramiana*

**Habit/Leaves** a bushy shrub, 2–2.5 m in height, the most common of the several *Amelanchier* species in Newfoundland, oval leaves are about 5 cm long and finely toothed. **Flowers** about 2–3 cm across. **Fruit** a purple-black edible berry 1–1.5 cm long. **Blooms** early in the season. **Habitat** woodland edges, clearings, and thickets.

## Dewberry (Plumboy)

*Rubus pubescens*

**Habit/Leaves** a low sub-shrub 10–25 cm tall with trailing stems, leaves are palmately compound of usually 3 sometimes 5 leaflets, each 2–7 cm long. **Flowers** upright flowering stems each bear one or more 5-petalled white flowers 6–10 mm long. **Fruit** red edible raspberry-like fruit, 10–15 mm long. **Blooms** mid-season. **Habitat** damp woodlands and clearings.

## Largeleaf Avens

*Geum macrophyllum*

**Habit/Leaves** an upright herb 0.3–1 m in height with pinnately compound or lobed leaves, larger and smaller leaflets, the terminal segment large and rounded. **Flowers** yellow, 5-petalled, 1–1.5 cm across. **Fruit** a bristly globular cluster of achenes 1.5 cm diameter. **Blooms** mid-season. **Habitat** damp open woods and clearings.

## Virginia Rose

*Rosa virginiana*

**Habit/Leaves** an upright shrub 1–2 m in height with alternate compound leaves (5–11 toothed leaflets), scattered spines on stems, but not highly bristly like our other native rose (*R. nitida*). **Flowers** 3–5 cm across. **Fruit** a red hip with a few bristles, 1–1.5 cm diameter. **Blooms** mid-season. **Habitat** woodland edges, clearings, and shrubby barrens.

# FAMILY RANUNCULACEAE (BUTTERCUP FAMILY)

## Tall Meadow Rue

*Thalictrum pubescens*

**Habit/Leaves** a tall herb of 1–2 m with pinnately compound leaves similar to the garden columbine, leaflets lobed near tip. **Flowers** male and female flowers usually without petals are on separate plants. **Fruit** a cluster of beaked achenes, each achene 5 mm long. **Blooms** mid-season. **Habitat** moist woods clearings, stream banks, and meadows.

# FAMILY ASTERACEAE (ASTER FAMILY)

### Flat-Topped White Aster
*Doellingeria umbellata*

**Habit/Leaves** a tall stout herb 1–1.5 m in height with lanceolate entire leaves up to 15 cm long. **Flowers** flowering heads are 1–2 cm in diameter and have white ray florets and yellow central disc florets, arranged in a flat-topped inflorescence. **Fruit** achenes, each 3–4 mm long with hairy tips. **Blooms** late in season. **Habitat** woodland edges, thickets, and meadows.

### Purple-Stemmed Aster
*Symphyotrichum puniceum*

**Habit/Leaves** a stout herb 1–1.5 m in height with large lanceolate entire leaves (to 20 cm long) that clasp the upright purple stem. **Flowers** heads with lilac to bluish rays and yellow central disc florets, heads 2–3 cm across. **Fruit** a bristly achene 2–3 mm long with tuft of white hairs. **Blooms** late in the season. **Habitat** moist soils of woodland clearings, stream banks, and meadows.

# FAMILY GROSSULARIACEAE (CURRANT FAMILY)

### Skunk Currant
*Ribes glandulosum*

**Habit/Leaves** a sprawling shrub 30–90 cm in height with 5-pointed petioled palmately lobed alternate leaves, toothed blades 2–8 cm long, produces a skunky odour when crushed. **Flowers** white to pink 5–6 mm across, flower stalks glandular sticky. **Fruit** a red bristly edible berry, 6 mm diameter. **Blooms** early in the season. **Habitat** woodlands and clearings.

### Bristly Black Currant
*Ribes lacustre*

**Habit/Leaves** a shrub 0.5–1 m in height with leaf blades palmately lobed and with toothed margins, blades 4–8 cm long, stems densely covered with bristly prickles. **Flowers** 6 mm across, pinkish green in loose drooping clusters. **Fruit** black bristly edible berries, 9–12 mm diameter. **Blooms** early season. **Habitat** wet woods, clearings, and edges.

# FAMILY ASPARAGACEAE (ASPARAGUS FAMILY)

### Wild Lily of the Valley
*Maianthemum canadense*

**Habit/Leaves** a herb 10–20 cm tall with 2–3 shiny leaves each 2–8 cm long. **Flowers** an elongated cluster of tiny 4-petalled flowers, each 3–5 mm across. **Fruit** brown-speckled berries 3–4 mm across turning reddish in the fall. **Blooms** mid-season. **Habitat** forest edges, clearings, and sometimes in open peatlands and barrens.

# FAMILY LILIACEAE (LILY FAMILY)

### Corn Lily (Blue-Bead Lily)
*Clintonia borealis*

**Habit/Leaves** an upright herb 25–30 cm tall with 2–3 smooth entire elliptical elongate basal leaves, each up to 20 cm long. **Flowers** stalks with 3–8 yellow bell-shaped flowers, each 15–18 mm long. **Fruit** dark bluish berries each 7–9 mm diameter. **Blooms** mid-season. **Habitat** shady areas of the forest floor, and occasionally in open localities.

# FAMILY ONAGRACEAE (EVENING PRIMROSE FAMILY)

### Fireweed
*Chamerion angustifolium*

**Habit/Leaves** an upright leafy herb 1–2 m in height, leaves lanceolate and smooth margined, 15–20 cm long. **Flowers** produced in an elongated terminal raceme, magenta and 4-petalled with conspicuous 4-divided stigma, each 1.5–3 cm wide. **Fruit** an elongated capsule up to 6 cm long. **Blooms** mid to late season. **Habitat** forest clearings, cut-overs, burns, and disturbed habitats.

# FAMILY CAPRIFOLIACEAE (HONEYSUCKLE FAMILY)

### Twinflower
*Linnaea borealis*

**Habit/Leaves** a trailing sub-shrub 5–10 cm in height with opposite oval evergreen leaves 1–2 cm long with a few teeth. **Flowers** flowering stalks topped by two pink flowers each 8–15 mm long. **Fruit** a tiny dry one-seeded capsule. **Blooms** mid-season. **Habitat** forest clearings, peatlands, and barrens.

# FAMILY PLANTAGINACEAE (PLANTAIN FAMILY)

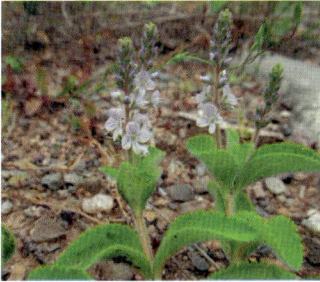

## Common Speedwell
*Veronica officinalis*

**Habit/Leaves** a hairy trailing herb with branch ends curving upward and becoming erect, flowering stems 15–20 cm tall, leaves elliptic opposite and toothed, 2–5 cm long. **Flowers** pale blue with darker lines, 4-lobed and 5–7 mm wide. **Fruit** flat heart-shaped capsules, 4–5 mm long. **Blooms** mid-season. **Habitat** drier mixed woods, edges, and clearings.

# FAMILY SAXIFRAGACEAE (SAXIFRAGE FAMILY)

## Naked Mitrewort
*Mitella nuda*

**Habit/Leaves** a herb 15–20 cm tall with basal long-stalked leaves, blades rounded 1–5 cm wide, hairy with heart-shaped bases. **Flowers** five petal-like sepals and five much-divided 'feathery' true petals, 6–8 mm across. **Fruit** a capsule 2–3 mm long. **Blooms** mid-season. **Habitat** moist woodlands.

# FAMILY ARALIACEAE (GINSENG FAMILY)

## Wild Sarsaparilla
*Aralia nudicaulis*

**Habit/Leaves** a large compound leaf arises at ground level on a long petiole to 30–40 cm in height. **Flowers** the flowering stalk arises from ground level, topped by a spherical cluster of tiny greenish flowers with white anthers. **Fruit** black berries, each about 5 mm across. **Blooms** mid-season. **Habitat** shaded woodlands and clearings.

# FAMILY ORCHIDACEAE (ORCHID FAMILY)

## Pink Lady's Slipper
*Cypripedium acaule*

**Habit/Leaves** from the centre of two basal sheathing entire leaves, each about 10–20 cm long, arises a flowering stalk, 25–40 cm tall. **Flowers** a single pink flower; slipper 3–6 cm long. **Fruit** a dry upright capsule about 3 cm long. **Blooms** early in the season. **Habitat** open dry woodlands and drier shrubby peatlands.

### Early Coralroot
*Corallorhiza trifida*

**Habit/Leaves** yellowish-green upright stems to 25 cm tall are leafless except for a few sheaths near base. **Flowers** greenish-yellow except for whitish lip petal 3–4 mm long, which may be red-spotted. **Fruit** a greenish capsule about 1 cm long. **Blooms** early in the season. **Habitat** shady woodlands, edges, and thickets.

## BARRENS AND HEATHLANDS

## FAMILY CARYOPHYLLACEAE (PINK FAMILY)

### Field Chickweed
*Cerastium arvense*

**Habit/Leaves** a matted trailing herb 10–20 cm in height with longer trailing stems, narrow opposite leaves 2–4 cm long. **Flowers** 1–2 cm across, each with 5 notched white petals. **Fruit** a capsule 6–10 mm long. **Blooms** mid-season. **Habitat** rocky and turfy barrens, especially limestone and serpentine, and coastal headlands.

### Moss Campion
*Silene acaulis*

**Habit/Leaves** plants 5–10 cm tall form low tight cushions of narrow opposite leaves, each 0.5–1 cm long. **Flowers** 5-petalled pink flowers 1–1.5 cm across are produced on short stems. **Fruit** a capsule 6–8 mm long. **Blooms** early season, and may reflower in the fall. **Habitat** rocky coastal, limestone, and serpentine barrens.

## FAMILY POLYGONACEAE (BUCKWHEAT FAMILY)

### Alpine Bistort
*Bistorta vivipara*

**Habit/Leaves** a herb 15–25 cm tall, with long-petiole basal leaves, narrowly elliptic, dark green and shiny blades 1–5 cm long, stem leaves narrow. **Flowers** tiny, 5 petal-like sepals white or pink, inflorescence in a long narrow spike, the lower flowers replaced by bulblets, which fall off and grow into new plants. **Fruit** a 3-sided achene 2–3 mm long. **Blooms** mid-season. **Habitat** barrens, headlands, and coastal meadows.

# FAMILY DIAPENSIACEAE (DIAPENSIA FAMILY)

## Lapland Diapensia
### *Diapensia lapponica*

**Habit/Leaves** an evergreen sub-shrub, 5–8 cm high, forming tight clusters or small mounds of tiny opposite entire spatulate leaves 1–2 cm long. **Flowers** 5-petalled white flowers are 1–1.5 cm across. **Fruit** a capsule 2–3 mm long. **Blooms** an early bloomer, sometimes populations bloom mid to late season. **Habitat** rocky outcrops and exposed gravels, and turfy headlands.

# FAMILY ROSACEAE (ROSE FAMILY)

## White Mountain Avens
### *Dryas integrifolia*

**Habit/Leaves** a partially evergreen mat-forming shrub, 5–10 cm in height, with alternate elliptical entire leaves 0.5–1 cm long, shiny on upper surface, white-hairy beneath. **Flowers** white 7–10 petalled flowers are about 1.5 cm across. **Fruit** a cluster of achenes with long feathery styles that often twist together. **Blooms** mid-season. **Habitat** rocky limestone barrens and cliffs.

## Three-Toothed Cinquefoil
### *Sibbaldia tridentata*

**Habit/Leaves** plants 5–20 cm in height, the evergreen leaves are composed of three leaflets, each leaflet has characteristic three teeth at its tip. **Flowers** white, 5-petalled, 1–1.5 cm wide. **Fruit** a cluster of achenes. **Blooms** mid-season. **Habitat** coastal barrens, meadows, and headlands.

## Shrubby Cinquefoil
### *Dasiphora fruticosa*

**Habit/Leaves** a deciduous shrub 0.2–1 m tall (but variable depending on exposure) with alternate pinnately compound leaves of 5–7 smooth-edged leaflets. **Flowers** yellow, 5-petalled, and about 2–3 cm across. **Fruit** a cluster of achenes. **Blooms** mid to late season. **Habitat** open rocky barrens to open shrubby sites and wetlands.

## Arctic Raspberry
### *Rubus arcticus*

**Habit/Leaves** a low sub-shrub, 5–15 cm tall, with compound leaves of three leaflets, each 1–4 cm long. **Flowers** often with just a single pink flower 15–25 mm across that is produced at each stem tip. **Fruit** a red raspberry-like fruit about 1 cm diameter. **Blooms** mid-season. **Habitat** turfy barrens.

# FAMILY ERICACEAE (HEATH FAMILY)

## Lowbush Blueberry

*Vaccinium angustifolium*

**Habit/Leaves** a deciduous shrub, 30–50 cm tall, with elliptical to lanceolate finely toothed leaves. **Flowers** urn-shaped, white to pinkish, 5–6 mm long and produced in clusters on branch ends. **Fruit** a bluish edible berry 5–15 mm diameter often with a waxy bloom. **Blooms** early to mid-season. **Habitat** barrens, open woodlands, and burns.

## Alpine Bilberry

*Vaccinium uliginosum*

**Habit/Leaves** a sprawling, often prostrate deciduous shrub 10–30 cm tall, with alternate entire oval leaves 1–2 cm long. **Flowers** white to pink urn-shaped flowers 5 mm long produced at stem tips. **Fruit** a dark bluish berry with a waxy bloom, 6 mm diameter. **Blooms** early season. **Habitat** exposed barrens and coastal headlands.

## Alpine Bearberry

*Arctous alpina*

**Habit/Leaves** a deciduous sub-shrub, 3–5 cm tall, with wrinkled alternate leaves 2–3 cm long, deep green turning bright red in fall. **Flowers** whitish urn-shaped flowers 5 mm long are produced as new leaves are forming. **Fruit** a purple-black berry 6–10 mm diameter; a rare, similar, species with red mature fruits also occurs (*A. rubra*). **Blooms** very early season. **Habitat** exposed rocky barrens and on headlands.

## Partridgeberry (Mountain Cranberry)

*Vaccinium vitis-idaea*

**Habit/Leaves** a trailing evergreen sub-shrub, 5–10 cm in height, with shiny oval entire leathery leaves 1–1.5 cm long. **Flowers** bell-shaped, pink, nodding and about 6 mm long. **Fruit** a red edible berry 6–8 mm in diameter. **Blooms** mid-season. **Habitat** barrens, headlands, and sandy and rocky open woods.

## Common Bearberry

*Arctostaphylos uva-ursi*

**Habit/Leaves** a trailing evergreen shrub 5–10 cm tall with smooth entire shiny oval to spatulate leaves 1–2 cm long. **Flowers** clusters of pink urn-shaped flowers 5 mm long. **Fruit** a red berry 8–10 mm diameter. **Blooms** early season. **Habitat** exposed rocky barrens and alpine areas.

## Alpine Azalea

*Kalmia procumbens*

**Habit/Leaves** a prostrate evergreen sub-shrub 2–5 cm tall, leaves opposite shiny and less than 1 cm long. **Flowers** pink, 5-petalled, and about 0.5 cm across. **Fruit** roundish reddish capsules 3–4 mm long. **Blooms** early season. **Habitat** alpine and coastal barrens and headlands.

## Black Crowberry

*Empetrum nigrum*

**Habit/Leaves** a mat-forming evergreen shrub 5–10 cm tall, with alternate needle-like leaves 3–7 mm long with a white groove on underside. **Flowers** tiny, 2 mm across and not usually noticed with the naked eye; most commonly recognized by leaves and fruits, which remain over winter. **Fruit** black berry-like drupes 6–10 mm diameter; red and purple fruited species also occur. **Blooms** very early season. **Habitat** barrens, coastal headlands, bogs, and open woodlands.

## Lapland Rosebay

*Rhododendron lapponicum*

**Habit/Leaves** a straggling low evergreen shrub 15–30 cm tall, with leathery and rusty scurfy elliptic/oval entire leaves 1–2 cm long; young twigs rusty-scaly. **Flowers** deep purple, 5-petalled, 1–2 cm across in terminal clusters. **Fruit** erect rusty capsules 5–7 mm long. **Blooms** early season. **Habitat** rocky alkaline soils of the limestone and serpentine barrens.

# FAMILY ORCHIDACEAE (ORCHID FAMILY)

## Large Yellow Lady's Slipper

*Cypripedium parviflorum* var. *pubescens*

**Habit/Leaves** this short compact orchid of the limestone barrens is 15–20 cm tall. **Flowers** typical yellow slipper-type flowers that have flattish, undulating or only slightly twisted yellowish side petals as opposed to the taller wildlands variant with maroon highly-twisted side petals. **Fruit** an erect capsule 2–3 cm long. **Blooms** early to mid-season. **Habitat** open turfy limestone barrens.

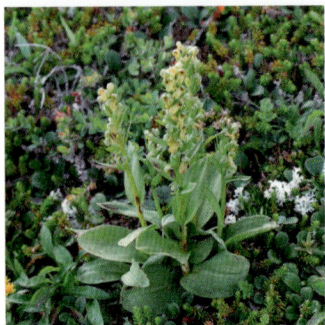

### Longbract Frog Orchid

*Coeloglossum viride*

**Habit/Leaves** an upright herb 6–20 cm tall with 2–4 lanceolate sheathing leaves. **Flowers** each flower of the inflorescence subtended by a conspicuous leaf-like bract, upper greenish flower parts forming a hood, lip petal elongate with a distinctively notched tip sometimes coloured red. **Fruit** a capsule 1 cm long. **Blooms** mid-season. **Habitat** shrubby turfy barrens and coastal meadows, often over limestone.

## FAMILY ASTERACEAE (ASTER FAMILY)

### Northern Goldenrod

*Solidago multiradiata*

**Habit/Leaves** a low herb, 10–20 cm in height, with narrow alternate, mostly entire leaves tapering to both ends, blades 2–5 cm long. **Flowers** bright yellow flower heads are grouped into large clusters on stem ends. **Fruit** a 1.5 mm achene with terminal hair tuft. **Blooms** mid-season. **Habitat** coastal, limestone, and serpentine barrens.

### Gall of the Earth

*Nabalus trifoliolatus*

**Habit/Leaves** an upright herb with milky sap, 20–50 cm tall, lower leaves usually divided into 3, but upper ones are simple and arrowhead-shaped. **Flowers** the composite flowering heads about 2 cm long have pale-yellow rays and droop. **Fruit** fluffy 'seed heads,' each individual achene 5 mm long with its own dandelion-like 'parachute.' **Blooms** mid to late season. **Habitat** barrens, clearings, headlands, and thickets.

## FAMILY ONAGRACEAE (EVENING PRIMROSE FAMILY)

### River Beauty

*Chamerion latifolium*

**Habit/Leaves** a herb 15–30 cm tall, with alternate entire lanceolate blue-green leaves 3–5 cm long. **Flowers** the 4-petalled pink flowers are over 2 cm across. **Fruit** an elongate capsule 5–6 cm long. **Blooms** mid-season. **Habitat** moist gravelly soils, barrens, and flood plains.

# FAMILY PLUMBAGINACEAE (LEADWORT FAMILY)

## Sea Thrift

*Armeria maritima*

**Habit/Leaves** a herb, 15–20 cm tall, with a cluster of basal grass-like leaves 5–10 cm long. **Flowers** upright flowering stems each bear a tight 2–3 cm wide head of pink 5-petalled flowers. **Fruit** a tiny single-seeded capsule. **Blooms** mid-season. **Habitat** coastal rocky barrens, especially limestone and serpentine.

# FAMILY FABACEAE (LEGUME FAMILY)

## Field Oxytrope

*Oxytropis campestris*

**Habit/Leaves** a herb 5–10 cm tall, with a basal rosette of compound leaves, each with 13–25 small leaflets 2–8 mm long. **Flowers** flowering stems terminate in clusters of pea-like flowers which lay on the leafy rosette. **Fruit** pointed pea-pods (legumes) 1–1.5 cm long. **Blooms** early to mid-season. **Habitat** limestone and gravelly coastal barrens.

# FAMILY CORNACEAE (DOGWOOD FAMILY)

## Swedish Bunchberry

*Cornus suecica*

**Habit/Leaves** 10–20 cm in height and similar to the common Crackerberry or Bunchberry, but leaves are spaced in several (3–7) pairs down the stem. **Flowers** tiny purple flowers 1 mm across are clustered above the four white bracts. **Fruit** a red berry about 5 mm diameter. **Blooms** mid-season. **Habitat** coastal headlands, barrens, and meadows.

# FAMILY CAMPANULACEAE (BELLFLOWER FAMILY)

## Harebell

*Campanula gieseckeana*

**Habit/Leaves** a herb 10–30 cm tall with basal leaves long-stalked round and toothed, stem leaves narrow, entire, 1–6 cm long. **Flowers** the 2 cm long bell-shaped flowers are distinctive, blue or rarely white. **Fruit** cylindric capsules 5–8 mm long. **Blooms** mid to late season. **Habitat** barrens, coastal shores, headlands, and meadows.

**PEATLANDS**

# FAMILY RANUNCULACEAE (BUTTERCUP FAMILY)

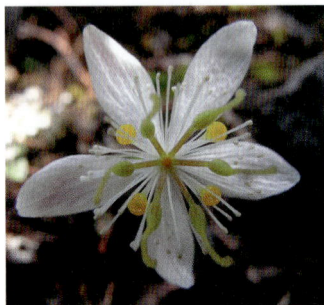

### Goldthread

*Coptis trifolia*

**Habit/Leaves** a low herb 5–10 cm in height with compound trifoliate leathery shiny leaves having toothed margins. **Flowers** each thin flowering stem produces a single flower 1–1.5 cm wide with 5–7 white petal-like sepals. **Fruit** a cluster of dry follicle fruits. **Blooms** early to mid-season. **Habitat** peatlands, moist open woodlands, and moist barrens.

# FAMILY ROSACEAE (ROSE FAMILY)

### Bakeapple (Cloudberry)

*Rubus chamaemorus*

**Habit/Leaves** a low deciduous subshrub 10–20 cm in height with 5-lobed toothed wrinkled firm leaves. **Flowers** with 4–7 white petals about 2–4 cm across; male and female flowers are on separate plants. **Fruit** edible orange and raspberry-like fruit. **Blooms** early to mid-season. **Habitat** acidic bogs.

# FAMILY DROSERACEAE (SUNDEW FAMILY)

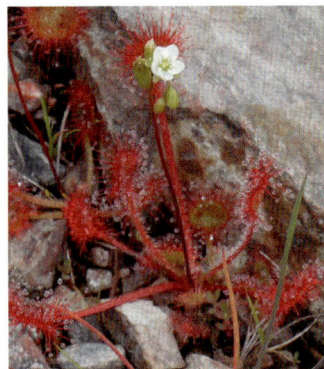

### Roundleaf Sundew

*Drosera rotundifolia*

**Habit/Leaves** a carnivorous plant 5–15 cm tall with a basal rosette of rounded reddish leaf blades covered with sticky glandular hairs that capture tiny insects. **Flowers** the raceme slowly uncoils and white 5-petalled flowers open one at a time in sunshine. **Fruit** an ellipsoidal many- seeded capsule 5 mm long. **Blooms** mid-season. **Habitat** bogs, but also in many other wet habitats.

# FAMILY ASPARAGACEAE (ASPARAGUS FAMILY)

## Threeleaf False Solomon's Seal
*Maianthemum trifolium*

**Habit/Leaves** a herb 10–20 cm in height with 2–4 (usually 3) lanceolate sheathing entire leaves 5–10 cm long. **Flowers** 3–8 flowers in a loose inflorescence each with six white petals, 7–10 mm across. **Fruit** a red berry 4–6 mm diameter. **Blooms** mid-season. **Habitat** peatlands and other wet open areas.

# FAMILY ORCHIDACEAE (ORCHID FAMILY)

## Rose Pogonia
*Pogonia ophioglossoides*

**Habit/Leaves** a herb 10–20 cm tall with a single elongate entire leaf sheathing the stem near the middle. **Flowers** the single pink flower is 1.5–3 cm long with a showy bottom fringe and hairy lip. **Fruit** a capsule 2 cm long. **Blooms** mid-season. **Habitat** wet peatlands.

## White Fringed Orchid
*Platanthera blephariglottis*

**Habit/Leaves** an upright herb 20–40 cm tall with 2–3 entire lanceolate leaves and 1 or 2 small bracts beneath inflorescence. **Flowers** 15–30 white flowers produced with the lower elongate lip petal conspicuously fringed. **Fruit** a capsule about 1 cm long. **Blooms** mid-season. **Habitat** peatlands.

## Club-Spur Orchid
*Platanthera clavellata*

**Habit/Leaves** a herb 10–20 cm tall with a single elongate elliptic sheathing leaf near base and 1 or 2 small bract-leaves up the stem. **Flowers** 5–15 small greenish flowers each with a curved spur enlarging at the tip (club-shaped). **Fruit** a capsule about 8 mm long. **Blooms** mid-season. **Habitat** peatlands and other open wet areas.

## Dragon's Mouth Orchid
*Arethusa bulbosa*

**Habit/Leaves** a herb 15–25 cm tall with a single elongate entire sheathing basal leaf. **Flowers** the stem produces a terminal large 3–5 cm long flower with a conspicuous showy lip petal and upright 'ears,' flowers pink but occasionally ranging to white. **Fruit** a ridged capsule 2 cm long. **Blooms** mid-season. **Habitat** open peatlands.

### Grasspink

*Calopogon tuberosus*

**Habit/Leaves** a herb 10–25 cm in height with a single elongate entire sheathing basal leaf. **Flowers** each flowering stem produces 2–7 large flowers 2–4 cm wide with the hairy lip petal uppermost. **Fruit** an oval capsule about 1.5 cm long. **Blooms** mid-season. **Habitat** open bogs.

## FAMILY ERICACEAE (HEATH FAMILY)

### Leatherleaf

*Chamaedaphne calyculata*

**Habit/Leaves** an evergreen shrub, 0.6–1 m tall, with leathery alternate elliptic to ovate leaves up to 3 cm long, margins with fine teeth, both surfaces brown-scurfy. **Flowers** urn-shaped flowers 6 mm long droop from a leafy end branch. **Fruit** a rounded seed capsule about 5 mm in diameter. **Blooms** early in the season. **Habitat** peatlands and wetlands.

### Labrador Tea

*Rhododendron groenlandicum*

**Habit/Leaves** an upright alternate leaved evergreen shrub 0.6–1 m tall, leaves are elliptic, 2–5 cm long, upper surface veined, underside with in-rolled entire margins, mature leaves densely rusty and hairy beneath. **Flowers** white 5-petalled flowers produced in terminal clusters. **Fruit** a rounded seed capsule about 5 mm long. **Blooms** mid-season. **Habitat** peatlands, wetlands, and moist barrens.

### Dwarf Huckleberry

*Gaylussacia bigeloviana*

**Habit/Leaves** a deciduous shrub 20–30 cm in height with alternate elliptic to spatulate hairy-fringed leaves 3–5 cm long, each with a distinctly pointed tip, leaves are glandular dotted, turn bright red in autumn. **Flowers** white bell-shaped drooping flowers 5–9 mm long. **Fruit** a black berry-like drupe 6–7 mm diameter. **Blooms** mid-season. **Habitat** peatlands.

### Sheep Laurel

*Kalmia angustifolia*

**Habit/Leaves** an evergreen shrub 0.8–1.2 m tall with leaves usually in whorls of three, leaves elliptic, entire, and 2–5 cm long with short petioles. **Flowers** 5-lobed, saucer-shaped with tiny anther pouches. **Fruit** a rounded capsule 6 mm in diameter. **Blooms** mid-season. **Habitat** widespread in peatlands, wetlands, forest clearings, and burns.

### Marshberry (Small Cranberry)

*Vaccinium oxycoccos*

**Habit/Leaves** a small trailing evergreen shrub 2–5 cm high, leaves ovate entire shiny green above, pale beneath, 4–8 mm long. **Flowers** nodding flowers have 4 folded-back petals and united beak-like stamens. **Fruit** a red berry often overwintering, 0.5–1 cm diameter. **Blooms** mid-season. **Habitat** peatlands and wetlands.

### Bog Laurel

*Kalmia polifolia*

**Habit/Leaves** a shrub 20–30 cm tall with opposite narrow leaves up to 3 cm long, the upper surface shiny green, the underside white with in-rolled entire margins. **Flowers** 5-lobed and saucer-shaped with tiny anther pouches. **Fruit** rounded reddish-brown seed capsules about 5 mm long. **Blooms** early to mid-season. **Habitat** peatlands and wetlands.

### Bog Rosemary

*Andromeda polifolia* var. *latifolia*

**Habit/Leaves** an evergreen shrub 30–50 cm tall with narrow alternate entire leaves up to 5 cm long, the edges in-rolled, the upper surface veiny and blue-green, the undersurface white with fine hairs. **Flowers** pink urn-shaped flowers are about 5–8 mm long. **Fruit** a globular 5-lobed pink seed capsule about 6 mm diameter. **Blooms** in mid-season. **Habitat** peatlands and wetlands.

### Rhodora

*Rhododendron canadense*

**Habit/Leaves** a deciduous shrub 0.6–1 m tall with elliptical entire alternate, somewhat hairy, grey-green leaves. **Flowers** large and showy, 2–3 cm long with narrow partly fused petals. **Fruit** an oval hairy seed capsule, 1–1.5 cm long. **Blooms** early in the season. **Habitat** peatlands, barrens, and open wet clearings.

### Black Huckleberry

*Gaylussacia baccata*

**Habit/Leaves** a deciduous shrub 30–50 cm tall with ovate oblong entire leaves 3–5 cm long, margins have a fringe of hairs and a tiny stub at the tip, turning brilliant scarlet in autumn. **Flowers** clusters of reddish flowers droop from branches each about 6 mm long. **Fruit** a black berry-like drupe 6–7 mm diameter. **Blooms** mid-season. **Habitat** peatlands and wet barrens.

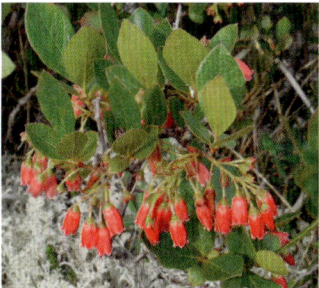

## FAMILY LENTIBULARIACEAE (BLADDERWORT FAMILY)

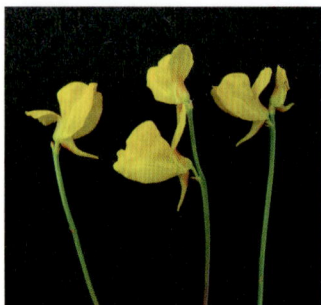

### Horned Bladderwort

*Utricularia cornuta*

**Habit/Leaves** a carnivorous species with leafless flowering stalks 10–20 cm in height arising from peaty substrate, unseen thread-like leaves with bladders are submerged in the substrate. **Flowers** bright yellow, 2-lipped with a distinct downward-pointing sharp spur. **Fruit** a capsule about 4 mm long. **Blooms** mid-season. **Habitat** wet peaty depressions and shallow bog and fen pools.

## FAMILY CAPRIFOLIACEAE (HONEYSUCKLE FAMILY)

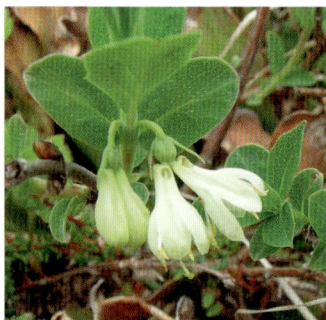

### Mountain Fly Honeysuckle

*Lonicera villosa*

**Habit/Leaves** a sprawling shrub, 30–80 cm in height with opposite elliptical to oblong leaves 2–5 cm long having hairy surfaces and margins. **Flowers** pale yellow, funnel-shaped with 5-petalled lobes borne in pairs. **Fruit** a blue 'two-eyed' berry up to 1 cm long. **Blooms** early to mid-season. **Habitat** wet peatlands, stream and pond margins, and wet barrens.

## FAMILY SARRACENIACEAE (PITCHER PLANT FAMILY)

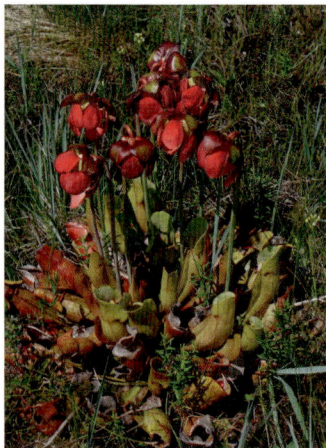

### Pitcher Plant

*Sarracenia purpurea*

**Habit/Leaves** the provincial flower of Newfoundland and Labrador, 25–45 cm in height, producing a basal rosette of upright pitcher-shaped leaves collecting water and drowning small insects to absorb nutrients from decayed bodies. **Flowers** the large single nodding flower on each stalk has reddish petals (occasionally yellow) that fall early, exposing the inverted umbrella-like stigma. **Fruit** an ovoid capsule 1–2 cm in diameter. **Blooms** mid-season. **Habitat** bogs and wet seepages.

# FAMILY ASTERACEAE (ASTER FAMILY)

### Bog Goldenrod

*Solidago uliginosa*

**Habit/Leaves** a herb 40-80 cm tall with one to several unbranched stems, upper leaves are simple, sessile, toothed or not, narrow tapering to both ends, linear-lanceolate, lower leaves long stalked. **Flowers** elongate club-shaped inflorescences of many tiny yellow composite heads terminate the stems. **Fruit** an achene with a short terminal tuft of hairs. **Blooms** mid to late season. **Habitat** peatlands and other wet habitats.

### Bog Aster

*Oclemena nemoralis*

**Habit/Leaves** a single-stemmed aster 20–50 cm tall with alternate narrow sessile entire lanceolate leaves about 2–3 cm long. **Flowers** often just a single flowering head, occasionally a few ray florets of flowering head pale-lilac, central disc florets yellow. **Fruit** an achene with terminal fluffy hair tuft. **Blooms** mid to late season. **Habitat** bogs, fens, and other open wet sites.

### Rough Aster

*Eurybia radula*

**Habit/Leaves** a herb 20–50 cm tall with a single unbranched stem terminating in one to a few flowering heads, leaves sessile lanceolate rough-hairy with sparsely-toothed margins, 4–8 cm long. **Flowers** ray florets pale blue, central disc florets yellow. **Blooms** mid to late season. **Habitat** peatlands and other wet habitats.

# FAMILY MYRICACEAE (WAX-MYRTLE FAMILY)

*Sweet Gale flowers: (top) female catkins; (bottom) male catkins*

### Sweet Gale

*Myrica gale*

**Habit/Leaves** an upright shrub up to 1 m tall with alternate leaves broadest and only toothed near the tip, leaves hairy-glandular about 2–5 cm long, plant fragrant when crushed. **Flowers** arranged in catkins, male and female on separate plants, female flowers have bright red styles. **Fruit** cone-like clusters of hard nutlets, about 1 cm long. **Blooms** very early in the season. **Habitat** peatlands, pond and stream margins, and other wet open areas.

## FRESHWATER WETLANDS

# FAMILY NYMPHAEACEAE (WATERLILY FAMILY)

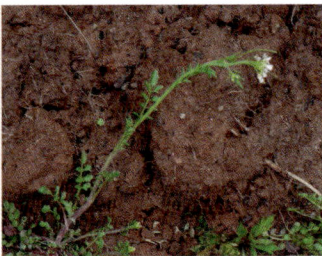

### Fragrant Water Lily
*Nymphaea odorata*

**Habit/Leaves** an aquatic herb with rounded floating leaf blades 7–30 cm long and a narrow v-shaped notch at base of blade, purplish on underside. **Flowers** white, 7–12 cm across held above water surface. **Fruit** a leathery berry 2–4 cm across. **Blooms** mid-season. **Habitat** shallow ponds up to 2 m deep.

### Yellow Pond Lily
*Nuphar variegata*

**Habit/Leaves** an aquatic herb, leaf blades floating on water surface, rounded with heart-shaped bases, blades 10–25 cm long. **Flowers** yellow, 4–5 cm across, solitary on stalks held several centimetres above surface. **Fruit** a reddish berry 3–5 cm long. **Blooms** mid-season. **Habitat** shallow ponds and pools up to 2 m deep.

# FAMILY BRASSICACEAE (MUSTARD FAMILY)

### Cuckoo Flower
*Cardamine pratensis*

**Habit/Leaves** an upright herb 20–50 cm tall showing long-petioled compound basal leaves with 3–5 pairs of broad slightly lobed leaflets and a longer terminal leaflet, stem leaves with 3–8 pairs of narrow oval to linear leaflets. **Flowers** 4-petalled, 1–1.5 cm across, white to pink. **Fruit** an elongate narrow pod (silique) 2.5–4 cm long. **Blooms** early season. **Habitat** pond margins, wet woods, and ditches.

### Pennsylvania Bittercress
*Cardamine pensylvanica*

**Habit/Leaves** an erect or reclining herb 10–35 cm in height with alternate compound leaves of 3–5 pairs in narrow leaflets and a broader slightly lobed terminal leaflet. **Flowers** 4-petalled, white and about 4 mm across. **Fruit** a slender pod (silique) 2–3 cm long. **Blooms** in mid-season. **Habitat** wet muddy shores, and wet open woods.

# FAMILY PLANTAGINACEAE (PLANTAIN FAMILY)

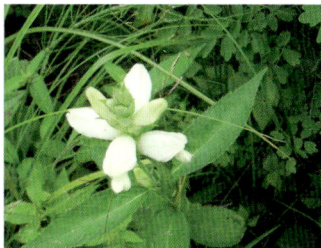

## White Turtlehead
*Chelone glabra*

**Habit/Leaves** a herb 30–90 cm tall with opposite almost sessile toothed pointy-tipped leaves. **Flowers** white or pinkish, 2-lipped, about 2.5 cm long, hairy within. **Fruit** an ovoid capsule 12 mm long. **Blooms** mid to late season. **Habitat** shorelines, marshes, wet thickets, and ditches.

# FAMILY PRIMULACEAE (PRIMROSE FAMILY)

## Swamp Candle
*Lysimachia terrestris*

**Habit/Leaves** a herb 30–60 cm in height with an erect square stem, leaves opposite entire narrowly lanceolate, 5–10 cm long, reddish bulblets produced in lower leaf axils. **Flowers** a 10–30 cm long raceme, each flower 1–1.5 cm across, dark lines on yellow petals with red dots at petal bases. **Fruit** a capsule 3–3.5 mm long. **Blooms** mid-season. **Habitat** shallow margins, wet shores, and marshes.

## Mistassini Primrose (Bird's-Eye Primrose)
*Primula mistassinica*

**Habit/Leaves** a herb 5–20 cm tall with basal leaves broadest towards tip, leaves toothed, 2–7 cm long, white-powdery below. **Flowers** a cluster on a leafless stalk, flowers white or lilac with a yellow 'eye,' 1–1.5 cm across. **Fruit** a capsule 1 cm long. **Blooms** early to mid-season. **Habitat** shorelines, fens, calcium-rich moist meadows, and mineral seepages.

# FAMILY MENYANTHACEAE (BUCKBEAN FAMILY)

## Bogbean
*Menyanthes trifoliata*

**Habit/Leaves** a herb 15–30 cm in height with emergent long-stalked compound leaves of 3 elliptical entire leaflets each 8–12 cm long. **Flowers** racemes of white conspicuously hairy 5-petalled flowers. **Fruit** an ovoid capsule 6–15 mm long. **Blooms** early season. **Habitat** shallow pond and pool margins.

### Common Pipewort
*Eriocaulon aquaticum*

**Habit/Leaves** an erect aquatic with submerged narrow pointed basal leaves, 2–10 cm long having conspicuous cross veins. **Flowers** tiny in head-like 'button' clusters, 5–8 mm across, whitish-hairy, emergent on stalks above water surface. **Fruit** a tiny capsule. **Blooms** mid-season. **Habitat** shallow ponds and pools.

## FAMILY TOFIELDIACEAE (FALSE ASPHODEL FAMILY)

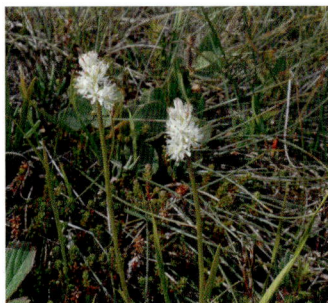

### Sticky Tofielda
*Triantha glutinosa*

**Habit/Leaves** a herb 20–50 cm tall with 2–4 basal upright linear entire sword-shaped leaves 6–15 cm long. **Flowers** about 1 cm across with 6 white 'petals,' anthers reddish, flower stalk sticky glandular-hairy, often with a single bract. **Fruit** a reddish capsule 5–6 mm long. **Blooms** mid-season. **Habitat** shores, fens, calcium-rich moist meadows, and mineral seepages.

## FAMILY ORCHIDACEAE (ORCHID FAMILY)

### Scentbottle (Bog Candle)
*Platanthera dilatata*

**Habit/Leaves** an erect orchid 10–80 cm in height with sheathing narrow lanceolate entire leaves 20–30 cm long on lower stem. **Flowers** white in a long narrow raceme with a strong spicy fragrance, lip petal 5–10 mm long abruptly broadening at base. **Fruit** a capsule 8 mm long. **Blooms** mid-season. **Habitat** fens, bogs, wet meadows, and wet roadsides.

### Lesser Purple Fringed Orchid
*Platanthera psycodes*

**Habit/Leaves** an upright herb 20–60 cm tall with 2–5 entire lanceolate or elliptic leaves 5–15 cm long and a few smaller upper bracts. **Flowers** pink to purple with a 3-parted lower lip 9–13 mm long, each part fringed, spur opening dumbell-shaped (in similar *P. grandiflora* opening is circular). **Fruit** a capsule 1 cm long. **Blooms** mid-season. **Habitat** wet meadows, marshes, fens, and bogs.

### Showy Lady's Slipper

*Cypripedium reginae*

**Habit/Leaves** an orchid with an upright stem 40–70 cm tall and 4–7 large hairy strongly ribbed entire leaves 10–25 cm long, sheathing at base. **Flowers** with a reddish-purple inflated lip petal (slipper) 3–5 cm long. **Fruit** a capsule 3–4 cm long. **Blooms** mid-season. **Habitat** fens, wet meadows, and open wet calcareous woodlands.

## FAMILY RANUNCULACEAE (BUTTERCUP FAMILY)

### Marsh Marigold

*Caltha palustris*

**Habit/Leaves** a herb 20–50 cm tall with long-petioled leaves with rounded heart-shaped blades 5–10 cm wide, dark green shiny with toothed margins. **Flowers** stalks with several flowers, each flower 2–4 cm wide with 5–9 bright yellow petal-like sepals. **Fruit** a dry elongate fruit 5–15 mm long, in clusters. **Blooms** early season. **Habitat** stream edges, margins of pools, swamps, and ditches.

## FAMILY LYTHRACEAE (LOOSESTRIFE FAMILY)

### Purple Loosestrife

*Lythrum salicaria*

**Habit/Leaves** a herb 20–50 cm tall with long-petioled leaves with rounded heart-shaped blades 5–10 cm wide, dark green shiny with toothed margins. **Flowers** stalks with several flowers, each flower 2–4 cm wide with 5–9 bright yellow petal-like sepals. **Fruit** a dry elongate fruit 5–15 mm long, in clusters. **Blooms** early season. **Habitat** stream edges, margins of pools, swamps, and ditches.

## FAMILY ROSACEAE (ROSE FAMILY)

### Marsh Cinquefoil

*Comarum palustre*

**Habit/Leaves** a somewhat sprawling stout-stemmed herb up to 50 cm tall with long-stalked alternate pinnately compound leaves of 5–7 toothed leaflets. **Flowers** five large purplish sepals and smaller petals, flowers about 2 cm wide. **Fruit** a cluster of achenes. **Blooms** mid-season. **Habitat** wet meadows, marshes, and pool margins.

# FAMILY IRIDACEAE (IRIS FAMILY)

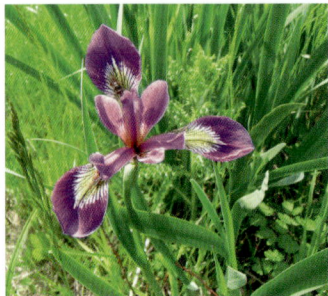

### Blue Flag Iris

*Iris versicolor*

**Habit/Leaves** a herb 60–100 cm tall with erect basal sword-shaped entire leaves arching at tips. **Flowers** large showy flower sepals (falls) blue to purple, striped and yellowish at base, the inner 3 true petals conspicuous and well developed, flowers 6–10 cm across. **Fruit** a cylindrical capsule 3–5 cm long. **Blooms** mid-season. **Habitat** wet margins, meadows, and marshes.

# FAMILY LENTIBULARIACEAE (BLADDERWORT FAMILY)

### Common Bladderwort

*Utricularia vulgaris*

**Habit/Leaves** a free floating submerged aquatic herb with finely divided thread-like leaves on branching large and 'bushy' stems. **Flowers** several on stout purplish emergent stalks, 2-lipped with a conspicuous curved upturned spur tip. **Fruit** a 2-chambered globose casule 5–6 mm diameter. **Blooms** mid-season. **Habitat** shallow ponds, pools, and streams.

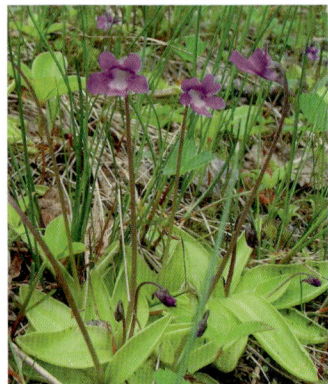

### Flatleaf Bladderwort

*Utricularia intermedia*

**Habit/Leaves** an aquatic herb with submerged green leafy branches on the substrate surface, leaves flattened, finely divided, leafless whitish branches within substrate have insect-trapping bladders. **Flowers** one to several on an erect emergent stalk, flowers 2-lipped with raised bump (palate) at base of lower petal, spur stout and curved, on underside of lip petal, about as long as lip petal. **Fruit** a rounded 2-chambered capsule 3–4 mm diameter. **Blooms** mid-season. **Habitat** shallow pond margins, marsh pools, and fen pools.

### Common Butterwort

*Pinguicula vulgaris*

**Habit/Leaves** a carnivorous herb 5–15 cm high, with a basal rosette of yellow-green leaves each 3–8 cm long, leaf edges rolled inward, upper surface glandular greasy-sticky. **Flowers** single on leafless stalks, each 10–20 cm long with a short spur. **Fruit** a 2-chambered capsule 5–8 mm long. **Blooms** mid-season. **Habitat** wet shores, fens, and mineral seepages, often in calcium-rich sites.

# FAMILY LAMIACEAE (MINT FAMILY)

### Canadian Mint
*Mentha canadensis*

**Habit/Leaves**s a square stemmed herb 30–60 cm in height with opposite short-petioled lanceolate leaves 2–8 cm long having toothed margins, producing a minty aroma when crushed. **Flowers** produced in dense clusters in leaf axils, each with a pinkish 4-lobed corolla about 6 mm long. **Fruit** a dry 4-parted cluster of nutlets. **Blooms** mid-season. **Habitat** stream margins, marshes, and moist open areas.

### Marsh Skullcap
*Scutellaria galericulata*

**Habit/Leaves** a square-stemmed upright plant 30–60 cm in height with opposite short-stalked lanceolate leaves, 3–5 cm long with toothed margins. **Flowers** blue to purple, 15–20 cm long in pairs with leaf axils, tubular and 2-lipped with a prominent bump on the upper calyx. **Fruit** a cluster of four dry nutlets. **Blooms** mid-season. **Habitat** wet shores, moist meadows, and swamps.

# FAMILY VIOLACEAE (VIOLET FAMILY)

### Marsh Blue Violet
*Viola cucullata*

**Habit/Leaves** a herb 15–30 cm in height with long-stalked basal leaves, leaf blade 5–10 cm wide, ovate with pointed tip, margins toothed, heart-shaped at base. **Flowers** on slender stalks overtopping leaves, two side flower petals with swollen-tipped hairs. **Fruit** a cylindrical-ovoid capsule 10–15 mm long. **Blooms** early to mid-season. **Habitat** wet margins, depressions, wet meadows, and thickets.

# FAMILY CAMPANULACEAE (BELLFLOWER FAMILY)

### Kalm's Lobelia
*Lobelia kalmii*

**Habit/Leaves** an erect herb 10–30 cm tall, stem leaves alternate entire or slightly toothed, narrow elongate and often broadest near tip, 1–5 cm long. **Flowers** 2-lipped, upper lip 2-lobed, lower lip 3-lobed, about 1 cm across. **Fruit** a capsule 4–8 mm long. **Blooms** mid-season. **Habitat** shores, fens, and wet calcareous meadows.

# FAMILY TYPHACEAE (CATTAIL FAMILY)

## Common Cattail
*Typha latifolia*

**Habit/Leaves** a robust herb 1–2.5 m in height, with erect sword-shaped entire leaves 2.5 cm wide. **Flowers** stems terminating in a brown spike of tightly packed miniature female flowers above which is a spike of male flowers. **Fruit** dry one-seeded and with brownish silky hairs, 1–2 mm long. **Blooms** mid-season. **Habitat** shallow pond margins, marshes, and wet ditches.

## SEASHORES AND SALT MARSHES

# FAMILY BRASSICACEAE (MUSTARD FAMILY)

## Greenland Scurvy Grass
*Cochlearia groenlandica*

**Habit/Leaves** a low plant 5–30 cm tall with long-petioled basal leaves containing ovate blades 5–12 mm long, stem leaves sessile. **Flowers** flowering stems with clusters of 15–20 white 4-petalled flowers each about 5 mm across. **Fruit** a rounded capsule-like pod 5–7 mm long. **Blooms** early to mid-season. **Habitat** rocky coastal shores, cliffs, and wet coastal meadows.

## Sea Rocket
*Cakile edentula*

**Habit/Leaves** an annual herb 10–50 cm tall with spatulate alternate toothed fleshy leaves. **Flowers** each with 4 white to lavender petals, about 1 cm across. **Fruit** a 2-segmented pod 1–3 cm long. **Blooms** mid to late season. **Habitat** sea beaches.

# FAMILY CARYOPHYLLACEAE (PINK FAMILY)

## Grove Sandwort
*Moehringia lateriflora*

**Habit/Leaves** a slender herb 5–15 cm tall with opposite entire elliptic leaves on short petioles, leaves 1–3 cm long. **Flowers** white 5-petalled flowers about 1 cm across. **Fruit** a rounded capsule 5 mm long. **Blooms** mid-season. **Habitat** coastal gravels, meadows, and headlands.

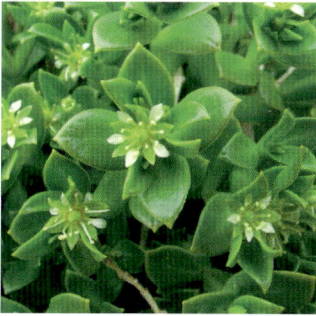

## Seabeach Sandwort
*Honckenya peploides*

**Habit/Leaves** a herb with fleshy ovate entire opposite leaves crowded on fleshy reclining stems, 10–25 cm in height, plants often forming thick mounds. **Flowers** either male or female, sometimes both, with five small white petals, about 1 cm or less across. **Fruit** a yellowish capsule 6–8 mm long. **Blooms** mid to late season. **Habitat** sandy or gravelly coastal beaches.

## Knotty Pearlwort
*Sagina nodosa*

**Habit/Leaves** a tiny rosette forming herb 5–10 cm in height, with narrow basal opposite leaves 5–12 mm long, thin upright or reclining stems with clusters of reduced rounded leaves at the upper nodes producing a knotty appearance. **Flowers** white 5-petalled, 5–12 mm across. **Fruit** a capsule 3–4 mm long. **Blooms** mid-season. **Habitat** gravelly or peaty coastal areas, salt marsh edges.

# FAMILY APIACEAE (CARROT FAMILY)

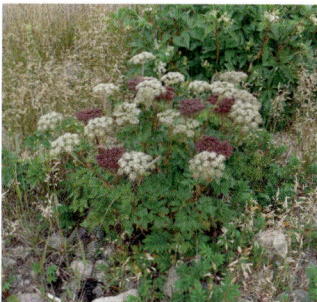

## Seaside Angelica
*Angelica lucida*

**Habit/Leaves** a herb 50–100 cm in height with large compound leaves several times divided into threes, leaflets 4–7 cm long, irregularly toothed, petioles sheathing stem. **Flowers** tiny white-petalled flowers arranged in large flat-topped compound inflorescences. **Fruit** dry elliptic flattened ribbed fruits, each 5–9 mm long. **Blooms** mid to late season. **Habitat** gravelly and rocky coastlines.

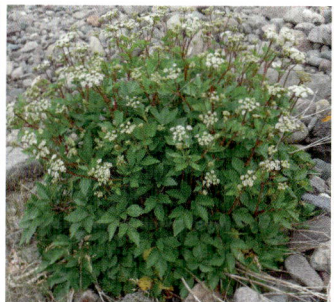

## Scotch Lovage
*Ligusticum scoticum*

**Habit/Leaves** a herb forming bushy clumps 40–60 cm tall, leaves large, compound divided into 3 segments of 3 leaflets, each leaflet 2–5 cm long long, shiny and aromatic, petioles sheath stem at base. **Flowers** tiny white-petalled flowers produced in large compound flat-topped inflorescences. **Fruit** dry, ovate, ridged, and winged, 4–7 mm long, not flattened. **Blooms** mid to late season. **Habitat** sandy to rocky seashores.

# FAMILY ASPARAGACEAE (ASPARAGUS FAMILY)

### Starry False Solomon's Seal
*Maianthemum stellatum*

**Habit/Leaves** an upright herb 10–50 cm in height with smooth entire alternate lanceolate leaves that clasp stem, 5–15 cm long. **Flowers** about 1 cm across, star-like with 6 white 'petals.' **Fruit** greenish berries with reddish-brown stripes, 6–10 mm across. **Blooms** mid-season. **Habitat** coastal beaches, meadows, and headlands.

# FAMILY RANUNCULACEAE (BUTTERCUP FAMILY)

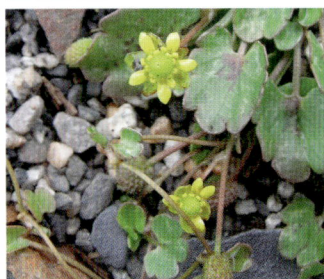

### Seaside Crowfoot
*Halerpestes cymbalaria*

**Habit/Leaves** a small herb 5–20 cm in height with creeping stolons, leaves 1–4 cm long with long petioles and rounded wavy-margined blades. **Flowers** a single yellow flower 5–8 mm across atop each leafless erect stem. **Fruit** a compact head of achenes about 1 cm long. **Blooms** mid-season. **Habitat** coastal shores, wet meadow margins, and salt marshes.

# FAMILY ROSACEAE (ROSE FAMILY)

### Silverweed
*Argentina anserina*

**Habit/Leaves** a prostrate herb spreading by reddish stolons, 3–10 cm tall, leaves 10–20 cm long, pinnately divided into 7–25 toothed leaflets, topside shiny green, underside silvery-hairy. **Flowers** each about 2.5 cm across, with 5 yellow petals. **Fruit** a cluster of hard reddish achenes. **Blooms** mid to late season. **Habitat** coastal shorelines and disturbed gravelly places.

# FAMILY PRIMULACEAE (PRIMROSE FAMILY)

### Sea Milkwort
*Lysimachia maritima*

**Habit/Leaves** a fleshy herb 5–15 cm in height with narrowly oval entire sessile opposite leaves 6–12 mm long. **Flowers** borne in leaf axils, pinkish with 5 petal-like sepal lobes, petals absent, each about 5 mm long. **Fruit** a capsule 2–3 mm long. **Blooms** mid-season. **Habitat** marine shores and salt marshes.

# FAMILY CRASSULACEAE (STONECROP FAMILY)

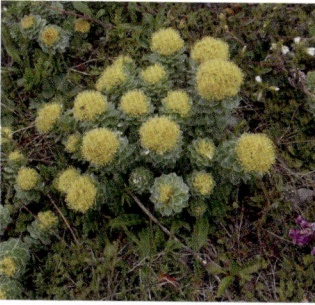

## Roseroot
*Rhodiola rosea*

**Habit/Leaves** a fleshy herb 10–30 cm in height with densely arranged alternate entire blue-green leaves, 1–4 cm long. **Flowers** in large terminal flat-topped clusters, yellowish-green to pinkish purple, male and female flowers on separate plants. **Fruit** cylindrical-elongate capsule-like achenes, 4–6 mm, reddish at maturity. **Blooms** mid-season. **Habitat** gravelly and rocky coastal areas.

# FAMILY ASTERACEAE (ASTER FAMILY)

## Seabeach Ragwort
*Senecio pseudoarnica*

**Habit/Leaves** a stout herb 30–100 cm tall with alternate elongate ovate sessile or short stalked leaves, margins toothed, mature upper surface shiny green, lower surface white woolly-haired, leaves up to 25 cm long. **Flowers** flowering heads large, sunflower-like, up to 4.5 cm across on white woolly stalks. **Fruit** achenes with terminal tufts of white hairs. **Blooms** mid-season. **Habitat** coastal sandy and gravelly beaches.

## Prickly Sowthistle
*Sonchus asper*

**Habit/Leaves** an annual herb with milky sap 30–100 cm or more in height, leaves alternate 6–30 cm long, stalkless and clasping stem with large rounded lobes, margins lobed and spiny-toothed. **Flowers** flowering heads 9–12 mm long, pear-shaped with only yellow ray flowers. **Fruit** an achene with a terminal tuft of hairs. **Blooms** mid-season. **Habitat** sandy, gravelly shores, disturbed areas, and waste places.

## Seaside Goldenrod
*Solidago sempervirens*

**Habit/Leaves** a herb with several erect stems 30–100 cm or more in height, plant mostly smooth, hairless, leaves entire lanceolate narrow, 10–30 cm long, decreasing upwards, somewhat fleshy. **Flowers** many flowering heads, each 1 cm long. **Fruit** achenes with hair tufts. **Blooms** late season. **Habitat** coastal beaches, salt marshes, and saline wet soils.

## FAMILY FABACEAE (LEGUME FAMILY)

### Beach Pea
*Lathyrus japonicus*

**Habit/Leaves** a viney herb 25–45 cm in height with alternate pinnately compound leaves of 2–5 pairs of oval smooth-edged leaflets, each 2–5 cm long, leaf terminating in a twining tendril. **Flowers** purple pea-type flowers 1.5–2.5 cm long. **Fruit** a pea pod (legume) 2–6 cm long. **Blooms** mid to late season. **Habitat** coastal beaches.

### Marsh Vetchling
*Lathyrus palustris*

**Habit/Leaves** a viney weak-stemmed plant 20–60 cm tall with tendrils attaching to nearby plants, stems winged, leaves alternate and compound, each with 2–4 pairs of leaflets broadly elliptic to narrowly elliptic, each up to 6 cm long, leaf terminating in a twining tendril. **Flowers** pea-like on stalks from leaf axils, 1.5–2 cm long. **Fruit** a pea pod (legume) 3–6 cm long. **Blooms** mid-season. **Habitat** wet shores, marshes, wet meadows, and in swamps.

## FAMILY IRIDACEAE (IRIS FAMILY)

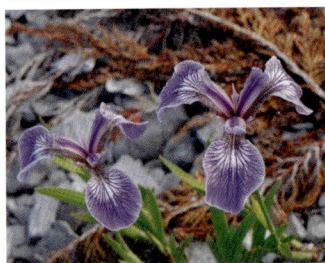

### Hooker's Iris
*Iris hookeriana*

**Habit/Leaves** a herb 20–40 cm tall with upright sword-like basal leaves. **Flowers** three large showy sepals (falls), blue to purple with darker veins, 2.5–4 cm broad, true petals tiny, 1–2 cm long with pointed tips. **Fruit** a 2–4 cm capsule. **Blooms** mid-season. **Habitat** coastal shorelines, meadows, and headlands.

## FAMILY PLUMBAGINACEAE (LEADWORT FAMILY)

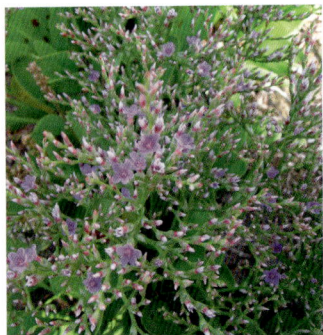

### Coralina Sea Lavender
*Limonium carolinianum*

**Habit/Leaves**: an erect herb 10–60 cm tall with basal leaves and a much branched upper stem and inflorescence, leaves entire elongate spatulate, tip with a sharp spine, which may break off, leaves to 25 cm in length including petiole. **Flowers** tiny, tubular, lavender, 5–7 mm long. **Fruit** a one-seeded fruit 4–5 mm long. **Blooms** mid to late season. **Habitat** salt marshes, and on tidal coastal flats.

# FAMILY BORAGINACEAE (BORAGE FAMILY)

### Oyster Leaf
*Mertensia maritima*

**Habit/Leaves** a trailing herb 3–20 cm in height with alternate fleshy entire oval blue-green leaves. **Flowers** tubular with 5-petalled lobes, 0.5–1 cm long, pink in bud turning blue. **Fruit** a cluster of four brown rounded nutlets each 4–5 mm long. **Blooms** mid-season. **Habitat** sandy or gravelly sea shores.

# FAMILY AMARANTHACEAE (AMARANTH FAMILY)

### Maritime Glasswort
*Salicornia maritima*

**Habit/Leaves** usually an erect fleshy branching jointed-stemmed annual herb 5–25 cm in height, greenish or becoming reddish, leaves tiny, opposite and scale-like. **Flowers** tiny green flowers in groups of three at the nodes sunken into fleshy stems. **Fruit** tiny one-seeded inflated fruits. **Blooms** late season. **Habitat** salt marshes and on muddy saline shores.

### Lamb's Quarters
*Chenopodium album*

**Habit/Leaves** an erect annual herb 15–100 cm tall, but highly variable, with alternate triangular to lanceolate leaves 3–10 cm long, toothed, white and mealy underneath. **Flowers** in white mealy dense clusters, bluish-green, 2–3 mm wide. **Fruit** shiny black 'curling rock' shape, 1–1.5 mm broad. **Blooms** mid to late season. **Habitat** sandy, gravelly marine shores and in disturbed areas and waste places.

# FAMILY PLANTAGINACEAE (PLANTAIN FAMILY)

### Seaside Plantain
*Plantago maritima*

**Habit/Leaves** a herb 5–20 cm tall forming a rosette of long narrow fleshy mostly entire leaves up to 15 cm long. **Flowers** tiny inconspicuous in spike-like clusters on leafless stems. **Fruit** a 2–3 mm long capsule. **Blooms** mid-season. **Habitat** coastal rocky and gravelly areas.

# FAMILY JUNCAGINACEAE (ARROW GRASS FAMILY)

### Seaside Arrowgrass
*Triglochin maritima*

**Habit/Leaves** a herb 20–80 cm tall with narrow erect grass-like fleshy leaves to 50 cm long, sheathing at base. **Flowers** leafless flower stalks with a long terminal spike-like inflorescence, flowers greenish-purple, 1–2 mm long with feathery stigmas. **Fruit** capsule-like, 5 mm long. **Blooms** mid-season. **Habitat** brackish shores, and in peatlands and wetlands.

# FAMILY POACEAE (GRASS FAMILY)

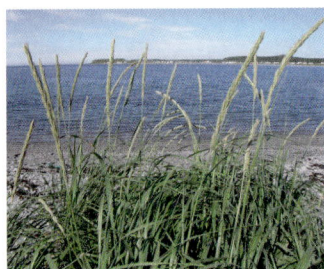

### Strand Wheat (American Dune Grass)
*Leymus mollis*

**Habit/Leaves** a grass 70–100 cm tall with narrow blue-green leaves 40–60 cm long. **Flowers** large, flowering spikes up to 15 cm long of crowded inconspicuous tiny flowers. **Fruit** a grain 7–10 mm long. **Blooms** mid-season. **Habitat** coastal sandy and gravelly beaches, and in disturbed areas.

## FIELDS AND DISTURBED SITES

# FAMILY ROSACEAE (ROSE FAMILY)

### Wild Strawberry
*Fragaria virginiana*

**Habit/Leaves** a herb 5-15 cm tall spreading by stolons, leaves basal, long stalked, compound with 3-toothed ovate leaflets each 2.5-4 cm long. **Flowers** 10-20 mm across, flowering stalks shorter, or as long as leaves. **Fruit** red fleshy fruits 5-20 mm across with embedded achenes ('seeds'). **Blooms** early season. **Habitat** roadsides, meadows, and old fields.

# FAMILY LINACEAE (FLAX FAMILY)

### Fairy Flax
*Linum catharticum*

**Habit/Leaves** a very thin-stemmed delicate annual herb 5-25 cm tall with opposite entire elliptic leaves each 6-15 mm long. **Flowers** 6-10 mm across, five white petals. **Fruit** a capsule 2-3 mm long. **Blooms** mid-season. **Habitat** roadsides, disturbed sites, and meadows.

# FAMILY ORCHIDACEAE (ORCHID FAMILY)

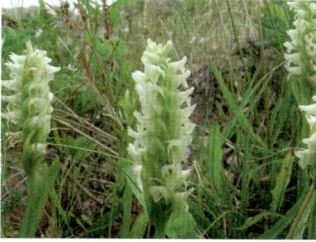

## Hooded Ladies'-Tresses

*Spiranthes romanzoffiana*

**Habit/Leaves** an erect herb 10–20 cm tall with 2–5 narrowly lanceolate entire sheathing leaves. **Flowers** arranged in a dense spiral of three rows, flowers fragrant, 7–12 mm long. **Fruit** an ellipsoid capsule 8 mm long. **Blooms** mid to late season. **Habitat** fens, meadows, and moist open grassy sites.

# FAMILY CARYOPHYLLACEAE (PINK FAMILY)

## Grassleaf Starwort

*Stellaria graminea*

**Habit/Leaves** a slender-stemmed branched herb 20–40 cm tall, with opposite sessile entire narrow lanceolate leaves 15–30 mm long. **Flowers** 8–14 mm wide, with 5-deeply cleft petals appearing as 10, reddish-brown anthers. **Fruit** a capsule 5–7 mm long. **Blooms** mid-season. **Habitat** roadsides, meadows, and old fields.

## Red Sandspurry

*Spergularia rubra*

**Habit/Leaves** an annual prostrate or ascending herb 5–20 cm tall with opposite entire narrow leaves 4–20 mm long with sharp tips, smaller leaves clustered in axils. **Flowers** 8–10 mm across. **Fruit** capsules 3.5–5 mm long. **Blooms** mid-season. **Habitat** roadsides, disturbed sites, and sandy-gravelly soils.

# FAMILY OROBANCHACEAE (BROOMRAPE FAMILY)

## Yellow Rattle

*Rhinanthus minor*

**Habit/Leaves** an upright herb 15–30 cm tall with simple opposite toothed sessile lanceolate leaves 2–6 cm long. **Flowers** 2-lipped with upper hooded lip, 15–18 mm long. **Fruit** a flattened dry capsule with loose 'rattling' seeds, 1 cm wide. **Blooms** mid-season. **Habitat** roadsides, meadows, open woods, and barrens.

## Common Eyebright

*Euphrasia nemorosa*

**Habit/Leaves** a branched annual herb 10–30 cm tall, with lower opposite, broadly-ovate, sharply-toothed leaves 5–15 mm long, upper bract-leaves with bristle-tipped teeth. **Flowers** 2-lipped, 5–10 mm long, lower lip 3-lobed, white to lavender with yellow spot. **Fruit** a flattened capsule 4–8 mm long. **Blooms** mid to late season. **Habitat** roadsides, disturbed sites, and waste places.

# FAMILY ASTERACEAE (ASTER FAMILY)

## Yarrow

*Achillea millefolium*

**Habit/Leaves** an upright aromatic herb 20–60 cm tall with much divided feathery leaves, basal leaves stalked, stem leaves sessile, alternate. **Flowers** in flat-topped clusters, heads 3–7 mm across, ray florets with white to sometimes pink ray petals, central disc florets yellow. **Fruit** a flattened achene 2 mm long. **Blooms** mid to late season. **Habitat** roadsides, disturbed sites, old fields, and gravelly barrens.

## Pearly Everlasting

*Anaphalis margaritacea*

**Habit/Leaves** an erect herb 20–60 cm tall with woolly stem, leaves alternate stalkless entire, white-woolly below, narrow elongate-lanceolate, 3–10 cm long. **Flowers** heads in dense terminal flattened cluster, each head 6–10 mm across, yellow disc florets surrounded by pearly white papery bracts (phyllaries). **Fruit** an achene 1 mm long with white hairs. **Blooms** mid-season. **Habitat** roadsides, disturbed sites, and open woodlands.

## Wild Chicory

*Cichorium intybus*

**Habit/Leaves** a branched herb 50–100 cm or more in height with a hollow stem and milky juice, basal leaves elongate, 7–15 cm long, toothed or lobed, stem leaves smaller, sessile, entire or toothed, clasping stem. **Flowers** heads 3–4 cm across with blue ray florets. **Fruit** 2–3 mm long achenes. **Blooms** mid to late season. **Habitat** roadsides, disturbed sites, and old fields.

## Pineapple Weed

*Matricaria discoidea*

**Habit/Leaves** an erect annual leafy plant 5–30 cm tall, fragrant when crushed, leaves alternate, 1–5 cm long and divided into many narrow segments. **Flowers** heads cone-shaped, greenish-yellow, compact, all disc florets, 5–10 mm across. **Fruit** a tiny achene 1 mm long. **Blooms** mid to late season. **Habitat** roadsides, disturbed areas, and waste places.

## Coltsfoot
### *Tussilago farfara*

**Habit/Leaves** a herb 10–30 cm tall, flowering stems with alternate purplish leaf-like bracts, basal leaves develop after flowering, long-stalked with broad ovate toothed blade and heart-shaped base, 5–20 cm broad, white-woolly below. **Flowers** heads 2.5 cm wide with yellow disc and ray florets. **Fruit** an achene 3–4 mm long with terminal white hair tuft. **Blooms** very early, a spring 'first bloomer.' **Habitat** moist disturbed soils, roadsides, embankments, and open disturbed woods.

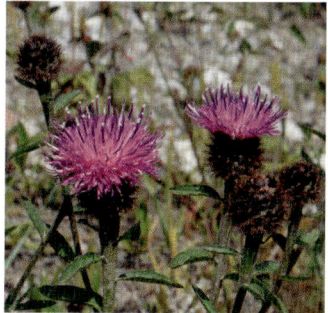

## Black Knapweed
### *Centaurea nigra*

**Habit/Leaves** an erect branched herb 30–80 cm tall, basal leaves long-stalked and toothed or shallowly lobed, blade to 15 cm long, upper leaves smaller, sessile. **Flowers** a single flowering head on the tip of each branch, heads 20–25 mm high with purple florets and dark brown to black comb-fringed phyllaries. **Fruit** a hairy achene 3–4 mm long. **Blooms** mid-season. **Habitat** roadsides, disturbed sites, and fields.

## Orange Hawkweed
### *Pilosella aurantiaca*

**Habit/Leaves** an erect herb 20–60 cm tall with milky juice, mostly basal leaves covered with black hairs, basal leaves elongate entire 5–15 cm long, stem leaves small or absent. **Flowers** crowded flowering heads 2–2.5 cm across with all ray florets, florets bright orange. **Fruit** an achene 3 mm long with tuft of white hairs. **Blooms** mid-season. **Habitat** roadsides, disturbed sites, and old fields.

## Oxeye Daisy
### *Leucanthemum vulgare*

**Habit/Leaves** an erect herb 30–60 cm tall with stalked toothed to lobed leaves broadening towards tip, 4–15 cm long, stem leaves smaller, sessile clasping, toothed to lobed. **Flowers** heads 2–6 cm across, white ray florets surround centre of yellow disc florets. **Fruit** an achene 1–2 mm long. **Blooms** mid-season. **Habitat** roadsides, disturbed sites, and fields.

# FAMILY ONAGRACEAE (EVENING PRIMROSE FAMILY)

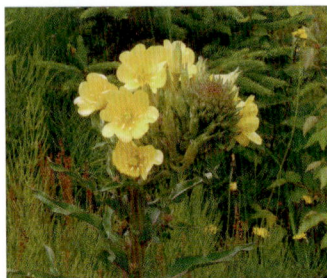

### Common Evening Primrose

*Oenothera biennis*

**Habit/Leaves** an erect stout herb 50–100 cm tall with basal leaves in a rosette, broadest towards tip, stem leaves alternate, lanceolate, entire to slightly toothed, 2–12 cm long. **Flowers** from narrow tube terminating in four broad petals, flowers 2–5 cm across. **Fruit** an elongate capsule 2–3 cm long. **Blooms** mid to late season. **Habitat** roadsides and dry disturbed sites.

# FAMILY PLANTAGINACEAE (PLANTAIN FAMILY)

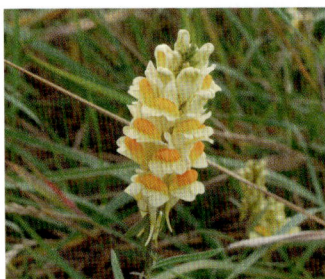

### Butter and Eggs

*Linaria vulgaris*

**Habit/Leaves** an upright herb 20–60 cm tall with crowded leafy stems; leaves alternate stalkless entire narrow, 2–10 cm long. **Flowers** 2–3 cm long with varying shades of yellow, 2-lipped with a prominent downward pointing spur. **Fruit** an oval capsule 8–12 mm long. **Blooms** late season. **Habitat** roadsides, disturbed sites, and meadows.

# FAMILY IRIDACEAE (IRIS FAMILY)

### Blue-Eyed Grass

*Sisyrinchium montanum*

**Habit/Leaves** a herb 10–30 cm tall with flattened stems and basal narrow grass-like leaves 2–6 cm long and 2–3 mm wide. **Flowers** 6 blue to purple 'petals' and a yellow centre. **Fruit** a globe-shaped capsule 4–6 mm long. **Blooms** mid-season. **Habitat** moist open grassy fields and meadows.

# FAMILY MALVACEAE (MALLOW FAMILY)

### Musk Mallow

*Malva moschata*

**Habit/Leaves** a herb 40–70 cm tall with stalked stem-leaves palmately divided into 5–7 narrow lobes, often further divided. **Flowers** pink or white, 3–5 cm across with five petals notched at their tips. **Fruit** produces a ring of flattened dry fruits separating at maturity. **Blooms** mid-season. **Habitat** roadsides, waste places, and old fields.

# FAMILY SOLANACEAE (NIGHTSHADE FAMILY)

## Bittersweet
### *Solanum dulcamara*

**Habit/Leaves** a herbaceous to semi-woody vine up to 3 m in height, climbing on other plants or trailing, leaves alternate entire stalked, 5–12 cm long with simple ovate blades or blades with 2 basal lobes. **Flowers** blue about 1 cm across with 5 petal lobes and a central yellow cone of stamens. **Fruit** an oval red berry 8–12 mm long. **Blooms** mid to late season. **Habitat** waste areas, thickets, and forest edges.

# FAMILY LAMIACEAE (MINT FAMILY)

## Heal-all (Self-heal)
### *Prunella vulgaris*

**Habit/Leaves** a herb 10–30 cm tall with square upright stems, leaves opposite, stalked, more or less entire, lanceolate, 2.5–5 cm long. **Flowers** in axils of purplish bracts in a tight spike, flowers 2-lipped, pinkish-purple, 8–12 mm long. **Fruit** a cluster of four nutlets. **Blooms** mid to late season. **Habitat** disturbed sites, meadows, and forest clearings.

## Common Hempnettle
### *Galeopsis tetrahit*

**Habit/Leaves** an erect plant 25–70 cm tall with square bristly-hairy stems, leaves broadly lanceolate, stalked, toothed, bristly-hairy. **Flowers** pink, white or variegated, 2-lipped, lower lip prominently 3-lobed, sepals bristle-tipped. **Fruit** a cluster of four nutlets. **Blooms** mid to late season. **Habitat** roadsides, disturbed sites, and open woods.

# FAMILY FABACEAE (LEGUME) FAMILY

## White Clover
### *Trifolium repens*

**Habit/Leaves** a creeping to trailing herb up to 20 cm in height with stems to 50 cm long, leaves alternate, long stalked, compound with three oval to elliptic leaflets, finely toothed, 1–2 cm long. **Flowers** white to pinkish, pea-like, 8–9 mm long in a compact head-like cluster. **Fruit** a pod (legume) 5–8 mm long. **Blooms** mid to late season. **Habitat** disturbed areas and lawns.

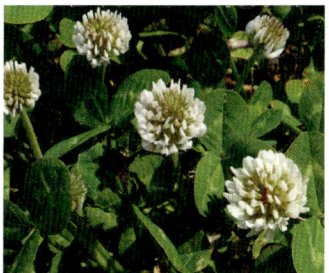

Four other *Trifolium* clovers also commonly occur in similar disturbed habitats:

**Alsike Clover**
*T. hybridum*

**Red Clover**
*T. pratense*

**Hop Clover**
*T. aureum*

**Rabbitfoot Clover**
*T. arvense*

**Black Medick**
*Medicago lupulina*

**Habit/Leaves** a trailing semi-prostrate herb 5–15 cm tall on longer trailing stems, with alternate compound leaves of three leaflets, leaflets oval toothed hairy, 5–30 mm long. **Flowers** pea-type, 3–4 mm long in a compact head 10–12 mm across. **Fruit** black kidney-shaped pods, 2–3 mm long. **Blooms** mid to late season. **Habitat** roadsides and disturbed sites.

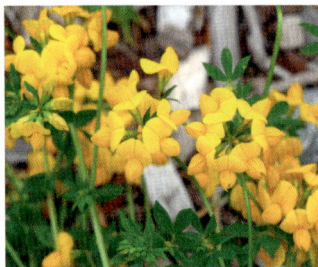

**Birdsfoot Trefoil**
*Lotus corniculatus*

**Habit/Leaves** a reclining or sub-erect herb 10–40 cm tall with alternate compound leaves of 5 elliptical finely toothed leaflets each 5–15 mm long. **Flowers** in clusters borne on leafless stalks from leaf axils, pea-like flowers 12–15 mm long. **Fruit** a brown pod (legume) 2–4 cm long. **Blooms** mid-season. **Habitat** roadsides, disturbed sites, and meadows.

## PLANTS GLOSSARY

NOTE: THE DEFINITIONS PROVIDED FOR THE PURPOSES OF THIS GUIDE ARE BROAD AND GENERAL. IN DEDICATED BOTANICAL WORKS THEY ARE TYPICALLY MORE DETAILED.

**achene:** fruit with single seed.

**alternate leaves:** leaves attached singly up and down the stem.

**berry:** a fleshy many-seeded fruit.

**blade:** the expanded flattened portion of a leaf.

**bloom:** a thin waxy coating on fruit.

**capsule:** a dry thin-walled fruit with usually several to many seeds.

**catkin:** an elongated cluster of tiny reduced flowers.

**compound leaf:** the blade portion of the leaf divided into several separate leaflets.

**cone:** dry, hard, seed containing fruits of conifers.

**double-toothed:** margins of leaf with larger and smaller teeth.

**drupe:** a fleshy one-seeded fruit, the seed enclosed in a hard stoney structure.

**entire:** leaf with smooth margins without teeth..

**gland:** a tiny dot-like or spherical structure, sessile or at the tips of hairs, that produces some sort of secretion.

**herb:** seed-bearing plant without a woody stem.

**lanceolate:** lance-shaped; narrow and long-tapering to a sharp tip.

**leaflet:** one of the small separate blades of a compound leaf.

**lenticel:** a small circular or lens-shaped patch of cells noticeable on the bark of woody plants.

**lobed:** broadly indented.

**needle:** narrow, slender, elongated leaf of a conifer.

**node:** a point on a stem where a leaf is attached.

**nutlet:** a small hard single-seeded fruit or fruit portion.

**opposite leaves**: two leaves attached opposite each other at a point on the stem.

**oval:** broadly elliptic (some authors use this as a synonym for ovate).

**petiole:** a stalk joining the leaf blade to the stem.

**raceme:** an elongate flower cluster where each flower is attached to the stem by a stalk (pedicel).

**sessile:** attached without a stalk or petiole.

**shrub:** a bushy woody plant with many stems and rarely exceeding 3 m in height.

**tree:** an upright single or few-stemmed woody plant in excess of 5 m, trunks greater than 10 cm in diameter.

**winged:** having flat, thin margins that help catch the wind for dispersal.

## BLOOMING TIMES

Flowering times are divided into three main seasons.

Most of the island's wildflowers are mid-season bloomers in July and August.

| |
|---|
| **Early** (May–June) |
| **Mid-season** (July–mid August) |
| **Late** (mid August–September) |

## INSECTS

The Class Insecta is the largest group within the Phylum Arthropoda, which includes those animals not possessing a backbone (invertebrates) but that do have a hard external skeleton to which the muscles are attached, and jointed appendages. The arthropod body is divided into different segments each of which may have attached jointed appendages. The Phylum Arthropoda also includes Crustacea (crabs, lobsters etc.), Diplopoda (millipedes), Chilopoda (centipedes), as well as Arachnida (spiders).

The external skeleton of an insect is composed of a light, water-resistant material called chitin (hard, chalky material). An insect's body is divided into three sections, namely the head, thorax (middle section), and the abdomen (tail section). The head typically bears a pair of antennae (feelers), mouth parts (which vary according to diet), and eyes. The thorax has three segments, each bearing a pair of jointed legs (spiders have four pairs of legs), and usually one or two pairs of wings. The abdomen has a number of segments, but none bear legs or wings. The end of the abdomen may bear a stinger or pincers. Insects do not possess lungs but breathe through openings in the 'cuticle' (exoskeleton) called 'spiracles,' which are connected to an internal network of tubes called 'tracheae.'

Most insects go through a 'metamorphosis' during their life cycle. The egg develops into a larva, which feeds and grows in size though a number of stages called 'instars.' The exoskeleton is moulted at the end of each instar. After the last moult the larva becomes a 'pupa.' Within the pupa the larval body is transformed into the adult whose form can be startlingly different from the larva (e.g., caterpillar and butterfly). There are a number of simpler insects (e.g., silverfish) that exhibit little or no metamorphosis, growing larger until they become reproductive adults (i.e., the adult is simply a larger version of the larva). A number of insects exhibit yet another form of metamorphosis whereby the egg hatches into a 'nymph' (terrestrial form) or 'naiad' (aquatic form), which gradually change into adults through slight changes at each moult.

Quite a few of our insects start life as larvae in streams, rivers, and ponds, with adults being released into the air in summer. Dragonflies, blackflies, mosquitoes, mayflies, and caddis flies all start life as larvae in water before spending their adult lives on land.

The number and variety of insects is astonishing, and insects are the most numerous animal species known. Over one million insect species have been identified so far, but it is estimated that there might be over ten million different species alive today! Of the one million or so known species, over one third are beetles, and there are more than one hundred thousand species of flies, butterflies, and moths!

Insects seem to fill every available niche in our world and interact with us in many ways. Butterflies are renowned for their beauty, and many more are useful to humans (e.g., bees, ladybugs, dragonflies), while others are agricultural pests (e.g., aphids, locusts). And then of course there are those insects that are responsible for the transmission of human diseases such as malaria, sleeping sickness, West Nile virus, and the like. Insects have such a great impact on our lives that it is impossible to ignore them!

## ORDER: LEPIDOPTERA

### Eastern Tiger Swallowtail
*Papilio glaucus*

Our most common butterfly. Adult is yellow with black stripes. Larvae are green to rusty brown with distinctive false eye spots toward front. Found in meadows and mixed forests throughout Newfoundland.

### Short-Tailed Swallowtail
*Papilio brevicauda*

Mostly black with yellow markings toward wing margins. Young larvae resemble bird droppings. Mature larvae are black with green stripes. This butterfly is found in Newfoundland and coastal areas of the Gulf of St. Lawrence, where it feeds on cow parsnip, parsley, and angelica.

## Clouded Sulphur

*Colias philodice*

Yellow butterfly with dark brown wing margins. Caterpillar is green with a white stripe on each side running from head to tail. Larvae feed on alfalfa, clover, and vetch. Found around gravel pits, roadsides, and fields.

## Cabbage White

*Pieris rapae*

White butterfly with dark spots on forewings and wing tips. Larvae are green with faint yellow line down the sides. Larvae feed on plants of the mustard family and are often pests on cabbage and broccoli. This species was imported and is not native to the province.

## Monarch

*Danaus plexippus*

This orange and black butterfly is an infrequent visitor to Newfoundland. The larval food plant, milkweed, is not found on the island, so the adults we see are carried here from mainland Canada. This butterfly is well known for its migration south, which takes it to Mexico where it overwinters.

## McIsaac's Ringlet

*Coenonympha inornata mcisaaci*

This small, brown butterfly is common in Newfoundland during June and July. It frequents cultivated meadows, bogs, and marshy ground. Larvae are green and feed on grasses.

## Silver-Bordered Fritillary

*Boloria selene*

This small brown and black speckled butterfly can be seen flying from late June to early September. It is most common in moist meadows. The larvae are greenish brown with prominent spines and feed on violets.

### Green Comma
*Polygonia faunus*

These butterflies can be seen from mid-May to September. They overwinter as adults, and therefore, the ones seen in the spring are very tattered and dull while the late summer specimens are much more vibrant in colour. The brownish adults have sculpted wing margins and a distinctive green band on the underside of the hind wing. Larvae are reddish or yellowish brown with a distinctive saddle near the centre of the back and are heavily spined. It feeds on birch, willow, and alder.

### Compton Tortoiseshell
*Nymphalis vaualbum*

This large brown mottled butterfly prefers densely wooded areas and is most often seen on gravel roads and trails in forested areas. It can be seen throughout the summer and overwinters as an adult. Larvae are light green and somewhat speckled and striped. It feeds on birch, willow, and poplar.

### Milbert's Tortoiseshell
*Aglais milberti*

A common mottled butterfly that is in flight from early May to early November. It prefers fields and meadows as well as river valleys, where adults lay their eggs on the host plant, nettle. The spiny larvae are black with green along the sides.

### Mourning Cloak
*Nymphalis antiopa*

This is one of the most recognized butterflies in Newfoundland and one of the first to fly in the spring. The distinctive brown colour and pale yellow wing margins make it easy to identify. The larvae, called spiny elm caterpillars, are black speckled with red and feed on willow and elm. Larvae are often found feeding in large clusters.

### Red Admiral
*Vanessa atalanta*

This is a migrant butterfly that overwinters in the south and flies north each spring to breed. They can be seen from May to mid-October in meadows, fields, and along river courses. The adult is black with orange and white markings. Larvae feed on species of nettle and vary greatly in colour.

## Painted Lady

*Vanessa cardui*

This butterfly arrives in early spring and lays its eggs on a variety of plants including thistle, lupin, and hollyhock. The adults are orange with black and white markings. Larvae are highly variable in colour and have branched spines. They build nests from which they feed on host plants.

## White Admiral

*Limenitis arthemis*

A distinctive black and white butterfly that is uncommon in Newfoundland. It can be seen from early to late July. The eggs are laid on birch, poplar, and willow. The fully-grown larva is black with spines and a white saddle.

## Bog Copper

*Lycaena epixanthe*

This small, copper-coloured butterfly is found around bogs and marshy areas. It is in flight from early July to early August. The males have a more distinctive copper colouring while the females are greyer and duller. Larvae are a velvet green and feed on species of cranberry.

## Common Blue

*Celastrina argiolus*

This beautiful little butterfly is in flight from early June to mid-August. The sky-blue males can be distinguished from the females, which have black edges on their front wings. The larva is mostly white, tinged with pale rose, and covered with white hairs. Host plants are dogwood, sumac, and blueberry, among others.

## European Skipper

*Thymelicus lineola*

This imported species was first reported in Newfoundland in 1976. It has since spread throughout the island and is often found in great numbers. It can be a serious pest of hay fields. The reddish-brown butterfly has a lazy flight and can be seen feeding on flowers. The larva is pale green with faint stripes and white lines on its head. It feeds on a variety of grasses.

### Twin-Spotted Sphinx Moth

*Smerinthus jamaicensis*

The most common of our large moths. It is often attracted to lights and may remain on a building all day. The brownish adult has distinctive red hind wings with a blue spot. A black bar across the spot distinguishes it from the closely related Cerisy's Sphinx. The green larva has a short horn at the back end. It feeds on a variety of trees including cherry, willow, and aspen.

### Hummingbird Clearwing Moth

*Hemaris thysbe*

This moth is easily distinguished from other hawk moths by the clear patch on the front wings. It is uncommon in Newfoundland and is most often spotted feeding on lilacs. It is often mistaken for a hummingbird. The larva is lime green with a prominent white stripe along each side. It feeds on viburnum, honeysuckle, hawthorn, and snowberry.

### Virginia Ctenucha

*Ctenucha virginica*

This small moth is a dark metallic blue with a yellowish-orange head, making it easy to identify. It has become quite common in parts of Newfoundland over the past several years. The larva feeds on a variety of grasses and is yellowish and quite fuzzy. Like most caterpillars in the tiger moth family, it curls up in a ball when disturbed.

### Spotted Tussock Moth

*Lophocampa maculata*

A common moth in Newfoundland, recognizable by the brown and yellow speckled front wings and whitish hind wings. Adults prefer wooded areas and edges of fields. The larvae are often seen crawling on the ground. They are very furry, yellow in the middle, and black on both ends. They feed on alder, willow, poplar, and maple. They have been known to cause a skin rash if touched.

### Herald Moth (Scalloped Owlet)

*Scoliopteryx libatrix*

This is one of the most beautiful moths in the province. The wings are orange with white markings and sculpted on the edges. It is often seen around porch lights and is in flight from mid-June to late August. The larva is smooth and green with a faint line along each side. It feeds on willow.

## White Dotted Prominent

*Nadata gibbosa*

A medium-sized, tan-coloured moth with two white dots on each of the front wings. They are in flight from late June to mid-August. The larva is sea green and stocky, with a faint stripe down each side. It feeds on birch, willow, maple, and oak. When threatened, the larva curls up and exposes its bright green mandibles (chewing mouth parts).

## Lettered Habrosyne

*Habrosyne scripta*

This beautiful little moth is one of the most distinctive moths in the province. The brown front wings have a series of delicate lines that give it the appearance of a piece of artwork. The adults are in flight from late June to mid-August. The larva has a dull, slightly wrinkled head and feeds on blackberry and other members of the Rosaceae family.

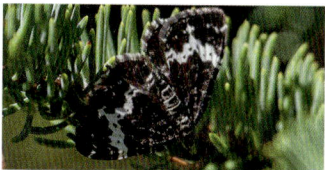

## Spear-Marked Black

*Rheumaptera hastata*

This attractive moth is diurnal (daytime flying) and is very common in Newfoundland. The adult is black with white markings and a distinctive white spear in the front wings. They are in flight from mid-June to late July. The larva is dark brown to black with a brown head. They feed on birch, alder, and willow.

## Light Emerald (Pale Beauty)

*Campaea perlata*

This is a delicate, medium-sized, greenish-white moth. The adults are in flight from June to August. The mature larva resembles a piece of bark. It is a generalized feeder and has been recorded on over 65 species of host trees and shrubs. Commonly found on trembling aspen, white birch, willow, and tamarack.

## St. Lawrence Tiger Moth

*Arctia parthenos*

One of the most spectacular moths in the province with its rusty-brown front wings and the orange and black hind wings. The adults are in flight from early July to mid-August. Larvae are black with some white warts and long, irregular hairs. They feed on a variety of trees and shrubs, including willow, alder, and birch.

## Hemlock Looper

*Lambdina fiscellaria*

This greyish-brown moth has two black bands on the front wings and one on the back wing. The mottled inchworm feeds on a variety of trees but has been most problematic as a defoliator of balsam fir. Millions of acres have been infected in Newfoundland in the past, and thousands of hectares of forest have been killed during some of the most severe outbreaks.

# ORDER: ODONATA

### Sedge Darner

*Aeshna juncea*

There are about 10 species of large Darner dragonflies in Newfoundland. They vary in colour, from blue to green, and are in flight most of the summer and into the fall. They feed on a variety of insects that they capture on the wing. The larvae can take up to 4 years to reach maturity and are voracious predators that capture insect larvae, tadpoles, and even small fish.

### Black Meadowhawk

*Sympetrum danae*

This small member of the dragonfly family is usually associated with meadows, where they can be very numerous. The males are black while the females are pale yellow. They are in flight from midsummer to the fall. Larvae feed on aquatic insects and are found in marshy or boggy ponds and small lakes.

### Four-Spotted Skimmer

*Libellula quadrimaculata*

This is the most common of the skimmer dragonflies. The distinctive spotted wings and large size make it one of the most easily identifiable dragonflies in the province. They are formidable predators and will even prey on other dragonflies such as meadowhawks. This species is circumpolar, ranging from North America to Europe and Japan. Larvae feed on aquatic insects in bog pools, slow moving streams, and ponds.

### Boreal Bluet

*Enallagma boreale*

One of the earliest damselflies on the wing with adults in flight from early June to August. Adults average 3 cm and are blue with black markings. They are usually found near ponds and bog pools. This is also one of the most abundant damselflies in our area. Larvae and adults feed on small insects.

# ORDER: EPHEMEROPTERA

## Stream Mayfly

Heptageniidae Family

There are a number of mayfly species found in this province. They range from small species to giant mayflies with a 5 cm wing span. All species have soft, membranous wings and two or three tails at the end of their abdomens. Their wings are held together, above the body, when at rest. Nymphs are aquatic and an important food source for freshwater fish. Adults have non-functioning mouth parts and do not feed. They therefore only live for a day or two.

# ORDER: ORTHOPTERA

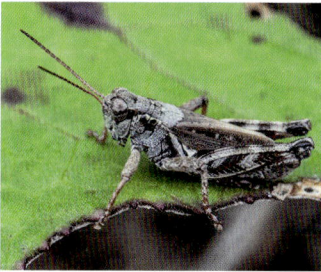

## Short-Horned Grasshopper

*Melanoplus* sp.

When fully grown these grasshoppers are about 3.5 to 4 cm long. Though common in fields and along roadsides, they can also be found in bogs and barren areas. They overwinter as eggs in elongated egg pods, hatching in the spring and developing throughout the summer. Adults, the only stage that can fly, are present in August and September.

# ORDER: DERMAPTERA

## European Earwig

*Forficula auricularia*

This insect is one of the most disliked in the province. The brown adults are up to 1.5 cm long and often invade homes and basements. They are not native to the province but have been here for many years, with some reports as early as the 1800s. The males can be easily distinguished from the females by the inward curve of the cerci (appendages at the end of the abdomen). They are nocturnal, hiding during the day in cracks and crevices. Earwigs are harmless and do not crawl into people's ears, despite the name and superstition.

# ORDER: HEMIPTERA

## Giant American Water Bug

*Lethocerus americanus*

This is the largest insect in the province with some specimens reaching 7 or 8 cm in length. They range from a dark brown to a greenish colour, have powerful front legs for grasping prey, and a beak-like mouth which punctures the victim. They are formidable predators, catching other insects, tadpoles, and even small fish. They are found in ponds and large bog pools and occasionally fly around on warm summer evenings. They have a very painful bite.

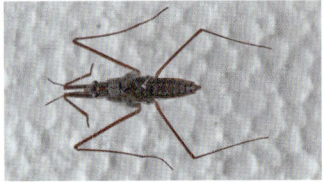

## Common Water Strider

*Aquarius remigis*

These insects are black and are commonly found on the surface of slow moving streams and rivers. They propel themselves along with their middle and hind legs, capturing prey that falls onto the water surface with their front legs. Many places in Newfoundland have their own localized name for these insects, including water doctors, water hoppers, and cleaners.

## Red-Crossed Stink Bug

*Elasmostethus cruciatus*

One of the most common bugs in Newfoundland, they have a shield-like appearance. The distinguishing red X on the back of this insect gives it its name. Stink bugs can produce a disagreeable odour when handled, which discourages predators from eating them.

## Froghoppers (Spittlebug)

*Philaenus* sp.

These insects are less that 1 cm in length and hop about on plants in meadows. The nymph stage surrounds itself with a frothy, spittle-like mass from which they get their name. This mass protects them from predators and provides them with a moist habitat. They feed on shrubs and herbaceous plants.

# ORDER: NEUROPTERA

## Green Lacewing

*Chrysopa* sp.

These delicate, light green insects are common on grasses, weeds, and the foliage of trees. Both the larvae and adults are predators of aphids. The eggs are laid on foliage at the end of a tiny stalk. When handled, the adults can give off a disagreeable odour and are sometimes called stinkflies.

# ORDER: COLEOPTERA

## Ground Beetle

*Carabus nemoralis*

This is one of the largest families of beetles in Newfoundland. This species is black with a metallic-blue sheen on many specimens and is approximately 3 cm long. It was imported from Europe and has taken over the habitat of our native species. Ground beetles are predators and are excellent around the garden for controlling caterpillars that sometimes damage crops.

## Tiger Beetle

*Cicindela* sp.

This beautiful metallic-green beetle can be found on sandy beaches along our rivers and lakes, and is also found in sandy gravel pits. The adults are predators that catch a variety of insects. The larvae are also predaceous and live in vertical burrows where they capture passing insects. Adults are difficult to approach and will fly a short distance when disturbed.

## Predaceous Diving Beetle

*Dytiscus* sp.

These black beetles are common in ponds and quiet streams as well as large bog pools. They are the largest beetles in the province, reaching a length of 4 cm. The adults and larvae are predators of other aquatic insects. They sometimes leave the water at night to fly to a new location and are attracted to lights, which can leave them stranded.

## Carrion Beetle

*Nicrophorus* sp.

These beetles are black with yellow markings and are about 2.5 cm long. Both the adults and larvae feed on carrion. The adults excavate the soil beneath a dead body, such as a mouse or small bird, and the body sinks into the ground. Eggs are then laid on it. When found, the adults often have a large number of mites on the underside of their body. These mites are actually hitching a ride from one burial site to another and are harmless to the beetle.

## Golden Rove Beetle

*Ontholestes cingulatus*

Rove beetles are the largest family of beetles in the province with many species found here. The golden rove beetle is one of the largest and gets its name from the gold colouring at the end of the abdomen. They are about 2 cm long. Most species are predators of other insects and occur around decaying animal and vegetable matter. Often found near compost bins.

## Larder Beetle

*Dermestes lardarius*

These small beetles are about 7 mm long. They are black with a light-brown band across their backs. They are often found in homes where they feed on a variety of stored foods, including meats and cereals. The larvae are brownish and covered with long hairs.

## Two-Spotted Ladybug

*Adalia bipunctata*

This is the most recognized of the ladybugs in our area. Adults are red with two black spots. Both adults and larvae of ladybugs are predators, feeding on aphids. They are very beneficial insects and gardeners like to see them on their crops. They overwinter as adults, sometimes seeking shelter in homes. They are considered to bring good luck.

## June Beetle (June Bug)

*Phyllophaga anxia*

These beetles are very common in areas with sandy soil. The larvae are called white grubs and feed on the roots of grasses and other plants. They can cause damage to commercial crops such a hay, potatoes, strawberries, and corn. The adults are about 2 cm long and active at night. They can be found around buildings in the morning after being attracted to the lights during the night. They do not bite.

## White-Spotted Sawyer Beetle

*Monochamus scutellatus*

These long-horned beetles are found around freshly cut logs and lumber. The adults lay their eggs on the bark, and the larvae make large holes in the wood. Adults are black with very fine white spots and a larger white mark on the back. The antennae of the males can be twice as long as the body, while the female antennae are the length of the body. They are quite common in the province.

## Black Vine Weevil

*Otiorhynchus sulcatus*

These black beetles are sometimes called snout beetles because the head is prolonged into a beak or snout. In this province, they are often called 'hard shells' because they are so resilient. They feed on plant material and often wander into homes. They are harmless to humans.

# ORDER: TRICHOPTERA

### Northern Caddisfly

Limnephilidae Family

Caddisflies are aquatic insects that spend most of their lives in ponds and streams. The adults are moth-like but lack scales on the wings and are usually brownish in colour. Both larvae and adults are an important food source for freshwater fish. The larvae construct a case in which they live, which is made from a variety of materials.

# ORDER: DIPTERA

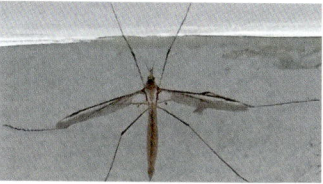

### Common Crane Fly

*Tipula* sp.

Crane flies resemble overgrown mosquitoes. The larvae are known as leatherjackets and feed on the roots of plants. They can sometimes be very destructive, especially to areas of lawn and grassland. Adults are between 3 and 4 cm long. They do not bite. In Newfoundland, they are sometimes called 'Dandy Longlegs' or 'Daddy Longlegs.'

### Mosquito

*Aedes* sp.

There are a number of species of mosquitoes in this province. The larval stages of all species are aquatic with one species found only in the reservoirs of the pitcher plant. Female mosquitoes require a blood meal before laying their eggs. Several species are carriers of disease. They are considered a major pest species in this province.

### Horse Fly

*Tabanus* sp.

Horse flies are large black flies, about 25 mm long, which can give a painful bite. Females require a blood meal for their offspring, but males feed on pollen and nectar. The larvae of most species are aquatic and prey on other insects. These flies are often a nuisance when people are hiking, fishing, or berry picking.

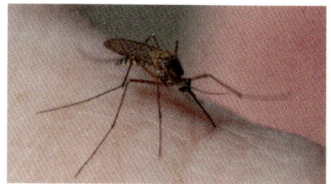

### Deer Fly

*Chrysops* sp.

Deer flies are often called 'stouts' in this province. They are a little over 1 cm long and typically have green, metallic eyes. They are most often found around marshes or streams and frequently buzz around people's heads or get in their hair. They have a very strong bite.

## Flower Fly

Syrphidae Family

There are several species of flower flies in this province. Most species resemble bees or wasps, which gives them some protection from predators such as birds. They are common around flowers, especially in late summer, and often do a lot of hovering. They do not bite.

## Blow Fly

Calliphoridae Family

Blow flies are a very common group of insects that are found around carrion and excrement, where the adults lay their eggs. The larvae develop in this material. Most flies in this group are often metallic green or blue in colour. They can be of considerable importance in assisting with the removal of dead animals from the landscape.

## House Fly

*Musca domestica*

This insect is probably the most recognized species of fly. They are found in nearly every home at some point during the year. They gather around exposed food and are often a nuisance. Most enter our homes through open doors and windows. Although they do not bite, in some parts of the world, they can be carriers of several diseases including typhoid fever, dysentery, and cholera.

## Blackfly

Simuliidae Family

Small black or grey flies, less than 5 mm. A number of different species are found in Newfoundland. Adult females feed on the blood of mammals, including humans. They are major pests of the outdoors. Larvae are aquatic, hatching from eggs laid in running water. They pupate in the water and the adults are released into the air. Widespread across the island particularly near running water.

# ORDER: HYMENOPTERA

## Elm Sawfly

*Cimbex americana*

This is the largest species of sawfly in the province. The dark blue adult is 18 to 25 mm in length and the female has four small, yellow spots on each side of the abdomen. The larvae are greenish yellow, with a black stripe down the back, and feed on elm and willow. It overwinters as a fully grown larva in a cocoon on the ground. Adults appear in early summer.

## Horntail Sawfly

Siricidae Family

These insects are called 'Timber Flies' in Newfoundland and Labrador. Females can be up to 3 cm in length with the males being smaller. They are black and often have yellow markings on the abdomen. The larvae are wood-boring insects, and the adults are often found around sawmills and freshly cut wood. Although they do not have a stinger, many people have had severe allergic reactions from being stuck by the female's ovipositor (a tube-like organ for laying eggs).

## Carpenter Ant

*Camponotus* sp.

This ant is widespread in the province and often causes damage to wooden structures when they excavate cavities for nests. On warm summer evenings, newly emerged queens can sometimes be seen by the hundreds when they leave the nest to mate. They shed their wings shortly afterward and attempt to start a new colony. In this province, ants are often called 'emmets.'

## Paper Wasp (Hornet)

*Vespula* sp.

These insects are black with yellow markings and are up to 2 cm long. They build nests constructed from wood and foliage, which is chewed and made into a papery substance. At the end of the summer, the nest is abandoned, and only the queens overwinter. They start new nests in the spring. Larvae are fed mainly on insects such as caterpillars. These insects have a very painful sting.

## Bumble Bee

*Bombus* sp.

Several species of bumble bee occur on the island. They are all characterized by robust bodies covered in dense hair. Most species are black and yellow, but one local species is black and orange. Bumble bees usually nest in the ground in abandoned rodent burrows. In the fall, they all die except the queens, who hibernate in sheltered locations. These queens start new colonies in the spring.

## Honey Bee

*Apis mellifera*

Honey bees are not native to North America. They are kept by bee keepers who harvest the honey that they produce. Adults are about 1.5 cm long and look more like wasps than bees. They harvest nectar and pollen from flowers. The nectar is made into honey. Workers have a very elaborate 'dance' in which they communicate the direction and distance to a source of nectar. The females can sting.

# AMPHIBIANS

For reasons explained in the introduction, there are no native amphibians on the island of Newfoundland, although there are several native species in Labrador, the mainland portion of the province. While there are no native amphibians, this does not mean that there are no amphibians living on the island, as a number of frog species and one toad species have been introduced by humans.

The most common amphibian is the green frog, introduced to the St. John's area in the mid-1800s and now widely distributed throughout the island. It has been historically deemed an accidental introduction, through hay shipments from Nova Scotia, but appears most likely to have been an intentional introduction. The green frog population is now widely transplanted, occurring throughout most of the island, at least as far north as Gros Morne National Park.

Eastern American toads were introduced into the Corner Brook area annually from 1963–1966, and possibly at the northern tip of Newfoundland. Toads from the original introductions were successfully transplanted to other localities throughout the island, including, in particular, Deer Lake, the Port au Port Peninsula, the Gros Morne National Park area, and the central and northeastern Avalon Peninsula. The species has also spread widely through its own devices, however, and now occurs 'naturally' as far east as the Bay d'Espoir Highway, and as far south as the Codroy Valley and La Poile Bay. Isolated populations have also been recorded from L'Anse aux Meadows and near the Main Brook watershed; both of these Great Northern Peninsula populations are separated, geographically, from the populations further to the south. These more northerly toads are brick red, like many Labrador toads, and may, perhaps, have been brought to the island across the Strait of Belle Isle.

The wood frog was first introduced in the Corner Brook area in 1963 and seems to be dispersing slowly. It is found as far north as Gros Morne National Park, as far south as the Codroy Valley, and on the central Avalon Peninsula, where it was transplanted from the Corner Brook area in 1979 and 1984.

The introduced mink frog was first discovered in the Corner Brook area in 2001. The source of the original animals is so far unknown. It is presently found as far south as the Lewis Hills, as far west as the Blomidon Mountains, and, perhaps, as far east as Humber Village (between Corner Brook and Pasadena).

The Northern leopard frog, introduced to the Corner Brook area in 1996, was found in ponds south of Corner Brook and was also transplanted, apparently unsuccessfully, to the central Avalon Peninsula in 1978. No animals have been seen since 1989 (or, possibly, 1994) and the frog is thought to no longer exist on the island.

The chorus frog was introduced to the Corner Brook area in 1963. The Ontario collecting area was proximal to where the boreal chorus frog and the Western chorus frog ranges meet. Since only a few voucher specimens were ever collected in Newfoundland and the species appears to be eradicated from the island, it would be difficult to determine which of these two species was actually introduced, or, for that matter, whether both species were. The literature is of no help, since it lists the Newfoundland animals under several names, both common and scientific. The frog was transplanted widely throughout the island, without apparent success, and failed to thrive. Since no animals have been seen since 1982, it is thought to no longer occur.

A seemingly self-sustaining population of Eastern red-backed salamanders (*Plethodon cinereus*) has been reported from piles of old timber in Conception Bay South. The origin and extent of these new invaders have yet to be determined.

*Manuels River Trail looking toward Little Bell Island*

## Eastern American Toad

*Anaxyrus americanus americanus*

**Descr** large, squat, fat-bodied, with thick rough skin and short legs. Large head and prominent eyes with oval pupils. Prominent crests (ridges) tapering to lateral extensions (spurs) between eyes. Large, narrow, kidney-shaped secretory (parotid) glands behind crests. Dorsal (back) surface with large, dark spots containing 1–2 warts. Body colour variable, usually brown to yellow, greenish, reddish, or even grey. Sides may be mottled black or brown. Belly lighter; yellow to dirty white to cream. Toads at the tip of the Great Northern Peninsula can be brick-red. **Size** 5–11 cm long. **Activity** mostly, but not exclusively, active at night. **Habitat** woods, fields, gardens, marshes, and shallow bodies of water. **Distribution** currently found in many localities across the island to which it has been transplanted, including Corner Brook, Deer Lake, the Port-au-Port Peninsula, the Gros Morne National Park area, and central and northeastern Avalon Peninsula.

## Wood Frog

*Rana sylvatica*

**Descr** smaller frog with dark brown or black wide face mask extending from snout, along bottom of eye, to end behind eardrum. Prominent, light, dorsolateral ridges run along back. Tympanum (circular eardrum) smaller than eyes. Webbing extends half way along slender toes. Body colour very variable; grey, tan, brown or red. Belly greyish-white to cream to white. Sides possibly with black spots; legs may have dark spots or bars. **Size** 3.5–6.5 cm long. **Activity** mostly diurnal. **Habitat** found in damp woods and forests; bodies of water are used only for egg laying. **Distribution** mostly on the west coast of the island, as far north as Gros Morne National Park, and as far south as the Codroy Valley. It is also found on the Avalon Peninsula.

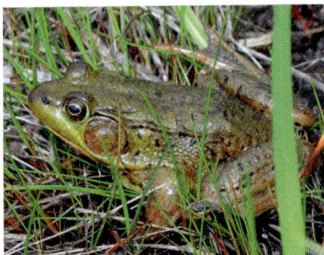

## Green Frog

*Rana clamitans*

**Descr** large frog with distinct dorso-lateral (back-side) ridges from the eye towards end of the body. Eardrums (tympana) large; in males may be larger than eyes. Variable body colour, mostly green; can also be brown, bronze, yellow, and spotted black. Belly greyish-white to white with darker lines or spots. Hind limbs may have dark coloured bars at right angles to legs (compare with similar Mink Frog). **Size** 5–10 cm. **Activity** usually nocturnal. **Habitat** found near brooks, streams, and along pond and lake edges. **Distribution** occurs throughout most of the island, at least as far north as Gros Morne National Park.

## Mink Frog

*Lithobates septentrionalis*

**Descr** moderate sized frog; large eardrum equal to, or larger than, eye. Dorsolateral ridges partial, prominent, or absent. Olive to brown, possibly with dark spots/mottling (network or reticulated pattern) on sides and hind legs (compare with the similar Green Frog). Green on head and lips. Belly cream, yellowish, or white; with or without grey markings. Webbing on hind foot reaches last joint of longest toe. Exudes pungent, musky odour. **Size** up to 7 cm long. **Activity** both diurnal and nocturnal (calling mates). **Habitat** aquatic, preferring large, cold, permanent ponds, lakes, and vegetated slower areas of moving rivers; rarely found on land. **Distribution** first discovered in the Corner Brook area in 2001, presently restricted to parts of the west coast.

# REPTILES

While there are no native reptiles on the island, for reasons explained in the introduction, the mainland portion of the province does have native reptiles most of which would be able to survive on the island if they had managed to reach it. From time to time there have been reports of common (or eastern) garter snakes in the wild, which may have been escaped pets or passengers in hay bales from the mainland. In 2010 a population of garter snakes (*Thamnophis sirtalis*) was reported from near St. David's on the island's west coast, which included a few yearlings and a gravid female. Since then, there have been reports of garter snakes elsewhere on the island. In 2023 a research project was launched to ferret out the snakes' stories. But other than garter snakes, there are no records of wild reptiles on the island.

*Eastern Garter Snake*

## BIRDS

B irds are the only living descendants of the dinosaurs; the structure of their reptilian ancestors has been transformed into a form optimized for flight. Their bones are lightweight with a sponge-like structure, forelimbs have become wings, and feathers cover their bodies. Variation in wing shape allows some birds to soar through the air with incredible speed and agility, while others gracefully hover from flower to flower. Hind limbs are also adapted for specific tasks such as running, grasping, perching, or swimming. Such abilities have made birds an endless source of joy and wonder for human observers.

When early explorers first came to Newfoundland, they not only discovered a bounty of fish, but also an abundance of birds. As the eastern precipice of North America, Newfoundland extends into the productive waters of the North Atlantic Ocean where the Labrador Current and the Gulf Stream meet. The island, and its surrounding waters, thus provides prime habitat for millions of seabirds. Seabirds spend most of their lives at sea, but numerous seabirds come to land, laying their eggs and rearing their young along the island's coastline. Colonies such as those at Cape St. Mary's, Witless Bay, Baccalieu Island, and Funk Island host globally significant numbers of seabirds. These dense colonies are natural spectacles and have fascinated visitors and residents for centuries.

Millions of terrestrial birds also visit the island to inhabit our pristine boreal forests, barrens, bogs, lakes, rivers, and coastlines. Though the diversity of birds is lower than in the rest of Canada, the province is visited by an array of inland birds that many Canadians rarely see. Birds that breed in the Arctic frequently visit the island to refuel during their spring and fall migrations. Many birds that breed in Canada's boreal forests, however, tend to migrate only over land and do not venture across the Gulf of St. Lawrence to reach Newfoundland. Yet being situated on the edge of the continent makes Newfoundland the first landfall for vagrant birds. Quidi Vidi Lake in St. John's, for instance, seems to attract many rare gull species and, as a result, the lake now enthralls an increasing number of birding tourists from around the world.

Being bathed by Arctic and temperate waters on the edge of North America gives Newfoundland an unique climate that attracts a mixture of birds. Moreover, each season is unique and brings a different pulse of birds. All of this makes Newfoundland a remarkable place for birding.

Birding terminology can be very technical and so to make this guide as accessible as possible, the use of specific descriptors has been minimized—instead everyday terms such as bill, face, head, breast, wings, and tail are used. Actual sizes for each species are not given; rather comparison is made to that of well known common species such as junco, starling, robin, jay, or crow. To help quickly tease apart some groups with many similar members, an introduction is provided that outlines the key features that distinguish them. Many juvenile birds look very different from the adults, but for brevity, descriptions are not provided for all juveniles. For more detail you are referred to larger field guides such as *Birds of Newfoundland*, *The Sibley Guide to Birds*, *National Geographic Field Guide to the Birds of North America*, *Peterson Field Guide to Birds of North America*, *The Crossley 1D Guide: Eastern Birds*, *Kaufman Field Guide to Birds of North America,* and the like.

## FRESHWATER BIRDS

## FAMILY ANATIDAE (DUCKS, GEESE)

### Canada Goose
*Branta canadensis*

**Adult** large goose with long, black neck. Head with a white vertical band on face. Upper parts of body dark brown, underparts light brown. **Habitat** ponds and estuaries throughout the island, often in large flocks. **Season** found in summer, but some overwinter.

### American Wigeon
*Mareca americana*

**Male** small duck with distinctive white head and green face, grey neck, and light brown body. White patch in wing. Blue bill with a black tip. **Female** small duck with light brown body and grey head and neck. White patch in wing. **Habitat** in ponds and bogs. **Season** summer resident.

## American Black Duck

*Anas rubripes*

**Male** dark brown body with lighter grey head, yellow beak. **Female** slightly lighter brown than male, and with browner beak. **Habitat** on ponds and in rivers. **Season** our most common duck, found all year round.

## Northern Pintail

*Anas acuta*

**Male** elegant long-necked duck. Head dark brown, neck white, back and body grey. Long thin tail (hence the common name). **Female** light brown mottled body with shorter neck. Tail not as long as on male. **Habitat** ponds. **Season** summer resident.

## Green-Winged Teal

*Anas carolinensis*

**Male** small grey duck with brown head and green area on side of head; obvious white mark in front of wing; cream-coloured patch near tail. **Female** small brown, speckled duck. **Habitat** on ponds. **Season** summer resident but may be seen in winter.

## Ring-Necked Duck

*Aythya collaris*

**Male** small duck with black head, back, and breast; light grey sides and undersides, with an obvious white mark in front of wing; grey bill with distinctive white band. **Female** small brown duck; undersides white; grey stripe on wing; dark bill with more subtle white band than the male. **Habitat** ponds. **Season** summer resident.

## Mallard

*Anas platyrhynchos*

**Male** greyish with a green head and a prominent white ring around the neck. Reddish brown breast and white tail. **Female** brownish (paler than the American Black Duck) with whitish tail and obvious metallic blue flashes on the wings. **Note** sometimes difficult to distinguish from crosses with black ducks. The narrow, regular ring around the neck is the best way of distinguishing 'wild' mallards from hybrids. **Habitat** on ponds and in rivers. **Season** common all year round.

# FAMILY GAVIIDAE (LOONS)

## Common Loon
*Gavia immer*

**Adult** large aquatic bird—symbol of the north with its haunting calls. Swims low in the water, so typically only the head and neck are visible above water. Black head and black neck; back chequered black and white, and white undersides. In winter greyish above and white underparts. **Habitat** on ponds and lakes in summer; more common in coastal waters in winter. **Season** year-round resident.

# FAMILY ARDEIDAE (BITTERNS)

## American Bittern
*Botaurus lentiginosus*

**Adult** stocky bird of wetlands. Upper parts brown with streaks, paler underparts streaked with brown. Long pointed yellow bill, white throat, with black mark on neck. Short yellow-green legs. When standing still, bill points upwards as camouflage among wetland plants. Males slightly larger than females. **Habitat** wetlands. **Season** summer visitor.

# SEABIRDS

# FAMILY ANATIDAE (SEA DUCKS)

## Greater Scaup
*Aythya marila nearctica*

**Male** small duck with black head, breast and tail; light grey back, white sides and undersides; blue bill with black tip. **Female** small duck with brownish body and white patch on head next to bill. **Habitat** Coastal waters. **Season** spends much of year in ice-free bays and estuaries.

## Common Eider
*Somateria mollissima*

**Male** large black and white duck. Head white with a black crown; white back, head and breast; black undersides and tail. **Female** large reddish brown duck. **Note** both sexes have a large bill which is yellow in summer and grey in winter. **Habitat** coastal waters. **Season** year-round resident.

## Common Golden Eye

*Bucephala clangula*

**Male** white duck with black back and an iridescent dark green head; large round eyespot between bill and eye; bright yellow eye, hence the common name. **Female** mostly greyish duck with brown head, white neck, and white underparts. **Habitat** spends summers in ponds and moves to coastal waters for the winter. **Season** year-round resident.

## Common Merganser

*Mergus merganser*

**Male** large slender duck with white body, dark green head and black back; long, narrow, toothed orange-red bill. **Female** large, slender and greyish duck with rust-coloured head showing a crest (not present in male); white patch on side of head; white breast; bill long, narrow, toothed, and red in colour. **Habitat** ponds and lakes. **Season** year-round resident.

## Red-Breasted Merganser

*Mergus serrator*

**Male** large slender duck with dark green head and prominent crest; a white ring around most of the neck, brown breast, dark back, and grey sides. Long, narrow, toothed, red bill. **Female** large, slender and greyish duck with reddish brown head and crest; white patch on wing; neck and breast colour not clearly distinguished (as in Common Merganser); long, narrow, toothed, red bill. **Habitat** more marine than Common Merganser, found in sheltered bays and estuaries. **Season** year-round resident.

## Long-Tailed Duck

*Clangula hyemalis*

**Male** medium sized duck with very striking appearance. In winter, when most likely to be seen, they are black and white, with an extremely long, black tail, almost as long as the body. Black patch on side of head; black bill with pinkish central band. **Female** smaller than male, in winter they are dark above and white below; head white with black crown and spot on cheek; lack male's long tail. **Habitat/Season** found in coastal ice-free waters in winter.

# FAMILY PROCELLARIIDAE (SHEARWATERS, FULMARS)

## Northern Fulmar
*Fulmarus glacialis*

**Adult** similar to seagulls but not closely related; separated by the tube nose on the bill. White head and breast, greyish atop wings. Hooked yellow bill with a prominent tube on top. **Habitat** breeds on offshore islands and headlands. **Season** found year round.

## Great Shearwater
*Ardenna gravis*

**Adult** similar to gull, but with narrower wings; dark above and white below. Black cap, white throat, and white band at base of tail. Dark beak has a clear hook at its tip. **Habitat** coastal waters. **Season** summer visitor.

## Sooty Shearwater
*Ardenna grisea*

**Adult** similar to Great Shearwater but slightly smaller and dark brown all over, except for undersurface of wings. Black bill with hooked tip is slightly narrower than in the Great Shearwater. **Habitat** coastal waters. **Season** summer visitor.

# FAMILY SULIDAE (GANNETS)

## Northern Gannet
*Morus bassanus*

**Adult** very large seabird, the largest in North America, with a wing span of 2 m. Body mostly white with a yellowish head. Large pale blue bill. Wings have black tips. Tail tapers to a point. **Habitat** colonies on cliffs and ledges. The colony at Cape St. Mary's is one of the easiest places to observe a gannet colony. **Season** summer resident.

# FAMILY PHALACROCORACIDAE (CORMORANTS)

### Double-Crested Cormorant
*Phalacrocorax auritus*

**Adult** large goose-sized water bird. Dark body with orange chin. Long thin hooked bill, and long curved neck. Typically seen standing upright on rocks, buoys, and wharves. **Habitat** coastal waters. **Season** summer resident.

### Great Cormorant
*Phalacrocorax carbo*

**Adult** large goose-sized water bird. Slightly larger than the Double-Crested Cormorant. Dark body, long hooked bill, yellowish chin (orange in Double-Crested) and a white patch on the throat. White patch on side of body ahead of the wing. **Habitat** south coast of the island where it nests on rock ledges. **Season** year-round resident.

# FAMILY SCOLOPACIDAE (PHALAROPES)

### Red Phalarope
*Phalaropus fulicarius*

**Adult** slightly larger than the Red-Necked Phalarope. Upper parts and crown of head dark, white face. Under parts deep red in female, less red in male. **Habitat** usually frequents open ocean. **Season** summer visitor.

### Red-Necked Phalarope
*Phalaropus lobatus*

**Adult** small, starling-sized sandpiper-like bird. Both sexes have grey upper parts and are whitish below. Head black with a white throat and a reddish brown area on the neck; this area is much larger in females. Upper parts browner in males. **Habitat** in coastal waters or the open sea. **Season** summer visitor.

# FAMILY LARIDAE (GULLS, TERNS)

Seabirds with long narrow wings. Typically observed far inland. Quidi Vidi Lake in St. John's has become a mecca for North American birders as a number of rare Arctic and European gulls visit the lake during winter (see Winter Gulls).

Gulls are not the easiest birds to distinguish from one another. In addition, immature birds typically have different plumage than adults and often resemble other immature gulls. For this reason immature gulls are not covered in this field guide. To identify immature gulls please refer to a Peterson or other bird guide. The pictures shown here are of mature gulls. Some physical differences to look for in adults are as follows.

## GULLS

**Black-Headed:** Brown head, dark red bill, orange legs

**Ring-billed:** Black ring around the yellow bill, yellow-green legs

**Herring:** Yellow bill with red spot, flesh-coloured legs

**Iceland:** No black in wings, pinkish legs, yellow bill with red spot

**Glaucous:** White wing tips—no black, yellow bill with red spot, pinkish legs

**Great Black-Backed:** Black back, yellow bill with red spot, pinkish legs

**Black-Legged Kittiwake:** Yellow bill—no spot, black legs

**Ivory:** All white body, black legs, black bill with yellow tip

## Black-Headed Gull

*Chroicocephalus ridibundus*

**Adult** Easy to distinguish in summer by its dark brown head and dark red bill. In winter it loses the brown head markings but does show a dark spot behind the eye. Upper parts grey, breast and underparts white. **Habitat** in bays and near the coast. **Season** while many of these gulls may migrate south for the winter, a number do overwinter here.

## Ring-Billed Gull

*Larus delawarensis*

**Male** a smaller gull that can be distinguished by a black ring around the bill near its tip. Upper parts grey, underparts white. Legs greenish yellow. **Habitat** around the coastline and inland. **Season** can be seen year round.

## Herring Gull
*Larus argentatus*

**Adut** our common large seagull. Large yellow bill with a prominent red spot on the lower part of the bill near the tip. Grey upperparts and white underparts. Legs pinkish. **Habitat** near coast as well as on inland lakes and ponds, and in urban areas. **Season** found year round.

## Iceland Gull
*Larus glaucoides*

**Adult** a very pale gull similar in size to the Herring Gull. Pale grey upperparts and white underparts. Wings do not show black markings as seen in the Herring Gull. Yellow bill has a red spot as in the Herring Gull. Legs are pinkish. Eye has a red ring around it (Herring Gull does not). **Habitat** in coastal areas. **Season** can be seen year round.

## Glaucous Gull
*Larus hyperboreus*

**Adult** a very large gull similar in size to the Great Black-Backed Gull. Light grey upperparts and white underparts. Wings lack any black areas. Red spot on lower part of the bill, as in the Herring Gull. Legs pinkish. **Habitat** in coastal areas and offshore. **Season** more commonly seen in winter than summer.

## Great Black-Backed Gull
*Larus marinus*

**Adult** our largest gull and the easiest to identify with its black back and wings. Underparts white. Legs pink. Has a red spot on the bill as in a number of other species. **Habitat** in coastal waters and in urban areas. **Season** found year round.

## Black-Legged Kittiwake
*Rissa tridactyla*

**Adult** a small gull with a small pale yellow bill but with no red spot. Tips of wings are black. Legs black. **Habitat** in coastal waters. **Season** found year round.

## Ivory Gull
*Pagophila eburnea*

**Adult** a small gull. Our only pure white gull (hence the name 'ivory'). Legs black. Bill black with a yellow tip. **Habitat/Season** usually seen in winter when pack ice comes close to the shore.

## Caspian Tern

*Hydroprogne caspia*

**Adult** a large gull-like bird similar in size to a Herring Gull. The top of the head is black and the large pointy bill is red. Wings grey above, underparts white. Legs black. **Habitat** in coastal areas. **Season** summer visitor.

## Common Tern

*Sterna hirundo*

**Adult** similar to Caspian Tern but much smaller (jay-sized). Top of head is black and the bill is reddish orange with a black tip. Feet are orange-red. **Habitat/Season** visitors during spring and fall migrations in coastal areas on their way to and from more northern breeding locations. Many nest on small islands along the coast.

## Arctic Tern

*Sterna paradisaea*

**Adult** very similar to Common Tern. Bill is orange-red to the tip (no black tip as in the common tern). **Habitat** in coastal areas. **Season** summer visitors that nest in colonies with Common Terns.

# FAMILY ALCIDAE (AUKS)

Auks are penguin-like birds usually black (or dark brown) above and white below. They dive into the ocean in search of food and, like penguins, use their wings under water to propel themselves.

The now extinct great auk was a member of this group. It bred on Funk Island until its extinction ca. 1810 due to overexploitation by humans. Originally called the penguin, the name was transferred to the Antarctic birds (now called penguins) because of their similarity to the North Atlantic birds with which mariners were familiar.

## Common Murre (Turr)

*Uria aalge*

**Adult** a duck-sized, penguin-like bird of coastal waters. Head is black, wings are dark brown, and underparts white. The bill is long, slender, and dark in colour. Many also show a white stripe called a 'bridle' running from the back of the eye. In winter they lose much of their dark brown colour on the face and throat. **Habitat** in coastal waters. Nest on rocky ledges of cliffs and headlands. There are a number of breeding colo-

nies on the island the biggest of which (1 million+ birds) is on the Funk Islands. **Season** year-round resident.

## Thick-Billed Murre (Turr)

*Uria lomvia*

**Adult** very similar to Common Murre, but blacker and slightly larger. Bill is thicker and has a thin white line along its upper edge. Like Common Murres, their throat turns white in winter but less dark brown is lost on their face. **Habitat** coastal waters. Nests in similar locations to the Common Murre. Much less numerous than the Common Murre in the summer but outnumber Common Murres in the winter. **Season** year-round resident.

## Razorbill (Tinker)

*Alca torda*

**Adult** can be distinguished from the murres by its much deeper bill with a vertical white stripe. Winter plumage, like the murres, has less black on the side of the head and throat. **Habitat** nests in similar situations to murres. Most breed in Labrador but there are a few colonies around the island. Overwinter in ice-free coastal waters. **Season** year-round resident.

## Black Guillemot (Sea Pigeon)

*Cepphus grylle*

**Adult** a mostly black bird with a large white wing patch. Feet are red (murres and razorbills have black feet). In winter they lose much of their black colour, showing white underparts and a mottled back, and black wings but white wing patch still visible. **Habitat** breeds along rocky coasts. Overwinters offshore. **Season** year-round resident.

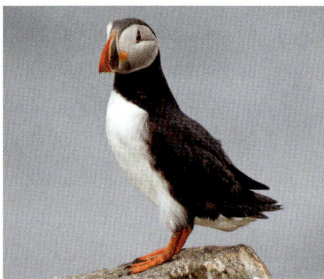

## Atlantic Puffin

*Fratercula arctica*

**Adult** this comical-looking, robin-sized bird, with its large, triangular orange-tinged bill is the provincial bird. Often seen flying back to nesting sites with several small fish in its bill. **Habitat** nests in burrows on offshore islands. The two largest North American colonies are here. Winters offshore. **Season** year-round resident.

## SHOREBIRDS (COASTAL AND FRESHWATER)

# FAMILY CHARADRIIDAE (PLOVERS)

### Black-Bellied Plover

*Pluvialis squatarola*

**Adult** a large wading bird, about the size of a jay. As the name implies it has a black belly, the black colouring extending through the neck to the lower face. Top of the head and back are grey speckled with black. White band from head through to the front of the wings. Black beak. Long dark legs. **Habitat** mud flats and sandy beaches. **Season** summer resident.

### American Golden Plover

*Pluvialis dominica*

**Adult** smaller than the Black-Bellied Plover. Similar pattern of colouring to the Black-Bellied Plover with black belly and white strip from above the eye to the front of the wing, but upper parts with brown mottling, not black. **Habitat** usually seen in coastal areas. **Season** summer visitor.

### Semipalmated Plover

*Charadrius semipalmatus*

**Adult** the smallest of our common plovers, slightly larger than a junco. Brown head and back, white underparts, with black collar band. Short yellow bill with black tip. Yellowish legs. **Habitat** found near ponds and rivers. **Season** summer visitor.

# FAMILY SCOLOPACIDAE (SANDPIPERS AND OTHER SHOREBIRDS)

### SANDPIPERS

Sandpipers are shorebirds with long legs and longish to very long bills. They are usually small (robin-sized) to medium sized (crow-sized). A number of them tend to resemble one another quite closely so small details must be noted to separate some of these species.

## SANDPIPERS

**Spotted:** Dark back, white underparts with black spots

**Red Knot:** Breast and underparts brick red in colour

**Sanderling:** Black bill, black legs

**Semipalmated:** Greyer above, black legs

**Least:** Smallest of the group, legs greenish

**White-rumped:** White rump, breast streaking extends below wings

**Pectoral:** Long neck, breast streaks end in a straight line halfway down breast, legs yellow-green

**Purple:** Legs short and yellow, bill droops slightly at tip, eye surrounded by white ring

### Spotted Sandpiper
*Actitis macularius*

**Adult** starling-sized wading bird. Dark brown above, white below with brown spots. Identified by its habit of 'teetering' as it walks. **Habitat** found near ponds and rivers. **Season** summer visitor.

### Red Knot
*Calidris canutus*

**Adult** a robin-sized shorebird with a longish bill. Dark, mottled underparts with a characteristic red-brown, hence the name. **Habitat** found on seashores and mud flats. **Season** summer visitor. **Note** designated as endangered. Frequents a few sites every year on the west coast of the island.

### Sanderling
*Calidris alba*

**Adult** a small sandpiper with a longish bill and long black legs. In summer upper parts are dark brown speckled with black. Under parts are white. **Habitat** frequent beaches and sandy areas where they have the habit of running down the beach as the waves go out, in search of food. **Season** summer visitor.

## Semipalmated Sandpiper
*Calidris pusilla*

**Adult** a small junco-sized sandpiper. Plumage similar to Sanderling but greyer upper parts. Legs usually black. **Habitat** usually seen on beaches and mud flats. **Season** summer visitor.

## Least Sandpiper
*Calidris minutilla*

**Adult** our smallest sandpiper, which is very similar to the Semipalmated but with browner plumage. The legs are greenish yellow rather than black as in the two previous species. **Habitat** frequent mud flats, sandy beaches, and even ponds and lakes. **Season** summer visitor.

## White-Rumped Sandpiper
*Calidris fuscicollis*

**Adult** slightly larger than the two previous species. Can be distinguished from other sandpipers by the white rump and breast streaking, which extends below the wings. **Habitat** found on sandy shores. **Season** summer visitor.

## Purple Sandpiper
*Calidris maritima*

**Adult** small sandpiper. Upper parts brown, streaking on upper and under parts. Legs are short and yellow. The dark bill droops slightly at the tip, which is dark with a yellowish base. Eye is surrounded by white ring. Adults in winter are greyish rather than brown. **Habitat** common in coastal areas. **Season** year-round resident, overwintering in more southern parts of the island.

## Pectoral Sandpiper
*Calidris melanotos*

**Adult** similar to White-Rumped Sandpiper but the breast streaks end halfway down the breast in a straight line, and the neck is longer. Legs are yellowish green. **Habitat** frequents wetland areas on the southern parts of the island. **Season** summer visitor.

## OTHER SHOREBIRDS

### Greater Yellowlegs

*Tringa melanoleuca*

**Adult** a wading bird with long legs and a long bill for catching prey in the water. Dark grey spotted with white above, and white underparts with some black streaks. Obvious yellow legs. Bill slightly upturned at the base. **Habitat** common around ponds; also feeds on marine mud flats and estuaries. **Season** summer visitor.

### Lesser Yellowlegs

*Tringa flavipes*

**Adult** a much smaller version of the Greater Yellowlegs, but the bill is straight. Dark grey spotted with white above, and white below with some darker streaking. Yellow legs. **Habitat** not as common as the Greater Yellowlegs. Frequents ponds and mud flats. **Season** summer visitor.

### Dunlin

*Calidris alpina*

**Adult** distinguished from similar species by the slight downward droop of the long bill towards the tip. Back reddish brown with streaks, and a black patch on the underside. Legs black. **Habitat** frequents sandy beaches and mud flats. **Season** summer visitor.

### Short-Billed Dowitcher

*Limnodromus griseus*

**Adult** larger than the sandpipers. Distinguished by the extremely long bill. Upper parts mottled black, breast reddish brown. Legs long and greenish. **Habitat** found in estuaries and mud flats. **Season** summer visitor.

### Wilson's Snipe

*Gallinago delicata*

**Adult** has an extremely long bill. Back dark brown with dark stripes on the head. Breast white, dappled above. Legs greenish. **Habitat** common around bogs, ponds, and streams. **Season** summer visitor.

## Whimbrel

*Numenius phaeopus*

**Adult** a large, crow-sized shorebird with a long downward curving bill and long legs. Grey brown with whiter underparts. Top of head is striped. **Habitat** found in estuaries, mud flats, and coastal barrens. **Season** summer visitor.

## Ruddy Turnstone

*Arenaria interpres*

**Adult** a robin-sized bird with a 'harlequin-like' plumage in the breeding season. Back reddish brown with white underparts. Head and breast show spectacular black and white patterning. **Habitat** common on seashores among seaweed searching for food. **Season** summer visitor.

## TERRESTRIAL BIRDS

# FAMILY ACCIPITRIDAE (BIRDS OF PREY)

## Bald Eagle

*Haliaeetus leucocephalus*

**Adult** our largest bird of prey. Characteristic white head and tail, and brownish black body. **Habitat** often seen flying over coastal waters, as well as lakes and ponds. **Season** year-round resident.

## Osprey

*Pandion haliaetus*

**Adult** large eagle-like bird. Blackish above and white below. Black band runs through eyes and down neck. Very characteristic 'bent' wings in flight. Commonly seen hovering over water before plunging feet first and catching a fish in its talons. **Habitat** in the vicinity of ponds and lakes, and in coastal waters. **Season** summer visitor.

## Northern Harrier
*Circus cyaneus*

**Adult** males are light grey, and females are streaked with brown. Both sexes have a white patch on the rump. When soaring, they hold their long wings in a shallow 'V.' **Habitat** on barrens and in wetlands. **Season** mostly seen in summer.

## Sharp-Shinned Hawk
*Accipiter striatus*

**Adult** small hawk of woodlands with a long, slim tail and short wings. Dark grey upper parts, breast with reddish brown bars. **Habitat** woodlands. **Season** year-round resident. In winter will often frequent areas near bird feeders in search of small birds as prey.

## Northern Goshawk
*Accipiter gentilis*

**Adult** large hawk with long tail. Male upper parts grey, under parts light grey with fine bars. Head has a black crown and cheeks, with a white stripe over the eye. Female similar to males but browner. **Habitat** forests. **Season** year-round resident.

## Merlin
*Falco columbarius*

**Adult** small falcon with small, hooked beak. **Male** Blue grey above, lighter underparts mottled with brown. Tail banded. **Female** Brown above, lighter underparts mottled with brown. Tail banded. **Habitat** mostly seen during summer in open areas in and around forests; in winter may be seen on the barrens and near coasts. **Season** year-round resident.

## Rough-Legged Hawk
*Buteo lagopus*

**Adult** large grey-brown hawk. Often seen hovering in search of prey. Tail white with a wide black band near the tip. Breast with brown and white streaks. Head and neck also streaked. Legs bear feathers to their toes, hence the 'Rough-Legged' name. **Habitat** barrens. **Season** year-round resident.

## BIRDS OF PREY OUTLINES

Falcon

Buteo

Accipiter

Harrier

# FAMILY PHASIANIDAE (GROUSE, PHEASANTS)

### Ruffed Grouse
*Bonasa umbellus*

**Adult** chicken-like bird of woodlands. Greyish-brown with a fan-shaped tail that has a black band near its tip. Head has a short crest and dark feathers (ruff) on the sides of the neck, and a reddish comb above the eye. Female smaller with a less obvious ruff. **Habitat** woodlands. Tracks can be observed in winter snow. **Season** year-round resident. **Note** an introduced species.

### Spruce Grouse
*Falcipennis canadensis*

**Adult** chicken-like bird of coniferous forests often seen perching in trees. Similar to the Willow Ptarmigan. **Male** Grey upper parts with lighter bars. Underparts dark brown, breast mottled with white. Obvious red comb above the eye. Black neck. Tip of tail has lighter brown band. **Female** Smaller than male. Dark reddish brown and barred. Short tail. **Habitat** coniferous forests. **Season** year-round resident. **Note** an introduced species.

### Willow Ptarmigan (Partridge)
*Lagopus lagopus*

**Adult** summer plumage rusty brown with white wings. Winter plumage white with black tail. Male shows red comb above the eyes. Grows feathers around its feet in winter, which act as snowshoes. **Habitat** found in barrens and other open areas. **Season** year-round resident. Willow and Rock Ptarmigan are commonly referred to as Partridge in Newfoundland.

### Rock Ptarmigan (Partridge)

*Lagopus muta*

**Adult** very similar to Willow Ptarmigan but summer plumage less rusty brown; more like a rusty brown-black. In winter can be distinguished from Willow Ptarmigan by the black stripe that runs from the bill to the eye. **Habitat** found at higher altitudes than the Willow Ptarmigan, in tundra-like areas such as mountain tops. **Season** year-round resident.

## FAMILY COLUMBIDAE (PIGEONS, DOVES)

### Rock Pigeon

*Columba livia*

**Adult** this familiar pigeon is a common sight almost everywhere in the world. The wilder forms are mostly greyish in colour but interbreeding with domestic birds has produced a variety of colours from black to white and everything in between. **Habitat** urban areas. **Season** common year round.

### Mourning Dove

*Zenaida macroura*

**Adult** a slightly smaller and more slender bird than the pigeon. Distinguished by its long tail. Upperparts brownish, underparts olive-green in colour. **Habitat** uncommon and usually seen in summer in urban areas and fields. **Season** mostly summer but some do overwinter.

## FAMILIES STRIGIDAE (OWLS)

### Great Horned Owl

*Bubo virginianus*

**Adult** a large owl, the most common on the island. Has prominent 'horns' or ear tufts, and a white band across the throat. Dark above and barred beneath. **Habitat** forested areas and wetlands. **Season** year-round resident.

## Snowy Owl

*Bubo scandiacus*

**Adult** a large distinctive white owl more common in northerly locations. Unlike most owls it hunts by day. **Habitat** open areas such as barrens. **Season** mostly seen in winter but some remain here all year round.

## Boreal Owl

*Aegolius funereus*

**Adult** a small, robin-sized owl. Flat head lacking 'horns' and top of the head covered with white spots. Upperparts dark brown, underparts striped. Nocturnal hunter. **Habitat** old forests. **Season** year-round resident.

## Short-Eared Owl

*Asio flammeus*

**Adult** a smaller owl with short ear tufts. Upper and underparts are mottled brown. Pale grey face. Hunts by day and night. **Habitat** in coastal areas and open areas. **Season** summer visitor.

# FAMILY ALCEDINIDAE (KINGFISHER)

## Belted Kingfisher

*Megaceryle alcyon*

**Adult** a mostly blue bird similar in size to the blue jay. Head large and blue with a shaggy crest and long dark bill. White neck and breast with a blue band across the top of the breast. Female shows a red-brown band on the breast. **Habitat** often found near rivers and ponds, where they plunge into the water to catch fish. **Season** year-round resident but mostly seen in summer.

# FAMILY PICIDAE (WOODPECKERS)

### Downy Woodpecker
*Picoides pubescens*

**Adult** the smallest of our woodpeckers, about the size of a sparrow. Top of head and upper edge of wings black, white back, black areas on face. Male shows a clear red spot on top of its head. Small bill. **Habitat** coniferous forests, feeding on insects in the trees. **Season** year-round resident.

### Northern Flicker
*Colaptes auratus*

**Adult** a large jay-sized woodpecker. Magnificently multi-coloured. Brown back with black barring. Top and back of head grey, with prominent red spot on back of head in both sexes. Face and neck brown. Black patch at top of chest. Underparts fawn in colour with black spots. Underneath of wings yellow, which show prominently when it flies. **Habitat** forested areas but frequently seen in urban areas in winter. **Season** year-round resident.

### Black-Backed Woodpecker
*Picoides arcticus*

**Adult** similar in size to the Hairy Woodpecker but has a black back and black barring on the sides of the breast. Male has a yellow cap. It is unusual in that it has only three toes—most birds have four. **Habitat** coniferous forests. **Season** year-round resident.

### Hairy Woodpecker
*Leuconotopicus villosus*

**Adult** very similar to the Downy Woodpecker but much larger (robin-sized) and with a much longer bill. Male has a red spot on the back of the head. **Habitat** forests. **Season** year-round resident.

# FAMILY VIREONIDAE (VIREOS)

### Blue-Headed Vireo

*Vireo solitarius*

**Adult** junco-sized bird with olive-green back, white throat and underparts. Head is blue-grey. White eye rings connected by a white bar give the impression that the bird is wearing spectacles. **Habitat** found in coniferous forests. **Season** summer visitor.

# FAMILY CORVIDAE (CROWS, JAYS)

### Grey Jay

*Perisoreus canadensis*

**Adult** a large grey bird (larger than a robin). Has a black cap on the back of its head, and a white forehead. **Habitat** in coniferous forests. **Season** found year round.

### Blue Jay

*Cyanocitta cristata*

**Adult** a noisy blue bird larger than a robin. Underparts white and head is crested. **Habitat** in urban areas and forested areas. **Season** Common visitors to feeders all year round.

### American Crow

*Corvus brachyrhynchos*

**Adult** large black bird. Large black beak. Tail more square ended than in the Common Raven. The cawing of crows is unmistakable! Congregate in overnight roosts on trees. **Habitat** in forests and urban areas. Common throughout the island. **Season** year-round resident.

### Common Raven

*Corvus corax*

**Adult** a very large black bird, much bigger than a crow. Tail is rounded rather than straight as in the crow. Also has shaggy throat feathers. Usually solitary but sometimes seen in small groups. **Habitat** coastal areas and coniferous forests. **Season** year-round resident.

# FAMILY ALAUDIDAE (LARKS)

## Horned Lark

*Eremophila alpestris*

**Adult** a brown bird slightly larger than a junco. Yellow band above the eye, and a black band above and below the eye. Yellow throat. Black band at the top of the breast. The head has two small 'horns,' which are not always visible. Hind claw very long. Primarily a ground bird. **Habitat** found in open areas such as barrens and fields. **Season** summer visitor.

# FAMILY TYRANNIDAE (FLYCATCHERS)

## Yellow-Bellied Flycatcher

*Empidonax flaviventris*

**Adult** a small junco-sized bird with olive-green upperparts and yellowish underparts. Wings and tail black, wings with white bars. **Habitat** coniferous forests. **Season** summer visitors.

## Alder Flycatcher

*Empidonax alnorum*

**Adult** small junco-sized bird with grey-brown head and upperparts, white throat and whitish breast. Olive-brown band across the breast. **Habitat** found in alder thickets, and near water. **Season** summer visitor.

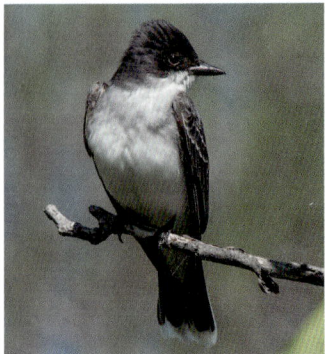

## Eastern Kingbird

*Tyrannus tyrannus*

**Adult** a starling-sized bird. Black head and back with a white band across the end of the tail. Lower part of the face and throat are white. Underparts white. Grey areas on upper sides of the breast. A red patch on the head is not always visible. **Habitat** found at forest edges, close to water, and roadsides. **Season** summer visitor.

# FAMILY HIRUNDINIDAE (SWALLOWS)

Junco-sized streamlined birds with long slender wings, which are more often seen when flying in search of their insect prey.

## Tree Swallow
*Tachycineta bicolor*

**Adult** sparrow-sized, blue-black above, underparts white. Tail forked only slightly. **Habitat** often seen when flying over fields, and pond and lake shores. **Season** summer visitor.

## Bank Swallow
*Riparia riparia*

**Adult** Similar to the Tree Swallow but smaller and with brown upperparts. White underparts with a dark band across the breast. Tail only slightly forked. **Habitat** colonies can be found burrowing into banks of rivers, cliffs, sandpits, gravel pits, etc. **Season** summer visitor.

## Barn Swallow
*Hirundo rustica*

**Adult** larger than the Tree and Bank Swallows and with a very deeply forked tail. Blue-black beneath and pale cream underparts. Underneath of face is reddish brown. Female has a shorter tail. **Habitat** its nests are usually on the outside of buildings underneath an overhang. **Season** summer visitor.

# FAMILY PARIDAE (CHICKADEES)

## Black-Capped Chickadee
*Poecile atricapillus*

**Adult** a small very familiar bird, and a regular visitor to bird feeders. Black cap (brown in females), white face, and black 'bib.' Upperparts dark grey, underparts light in colour. **Habitat** wooded urban areas. **Season** year-round resident.

## Boreal Chickadee
*Poecile hudsonicus*

**Adult** similar to the Black-Capped Chickadee but has a dark brown cap and is brown above, rather than grey. Face white with a black 'bib.' **Habitat** coniferous forests. Quite tame and will come close to observers. **Season** year-round resident.

# FAMILY SITTIDAE (NUTHATCHES)

### Red-Breasted Nuthatch

*Sitta canadensis*

**Adult** a small sparrow-sized bird with a superficial resemblance to chickadees. Black cap, white face with a black line through the eye. Back dark grey and underparts are reddish brown. Often seen upside down walking down a tree trunk in search of insects. **Habitat** coniferous forests, and will visit bird feeders in winter. **Season** year-round resident.

# FAMILY REGULIDAE (KINGLETS)

### Golden-Crowned Kinglet

*Regulus satrapa*

**Adult** minute bird. Head has a distinctive orange cap with yellow margins (male) or yellow cap (female). Both sexes have a black band above a white eye stripe. Olive green back and light grey underparts. **Habitat** coniferous forests. **Season** year-round resident.

### Ruby-Crowned Kinglet

*Corthylio calendula*

**Adult** a very small bird similar in size and appearance to the Golden-Crowned Kinglet, but the head markings are quite different. The male has a small red patch on the head, which is not present on the female. **Habitat** coniferous forests. **Season** unlike the previous species it is a summer visitor.

# FAMILY TURDIDAE (THRUSHES)

Local members of the thrush family are very similar and not easy to distinguish from one another, with one exception, the robin. The local species of thrush (excluding the robin) have brown backs and spotted breasts; only four are described here.

### Swainson's Thrush

*Catharus ustulatus*

**Adult** a thrush with a more evident eye ring and grey face. **Habitat** found in forested areas. **Season** summer visitor.

### Hermit Thrush

*Catharus guttatus*

**Adult** has a reddish tail and a pale eye ring. **Habitat** seen in mixed coniferous-deciduous forests. **Season** summer visitor.

### American Robin

*Turdus migratorius*

**Adult** our familiar red-breasted robin, which is the largest member of the thrush family. **Habitat** commonly seen in forested areas and in urban locations. **Season** summer visitor, usually considered to be a harbinger of spring.

### Grey-Cheeked Thrush

*Catharus minimus minimus*

**Adult** similar to other thrushes but is identified by its greyish face and lack of a clear eye ring. **Habitat** mountainous coniferous forests. **Season** summer visitor but 90% of breeding range on island. **Note** according to COSEWIC 'remains one of the least-studied songbirds of North America' and is classified as Threatened (2023) primarily due to invasive Red Squirrels.

## FAMILY STURNIDAE (STARLINGS)

### European Starling

*Sturnus vulgaris*

**Adult** slightly smaller than a robin. Irridescent blackish plumage with lighter spots. Juveniles have dark grey-brown plumage with brown beaks. Short tail and long yellow bill. **Habitat** common in summer in urban areas. Often found in very large flocks that can number in the thousands. **Season** seen all year round.

## FAMILY MOTACILLIDAE (PIPITS)

### American Pipit

*Anthus rubescens*

**Adult** a sparrow-sized brown bird with a very slender beak. Dark brown back, undersides lighter with dark brown stripes. Light eye stripe. Outer tail feathers white (as in the junco). **Habitat** seen in open areas. **Season** summer visitor.

# FAMILY BOMBYCILLIDAE (WAXWINGS)

### Cedar Waxwing
*Bombycilla cedrorum*

**Adult** intermediate in size between a sparrow and a robin. Brown, crested bird with a clear yellow band at the end of the tail, and a red spot on the wings. **Habitat** often seen in flocks feeding on dogberries (mountain ash berries). **Season** fall visitor.

### Bohemian Waxwing
*Bombycilla garrulus*

**Adult** larger than the Cedar Waxwing with a crest, and greyer, but with a clear white wing bar. **Habitat** often seen in flocks feeding on dogberries (mountain ash berries). **Season** fall visitor.

# FAMILY PARULIDAE (WARBLERS)

Small song birds that arrive here in spring and migrate south in fall. Often brightly coloured with thin sharp bills (finches have more massive bills). Most show some yellow colouring. Generally are slightly smaller than a house sparrow. In some species (e.g., American Redstart, Tennessee Warbler) there are colour differences between male and female.

### Yellow Warbler
*Setophaga petechia*

**Adult** our only all-yellow bird. Male also shows reddish streaks on the breast. **Habitat** alder and willow thickets, and often seen in urban areas. **Season** summer visitor.

### Magnolia Warbler
*Setophaga magnolia*

**Adult** blackish above, light grey head with yellow chin, black cheeks with a white eye stripe. Wings are dark grey with a prominent white spot. Breast is yellow with black stripes. Tail has white bars. In the fall they are brown above and yellow below, with a few black stripes on the breast. **Habitat** in coniferous forests. **Season** summer visitor.

## Yellow-Rumped Warbler

*Setophaga coronata*

**Adult** easily recognized by the yellow rump. **Male** has a grey back and wings with two white wing bars, a yellow cap on the head, and a white breast with a yellow patch at the front of the wing. **Female** brownish rather than greyish. **Habitat** wooded areas and also seen in urban settings. **Season** summer visitor.

## Black-Throated Green Warbler

*Setophaga virens*

**Male** has a yellow face, black throat, and white breast with some black stripes. Back and wings greenish with two yellow wing bars. **Female** similar but throat and underparts less black. **Habitat** coniferous forests. **Season** summer resident.

## Blackpoll Warbler

*Setophaga striata*

**Adult** sparrow-sized warbler. **Male** has a grey back, wings and tail and two yellow wing bars. Its head is black, with white cheeks and black stripes on the breast. **Female** similar to the male but lacks the black head, is greenish-grey above, and white below. In fall the adults are olive-green above and yellowish below. **Habitat** coniferous forests. **Season** summer resident.

## Black and White Warbler

*Mniotilta varia*

**Adult** easily distinguished by its black and white stripes (Blackpoll Warbler has a solid black cap). **Habitat** inhabits woodlands. **Season** summer visitor.

## American Redstart

*Setophaga ruticilla*

**Male** has a black head, back, tail, and wings, with bright orange patches on the wing and tail, and a white chest. **Female** mostly brownish above, white below, with yellow patches on the wings and tail. **Habitat** in deciduous woodlands. **Season** summer visitor.

### Common Yellowthroat

*Geothlypis trichas*

**Adult** a sparrow-sized bird with olive green upper parts and lighter underparts. Has a yellow breast. **Male** has a black 'mask' on its face. **Female** lacks the 'mask.' **Habitat** found in shrubby areas in the vicinity of water. **Season** summer visitor.

### Wilson's Warbler

*Cardellina pusilla*

**Adult** a small warbler, slightly smaller than a sparrow. Olive green above and yellow below. **Males** have a prominent black cap, which is missing or greatly reduced in females and young. **Habitat** usually found near water. **Season** summer visitor

### Northern Waterthrush

*Seiurus noveboracensis*

**Adult** a sparrow-sized bird usually found near water. Has a brown back, yellowish underparts with brownish streaks and a yellowish stripe above the eye. Tends to resemble a small sandpiper in its habit of teetering up and down when near water. **Habitat** found in the vicinity of water. **Season** summer visitor.

### Mourning Warbler

*Geothlypis philadelphia*

**Adult** sparrow-sized bird with olive-green back and yellow underparts. The head is dark grey with a black 'bib.' **Female** is similar to the male but lacks the black 'bib.' **Habitat** prefers regenerating forest areas. **Season** summer visitor.

### Tennessee Warbler

*Leiothlypis peregrina*

**Adult** has grey head, greenish back, black wings, white breast, and white eye stripe. Female similar to the male but has a less grey head and slightly yellowish underparts. In fall both adults and immature are greenish above and pale yellow below, with a yellowish line above the eye. **Habitat** in coniferous forests. **Season** summer visitor.

## WARBLERS WITH SOME YELLOW COLOURING

**Yellow Warbler:** All yellow; male has red streaks on the breast

**Yellow-Rumped Warbler:** Yellow rump, yellow patches on the head and wings

**Magnolia Warbler:** Yellow underparts, blackish upperparts

**Wilson's Warbler:** Olive green above, yellow underparts; male has a black cap

**Common Yellowthroat:** Olive green above, yellow underparts; male has a black face mask

**Mourning Warbler:** Olive green above, yellow underparts; head is dark grey; male has a black 'bib'

**Black-Throated Green Warbler:** Yellow face and black throat; female has less black on throat

**American Redstart (female):** Yellow patches on wings and tail, olive brown upperparts and white underparts

**Tennessee Warbler (female):** Greenish back, greyish head with white eyestripe, and yellowish underparts

**Blackpoll Warbler:** Yellow wing bars prominent in fall and immature

## WARBLERS LACKING ANY YELLOW COLOURING

**Tennessee Warbler (male):** Greenish back, greyish head and back, white eye stripe

**American Redstart (male):** Black body with orange patches on the wing and tail

**Black and White Warbler:** Black and white striped body

**Northern Waterthrush:** Brown head and upperparts, light underparts with brown streaks

# FAMILY PASSERELLIDAE (SPARROWS)

Small birds. The bills are used for cracking seeds and so are more massive than those of warblers. Sparrows are difficult to identify as they are similarly coloured and often lack clear identifying characteristics.

### Savannah Sparrow
*Passerculus sandwichensis*

**Adult** a sparrow with a black streaked brown back and light underparts with brown streaks. Long slightly forked tail. Has a yellowish stripe over the eye and a whitish stripe on the head. **Habitat** open areas. **Season** summer visitor.

### Fox Sparrow
*Passerella iliaca*

**Adult** a large sparrow with a bright reddish tail and heavily streaked breast. **Habitat** coniferous forests. **Season** year-round resident.

## Song Sparrow
*Melospiza melodia*

**Adult** a sparrow with a heavily streaked breast and a large dark spot on the breast. Top of head brown with a lighter stripe on the middle of the head, and a lighter stripe above the eye. Underparts white. **Habitat** low growing shrubs near water. **Season** summer visitor.

## Lincoln's Sparrow
*Melospiza lincolnii*

**Adult** similar to previous species but distinguished by whitish breast with finer streaks; central breast spot is usually absent. **Habitat** prefers boggy areas. **Season** summer visitor.

## Swamp Sparrow
*Melospiza georgiana*

**Adult** similar to the Song and Lincoln's Sparrows but breast is grey and lacks any streaking. Reddish brown cap on head. White throat. **Habitat** as the name suggests it prefers wetlands and especially those with cattails. **Season** mostly summer visitors but some may overwinter.

## White-Throated Sparrow
*Zonotrichia albicollis*

**Adult** a large sparrow with a grey breast, white throat patch, white stripe on the head, and white eye stripe. Juvenile immatures lack white head stripe. **Habitat** coniferous forests. **Season** summer resident.

## White-Crowned Sparrow
*Zonotrichia leucophrys*

**Adult** a large sparrow with a white stripe on the head and a white eye stripe, and unstriped greyish breast. Unlike the White-Throated Sparrow it does not have a white throat. Juvenile immatures have reddish brown stripes on the head rather than white. **Habitat** coniferous forests. **Season** summer resident.

## Dark-Eyed Junco
*Junco hyemalis*

**Adult** our most common bird. Slightly smaller than a sparrow. Outer tail feathers white and easily seen when the bird takes to flight. Male has a black head and back with white underparts. Female and immature have a dark grey head and back, and white underparts. **Habitat** coniferous forests and at bird feeders. **Season** common all year round.

## American Tree Sparrow
*Spizella arborea*

**Adult** a sparrow with dark brown, striped upperparts and grey underparts, slightly smaller than a House Sparrow. Has a reddish brown cap and a black spot on its breast. Has two white wing bars, and a short bill. Similar to the Swamp Sparrow but shows a black spot on the breast that is not present in the Swamp Sparrow. **Habitat** open areas. **Season** summer visitor.

## House Sparrow
*Passer domesticus*

**Adult** the familiar introduced European sparrow, which is not as common on the island as elsewhere in North America. **Male** dark brown above with black streaks, a whitish face, head dark grey on top and rust colour on side, black bib, and light grey underparts. **Female** similar but lacks the black bib, and the head is more brown than grey. **Habitat** urban areas. **Season** year-round resident.

### SPARROWS WITH UNSTREAKED BREASTS

**White-Throated Sparrow:** White throat patch, white stripe on head, white eye stripe

**White-Crowned Sparrow:** White stripe on head, white eye stripe

**American Tree Sparrow:** Reddish brown cap, dark spot on the breast

**Swamp Sparrow:** Reddish brown cap, white throat

**House Sparrow:** Light greyish face, black bib—
different family (Passeridae) than North American sparrows

### SPARROWS WITH STREAKED BREASTS

**Savannah Sparrow:** White stripe on the head, yellowish eye stripe

**Fox Sparrow:** Large sparrow with a bright reddish tail

**Song Sparrow:** Light stripe on top of the head, lighter stripe above the eye, and a large dark breast spot

**Lincoln's Sparrow:** Similar to song sparrow but does not have a breast spot

**Purple Finch (female):** Resembles a heavily streaked sparrow

# FAMILY CALCARIIDAE

## Lapland Longspur
*Calcarius lapponicus*

**Adult** a sparrow-like bird. Male has black colouring on the top of its head, face, throat, and upper breast, and a reddish brown area on the back of the neck. Dark upperparts and white underparts. Females are similar but lack black face and neck. Males in winter are similar to females. The name 'longspur' refers to the long claw on the hind toe. **Habitat** usually seen in open areas. **Season** mostly summer visitors although some may overwinter.

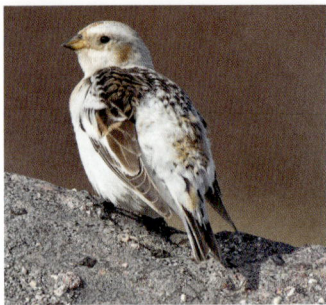

### Snow Bunting
*Plectrophenax nivalis*

**Adult** a sparrow-sized bird of the north. In summer the male is mostly white with a black back. In winter both sexes have brownish heads and upperparts, and are white below. Adults have white wing patches. Often seen in large flocks. **Habitat** open areas such as barrens. **Season** mostly seen in spring and fall as they move to and from their breeding grounds in the Arctic.

## FAMILY FRINGILLIDAE (FINCHES)

Small to medium-sized birds with short bills for cracking seeds. Many are quite colourful and easy to distinguish from one another.

### Pine Grosbeak
*Pinicola enucleator*

**Adult** a robin-sized finch. **Male** reddish with two white wing bars. **Female** greyish with the head and rump yellowish. Juveniles are similar to the female but with some red on the head and rump. **Habitat** coniferous forests. **Season** found year round.

### Purple Finch
*Haemorhous purpureus*

**Adult** a sparrow-sized finch. **Male** more raspberry coloured than purple, and is striped. **Female** quite unlike the male as it is not coloured and looks more like a striped, brown sparrow. Has a largish stout bill. Juveniles are similar to the female. **Habitat** common at bird feeders. **Season** found year round.

### White-Winged Crossbill
*Loxia leucoptera*

**Adult** a sparrow-sized bird with crossed upper and lower mandibles to prise out seeds from cones. **Male** rosy pink with a black tail and wings. The wings have two evident white wing bars. **Female** olive-grey with a yellowish rump, and also shows the two wing bars. The Red and White-Winged Crossbills are very similar but can be easily distinguished by the latter's white wing bars. **Habitat** coniferous forests. **Season** year-round resident.

## Red Crossbill

*Loxia curvirostra*

**Adult** similar to the previous species. **Male** brick red with black wings and tail. **Female** olive grey with yellowish underparts and tail. **Note** this species does not have the white wing bars seen in the previous species. **Habitat** coniferous forests. **Season** year-round resident.

## Common Redpoll

*Acanthis flammea*

**Adult** a small finch, slightly smaller than a sparrow. Upperparts greyish brown and streaked, underparts white. Both sexes have a bright red patch on the head, while the male may also show a pink breast and back. **Habitat** forests, and may be seen at bird feeders in winter. **Season** year-round resident.

## American Goldfinch

*Spinus tristis*

**Adult** a very distinctive sparrow-sized finch. Male very bright yellow with a black cap, and black wings with a white bar. Female olive-green upperparts and greenish yellow underparts. Juvenile immatures are similar to females. **Note** the male plumage is much more drab and less yellow in winter. **Habitat** common at bird feeders year round. Often seen in large flocks. **Season** found year round.

## Evening Grosbeak

*Coccothraustes vespertinus*

**Adult** a starling-sized finch with a yellow back and white wings. Female is not as yellow as male but more greyish. **Habitat** coniferous forests. Will also feed at bird feeders in winter. **Season** found year round.

## Pine Siskin

*Spinus pinus*

**Adult** a sparrow-sized finch. Dark brown and heavily streaked. Has yellow patches on wings and tail. Slender pointed beak. Sexes similar. Quite similar to female Purple Finch but with a slender bill and more deeply notched tail. **Habitat** coniferous forests. Common at bird feeders in winter. **Season** common year round.

# FAMILY ICTERIDAE (BLACKBIRDS)

### Red-Winged Blackbird

*Agelaius phoeniceus*

**Adult** a familiar bird of wetlands on mainland North America but less common here. **Male** very distinctive with its black body, and bright red wing patch bordered with a yellow edge. **Female** is quite different being brown with striping on its underparts, and no wing patches. **Habitat** frequents wetlands where the males can be seen clinging to taller plants. **Season** summer visitor.

### Rusty Blackbird

*Euphagus carolinus*

**Adult** a robin-sized black bird with a fairly long and slightly curved sharp bill. Only becomes rusty coloured in the fall. The tail is intermediate in length between the related Starling (short tail) and the Common Grackle (very long tail). **Habitat** prefers wetland areas. **Season** summer visitor.

### Common Grackle

*Quiscalus quiscula*

**Adult** a large, iridescent black bird with a very long tail. **Male** has more iridescence than females, particularly on the head. Typically seen in small flocks. Very often heard before seen as it very noisy, like a jay. **Habitat** often seen near agricultural areas, and in urban areas. Will frequent bird feeders in winter. **Season** year-round residents. **Note** a more recent newcomer to the island.

*A couple of occasional visitors to the island from Labrador:*

*Arctic Fox >*

*Polar Bear on ice >>*

# TERRESTRIAL MAMMALS

**M**ammals, the group of fur-bearing animals that give birth to and nurse their young, constitute a small group of species on the island of Newfoundland. The number of native mammals is small in comparison with the number of mammals in adjacent parts of the mainland and in Labrador, the mainland portion of the province. When the most recent ice age ended and animals started to recolonize the island, they had to be able to fly, swim through salt water, or cross over on winter sea ice. As a result, only fourteen species are known to have colonized the island. (One day we may also discover that some creatures survived in refugia). These were caribou, black bear, lynx, red fox, ermine, pine marten, Newfoundland wolf (now-extinct), beaver, muskrat, meadow vole, Arctic hare, little brown bat, northern long-eared bat, and river otter.

In the last few hundred years, a number of other mammals have been deliberately introduced to the island, including, strangely enough, two of our most common mammals: the moose and snowshoe hare. Other introduced species include mink, chipmunk, red squirrel, Norway rat, bank vole, deer mouse, red-backed vole, and masked shrew. In recent years, coyotes, which may have crossed from the mainland on winter ice, have colonized the island and are now widespread.

The island also receives a few winter visitors each year when polar bears and Arctic foxes ride down on ice floes from Labrador. In 2012, a wolf was shot on the island, which proved to be a Labrador wolf, raising the possibility that this species could make its way to the island and perhaps colonize it. A second pelt collected earlier and originally thought to be that of a large coyote, has also been proven to be that of a Labrador wolf.

## ORDER: CHIROPTERA

## FAMILY VESPERTILIONIDAE

### Little Brown Bat

*Myotis lucifugus*

**Descr** dark brown fur on the back and slightly paler underneath. **Size** wingspan 22–27 cm and average weight is 8 g. **Habitat** spring, summer, and fall they roost in trees, cavities, rock crevices, and buildings. They eat mostly insects, using echolocation to find prey. Females will gather in nursery colonies with their young, which are born in late spring. A few overwintering sites have been found in natural and man-made caves. One recently discovered hibernaculum contained more than 1000 bats. **Distribution** found throughout Newfoundland. **Status** indigenous.

### Northern Long-Eared Bat

*Myotis septentrionalis*

**Descr** quite similar to the Little Brown Bat, but with slightly larger ear and tragus (skin on nose), thought to be fewer in number. Dull brown fur on back and yellowish underneath. **Size** weighs between 5–10 g with a total length of 84 mm. **Habitat** forested areas. They primarily eat moths gleaned from a surface as opposed to moths in flight. Females gather in nursery colonies with their single young, which are born in late spring. Bats have been found in a few overwintering sites; however, it is uncertain if any of the sites contained Northern Long-Eared Bats. **Distribution** across the island. **Status** indigenous.

## ORDER: EULIPOTYPHIA

## FAMILY SORICIDAE

### Masked Shrew

*Sorex cinereus*

**Descr** grey-brown in colour with a lighter underbelly. **Size** 9 cm in length with about half of that tail. It weighs 5 g. **Habitat** relatively moist areas with good cover vegetation. It is opportunistic in its feeding habits and will consume insects, worms, carrion, seeds, and even small mammals. Prey to predators such as owls, foxes, trout, and weasels. **Distribution** most of the island. **Status** introduced in the late 1950s primarily to control Larch Sawfly.

## ORDER: LAGOMORPHA

## FAMILY LEPORIDAE

### Arctic Hare
*Lepus arcticus bangsii*

**Descr** In winter it has an almost pure white coat while its summer pelage is bluish grey with a whitish underbelly. **Size** 55–70 cm in length and weighs 3.5–6 kg. **Habitat** occupies barren land areas with adjacent suitable cover, and will move into forested areas during winter. They eat grasses, sedges and rushes, and woody plant material. Winter food may include a variety of plant material. The Red Fox is their primary predator. **Distribution** the Long Range Mountains and the Buchans and Topsail Plateaus with several smaller introduced populations on islands off the south and east coasts. Populations fluctuate and may range between 5000 and 20,000. **Status** indigenous.

### Snowshoe Hare
*Lepus americanus*

**Descr** summer fur is a rusty brown while in winter it is almost completely white. Has large hind feet, making it easier to travel over snow. **Size** weigh on average between 0.9 and 1.8 kg and are 41–51 cm in length. **Habitat** generally found in dense shrub layer in boreal forests. In summer, they will eat grasses, ferns, and leaves while in winter they consume woody plant material. Prey to carnivores such as Red Fox, Pine Marten, Coyote, Lynx, and Great Horned Owls. **Distribution** most of the island. **Status** introduced in the 1860s and 1870s.

## ORDER: RODENTIA

## FAMILY SCIURIDAE

### Red Squirrel
*Tamiasciurus hudsonicus*

**Descr** reddish fur with a whiter underbelly. **Size** an average length of 31 cm, which includes a reddish bushy tail. Weighs about 190 g. **Habitat** conifer and mixed-wood forests or areas with food and cover. While its diet is primarily seeds of cones from conifers, it also consumes other food such as eggs and young birds. **Distribution** entire island. **Status** introduced in the early 1960s.

## Eastern Chipmunk

*Tamias striatus*

**Descr** reddish brown fur on its back and a lighter colour on its belly. Highlighting the back are 5 dark brown stripes alternating with light brown stripes. **Size** average weight is 97 g with an overall length of 27 cm. **Habitat** relatively dry hardwood forests with coarse debris is its preferred habitat. They eat bulbs, nuts, berries, seeds, insects, worms, and eggs. **Distribution** slow to colonize from its original release points and is still restricted to those areas.

**Status** first introduced in 1962 on the west coast and later to the eastern Avalon Peninsula. **Note** while not true hibernators, they do enter a state of torpor during the winter.

# FAMILY CRICETIDAE

## Meadow Vole

*Microtus pennsylvanicus terraenovae*

**Descr** Newfoundland's only native small mammal and also a unique sub-species. Their long, dense fur is usually rusty brown. **Size** average about 16 cm long with a relatively short tail. Average weight about 36 g but can weigh over 70 g. **Habitat** meadows, bogs, fens, grassy openings in and adjacent to forests, and upland areas. Primarily eats herbaceous vegetation and is active year round. **Distribution** entire island. **Status** indigenous.

## Southern Red-Backed Vole

*Clethrionomys gapperi*

**Descr** dorsally the fur is a bright reddish colour while the underbelly is a pale grey. **Size** ranges from 12–16 cm in length with a relatively small tail and an average weight of 20 g. **Habitat** prefers forest habitats with ample coarse woody debris and access to water. It is omnivorous but seems to prefer broad-leaved herbaceous flowering plants and shrubs. **Distribution** has quickly spread to the east-central part of the island. **Status** first discovered in western Newfoundland in 1999.

## Deer Mouse

*Peromyscus maniculatus*

**Descr** fur described as bi-coloured, rufous on the back and whitish below. Notably large ears. Deer mice are sociable, often grouping together. **Size** can range from 12–22 cm, half of which is tail length, and weigh from 12–30 g. **Habitat** a broad range of habitats with dryness being a defining factor. Diet consists mostly of vegetable matter, but will also eat insects and eggs. Nocturnal creatures using a nest or den during the day. **Dis-**

**tribution** has slowly extended its range across western and into west-central Newfoundland. **Status** first discovered in southwestern Newfoundland in 1968.

## Muskrat

*Ondatra zibethicus obscurus*

**Descr** short brown fur that is a lighter brown on its ventral side. Scaly tail. **Size** about 40–60 cm long and weighs from 0.7–1.8 kg. **Habitat** a semi-aquatic rodent sharing a similar habitat to beavers: in streams, rivers, ponds, and lakes. Feeds on aquatic vegetation. **Distribution** occurs throughout Newfoundland. Seemingly not as common as Beavers, Muskrats in Newfoundland once went through a significant population decline but since appears to have re-bounded. They are also known to have population cycles. **Status** indigenous.

# FAMILY MURIDAE

## House Mouse

*Mus musculus*

**Descr** fur light to dark brown. Rounded ears. **Size** body length can range up to 10 cm. Tail length up to 10 cm. Weighs from 10–25 g. **Habitat** around homes, commercial structures, and open fields. Omnivorous, though diet consists mostly of plant matter. Mostly nocturnal. **Distribution** throughout the island. **Status** introduced.

## Norway Rat

*Rattus norvegicus*

**Descr** fur brown or grey. **Size** body up to 25 cm in length. Tail length up to 25 cm. Weighs between 250–350 g with males being larger than females. **Habitat** Anywhere humans live, mostly urban areas. **Distribution** generally confined to larger centres. **Status** introduced.

# FAMILY CASTORIDAE

## Newfoundland Beaver (Beaver, Canadian Beaver)

*Castor canadensis caecator*

**Descr** unique sub-species of the Canadian beaver. Its highly prized fur is brown, and it has a large flat tail. **Size** our largest rodent weighing 18–27 kg and measuring up to 1.3 m in length. **Habitat** semi-freshwater aquatic lifestyle along streams, rivers, ponds, and lakes. Builds dams to maintain desired water levels for its houses and to access aquatic vegetation. Also feeds on hardwood trees, which it also uses for dam and house construction. **Distribution** throughout the island. **Status** indigenous.

## ORDER: CARNIVORA

# FAMILY MUSTELIDAE

### Ermine (Short-Tailed Weasel)

*Mustela richardsonii*

**Descr** winter fur is completely white except for a black tipped tail. Summer fur is brown on the back and head and white on the underbelly. **Size** our smallest native mustelid, males are on average 27 cm in length and weigh 80 g. Males are twice the size of females. **Habitat** wide range of habitats, including forests, barrens, and riverbanks, but always staying close to cover. Prey primarily on small mammals, and are hunted by larger carnivores. **Distribution** probably throughout the island. **Status** indigenous.

### American Mink

*Neogale vison*

**Descr** relatively long and slender, with a dense, black-coloured coat. **Size** males are larger than females, measuring on average 34–45 cm in length. Weights vary between 0.5–1.5 kg. **Habitat** a semi-aquatic carnivorous mustelid, mink stay close to water and occupy rocky coastal and river shorelines. Diet primarily consists of fish but will also eat small mammals, crustaceans, amphibians, and birds. **Distribution** most of Newfoundland. **Status** escaped from mink farms into the wild in the mid-1930s.

### Northern River Otter

*Lontra canadensis canadensis*

**Descr** The fur of the otter is short and brown to black with some grey around the muzzle. **Size** about 1 m in length. Weighs about 7.5 kg. A third of their length is tail. **Habitat** a semi-aquatic carnivore found along the shore in both marine and freshwater environments. They eat primarily fish but will also take a wide variety of other foods, including shellfish, amphibians, and small semi-aquatic mammals. **Distribution** throughout Newfoundland. **Status** indigenous.

## Pine Marten (American Marten, Marten Cat, Newfoundland Marten)

*Martes americana atrata*

**Descr** typically have dark brown fur except for an orange/yellow throat patch. The Newfoundland population of marten is genetically unique. **Size** average male weighs 1.3 kg while a female weighs 772 g. **Habitat** restricted to forested landscapes. Diet consists of small mammals, Snowshoe Hare, berries, and carrion. **Distribution** now only found on the west coast with a smaller population in the Terra Nova National Park area. Once occurred throughout Newfoundland. Estimated between 286 and 556 adults. Currently listed as a threatened species, but showing signs of recovery. **Status** indigenous.

# FAMILY URSIDAE

## Newfoundland Black Bear (American Black Bear, North American Black Bear)

*Ursus americanus hamiltoni*

**Descr** the Newfoundland population is recognized as a unique sub-species. The pelage is thick and usually black. **Size** averaging 135 kg in weight, it is larger than other black bears across North America. Adults can be 1.2–2 m in length, and about 0.7–1 m in shoulder height. Males are larger than females. **Habitat** can be found on open barrens, but mostly inhabit areas with good cover such as forests. Omnivores, feeding on everything from berries to large ungulates. **Distribution** throughout Newfoundland, though rare on the Avalon Peninsula. Population estimated to be between 6000 and 10,000 animals. **Status** indigenous.

# FAMILY CANIDAE

## Newfoundland Fox (Red Fox)

*Vulpes vulpes deletrix*

**Descr** unique sub-species. Resembles a small dog with long fine red fur and pointed ears. Three recognized colour phases, namely red, silver, and black. **Size** weighs between 3.6–6.8 kg and about 1 m in length with females being smaller than males. **Habitat** a variety of semi-open habitats. They feed mostly on small mammals but will also eat birds, berries, and fish. **Distribution** found throughout Newfoundland. **Status** indigenous.

## Coyote

*Canis latrans*

**Descr** a medium-sized animal with long legs and a tawny-grey coat. **Size** males weigh on average 15.5 kg and may be about 1 m in length. Males are larger than females. Found singly or roaming in packs. **Habitat** variety of habitats, including wilderness and urban areas. Has been described as a versatile carnivore, meaning it will eat what is available. Hunts small mammals and also large ungulates such as caribou. **Distribution** most of the island. **Status** probably first arrived in 1985 over sea ice on the west coast, but not confirmed until 1987.

# FAMILY FELIDAE

## Canada Lynx (Newfoundland Lynx)

*Lynx canadensis subsolanus*

**Descr** this sub-species is unique to Newfoundland. Fur is long and thick, the back has a grey-frosted appearance while underparts are more buffy. A short tail and long pointed ears with tufts of hair. Black stripes on the face. Relatively short body, but long legs. **Size** males are larger than females, averaging 89 cm in length and weighing 10.6 kg. **Habitat** mostly in forested habitats. **Distribution** throughout the island at relatively low densities. Primary food is the Snowshoe Hare, and numbers fluctuate with hare cycles. They have also been known to take caribou calves. **Status** indigenous.

## ORDER: ARTIODACTYLA

# FAMILY CERVIDAE

### Newfoundland Caribou (Woodland Caribou)

*Rangifer tarandus caribou*

**Descr** males annually grow new antlers of impressive proportions. They possess adaptations to survive in cold northern climates such as unusually large feet to travel over snow and boggy ground. Generally dark brown with lighter patches. They seasonally shed hair. **Size** average weight for males is 180 kg and 135 kg for females. Between 1–1.2 m in height. **Habitat** herbivores, feeding primarily on lichens but also other plants such as grasses and hardwood leaves. Mostly seen in open areas. Black Bear is the primary predator. **Distribution** nineteen recognized herds, based on calving areas, are located from the Great Northern Peninsula to the Avalon Peninsula. In recent years, the overall population has been in decline and now numbers ca. 27,2115 (2021). **Status** indigenous.

### Moose

*Alces alces*

**Descr** our largest member of the deer family. Moose are dark brown with relatively long greyish white legs. **Size** males are larger than females and weigh 385–534 kg and 1.5–1.8 m in height. Males also grow impressive racks of antlers once a year. **Habitat** in winter this herbivore feeds on woody vegetation and so is usu-ally found in forested areas; in summer it feeds on leaves, herbaceous flowering plants, and aquatic plants and can be seen in forested areas, ponds, and road-sides. **Distribution** common through-out the island. **Status** was successfully introduced into Newfoundland in 1904 and today numbers more than 110,000 (2022). Because of their size they have few predators except for Black Bears.

## MARINE PLANTS

**M**any plants are salt tolerant and grow in proximity to the sea. On rocky shores they are found in the spray zones and are also abundant in reduced salinity areas such as estuaries and salt marshes. In Newfoundland there are two groups that are found immersed in full salinity environments: the sea grasses and the seaweeds.

Sea grasses are flowering plants found most abundantly in the tropics, in Newfoundland there is one species, *Zostera marina.*

Seaweeds are multicellular algae that, for the most part, grow for at least part of their day immersed in seawater. Algae are both unicellular and multicellular and are found in all terrestrial and aquatic environments, as well as forming complex symbiotic relationships, such as seen in lichens. The term 'algae' (singular alga) is difficult to define. Morphologically algae are often simple and, while they may become quite massive and elaborate in appearance, most retain a filamentous construction and do not show the tissue differentiation of higher plants, and—with the exception of some of the laminarians—lack specialized internal conductive tissues. The terms thallus or thalloid are used to describe such seaweeds. When algae form reproductive cells, whether these are gametes or spores, the structures producing them are naked to the environment; they are not surrounded by sterile tissue such as seen in even simple plants like mosses.

Seaweeds can be divided into three major groups. The green algae (Chlorophyta) possess photosynthetic pigments similar to flowering plants, with a dominance of chlorophyll. The brown algae (Phaeophyta) also possess chlorophyll but the dominant pigment is olive-green-brown fucoxanthin. Chlorophyll also occurs in the red algae (Rhodophyta), but is usually masked by the red pigment phycoerythrin. The use of colour to place seaweeds in these three divisions can be sometimes difficult. This is particularly true for the red algae, many of which become yellow, or even green, especially in warm nutrient-poor waters such as occur in the late summer and fall. In such instances the basal areas, which often retain the red colour, should be examined.

There are over 250 species of seaweed recorded from Newfoundland, but most are small and require microscopic examination for identification, and are beyond the scope of a field guide such as this one. About a fifth of these species are described here. As much as possible, specialized scientific terms and microscopic characters have been avoided in their descriptions. The species chosen are those most likely encountered in the intertidal, or cast on the beach after storms, and which might be identified from their overall appearance. Only the most abundant species have common names and these are given where appropriate.

## MARINE PLANTS GLOSSARY

**articulated:** with flexible joints, applied to otherwise rigid coralline algae.

**chloroplast (plastid):** the organelle inside an algal cell where photosynthesis occurs, they contain the chlorophyll and other pigments.

**coralline:** stone-like red algae, which have calcium carbonate in their cell walls, often mistakenly referred to as corals.

**cortex (cortical cell):** the outermost layer of some seaweeds, irregular to spherical shapes, but sometimes may be fine filaments. Usually highly pigmented.

**crust:** as the name suggests, thallus that grows predominantly horizontally, usually on a solid substrate.

**epiphyte:** grows on other seaweeds or on eel grass.

**filament (filamentous):** sometimes a single row of cells attached end to end forming a thread-like structure (fine filamentous), but often made up of multiple rows of cells bound together to form a more cord-like structure (coarse filamentous).

**holdfast:** a basal organ that attaches the seaweed to its substrate; it is commonly filamentous, discoid, or more massive in larger seaweeds.

**lamina** or **blade:** a structure in seaweeds analogous to a leaf in higher plants.

**multicellular:** numerous connected cells, may be microscopic or macroscopic.

**receptacle:** a reproductive body formed on seaweeds, in which are found the conceptacles where the sperm and eggs are produced.

**rhizoid:** fine filaments that are colourless and often form attachment structures such as holdfasts.

**siphon (pericentral siphons):** elongated cells that surround the central filament cell, as in *Polysiphonia*.

**sporophyll:** a blade-like structure that bears spore-forming tissue (as in *Alaria*).

**stipe (stalk, stem):** analogous to a stem in higher plants.

**substrate:** the surface on which seaweed grows.

**thallus (thalloid, thallose):** a term used to describe an algal body that is not obviously filamentous but is also not differentiated into distinct organs such as flowering plants are into leaves, flowers, stems, etc.

**tubular:** as the name suggests, a hollow tube-like thallus that, depending on species, may be constricted at intervals.

**unicellular:** microscopic, consists of a single cell.

# SEAGRASSES

## Eel Grass
*Zostera marina*

**Descr** Newfoundland's only true marine flowering plant; while other species may occur in estuaries, salt marshes, and in high intertidal zones, only *Zostera* is found subtidally in full-salinity waters. It produces upright narrow green leaves that arise from rhizomes growing horizontally through the substrate and are anchored by roots growing from nodes. Leaves are up to 1 m in length and more than 1 cm in width. **Habitat** forms extensive beds in the immediate subtidal region of soft-bottomed sheltered bays, lagoons, estuaries, and harbours. It catches sand and stabilizes its substrate as well as provides shelter for numerous invertebrates and juvenile fish. The upright blades are also an important habitat for numerous epiphytic seaweeds. **Season** year round.

# CHLOROPHYTA (THE GREEN SEAWEEDS)

## FINE MAT-FORMING GREEN SEEWEEDS

Microscopic individuals make up prominent mats.

*Prasiola stipitata*

**Descr** minute green blades are attached to rock by a distinct short stalk and form extensive mats. **Habitat** usually found on rocks in the splash zone above high-tide level where seabirds perch and is abundant under seabird colonies. It is always associated with nitrogen-rich environments and in other sites may indicate effluent from fish plants or municipal sewage. **Season** year round. **Note** a green filamentous species, *Rosenvingiella polyrhiza*, is associated with some *Prasiola* populations.

*Urospora penicilliformis*

**Descr** when submerged appears as waving filaments up to 20 cm long. **Habitat** common in the mid-tidal zone. **Season** late winter until late spring, may persist into summer in colder areas.

### Urospora wormskioldii

**Descr** this species is readily distinguished by its chain of large spherical cells, up to 1 mm diameter with filaments resembling a string of beads up to 15 cm in length. **Habitat** may form extensive mats in the low intertidal. **Season** Appears late winter and usually disappears by April. **Similar Species** *Ulothrix flacca* is abundant in the early spring on shores that have been subjected to winter ice scour. Several other species of the genera *Urospora* and *Ulothrix* may appear as fine woolly green ephemeral mats on rock in the intertidal in late winter and spring. While they may form extensive mats, individual filaments, which may reach several centimetres in length, are fine and difficult to distinguish without a microscope.

## HOLLOW GREEN SEAWEEDS

Several species of green seaweed grow as tubular hollow branched or unbranched forms. Species identification is difficult and relies on microscopic characters.

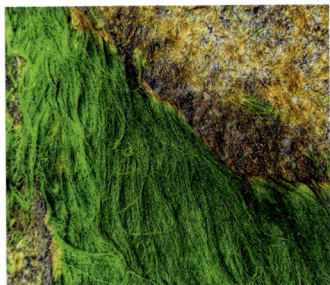

### Ulva intestinalis

**Descr** gas bubbles and irregular constrictions account for the descriptive name *intestinalis*, more than 20 cm in length and 1 cm in diameter. **Habitat** common in the intertidal particularly in rock pools and is frequently associated with freshwater seepage. It is also common in brackish areas and may form extensive mats in tidal flats and estuaries. **Season** year round.

### Ulva linza

**Descr** a larger broader species that arises from a tubular base, but then often grows without an obvious hollow tube up to 40 cm in length and more than 10 cm wide. **Habitat** widespread and frequently found growing on other seaweeds in the lower intertidal. **Season** Most abundant in summer and fall. **Similar Species** *Capsosiphon* *fulvescens* is irregularly branched, dark olive green, and forms extensive mats that are anchored to the substrate by numerous colourless rhizoids. It occurs on tidal flats and in estuaries, salt marshes and soft-bottomed harbours, especially where these are influenced by freshwater run-off. *Blidingia minima* has finer and smaller filaments than *Ulva*; it is widespread in the mid to high intertidal and is frequently seen on the sides of large boulders, where it may form extensive patches in the early spring, and where its growth is controlled by grazing gastropods.

## BLADED GREEN SEAWEEDS

There are several species of seaweed in Newfoundland that form green sheets one or two cell layers thick.

### Sea Lettuce
*Ulva lactuca*

**Descr** has two cell layers and grows as tough green flat irregularly oval-shaped, non-hollow blades that may be folded and perforated by holes, reaching more than 30 cm in length and sometimes equally wide. **Habitat** common and widespread in the intertidal attached to rocks, wharves, and other seaweeds. **Season** found year round but most abundant in early summer to fall.

*Monostroma grevillei*

**Descr** has a single layer of cells and is more delicate than *Ulva* and duller green. Young plants initially grow as a hollow sac that splits to form blades with ragged and pleated edges. **Habitat** common in the intertidal. **Season** winter and spring usually disappears by July. **Similar Species** *Protomonostroma undulatum* is more delicate still, with wavy edges and a darker more jade green colour. *Ulvaria obscura* also starts growth as a sac that splits to form blades stiffer and more rigid than *Monostroma*, while being darker green than *Ulva*. It is readily distinguished when dry by its dark brown colouration.

## FILAMENTOUS GREEN SEAWEEDS

May be branched or unbranched; they are more robust than *Ulothrix/Urospora* and obviously filamentous to the naked eye. Numerous species of *Chaetomorpha* have been described and are distinguished principally by the size of the cells in their unbranched filaments.

*Chaetomorpha melagonium*

**Descr** is quite distinct with wiry stiff filaments of thick-walled barrel-shaped cells up to 1 mm in diameter that are readily visible to the naked eye. **Habitat** grows attached to rock in the low intertidal and subtidal. **Season** year round. **Similar Species** *Rhizoclonium riparium* is distinguished from the finer filamentous *Chaetomorpha* species by its short colourless hook-like branches that, as well as serving for attachment, also cause it to tangle. It is widespread in Newfoundland occurring on all shores, including estuaries, salt marshes, and high-splash zones on rocky shores.

Regularly branched filamentous green seaweeds are likely to be either species of *Cladophora* or *Spongomorpha*. These genera appear morphologically very similar, but are not closely related and have very different reproductive systems.

## Chaetomorpha linum

**Descr** consists of rather coarse tangled unattached filaments, which are frequently clumped into balls or mats. **Habitat** on sheltered shores, in estuaries and lagoons. **Season** abundant in the summer months. **Similar Species** C. aerea, is not as tangled and grows attached to rock and shells in more exposed locations.

## Cladophora rupestris

**Descr** is the most distinctive species, with bushy dark green tufts of branched coarse filaments up to 10 cm in length. **Habitat** occurs commonly in the lower intertidal on rocks and epiphytically, in tide pools and as an understory plant in *Fucus* beds. **Season** year round with maximum growth in summer.

## Cladophora albida

**Descr** a common species, more delicate than C. rupestris; its branches are yellow-green in colour with rounded tips. Habitat widespread in high tide pools. **Season** widespread in summer but disappears in the fall. **Similar Species** C. sericea is more delicate than C. albida with pointed branch tips and is a darker green. It is also a summer annual found in high tide pools.

## Spongomorpha arcta

**Habitat** an important component of the green filamentous algal zone in the mid to low shore. **Season** winter to early spring. **Similar Species** S. aeruginosa is more delicate with a filament diameter less than half that of S. arcta and is found on intertidal rocks in the summer disappearing in the fall.

Two species of *Spongomorpha* are usually recognised in Newfoundland. Both resemble *Cladophora* species, but can be distinguished by seasonality and habitat.

# PHAEOPHYTA (THE BROWN SEAWEEDS)

## FINE FILAMENTOUS BROWN SEAWEEDS

Unlike the green and red seaweeds there are no unbranched brown filamentous seaweeds. Numerous fine-filamented branched species are found on Newfoundland shores. Their identification depends on microscopic details and is difficult even for the expert.

### *Pylaiella littoralis*

**Descr** one of the most abundant and widespread Newfoundland seaweeds. With filaments up to 50 cm in length it can completely cover other seaweeds with a sock-like brown fuzz. (With a microscope it is readily distinguished by its cells containing numerous disc-shaped chloroplasts as opposed to a few ribbon-shaped ones in other species). It is also distinguished by its predominantly opposite branching and having spore-producing cells in the main axes rather than borne on specialized small branches. **Habitat** in all habitats from the high intertidal to sub-tidal. **Season** year round. **Similar Species** *Ectocarpus fasciculatus* and *E. siliculosus* are two other common species that grow predominantly on rock. *Spongonema tomentosum* has short recurved branches that allow it to form twisted rope-like strands. It is abundant in the low intertidal often growing epiphytically.

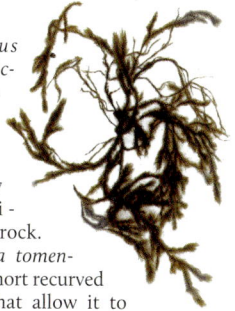

## CRUST-LIKE BROWN SEAWEEDS

There are numerous crust-like brown seaweeds found from the intertidal to deep subtidal, which range in size from the microscopic up to more than 15 cm in diameter. They are often difficult to identify and many are parts in the life cycles of other brown seaweeds.

### *Ralfsia fungiformis*

**Descr** has concentric growth rings and ruffled spreading lobes, and can resemble a bracket fungus. It commonly becomes more than 10 cm in diameter. **Habitat** grows attached to rocks in the lower intertidal. It is also common in shallow tide pools especially in sandy areas where it is resistant to scour. **Season** year round. **Similar Species** *Ralfsia verrucosa* is usually smaller and unlobed and is distinguished by its rough lumpy surface. It is particularly common on pebbles and stones on sheltered beaches.

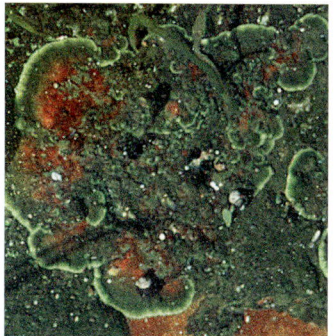

## THALLOID BROWN SEAWEEDS (EXCLUDING FUCOIDS AND LAMINARIANS)

There are a number of larger brown seaweeds ranging from coarse filamentous to tubular, bladed, or gelatinous forms, which also range in texture from soft and slippery to stiff and cartilaginous.

### Petalonia fascia

**Descr** forms short dark brown leathery blades up to 5–30 cm long and more than 1 cm wide. **Habitat** densely clustered on rocks in the low intertidal. **Season** year round but most abundant spring to fall. **Similar Species** *P. zosterifolia* has long narrower pale brown blades. It grows in the lower intertidal and upper subtidal in the winter. *Punctaria latifolia* has fairly delicate simple blades, which grow to more than 20 cm on sheltered to moderately exposed shores. *Punctaria plantaginea* is larger and more robust, growing to greater than 50 cm, it is usually found on rocks in the lower intertidal.

### Scytosiphon lomentaria

**Descr** an unbranched, olive-drab, frequently constricted tubular seaweed, which arises in clusters from a disc-like base, grows up to 50 cm long and 20–50 mm wide. **Habitat** found on mid to lower shores and on rocks and in tide pools. **Season** year round most abundant in summer. **Similar Species** *Melanosiphon intestinalis* can only be distinguished with certainty by microscopic characters. However, its distribution is different, being usually found in high intertidal and spray zone rock pools.

### Delamarea attenuata

**Descr** a tubular seaweed that is stiffer and more yellow with more crowded tufts and blunter tips than the previous species and is much less common, usually about 10 cm long but sometimes longer. **Habitat** grows on rocks in the mid to low intertidal. **Season** appearing in the early summer.

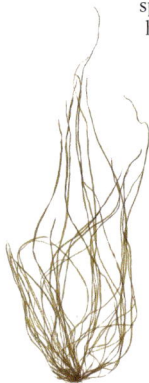

### Chordaria flagelliformis

**Descr** a dark brown to black slippery seaweed with round solid stems. It has mostly two orders of branching with a short main axis irregularly producing longer branches of similar diameter. The longest of these may produce other short branches towards their tips, but for the most part the secondary branches remain unbranched, growing to more than 50 cm in length with a diameter of about 1 mm. **Habitat** abundant and widely distributed occurring sometime on rock but usually epiphytic in the lower intertidal. **Season** common in spring and summer.

## Dictyosiphon foeniculaceus

**Descr** much paler than *Chordaria* and its cream coloured filaments, growing up to 50 cm in length, are finer and much more profusely branched. **Habitat** epiphytic on *Chordaria* as well as other tide-pool brown seaweeds such as *Scytosiphon*. **Season** year round but most abundant in the summer and fall.

## Elachista fucicola

**Descr** appears initially as a firm cushion, which later develops numerous short unbranched filaments up to 1.5 cm in length. **Habitat** grows epiphytically *Ascophyllum nodosum*. **Season** from May until the late fall.

## Leathesia marina

**Descr** forms gelatinous irregular hollow masses up to 5 cm or more in diameter. **Habitat** grows epiphytically on *Corallina officinalis* and other coarse tide pool seaweeds, especially at warmer locations on the south and west coasts of Newfoundland. **Season** late July until September.

## COARSE FILAMENTOUS SEAWEEDS (*DESMARESTIA*)

*Desmarestia* species are large bushy seaweeds up to 1 m in length with a unique mode of growth. The main stem consists of an outer sheath of filaments that grows down from the tip. In actively growing plants the tip is surmounted by a multi-cellular hair-like growth that can give a furry appearance.

## Desmarestia aculeata

**Descr** variable in appearance; plants are robust and have alternate branches arising in a single plane and giving a flattened appearance. Plants from sheltered habitats are more rounded forming more sparsely branched bushes. **Habitat** usually subtidal on exposed rocky shores. **Season** year round with maximum growth in late winter and spring.

## Desmarestia viridis

**Descr** distinguished by its opposite branching and generally a softer texture than *D. aculeata*. When damaged the plants become bright green due to the release of sulphuric acid, which causes rapid disintegration. **Habitat** Usually subtidal on exposed rocky shores. **Season** shows maximum growth in the late winter and spring.

## LAMINARIANS (THE KELPS)

This group contains Newfoundland's largest and most elaborate sea-weeds, some of which show complex tissue development analogous to terrestrial plants. These species have a number of features in common. They are attached to the substrate usually by a much branched holdfast. Arising from this is a stem-like stipe to which is usually attached a lamina. Growth in these species occurs at the junction of the stipe and lamina, producing stipe towards the base and lamina to the apex. While some species occur at low water mark on exposed shores, they are most abundant in the subtidal, and may produce extensive forest-like growths. They are cast ashore after storms. There are also two other laminarian seaweeds in Newfoundland that are whip-like in appearance and lack an obvious lamina.

### Laminaria digitata

**Descr** has a smooth slippery stipe more than 50 cm in length and has a lamina up to 1 m wide divided into numerous ribbons. **Habitat** occurs in dense populations on exposed shores in the immediate subtidal fringe. **Season** year round but with maximum lamina growth from winter until early summer.

### Saccorhiza dermatodea

**Descr** distinguished by its flattened stipe up to 50 cm long tapering without abrupt change into an undivided lamina reaching more than 1 m in length and bearing tufts of white hairs. **Habitat** Widespread on rocky shores, most abundant in the immediate subtidal. **Season** appears in winter, reaches full size in summer, and disappears by early fall.

### Saccharina latissima

**Descr** has a short solid stipe 50 cm in length and an undivided lamina, which may be rippled but usually lacks a ruffled margin, growing to 2 m or more in length. **Habitat** found in the lower intertidal and upper subtidal on exposed shores. **Season** year round with maximum growth in late winter and spring. **Similar Species** *Saccharina longicruris* is Newfoundland's largest seaweed; it resembles *S. latissima*, but is larger and typically has a long hollow stipe 1–2 m in length, which is frequently covered with epiphytes. It has a long undivided lamina 2–5 m in length with ruffled edges. Common on vertical surfaces in the immediate subtidal, but where sea urchins are absent it forms extensive closed canopies from low water mark to considerable depths.

## Winged Kelp

### Alaria esculenta

**Descr** a short stipe bears a lamina with midrib and ruffled edges growing up to 2–3 m in length with a width of more than 20 cm. Small blade-like sporophylls are borne at right angles on the stipe below the lamina. In older stable populations much larger plants occur and in sheltered areas both the lamina and the sporophylls may be more rounded. **Habitat** Common on exposed rocky shores in the extreme low intertidal and immediate subtidal. **Season** year round, with blade having maximum growth in late winter and spring and dying back in late summer and fall.

## Colander Weed

### Agarum clathratum

**Descr** A short stipe bears a lamina with a midrib and numerous colander-like perforations, grows to more than 50 cm wide and up to more than 1 m in length. **Habitat** A. clathratum is highly resistant to sea urchin grazing and forms extensive canopies most abundantly below 10 m in the subtidal to depths of more than 50 m. **Season** year round, with maximum growth rates in winter and spring.

## Brown Bootlace Seaweed

### Chorda filum

**Descr** long rubbery whip-like seaweed more than 5 mm in diameter which may have fine white hairs when young, but becomes smooth at maturity growing up to 3 m in length. **Habitat** grows in the immediate subtidal frequently on pebbles and shells in sandy areas. **Season** appears in the summer and disappears in the fall.

### Halosiphon tomentosa

**Descr** similar in appearance to C. filum, but covered in dark brown hairs making it appear of greater diameter. **Habitat** widespread in the immediate subtidal. **Season** appears earlier than C. filum, starting growth in March and disappearing in July.

## FUCOIDS (WRACKS AND ROCKWEEDS)

These are the dominant intertidal seaweeds. They occur in abundance on virtually all but the most exposed ice-scoured shores. There are two genera *Fucus*, with four to five species, and *Ascophyllum,* with a single species.

Species of *Fucus* are highly variable and their appearance is influenced by the environment. A disc-shaped holdfast supports a dichotomously dividing blade with a midrib bordered by a thinner wing. When fertile they produce inflated bladder-like receptacles at the tips of the thallus.

## Spiral Wrack
### Fucus spiralis
**Descr** typically found in dense clumps of twisted blades on rocks. When fertile, readily identified by the almost spherical receptacles encircled by a ribbon-like band. **Habitat** in the mid to upper intertidal. **Season** year round.

### Fucus distichus
**Descr** narrow blades up 5–10 cm in length with cylindrical receptacles. **Habitat** confined to rock pools at high tide levels. **Season** year round.

## Bladder Wrack
### Fucus vesiculosus
**Descr** probably the most abundant fucoid species; it is readily distinguished by paired air bladders on opposite sides of the mid rib. **Habitat** occurs from the mid to low intertidal. **Season** year round.

### Fucus evanescens
**Descr** has a broad lamina that lacks bladders and when reproductive has large broad, often forked, receptacles. **Habitat** commonly found in estuaries and on sheltered shores. **Season** year round. **Similar species** a similar, but narrower form with long narrow highly pointed forked receptacles is sometimes recognized as *Fucus edentatus*. It occurs on moderate to fully exposed rocky shores.

## Knotted Wrack
### Ascophyllum nodosum
**Descr** a yellowish to olive green seaweed with a central stem lacking lateral wings, which becomes swollen at regular intervals into single floats. Receptacles are produced on short lateral branches. **Habitat** widespread throughout Newfoundland, but is most abundant on the south coasts that are free from ice scour. In other locations it occurs in sheltered areas such as inlets and harbours as well as rocky shores with protective gullies and boulders. **Season** year round. **Note** *Elachista fucicola* and *Vertebrata lanosa* are epiphytic on *A. nodosum*.

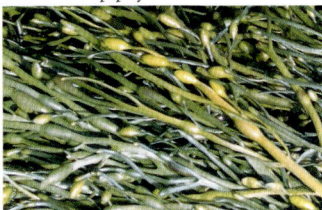

# RHODOPHYTA (THE RED SEAWEEDS)

All red seaweeds are filamentous, which are tightly bound together in many species forming complex, thallose, bladed, or crust-like structures.

## THALLOSE RED SEAWEEDS

May be soft, cartilaginous, or wiry; some are filamentous in appearance, but their internal anatomy is not obviously filamentous.

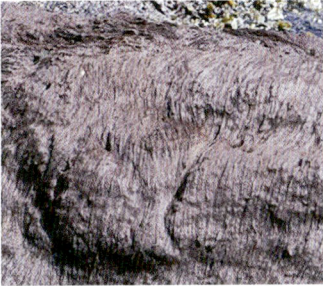

### Bangia fuscopurpurea

**Descr** fine threads up to 10–20 cm in length, less than 0.2 mm in diameter, form dark purple to reddish black dense woolly mats that fade to a light tan before disappearing. A phase in its life cycle appears as clumps of thin, filamentous, hair-like strands that can be purplish-brown growing on mollusc shells. **Habitat** may completely cover bare intertidal rock surfaces in moderate to exposed locations. **Season** late winter and spring.

### Ahnfeltia plicata

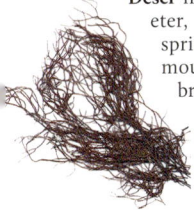

**Descr** has a 0.5-1 mm diameter, dark red to black springy wiry dichotomously to irregularly branched form up to 30 cm in length, which arises from a thin disc-like holdfast. **Habitat** widespread, particularly in low shore pools subject to sand scour where it is remarkably resistant to abrasion. It is commonly found in the drift. **Season** year round.

### Cystoclonium purpureum

**Descr** attached by filamentous threads supporting cylindrical branched stems up to 60 cm long and 3 mm wide. The numerous alternate branchlets may become recurved. Its colour is dull purplish pink to rosy red, becoming paler or even yellow in the late summer. **Habitat** in the low intertidal on rocks and epiphytically. **Season** year round.

### Irish Moss

#### Chondrus crispus

**Descr** forms bushy cartilaginous plants usually up to 10 cm in height, but sometimes much larger. A tapered stem arising from a holdfast bears dichotomous to irregularly branched flattened blades 5–10 mm wide. The tips may be fringed with small new branches. The colour is variable, typically brownish red to darker; with the lower portions greener, wet or submerged individuals often show a purple iridescence. The upper portions in summer may bleach to yellow green or straw colour. **Habitat** growing in midshore tide pools and on rock in the lower intertidal often under fucoids. It may be found in the subtidal particularly in sheltered areas and lagoons where it can form unattached balls. **Season** year round. **Note** it is harvested in the Maritimes for the food industry as a source of the gelling agent carrageenan. While not commercial in Newfoundland, experimental harvesting has been undertaken in Port-au-Port Bay.

## Devaleraea ramentacea

**Descr** one of Newfoundland's most variable seaweeds, consisting of cartilaginous, springy, usually hollow compressed fronds, which can grow to 50 cm in length. Its branching can vary from unbranched, to simple dichotomous, to having numerous lateral branches giving it a bottle brush appearance. Damaged tips of the thallus (apices) may also produce numerous branches. It is dark wine red to blackish red in colour in the winter and spring, but older plants in summer may become yellow green. Its coarse texture readily separates it from both *Dumontia* and *Cystoclonium*. **Habitat** found on rock in the low intertidal and upper subtidal and is widely distributed on moderate to fully exposed shores. **Season** year round.

## Dumontia contorta

**Descr** produces several very slippery flaccid red brown to yellowish fronds that arise from a disc-like holdfast. The young fronds are solid but become flattened and hollow at maturity and may grow to more than 30 cm long and 10 mm in width, they may branch, but the branchlets rarely branch again. Its slippery flaccid nature distinguishes it from *Devaleraea* and the disc-like attachment structure distinguishes it from some forms of *Cystoclonium*. **Habitat** mid intertidal pools and on rock in the lower intertidal. **Season** spring and summer disappearing in the fall.

## CALCAREOUS RED SEAWEEDS

Calcium carbonate depositions in their cell walls give a stony or 'hard coral–like' appearance to these seaweeds, which are collectively known as coralline algae.

## Corallina officinalis

**Descr** Newfoundland's only articulated calcareous species and is unmistakeable. It arises from a crust-like base and produces erect branches that are divided into segments, 1 mm wide, separated by non-calcified flexible joints. The branches are generally oppositely branched giving a feathery appearance. The colour is pale pink to mauve with white branch tips. **Habitat** found extensively on rock and in tide pools on exposed low shores. **Season** year round.

## Lithothamnion glaciale

**Descr** characterized by its short upright non-articulated protuberances and speckled rose pink appearance, this is probably Newfoundland's most abundant seaweed. **Habitat** can be found from the low intertidal, subtidally to depths in excess of 100 m on all rocky shores. It is frequently seen on glass bottles and pottery that have been discarded in harbours. On soft habitat in the Newfoundland subtidal, fragments of *L. glaciale* may grow into spherical balls called 'rhodoliths.' **Season** year round.

*Clathromorphum circumscriptum*

**Descr** paler, smoother and lacks the protuberances of *Lithothamnion gla-ciale*. When damaged it may develop a fungal infection, which produces greenish-grey ulcer-like sores on its surface. **Habitat** in the low intertidal and subtidal. **Season** year round. **Similar Species** *Phymatolithon lenormandii* is another species found in the intertidal. It has a thin rough crust with distinct ridges and grows under cover of fucoids. Should this shelter be removed it dies and the remains of its chalky white skeleton can be striking. About a dozen other species of coralline algae grow in Newfoundland.

## NON-CALCAREOUS ENCRUSTING RED SEAWEEDS

*Hildenbrandia rubra*

**Descr** one of the most abundant of several non-calcareous encrusting red seaweeds. Its crusts are less than 0.5 mm thick and are bright red, but may become browner in higher tide pools. **Habitat** extremely widespread in pools and on the lower shore on rocks and pebbles; it is particularly abundant in estuaries. **Season** year round.

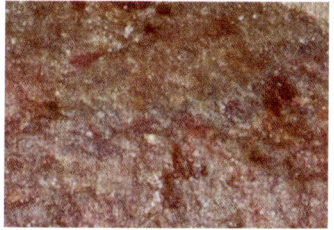

## COARSE FILAMENTOUS RED SEAWEEDS

These may be large and complex seaweeds but close examination, particularly of the branch tips, clearly shows their filamentous construction. In *Polysiphonia* and *Vertebrata* species the central filament cell is surrounded by a rosette of similar cells called pericentral siphons, these in turn may be covered with smaller more rounded cortical cells. At least 10 species of *Polysiphonia* occur in Newfoundland and their identity depends on their number of siphons and the degree of cortication.

*Ceramium virgatum*

**Descr** the most readily identified species of *Ceramium* reported from Newfoundland, it has a main stem up to 0.5 mm in diameter and 20 cm in length. Its dichotomous branches have a banded appearance and incurved pincer-like tips. **Habitat** growing on rocks and other seaweeds in the lower intertidal and immediate subtidal. **Season** year round.

## Polysiphonia flexicaulis

**Descr** its lateral branches are usually longer than the main axis giving it a bushy appearance and making the main axis (up to 25 cm in length) difficult to distinguish. Four pericentral siphons are covered by cortical cells on the lower parts of the plant. **Habitat** common in the lower intertidal to subtidal on rocks and other seaweeds. **Season** year round but most abundant in spring and early summer.

## Polysiphonia stricta

**Descr** more delicate than *P. flexicaulis* with four pericentral siphons lacking cortical cells, wine red in colour and up to 15 cm in length. **Habitat** abundant on exposed rocky shores from the mid-intertidal to subtidal. **Season** year round with maximum growth in the spring and summer.

## Vertebrata lanosa

**Descr** has 20–24 pericentral siphons and grows as reddish-brown to purple-brown springy tufts up to 5 cm long. **Habitat** epiphyte on *Ascophyllum nodosum*. **Season** year round.

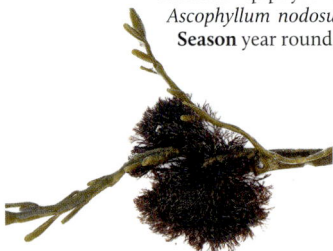

## Rhodomela confervoides

**Descr** similar to some species of *Polysiphonia* except that a dense growth of cortical cells replaces the pericentral siphons. It is extremely variable in appearance; large coarse plants may grow to 50 cm, while others found growing epiphytically in the early spring are much more delicate. **Habitat** in the lower intertidal and subtidal. **Season** year round but most abundant in the late winter and spring and dies back in summer.

## Ptilota serrata

**Descr** this is the most widespread and abundant non-coralline red seaweed in Newfoundland. It forms dark red irregular bushes with its ultimate branches flat with a coarse feathery appearance up to 15 cm tall. These have dissimilar opposite paired branchlets, one of which resembles the main branch tip while the other is unbranched, but has a serrated edge. When fertile these branches may be replaced by short black spore-bearing stalks. **Habitat** a subtidal species found growing in abundance from 5 m to over 50 m depth on most Newfoundland rocky shores. It is cast ashore in large amounts after storms. **Season** year round.

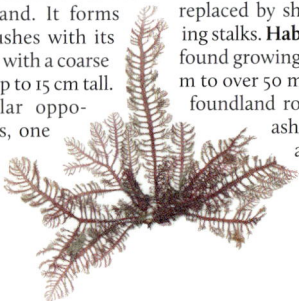

## BLADED RED SEAWEEDS

Bladed red seaweeds are very diverse in structure, ranging from flat blades of one to two cells in thickness, to coarse, almost cartilaginous forms, to delicate fronds borne on midribs.

*Porphyra* species have thin delicate blades, are rose-red to red-brown to olive green in colour, are one cell layer thick, and lack midribs; they may be attached to rocks by a short stalk of filamentous cells. The delimitation of species is contentious and identification of species even using microscopic characteristics is difficult. Like *Bangia*, *Porphyra* species also have an alternate phase in their reproductive cycles, forming rose red patches on shells, barnacle plates, and other calcareous substrates.

### *Porphyra umbilicalis* and *P. purpurea*

**Descr** these two species are superficially almost identical, with rounded ruffled blades attached by a short stalk. *P. umbilicalis* is more circular, greenish towards the base with a rubbery texture and a usually more centrally located stalk. *P. purpurea* is more delicate, more oblong in shape and with the stalk attached less centrally. They may grow 50 cm in length, but are usually much smaller. **Habitat** both are common on rocky shores. **Season** year round.

### *Porphyra linearis*

**Descr** much narrower than the two previous species, usually less than 2 cm wide with ruffled fronds and may grow up to 30 cm in length. **Habitat** may form a distinct band in the upper tidal of exposed rocky shores. **Season** fall and early winter. **Note** the aquaculture of some *Porphyra* species is a multi-billion dollar industry in East Asia and many people will be familiar with this as the black wrapper surrounding some types of sushi. However, with the exception of *P. linearis*, Newfoundland species are considered unpalatable.

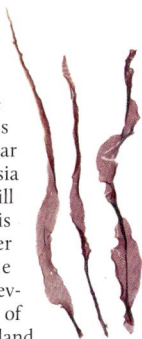

### *Wildemania miniata*

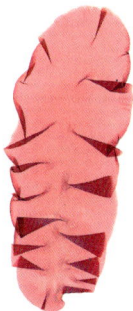

**Descr** very similar to a *Porphyra*, but is two cell layers thick and forms flat, oval sheets that lack ruffled edges, up to 50 cm in length and 30 cm wide. When young it is rose-pink, but becomes browner with age. **Habitat** grows in the low intertidal on rocks on exposed coasts. **Season** appearing in the spring and generally disappearing in the late summer.

## Dulce

### Palmaria palmata

**Descr** has a short stalk that arises from a disc and expands to form reddish brown, occasionally bleached yellow, membranous flattened fronds. Irregular dichotomous branching produces a palm shape with the lobes frequently covered with numerous leafy outgrowths. Growing to more than 50 cm in length. **Habitat** throughout Newfoundland in the low intertidal on rocks and epiphytically on *Laminaria* stipes. **Season** year round. **Note** fresh plants are unpalatable, but when dried are tasty, being rich in minerals, vitamins, amino acids, and sugar-like compounds that give the species its characteristic flavour.

### Phycodrys rubens

**Descr** one of Newfoundland's most attractive seaweeds. A short stalk bears a thin pink membranous, oak leaf–shaped, blade up to 5 cm wide with a prominent midrib and lateral veins and ultimately up to 15–20 cm long. As growth occurs, the membranous part of the blade erodes leaving the mid rib and the veins from which new blades arise. The margins of the blade may be smooth or bear numerous smaller blades. **Habitat** frequently found in the drift this subtidal species grows on rock, coralline algae, sessile animals, and other larger seaweeds. **Season** year round.

### Membranoptera alata

**Descr** like *Phycodrys rubens* this has a short stalk, but bears narrower membranous blades up to 1 cm width with prominent midribs. It is brownish crimson in colour. The blades branch dichotomously and the membranous margins are frequently missing with new blades arising from the mid rib growing to 10–15 cm in length. A much smaller form, less than 5 cm in length that lacks a prominent midrib, grows in deep water on *Ptilota serrata*. **Habitat** sub-tidal and frequently found on the stipes of *Laminaria*. **Season** year round.

# SEASHORE INVERTEBRATES

## SPONGES (PHYLUM PORIFERA)

Even though they do not appear to be very animal-like, the sponges are the simplest of the many celled (multicellular) animals. A sponge is basically a mass of individual cells supported by a skeleton of chalk-like, glass-like, or horn-like material. The cells surround internal canals with openings to the outside called 'oscula.' Water, containing microscopic food particles, is brought in through the oscula, and flows through the canals where the individual sponge cells capture the particles for food and digest them. They are mostly found in salt water, but there are a few freshwater forms, some of which are found in Newfoundland rivers and streams.

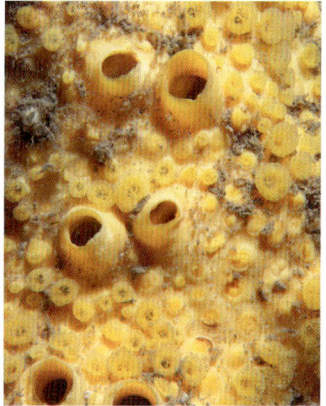

### Finger Sponge (Deadman's Fingers)

*Haliclona oculata*

**Descr** a yellow to brownish sponge with finger-like erect branches, and with prominent oscula at the tips of the branches. **Size** up to 50 cm in height. **Habitat** in the lower intertidal zone to depths of 20 m, especially at wave exposed locations growing on rocks.

### Boring Sponge

*Cliona celata*

**Descr** a yellow sponge that bores into mollusc and barnacle shells, appearing as pockmarks on the surface of the shell. Eventually the sponge can over-grow the whole shell and dissolve it completely. **Habitat** mollusc and barnacle shells.

### Bread Crumb Sponge

*Halichondria panicea*

**Descr** forms irregular cream-coloured or sometimes greenish masses. Upright extensions produce close set knobs, or fingers, and sometimes form hollow chimneys. Soft to the touch and crumbles in the hand, the pieces looking very much like bread crumbs, hence the common name. **Habitat** grows over rocks and stones on the lower shore and on wharf pilings, seaweeds, and rocks, often extending below tide level.

*< Bread Crumb Sponge*

## JELLYFISH, ANEMONES, AND HYDROIDS (PHYLUM CNIDARIA)

Simple animals made up of two layers of cells, an outer layer (ectoderm), and an inner layer (endoderm) that digests and absorbs food. The food, usually small swimming animals, is captured by the tentacles, and enters through the 'mouth' into the hollow centre (gastrovascular cavity) where it is digested. There is only the one opening to the 'gut,' so undigested remains must be disgorged through the 'mouth.'

The tentacles are armed with stinging cells (nematocysts), which are used to capture the prey and deter enemies. Each nematocyst can release a harpoon-like thread, which can either penetrate the prey and immobilize it or stick to it, thereby preventing it from escaping.

Most forms are marine, but there are a few freshwater forms, a number of which are found in Newfoundland ponds.

### Moon Jelly
*Aurelia aurita*

**Descr** a very common jellyfish of northern waters that often becomes stranded on the seashore. Has four very obvious horseshoe-shaped pinkish reproductive organs. Numerous tentacles along the outer edge of the bell. **Size** up to 250 mm across. **Habitat** in open waters but often stranded on the shore.

### Garland Sea Fir
*Dynamena pumila*

**Descr** a small colonial hydroid with the hydrothecae arising from the main stalks in opposite pairs. To the naked eye it looks like fur growing on the substrate. **Size** up to 5 cm tall. **Habitat** lower intertidal zone growing on rocks, pilings and seaweeds, especially *Ascophyllum*.

### Lion's Mane (Sea Blubber)
*Cyanea capillata*

**Descr** the largest known jellyfish in the world. Has large numbers of very long tentacles trailing up to 20 m below the bell. The colour changes with age but usually dark brown or reddish. **Size** up to 2 m in diameter but usually about 30 cm. **Habitat** coastal and open waters. **Note** Avoid touching the tentacles as they can produce a very bad sting, especially if you touch them and then rub delicate tissue like your lips or eyes.

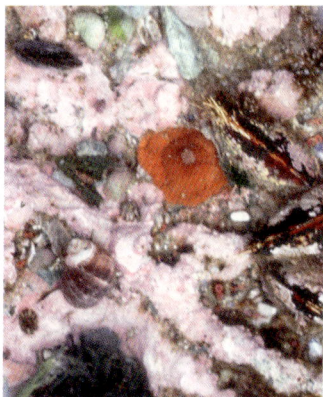
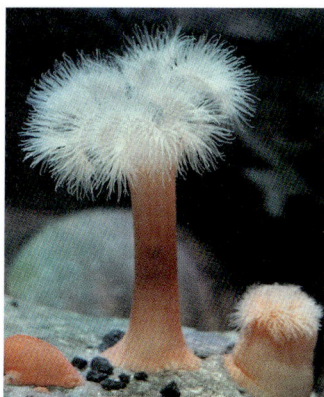

*Frilled Anemone: (left) contracted tentacles; (right) radiating tentacles*

## Frilled Anemone (Brown Anemone)

*Metridium senile*

**Descr** the column (stem) of the animal is smooth to the touch, and usually purple in colour although it can also be orange, yellow brown, pink, or even white. There are many short tentacles radiating from a central disk. In older, larger specimens this disk may be lobed and carry up to 1000 tentacles. When the tide is out and the animal is exposed, the column and tentacles contract and the animal then resembles nothing more than a blob of brownish jelly. **Size** usually measures up to 100 mm in height and 75 mm in width, but can be much larger in sheltered rock pools and in areas below low tide level. **Habitat** usually found in the lower shore area, in rock pools, and below low tide level.

## Northern Red Anemone (Dahlia Anemone)

*Urticina felina*

**Descr** column smooth, deep wine red to brownish or purplish, often streaked with green. Tentacles short, thick, and blunt, usually with one or two dark rings. **Size** up to 50 mm in height, and up to 100 mm wide. Like *Metridium*, contracts if out of water. **Habitat** intertidal zone and in tidepools, but more adundant in the subtidal.

## Silver-Spotted Anemone

*Aulactinia stella*

**Descr** column pale olive to bluish green, with rows of sticky bumps to which bits of shell and pebbles attach. Tentacles same colour as column with a pale ring about midway along each tentacle, and a silvery white spot at the base of each tentacle. **Size** up to 40 mm tall and 50 mm wide. **Habitat** in shallow water and rock pools.

## MARINE WORMS (PHYLUM ANNELIDA)

This phylum includes not only familiar garden earthworms, but also leeches and a number of marine worms called polychaetes. The members of this group have segmented bodies with many body parts repeated in each segment. The segments are revealed on the outside by rings around the body.

Polychaetes, the most common marine worms of this group, have long bristles called 'chaetae' on the sides of most segments, and side flaps called 'parapodia' that can be moved backwards and forwards like paddles, allowing the animals to swim quite rapidly. Polychaetes have distinctive heads possessing both 'eyes' and 'jaws.'

### Clam Worm
*Alitta virens*

**Descr** a long, robust, iridescent, greenish polychaete worm. Has well-developed parapodia, and a distinctive head with four or five pairs of short tentacle-like projections, four eyes, and a large pair of sickle like jaws. Carnivorous on other worms and small animals. **Size** up to 90 cm long. **Habitat** often found swimming in subtidal waters. Usually buried under the sand, often associated with clams but is not their predator.

### Hard Tube Worm
*Spirorbis borealis*

**Descr** a small polychaete worm that lives in a tiny, spiral, chalky tube on rockweeds and other seaweeds. White when young, it later is coloured green by associated algae. **Size** the distinctive tube measures up to 4 mm across and is easy to spot. **Habitat** rockweeds and other seaweeds. When the tide is in, the worm puts out head tentacles to catch floating plankton as food.

1 mm

### Twelve-Scaled Worm
*Lepidonotus squamatus*

**Descr** a very unwormlike polychaete that is covered by 12 or 13 pairs of scales, resembling a row of shields, on its upper side, hence the name. Each scale is roughened with knobs of various sizes, and coloured with various shades of brown, and often spotted with green, red, or yellow. It can curl itself up when disturbed. **Size** up to 50 mm in length. **Habitat** lower shore area in crevices and among anchored mussels and seaweeds.

### Lugworm
*Arenicola marina*

**Descr** a large worm that eats sizable quantities of sand, digesting bacteria and organic detritus and producing pyramidal fecal mounds of sand. Has small parapodia that bear setae, and reddish gills midway along the tubular body. **Size** up to 20 cm in length. **Habitat** usually found in U-shaped tubes in sediment.

# RIBBON WORMS (PHYLUM NEMERTEA)

Long, flattened worms with soft, unsegmented flat or cylindrical bodies. The head end may have light sensitive organs called 'ocelli.' The head end also has a tongue-like internal organ, the 'proboscis,' a feeding organ, which can be everted. When fully extended the proboscis can be almost as long as the body. One European species can attain the gigantic length of nearly 30 m. North American forms are, however, much smaller.

Ribbon worms feed on small animals, capturing them with the proboscis. They live in the mud and under rocks during the day, becoming active and crawling or swimming at night. Ribbon worms are sometimes found breeding in masses resembling a tangled ball of thread.

## Red Lineus

*Lineus ruber*

**Descr** body thread-like and rounded in cross section, usually red, but sometimes green or brownish-green. Ocelli appear as light dots around the edge of the head, usually visible only with the aid of a hand lens. **Size** can measure up to 15 cm in length. **Habitat** among pebbles, or burrowing in mud and sand.

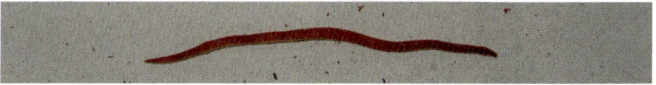

# MOSS ANIMALS (PHYLUM BRYOZOA)

This group of quite common, but easily overlooked and most unanimal-like organisms consists of very tiny animals living in colonies (attached groups) growing on the surfaces of rocks, seaweeds, and shelled animals. Somewhat moss-like in appearance as the name suggests. Each tiny microscopic individual has a horny body covering that may be hard and chalky. The body covering usually has a trap door through which an organ called the 'lophophore' is extended to catch microscopic marine life and particles.

## Sea Mat

*Membranipora membranacea*

**Descr** forms greyish-white encrusting lacy mat-like colonies. Each zooecium (host sac) is rectangular with short spines at each corner. A recent immigrant that is outcompeting local species and causing severe damage to Newfoundland kelp beds. **Habitat** grows on marine algae and, in particular, *Laminaria* and *Fucus*. Occurs on the lower shore into shallow water.

# CRABS, LOBSTERS, BARNACLES, AND SCUDS (PHYLUM ARTHROPODA)

This phylum contains the greatest variety of animal types, with over 90% of all known animal species belonging to this one group. Each animal has a partly segmented body (head is not segmented) covered by a hard shell made of chalk or protein. The head is well developed with antennae, eyes, and mouth parts. The body segments may bear jointed limbs (e.g., legs, wings). Nearly all marine arthropods are of the subphylum Crustacea, and all animals described in this field guide are Crustaceans.

## SCUDS

### Scud (Sideswimmer)

*Gammarus* sp.

**Descr** body flattened from side to side. First pair of antennae much longer than the second and are nearly half the length of the body. The eyes are kidney-shaped. **Size** varies with species, and can be 20 mm or more in length. Scuds are much larger than beach fleas. **Habitat** Different species found at variable shore levels, sheltering under seaweeds when tide is out, or in rock pools. Can be seen swimming on their sides in the water. Often seen in pairs with the larger male grasping the smaller female.

### Rockhopper

*Apohyale prevostii*

**Descr** body flattened from side to side. First pair of antennae on head not as long as the second pair. The eyes, on the sides of the head, are rounded. Is easily identifiable by its habit of jumping when disturbed out of water. Similar to the scud, but the latter are larger, have kidney-shaped eyes, and are not usually found out of water. Feeds on decaying matter. **Size** up to 7 mm in length. **Habitat** found in enormous numbers in water and around seaweeds in shallow water.

### Beach Flea

*Talorchestia* sp.

**Descr** small, scud-like creatures with long antennae. Jumps frantically when disturbed, hence the name 'flea.' **Size** up to 3 cm long. **Habitat** vast numbers burrow into the sand near the high water mark and come out at night to feed on decaying seaweed stranded by the high tides.

## Planktonic Amphipod

*Calliopius laeviusculus*

**Descr** a planktonic scud-type organism with huge eyes. Antennae are brush-like in appearance. **Size** usually 5–6 mm long. **Habitat** vast swarms live among surfy low shore seaweeds in the summer and retreat to the deeper subtidal for the winter.

## Kelp Sowbug

*Idotea baltica*

**Descr** body flattened from above to below; about four times longer than broad. Seven pairs of legs, the last four pairs being longer than the others. Has a large distinctive tail plate measuring one quarter of the total body length, with three distinct 'teeth' at the end. **Size** up to 25 mm in length. **Habitat** especially common swimming or crawling among estuarine eel grass beds and seaweeds, and in rock pools.

## BARNACLES

Barnacles are hardly typical arthropods, since they are permanently attached to rocks, and are covered by overlapping shell plates. In reality they are arthropods that have abandoned a free-moving way of life in favour of standing on their 'heads' attached to a solid base. The shell plates open when the barnacle is underwater and its legs are extended to capture floating plankton as food. Because they cannot move to mate, they possess a giant penis that can mate, in the fall, with neighboring barnacles several centimetres away. Two species are commonly found on Newfoundland shores.

## Common Barnacle (Northern Rock Barnacle)

*Semibalanus balanoides*

**Descr** the common shore barnacle crowded into large colonies. If the common barnacle is prised off the rock it leaves a thin, non-chalky membrane on the rock to which it was attached. **Size** the shell usually measures up to 25 mm in height and about 10 mm in width, though crowded barnacles can be very columnar, up to 40 mm tall and very narrow. **Habitat** on the rocks in the mid to upper shore region, often above the seaweeds.

## Rough Barnacle

*Balanus balanus*

**Descr** a taller species. If this barnacle is prised off the rock it leaves behind a thin chalky base (the common barnacle leaves a non-chalky base). The opening at the top of the shell plates is usually sharply toothed. **Size** up to 50 mm in height and up to 40 mm in diameter. **Habitat** more frequent in the lower shore region and in the subtidal area.

## CRABS AND LOBSTERS

## Common Rock Crab

*Cancer irroratus*

**Descr** the shell is roughly oval in out-line. Yellowish in background colour with purplish brown dots set so closely together as to give a brick red appear-ance. **Size** about 75 mm long and 125 mm wide. **Habitat** among rocks between tide marks and in the subtid-al zone. It is especially adapted to dig into the sand.

## European Green Crab

*Carcinus maenas*

**Descr** shell broader than long and with five teeth on each side. The males are irregularly mottled white to greenish in colour while the females are greeny reddish orange. **Size** up to 8 cm long. **Habitat** this is an aggressive invasive species that is expanding its territory as it outcompetes local crab species. It can tolerate much more brackish water than Rock Crab and is especially abundant in estuarine eel grass beds.

## Hermit Crab

*Pagurus* sp. (*bernhardus, pubescens, aca-dianus*)

**Descr** If you think you see a snail shell suddenly sprout legs and walk away, you are not 'seeing things' but prob-ably looking at a hermit crab. Unlike other crabs, the hermit crab has no hard shell encasing its soft body. To protect its soft body this species finds an empty snail shell of the right size to use as a 'mobile home.' This shell is large enough to protect the whole crab when it withdraws into it. When it wants to move, the front part of the body, including the head and legs, emerge from the shell, while the soft tail remains in the shell. As the crab grows and becomes too large for its current home, it casts off the old shell and searches for a new one to use as its home. **Habitat** in rock pools and on the lower shore.

### Toad Crab
*Hyas coarctatus*

**Descr** a small, reddish crab. The shell is roughly rectangular with tubercles (swellings) in rows on the side and also on the upper surface. **Size** up to 10 cm in length. **Habitat** usually found in the sub-tidal zone but occasionally seen in rock pools. Young animals stick bits of seaweed, hydrozoans, and debris to special spiky hairs on their bodies to serve as camouflage from predators, hence are sometimes called Decorator Crabs.

### American Lobster
*Homarus americanus*

**Descr** our familiar 'table' lobster. Usually greenish in colour above, but yellow to orange beneath, and bright blue on the limbs. The two large claws are unequal in size and shape, the right being more slender and used for grasping food, while the more massive left claw is used for crushing. The antennae are as long as the body. **Size** up to 60 cm in length. **Habitat** in deeper sub-tidal water.

## CHITONS, SNAILS, CLAMS, AND SQUIDS (PHYLUM MOLLUSCA)

A large group exhibiting a wide variety of body shapes. Common on land and in both fresh and salt water. A large number of the common seashore organisms belong to this group. The molluscs typically have one or more outer (external) shells, although in some forms (e.g., slugs and squids) the shell is small and inside the body (internal). The shell is produced by a special tissue called the 'mantle.' A mollusc usually has a muscular foot, typically used in movement, and highly developed sense organs (e.g., the eyes of a squid or octopus; antennae of a snail).

The main marine forms fall into one of the four distinct groups:

- CHITONS (many-plated external shell) e.g., chiton
- GASTROPODS (single twisted shell) e.g., snail, slug
- BIVALVES (two shells, usually hinged together) e.g., clam, mussel
- SQUIDS (small internal shell; very mobile, possessing large eyes and tentacles bearing suckers) e.g., squid, octopus

Only the first three of these groups are represented on the seashore, although an occasional squid may be washed up on the shore or become stranded in a tide pool. The internal shells of squid (called cuttlefish bones) are frequently found cast up among the flotsam and jetsam in the driftline on the seashore.

## CHITONS

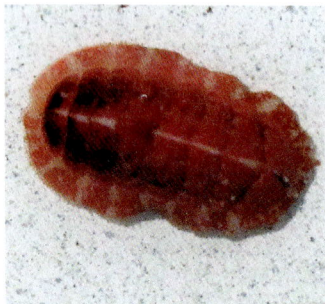

### Red Chiton
*Tonicella rubra*

**Descr** body covered by eight shell plates. Oval in shape. Reddish in colour with white and brown markings. They are practically invisible on coralline algae, that benefit from the chitons' diet of algae that would otherwise overgrow them—a perfect mutualistic relationship for both partners. **Size** up to 25 mm in length. **Habitat** live on rocks and coralline algae in the subtidal zone.

### Mottled Chiton
*Tonicella marmorea*

**Descr** similar to the Red Chiton but larger and lighter in colour. Body covered by eight shell plates. Oval to oblong in shape. Creamy brown or buff in colour mottled with dark red. **Size** up to 40 mm in length. **Habitat** usually attached to rocks in the subtidal region. Feeds by scraping off microscopic algae growing on the surfaces of rocks.

### White Chiton
*Ischnochiton albus*

**Descr** similar to the Red Chiton but the covering plates are white and the animal is smaller. **Size** only measuring up to 12 mm. **Habitat** found in the intertidal and subtidal zones. White chitons are nocturnal, hiding on rocks in daylight and venturing out to eat encrusting seaweeds in the night.

## GASTROPODS (SNAILS, SLUGS)

There are three different species of periwinkle (*Littorina*) snails commonly found on our seashores, namely, the common, rough, and smooth. They differ in size and location on the shore, but since both their sizes and distributions overlap, it is sometimes difficult to distinguish between them. The rough is the smallest of the three and is found on rocks as high as the high tide mark; the common is the largest and is found in the middle and lower shore regions; the smooth is often yellow or orange coloured and found in the middle shore area. If in doubt, the only definite way of distinguishing between these three different species is to closely examine the shell opening, as well as using the shell shape and colour. Another shell characteristic that can be useful in distinguishing between the species is the number of whorls, that is the number of turns in the shell. The differences between the three species are summarized below.

| | ROUGH | COMMON | SMOOTH |
|---|---|---|---|
| Shape | Tall pointed | Flat | Rounded |
| Habitat | Upper shore | Mid / lower shore | Middle shore |
| Size | 12 mm or less | Up to 30 mm | Up to 20 mm |
| Whorls | 4–5 | 7–8 | 3–4 |
| Colour | Dark grey, brown, black, sometimes yellow | Olive, dull brownish yellow, with spiral stripes | Yellow, shiny orange, red |

## Rough Periwinkle

*Littorina saxatilis*

**Descr** has a tall, pointed shell that is dark grey to black in colour, and sometimes banded with yellow, brown, or black. The shell has four to five whorls, and is rough in appearance. **Size** up to 12 mm. **Habitat** one of the few animal inhabitants of the splash zone and upper shore region. **Note** this species can withstand prolonged periods of exposure to the air, often for a week or more. It has adapted to life in an often dry environment by giving birth to live young, unlike its relatives lower on the shore, which lay their eggs into the water.

## Common Periwinkle (Shore Periwinkle, Edible Periwinkle)

*Littorina littorea*

**Descr** one of the most common seashore animals. The shell is flatter than that of the rough periwinkle, and has seven to eight whorls. The shell colour is variable, usually olive to brownish yellow or grey, and often banded with brown, dark red, or even black. **Size** up to 30 mm. **Habitat** common on rocks and seaweed from below high tide mark down, feeding on rock algae. **Note** this is an edible species.

## Smooth Periwinkle

*Littorina obtusata*

**Descr** has a small, rounded shell, lacking the pointed tip of the other periwinkles. The shell surface is smooth and shiny, and has three to four whorls. The shell colour is variable, usually yellow, brown, orange, or red, but even green or black, and sometimes banded. Colour matches the rockweeds with which they are always associated due to selective predation by seabirds, which eat all the highly visible individuals. **Size** up to 20 mm. **Habitat** abundant in the midshore region, and in tide pools. Feeds on rock algae.

## OTHER SNAILS

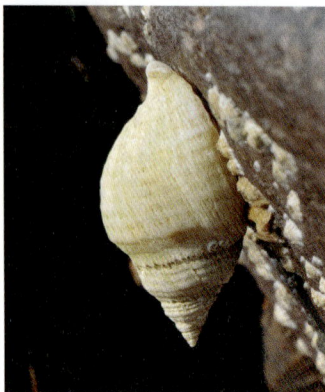

### Dogwhelk (Dogwinkle, Rock Purple, Common Drill)

*Nucella lapillus*

**Descr** typical snail shell but variable in shape and colour. Shell opening is oval, with the lip of the opening showing a conspicuous groove that distinguishes it from the periwinkles. Colour often dull greyish white, but other colours such as bright orange, yellow, dark brown, purple, and banded varieties are also common. The shell colour is, at least in part, due to changes in diet. White shelled forms are barnacle eaters, while brown and purple forms are mussel eaters. **Size** up to 50 mm. **Habitat** commonly found throughout the intertidal area, and often in large groups. Unlike the herbivorous periwinkles, the dogwhelk is carnivorous drilling through the shells of other molluscs, especially mussels, and also barnacles (hence the alternative name of common drill). **Note** this whelk lays individual straw coloured egg capsules the size of rice grains, which are often found attached to the rocks. It secretes a purple dye (hence the alternative name of rock purple), which was used by North American indigenous peoples. Population numbers vary greatly over time; booming when mussels and barnacles are abundant and dying off when they wipe out their prey.

### Moon Snail

*Lunatia heros*

**Descr** has a snail-like shell with a conspicuous small opening in the shell just above the main shell opening. Colour is greyish to brown. **Size** up to 100 mm. **Habitat** on sandy shores. Often found moving over the sand surface leaving behind a grooved track.

### Little Chink Shell (Atlantic Chink Shell )

*Lacuna vincta*

**Descr** looks like a thin, elongated periwinkle. The shell is fragile, conical in shape, and with a half-moon–shaped shell opening. It can be distinguished from the periwinkles by the little 'chink' in the lip of the shell opening. Shell has up to five whorls. Colour varies with brown banding on a whitish background, or purple banding on a whitish background. **Size** up to 10 mm. **Habitat** usually low intertidal and subtidal. **Note** these beautiful snails feed on kelps, quickly multiplying to vast concentrations, which can devastate kelp beds. Their egg masses resemble tiny gelatinous donuts 3–4 mm in diameter attached to the surface of seaweeds.

3 mm

## Smooth Top Shell

*Margarites helicinus*

**Descr** a small but beautiful shell that is thin and often iridescent with a stripy, pinkish brown, yellow, or yellow-green lustre. Shell opening is round, and has four to five whorls. **Size** up to 12 mm. **Habitat** usually subtidal. **Note** a major herbivore of kelps and other seaweeds, it reproduces rapidly with translucent brown egg masses attached to the surface of seaweeds and rocks.

## Tortoiseshell Limpet

*Testudinalia testudinalis*

**Descr** our only intertidal limpet. Has a cone-shaped shell that covers the whole animal. Becomes firmly clamped to rock when the tide is out. Usually marked with brown stripes or spots radiating outwards from the top of the shell, resembling a tortoiseshell pattern, hence the common name. **Size** can be up to 50 mm. **Habitat** An easily spotted animal usually found clamped tightly to the rock when the tide is out, or in tide pools. When underwater the limpet moves slowly over the rock scraping off algae for food. This animal is closely associated with the low intertidal coralline seaweed, *Clathromorphum*. When the tide retreats it moves back to its 'home' spot on the rock where the contour of the edge of the shell perfectly matches the rock contour. It is especially abundant in tide pools. In the clamped down position, it is almost impossible to prise this animal loose!

## SEA SLUGS

The sea slugs are marine molluscs that, like their dry land counterparts, have no shell. The common name of sea slug is an unfortunate one since they are among the most beautiful of marine animals with wonderful shapes and colours. The sea slugs are easily identified by the 'cerata,' which are outgrowths along their backs. These cerata are used for breathing, and are the equivalent to the gills of fish. The sea slugs are carnivorous, feeding on animals such as anemones, bryozoans, sponges, and tunicates.

## Bushy Backed Sea Slug

*Dendronotus frondosus*

**Descr** has a double row of branched, bushy cerata along its back, usually seven pairs in all. Body colour varies, but is usually brown or reddish, mottled with yellowish or whitish spots. **Size** our largest nudibranch, up to 75 mm long. **Habitat** usually found in tidepools among seaweeds, and especially with hydroids on which it feeds, and in the lower shore and subtidal regions.

## Common Grey Sea Slug (Maned Nudibranch)

*Aeolidia papillosa*

**Descr** the cerata of this sea slug are simple, elongated, tapering projections that tend to part in the middle and fall away to the sides, giving the animal the appearance of having a central parting, with hair combed to either side. May be up to 400 cerata per side. Body colour is grey or orange, spotted with white, green, or purple. This species also takes on the colour of the anemones, especially the brown anemone *Metridium* and hydroids on which it feeds. It can also extract the stinging cells (nematocysts) from its sea anemone prey and incorporate them in the cerata for its own defence. **Size** up to 40 mm long. **Habitat** in tidepools and shallow water among sea anemones.

## BIVALVES (MUSSELS, CLAMS)

Characterized by a pair of shells that completely cover the animal, and can be closed tight to protect them from predators or from drying out when exposed at low tide. Most attach themselves to rocks, although some, such as clams, can move. Bivalves feed by filtering plankton from the seawater.

## Blue Mussel

*Mytilus edulis*

**Descr** one of the most common intertidal animals, often found in large groups. Shell usually smooth and glossy, blue or black in colour, and pointed at one end. Anchored to the rock by byssal threads. **Size** can be up to 100 mm but often much smaller in crowded groups. **Habitat** found in the mid to low shore and subtidal zones, just below the barnacles. **Note** an edible species. It is now grown commercially at a number of sites around the island. Newfoundland beds usually contain *M. trossulus* as well, which is difficult to distinguish.

### Horse Mussel

*Modiolus modiolus*

**Descr** similar to blue mussel in shape, but shell usually longer, and rough. Colour usually mauvish white to dark blue. **Size** up to 150 mm long. **Habitat** in the subtidal region, but can extend into the lower shore area. Can burrow into gravel or sand, or become attached to rocks by threads. Typically very old, recruitment is seldom successful.

### Common Razor Clam

*Ensis directus*

**Descr** bivalve with two shells, each about six times longer than broad. Similar in shape to an old-fashioned cutthroat razor, hence the name. **Habitat** live animals burrow in the sand, but the white shells of dead animals are often found on the surface of the sand. Common on sandy beaches. These clams are expert diggers and outcompete all other clams where currents and surf reduce sediment stability.

### Baltic Macoma

*Limecola balthica*

**Descr** shells oval, chalky white. **Size** up to 40 mm long. **Habitat** in muddy estuarine areas. **Note** usually too small to eat although it is edible.

# SEA STARS, BRITTLE STARS, SEA URCHINS (PHYLUM ECHINODERMATA)

The members of this group only occur in seawater. Echinoderms, in common with Cnidarians (sea anemone group), possess 'radial symmetry,' that is a body plan arranged in a circular fashion with no distinct head end, tail end, or left and right sides. Most other animals show 'bilateral symmetry' where the body possesses a definite front end (head), back end (tail), upper (dorsal), and lower (ventral) sides, as well as left and right sides.

The outer covering of Echinoderms is usually made up of hard, chalky plates, often covered with spines. Echinoderms possess hollow, water filled projections called 'tube feet' with suction cups at the ends. Tube feet are used for attachment and movement.

Individual echinoderms produce both eggs and sperm (at different time periods), which are released into the water where fertilization takes place. The fertilized egg then develops into a free swimming larva that settles and develops into the adult form.

### Northern Sea Star (Purple Star, Boreal Sea Star)

*Asterias rubens*

**Descr** five radiating arms. Colour varies from purple or red to orange, yellow, brown, or greenish. The tube feet are in four parallel rows on the underside of each of the arms. Outer 'skin' is rough with many small spines. **Size** up to 80 cm across. **Habitat** in tidepools and in the subtidal region. **Note** sea stars crawl slowly over the rocks and seaweed using their tube feet, which can clamp tightly to surfaces. If you carefully pull a sea star off the rock to which it is attached and turn it upside down, you will see the tube feet waving back and forth. These animals feed mostly on mussels and other bivalve molluscs. They clamp their arms onto the two shells of a bivalve, and eventually, over several hours, when the clam tires and opens its shell, they are able to push in their mouth and stomach to digest the soft insides.

Because of their penchant for bivalves, sea stars can be a real menace in clam, mussel, and oyster beds. Fishermen dredging up molluscs, on finding a sea star would cut it up into pieces and throw the pieces back overboard. Unfortunately for these fishermen, parts of a sea star can regenerate their missing parts, and so rather than reducing the number of sea stars they were aiding their increase, the reverse of their intentions! Thus, if you find a sea star with four larger arms and one smaller arm, it is highly probable that this particular animal had lost an arm and is now regenerating a new one.

## Purple Sunstar

*Solaster endeca*

**Descr** a distinctive sea star with a large diameter disk and seven or more arms. Reddish to purplish in colour. **Size** can be 60 cm or more in diameter. **Habitat** lower intertidal and subtidal.

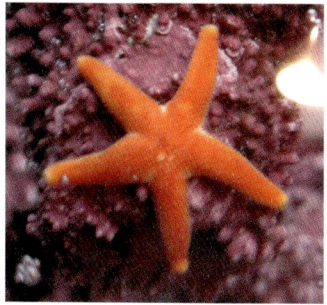

## Blood Star

*Henricia sanguinolenta*

**Descr** a small brightly coloured, usually reddish, sea star, with five slender arms. **Size** up to 10 cm or more in diameter. **Habitat** in rock pools and subtidally.

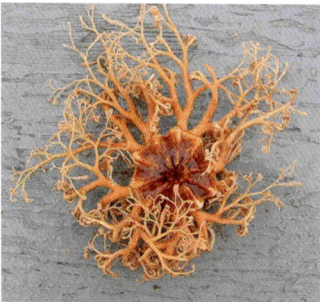

## Northern Basket Star

*Gorgonocephalus arcticus*

**Descr** a very distinctive type of brittle star with five long arms that are repeatedly branched. Yellowish to brownish in colour. **Size** can be over 60 cm in diameter. **Habitat** subtidal to deep water.

## Daisy Brittle Star

*Ophiopholis aculeata*

**Descr** the body has a central disk with five radiating, long, thin, flexible arms. Disk bears small spines. Colour varies from brownish red to blue, green, or brown. Disk usually mottled and arms banded. **Size** disk up to 20 mm across, and arms up to 75 mm long. **Habitat** often found hidden under rocks in tide pools in the lower shore region. **Note** when attacked by a predator like a codfish it can cast off its arms and regenerate new ones.

## Sand Dollar

*Echinarachnius parma*

**Descr** a flat sea urchin with five petal-shaped holes in the test. Usually purple coloured when alive and burrowing in the lowshore and subtidal sand. **Size** up to 75 mm. **Habitat** in the lowshore and subtidal sand, but the bleached white tests of dead animals are commonly found on the sand surface. **Note** they feed on algae and small organisms in the sand and are prey to flounders, plaice, eel pouts, and wolffish.

*(top) Sand Dollar, empty test; (bottom) Green Sea Urchin: (left) living animal with spines; (right) empty test*

## Green Sea Urchin

*Strongylocentrotus droebachiensis*

**Descr** hard spherical chalky shell (called a test) encases the body. This test is covered by bright green spines up to 10 mm long, and long extendible tube feet. Colour usually greenish brown. **Size** up to 90 mm in diameter. **Habitat** often numerous, attached to rocks in the water just below low water mark, and in tide pools. Sea urchins feed on the larger seaweeds, often stripping whole areas of the shore clean of seaweeds. **Note** they are eaten by cod, wolffish, and other fish, sea stars, and seabirds. Old empty tests are commonly found on the shore. Sea urchins are very intolerant of freshwater and thousands are killed whenever torrential rainstorms reduce shallow water salinity. Sea urchin eggs are considered a delicacy by many people and support a commercial fishery in Newfoundland.

# MARINE VERTEBRATES (PHYLUM CHORDATA)

Phylum Chordata, the most evolutionarily advanced of the animal groups, includes the vertebrates, back-boned animals, such as fish, amphibians, reptiles, birds, and mammals. Fish, of course, are the most common marine vertebrates around our coasts, and these are dealt with below. There are no local marine amphibians or reptiles, although occasionally a leatherback turtle, from more southerly waters, turns up around our coasts in the summer months. Many birds make their homes on the rocky cliffs around our coasts, but most feed in the open sea, and so are not often found on the seashore itself; seabirds are described above in the Animals section of this field guide. Marine mammals are very frequent around our coasts but only rarely come ashore; they are described below in Marine Mammals.

This phylum also includes, in addition to the familiar vertebrates, a number of simpler organisms, which at first glance bear little resemblance to vertebrates, but which possess features in common. These features include the notochord, a forerunner of the vertebrate backbone; the dorsal nerve cord, similar to the vertebrate spinal cord; and paired gill slits, as in fishes. One of these primitive groups, represented on our seashores, the Urochordates, or tunicates, show these characteristics, but only in the free-swimming larval form.

## TUNICATES (SEA SQUIRTS)

### Sea Peach
*Halocynthia pyriformis*

**Descr** a sea squirt has a body that is basically bag-like with two openings, called siphons, to the outside. Water is drawn into the body through one of these siphons, and food particles are filtered out on the gill slits. The water is then expelled through the second siphon. The sea peach is an orangey-yellow tunicate resembling a peach, hence the common name. It has two prominent siphons. **Size** up to 12 cm tall. **Habitat** found attached to rocky or gravelly bottoms below low water mark at sites with currents in surf.

# FISHES

All fish species share several characteristics. They are vertebrates; that is, they all possess a backbone composed of either cartilage or bone. Fish are cold-blooded—their body temperature being the same as the environment. Fish have a body covered by scales, though scales are minor or absent in some fishes. The body of a fish is covered by a protective mucus layer. Many fish species have a lateral line with sensory cells on the skin. Fish possess gills for respiration. Fish use fins and a tail to swim through their aquatic environment, but some fish lack certain fins. Whales, dolphins, porpoises, and seals are not fish, but rather warm-blooded marine mammals. Mammals give live birth and nurse their young. While some fish species give live birth, unlike mammals, no fish nurse their young.

Fish species fall within one of two major taxonomic categories: those with jaws and those without jaws. The fishes commonly observed in the estuarine and shallow coastal waters of Newfoundland and Labrador all possess jaws. Jawed fishes can be further divided into two classes: species with a cartilaginous skeleton (skates and sharks) and species with a bone skeleton (perch-shaped fishes and flatfishes).

## MARINE VERTEBRATES—FISHES GLOSSARY

**anadromus:** category of fishes that are born in freshwater, migrate to the ocean to feed and grow, and then return to freshwater to spawn (e.g., Atlantic salmon).

**brackish water:** seawater diluted with freshwater.

**catadromous:** category of fishes that are born in the ocean, migrate to freshwater to feed and grow, and then return to the ocean to spawn (e.g., American eel).

**demersal:** a sea-bottom dwelling way of life.

**estuary:** a coastal embayment where seawater is significantly diluted with freshwater draining from the land.

**flatfish:** pancake-shaped demersal fishes (e.g., flounders).

**groundfish:** commercially important fishes that live and feed near the bottom of the ocean.

**intertidal zone:** the shoreline between mean low tide and mean high tide.

**pelagic:** a water-column dwelling way of life.

**subtidal zone:** the sea bottom below the mean low tide line.

# CARTILAGINOUS FISHES

## SKATES

Skates are pancake-shaped fishes with a cartilaginous skeleton. The flattened body is an adaptation to a bottom-dwelling or 'demersal' way of life. The mouth is located on the ventral surface (underside) of the body. Skates have breathing holes or 'spiracles' on the topside of the head. A skate breathes by pulling water into the spiracles and across the gills located on the ventral surface. Large pectoral fins are attached to the sides of the head, giving the skate 'wings'. The skate swims with an undulating motion of the tips of the pectoral fins. A skate can bury itself by stirring up bottom sediment through flapping its fins.

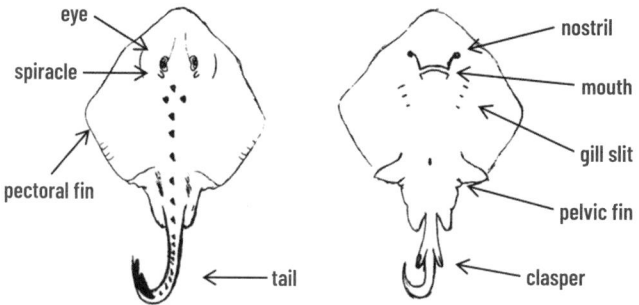

## SHARKS

Sharks are torpedo-shaped fishes with a cartilaginous skeleton. The body is formed for continuous swimming, an adaptation for a water-column dwelling or 'pelagic' way of life. Carnivorous sharks have a large head and mouth with sharp teeth. A few species of shark are planktivorous and feed on small, floating marine life.

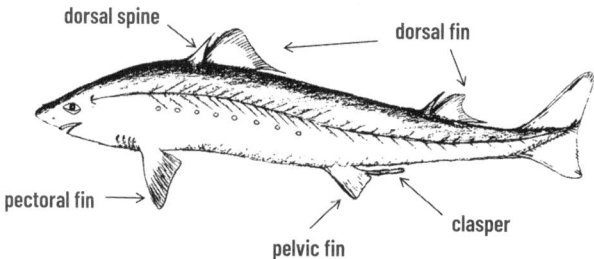

# BONY FISHES

## PERCH-SHAPED FISHES

Many estuarine and marine fishes have a skeleton of bone, fins with supportive soft rays, and a body shape similar to the freshwater yellow perch (*Perca flavescens*). The body is compressed side to side and tapered at the head and tail. Trout-like species (e.g., the Atlantic salmon [*Salmo salar*] and the brook trout [*Salvelinus fontinalis*]) have a fleshy dorsal fin, the adipose fin. The biological purpose of the adipose fin is unknown.

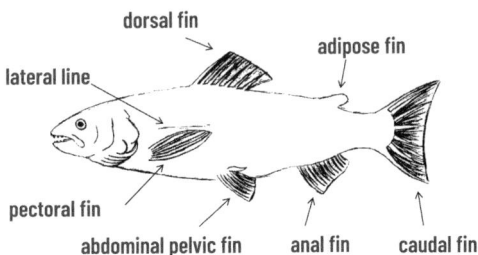

dorsal fin
adipose fin
lateral line
pectoral fin
abdominal pelvic fin      anal fin      caudal fin

## FLATFISHES

'Flatfish' is the generic name given to a fish species with a bone skeleton and rayed fins that lies on its side when resting on the sea bottom. Some flounder species lie on their right side while other flounder species lie on their left side. Both eyes are on the topside of the head, so the fish can see with both its eyes as it lies on the bottom. The underside of the body is pale while the topside is pigmented, so the flounder blends with the bottom habitat. The flatfish swims with its eyed side upward and the eyeless side downward toward the ocean floor.

As juvenile flounders grow, one eye migrates to the side of the body that becomes pigmented. Flounders are classified as left-eyed or right-eyed flatfish, depending on the side of the body that has both eyes.

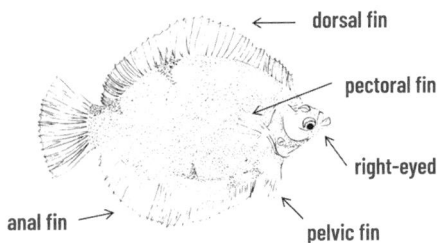

dorsal fin
pectoral fin
right-eyed
anal fin
pelvic fin

## HABITAT USE BY FISHES

The fishes found in estuarine and marine waters of Newfoundland and Labrador can be grouped according to their habitat use, specifically where they dwell, feed, and spawn. Common fishes can be grouped as:

- **ANADROMOUS FRESHWATER:** grow in sea /spawn in freshwater
- **CATADROMOUS MARINE:** grow in freshwater /spawn in the sea
- **ESTUARINE** and **MARINE:** live near the shoreline
- **MARINE:** live offshore in waters of the continental shelf

## ANADROMOUS FISHES

Anadromous species are fishes that are born in freshwater, migrate from freshwater to the sea to feed and grow, and then return to freshwater to spawn. Anadromous fishes commonly found in estuarine waters of Newfoundland and Labrador include the Atlantic salmon, sea-run brook trout, Arctic char, rainbow smelt, Atlantic tomcod, and alewife. The sea lamprey and Atlantic sturgeon are also anadromous fishes of Atlantic Canada, but are not commonly observed in the estuarine waters of Newfoundland.

## FAMILY SALMONIDAE

### Atlantic Salmon

*Salmo salar*

**Descr** body is elongate, spindle-shaped, tapering to tail. Adults stouter than juveniles; adipose fin behind single dorsal fin, just above the single anal fin; tail fin slightly forked; no spines. Colouration varies with lifecycle stage. One year olds, called 'post-yearling parr,' have dusky bars on the side called 'parr marks' and red dots between the parr marks (see photo). Three year olds, called 'smolts,' 15 cm in length, turn sil- very as they migrate to the sea. At sea, dorsal surface is black, sides are silvery, and belly is white; black flecks scattered along the sides. During spawning in freshwater, the salmon loses its silvery colour and becomes reddish brown. Breeding males have reddish-orange spots, and lower jaw may be hooked, forming a 'kype' (see photo next page). After spawning, surviving parents, known as 'kelts,' darken in colour. **Size** can grow to 1.5 m in length and weigh 38 kg. **Habitat** found in coastal waters, freshwater rivers, and some lakes.

*Atlantic Salmon: (above) with parr marks; (below) with kype*

## Brook Trout (Mud Trout)

*Salvelinus fontinalis*

**Descr** body is elongate, spindle-shaped, tapering to tail; adipose fin between dorsal fin and tail; tail fin slightly forked; single anal fin. Colouration varies with lifecycle stage. Adults back is dark brown or black; sides green to brown with pale spots, red spots surrounded by bluish halos (see photo); belly is white; pectoral, pelvic, and anal fins are white along the leading edge. Sea-run brook trout become silvery, but white leading edges on fins and red spots on sides remain. The silvery colouration of a sea-run brook trout is lost when it returns to freshwater. Brook trout in breeding condition have bright orange and red pigmentation, especially the belly of the male. Juvenile parr marks similar to juvenile salmon, but with blue circle around red dots on upper sides. **Size** up to 45 cm in length, weighing 6 kilograms. **Habitat** found in streams, ponds, and lakes.

*Brook Trout: (above) adult with red spots surrounded by bluish halos; (below) juvenile with parr marks*

## Arctic Char

*Salvelinus alpinus*

**Descr** body shape elongate, spindle-shaped, tapering to tail; lower jaw protrudes slightly; dorsal adipose fin is present; pectoral, pelvic, and anal fins are white along the leading edge; tail fin slightly forked. Sea-run char are bright silvery. In spawning condition highly coloured; males have silvery-blue sides; large reddish spots; lower sides and belly orange-red. Prized catch for recreational anglers. **Size** trophy-sized char can be 90 cm long and weigh 12 kg. **Habitat** circumpolar distribution in the Northern Hemisphere. Landlocked populations in cold highland ponds of the Long Range Mountains of insular Newfoundland, but the most southern anadromous Arctic Char inhabit the tip of the Great Northern Peninsula.

## FAMILY OSMERIDAE

## Rainbow Smelt

*Osmerus mordax*

**Descr** body is slender; lower jaw projects slightly beyond upper jaw; teeth on the tip of the tongue; small adipose fin behind dorsal fin and above anal fin; tail fin is forked; scales are relatively large; dark olive-green on back with silvery sides that reflect pink, blue, and purple iridescence, hence the common name; silvery belly has tiny, dusky dots. **Size** can grow to 33 cm in length. **Habitat** found along both the east coast and west coast of North America and in many inland freshwater systems.

## FAMILY GADIDAE

## Atlantic Tomcod

*Microgadus tomcod*

**Descr:** moderately elongate, tapering to tail; eye relatively small; snout rounded and a slender 'whisker' or barbell on underside of lower jaw; three dorsal fins and two anal fins; caudal fin is rounded; pelvic fins each have a long filament. The colouration is olive-green with yellowish tinges, paling on sides to a greyish or yellow-white belly; sides and fins are mottled with dark blotches; lateral line is pale. **Size** maximum length of about 40 cm. **Habitat** Found only in nearshore waters. Most abundant in estuaries around Newfoundland and Nova Scotia and in the St. Lawrence River. Inhabit shallow waters, especially the mouths of rivers and streams, eel grass beds, and salt marshes.

## FAMILY CLUPEIDAE

### Alewife (Gaspereau)

*Alosa pseudoharengus*

**Descr:** deep bodied; head relatively small; belly has a keel of saw-toothed 'scutes,' which are different from scales; single dorsal fin and single anal fin; tail fin is forked. Colouration is dark greyish green on the back, silvery on sides and belly. **Size** can grow to 40 cm in length. **Habitat** Found only in coastal waters and tributary freshwaters of the North-west Atlantic Ocean. Ranges from west coast of Newfoundland south to the coast of North Carolina, including the Gulf of St. Lawrence, the Bay of Fundy and Gulf of Maine. There are freshwater and marine populations of alewife.

### CATADROMOUS FISHES

Catadromous species are marine fishes that are born in the ocean, migrate to freshwater to feed and grow, and then return to the ocean to spawn. The American eel and the ninespine stickleback are the only catadromous species found in estuarine waters of Atlantic Canada.

## FAMILY ANGUILLIDAE

### American Eel

*Anguilla rostrata*

**Descr** body shape is serpentine; head is pointed; jaws have needle-like teeth; single dorsal fin is continuous with the rounded tail fin and anal fin; pelvic fins are absent; skin secretes notable amounts of mucus as a protective coating. Colouration varies with lifecycle stage. Immature eels, called 'yellow eels,' are black or olive-brown on the back and yellowish white on the belly. Mature eels, called 'silver eels,' beginning their catadromous migration to the sea turn silvery on the sides and belly. **Size** female eels can grow up to 1.5 m in length. Males have a smaller maximum size. **Habitat** inhabits the estuaries and freshwater tributaries of the east coast of North America, the Gulf of Mexico, and the Caribbean.

## FAMILY GASTEROSTEIDAE

### Ninespine Stickleback
*Pungitius pungitius*

**Descr** the most slender of the stickleback species found in Newfoundland. Head is relatively large and mouth is small; dorsal fin preceded by nine short spines, hence its common name; anal fin has one spine; tail fin is rounded or slightly forked; slender caudal peduncle has a keel formed by bony plates. Colouration is olive-brown or grey on the back, upper sides of body have faint barred marks; belly is silvery. **Size** maximum of about 7 cm. **Habitat** circumpolar distribution in the Northern Hemisphere. Inhabits both freshwater and saltwater environments. Freshwater populations may be catadromous, moving downstream into coastal salt marshes to spawn.

## ESTUARINE AND MARINE FISHES / SHORELINE

There are several estuarine and marine species that live near the shoreline. These fish are adapted to life in shallow waters affected by the tides. Two fishes commonly found in the rocky intertidal zone are the rock gunnel and the Atlantic snailfish. Fishes commonly observed in brackish lagoons and eel grass beds of river deltas are the threespine stickleback, fourspine stickleback, blackspotted stickleback, and northern pipefish. Schools of cunner are often seen at rock outcroppings near the shoreline. A small sculpin called the grubby can often be found in the shallows of estuaries and bays.

## FAMILY PHOLIDAE

### Rock Gunnel (Butterfish)
*Pholis gunnellus*

**Descr** body shape is elongate; head relatively small with a blunt snout; one dorsal fin extends from the head to tail; single anal fin also joins the tail; tail fin is rounded. Although dorsal and anal fins have tiny spines, the skin feels very smooth to the touch, hence the nickname 'butterfish.' Colouration varies with background environment, but usually olive to reddish brown; belly is pale white to yellowish white; dark streak across the eye and a row of black spots along the dorsal fin. **Size** maximum length of about 30 cm. **Habitat** found on both sides of the North Atlantic Ocean. Common species of the rocky intertidal zone where it remains under rocks and seaweeds at low tide.

## FAMILY LIPARIDAE

### Atlantic Snailfish (Seasnail)

*Liparis atlanticus*

**Descr** body shape is moderately elongate; one dorsal fin with a notch; single anal fin; tail fin is truncate or square; pectoral fins are fanlike; pelvic fins are modified to form a suction disk (see photo). Colouration is dark olive, with darker sides of the body; belly is greyish white. **Size** maximum length of about 13 cm. **Habitat** found only in the Northwest Atlantic Ocean. Lives in the rocky intertidal zone and the shallow subtidal zone. Often found attached by its suction disk to the lower sides of rocks.

## FAMILY GASTEROSTEIDAE

### Threespine Stickleback

*Gasterosteus aculeatus*

**Descr** body shape is tapered at the head and tail; mouth is small; three spines precede dorsal fin; anal fin has one spine; pelvic fins each have a spine; a lateral keel formed by bony plates on the body just before the tail, which can be felt if held between thumb and forefinger; three dorsal spines and the keel near the tail distinguish the threespine stickleback from other stickleback species. Colouration is dark olive on the back; sides are silvery, sometimes with dark mottling; belly is silvery; during breeding season males have red colouration on the belly. **Size** maximum recorded size is 10 cm in length. **Habitat** found in both freshwater environments and marine environments of the temperate Northern Hemisphere.

### Fourspine Stickleback

*Apeltes quadracus*

**Descr** body is moderately elongate; four spines precede dorsal fin; anal fin has one spine; each pelvic fin has a spine; tail fin is truncate with rounded corners; caudal peduncle is slender and there is no keel, as present in the Threespine Stickleback and Ninespine Stickleback. Colouration is olive green to brownish on the back and upper sides; lower sides and belly are silvery. **Size** maximum length of about 6 cm. **Habitat** found only in the Northwest Atlantic. Can be found in marine, brackish water, and freshwater.

## Blackspotted Stickleback

*Gasterosteus wheatlandi*

**Descr** body shape is stouter than the Threespine Stickleback; three spines precede dorsal fin; tail fin is truncate or square; no keel on the caudal peduncle, as present in the Threespine and Ninespine Stickleback. Colouration is yellowish green on the back; sides are silvery with black spots; belly is silvery. **Size** maximum length of about 7 cm. **Habitat** found only in the Northwest Atlantic. Can be found in estuarine waters, but does not enter the fully freshwater environments of rivers and streams.

## FAMILY LABRIDAE

## Cunner

*Tautogolabrus adspersus*

**Descr** head is pointed; mouth thick lipped and relatively small; dorsal, pelvic, and anal fins have spines; caudal fin is slightly rounded. Colouration can change with the environmental background, but the body is usually a dull olive-green with brown and reddish mottling; belly is bluish white. **Size** can grow to 43 cm in length and weigh 1 kg. **Habitat** found in the western North Atlantic. Present year round in the nearshore subtidal zone. Schools commonly seen around wharves. Commonly known as 'conner' in Newfoundland.

## FAMILY SYNGNATHIDAE

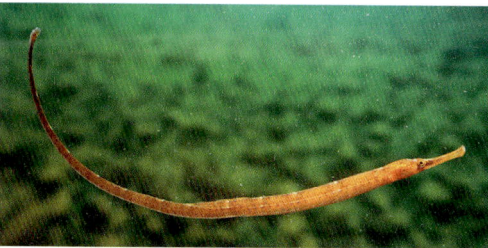

## Northern Pipefish

*Syngnathus fuscus*

**Descr** body is very elongate and armored by bony plates; mouth small and trumpet-shaped; one dorsal fin, but lacks pelvic fins; anal fin is tiny in females and absent in males; tail fin is rounded. Colouration may change to match its surroundings, but usually brownish with dark mottling; belly is golden yellow. **Size** maximum length of about 30 cm. **Habitat** found only in the western Atlantic. Lives in beds of seaweed and eel grass in coastal bays, salt marshes, and estuaries.

# FAMILY COTTIDAE

## Grubby

*Myoxocephalus aenaeus*

**Descr** body shape is moderately elongate, tapering from the head to a narrow tail; a ridge with two short spines runs along the top of the head over each eye; cheek spines are short; two dorsal fins and one anal fin; tail fin is rounded and the pectoral fins are fanlike. Colouration is greenish grey with dark broken bars on the sides; belly is pale grey. **Size** the smallest of the common sculpins, its maximum length is about 18 cm. **Habitat** found only in the Northwest Atlantic. Lives in coastal waters and on the continental shelf. Grubby can often be found in estuaries and in the shallow water of bays.

## MARINE FISHES / CONTINENTAL SHELF

Many species of marine fish live in subtidal waters of the continental shelf down to depths of about 200 m. Some of these marine fishes are demersal while others are pelagic. Some species migrate seasonally into shallow waters to feed (e.g., the Atlantic cod and the Atlantic mackerel). Other species migrate inshore to spawn (e.g., the Atlantic herring, the capelin, and the lumpfish). Several species have populations in the major deep bays of Newfound (e.g., Atlantic cod living in Bonavista Bay, Trinity Bay, and Placentia Bay).

### DEMERSAL SHELF FISHES

Common skates living on the sea bottom of the continental shelf are the winter skate and thorny skate. The Atlantic cod is considered a demersal fish, but it spends a considerable amount of time off the bottom, feeding in the water column. Other demersal fishes include the Greenland cod, white hake, Newfoundland eelpout, ocean pout, radiated shanny, Atlantic wolffish, spotted wolffish, sea raven, longhorn sculpin, shorthorn sculpin, and lumpfish. Common flatfish include the winter flounder, windowpane flounder, and yellowtail flounder.

# FAMILY RAJIDAE

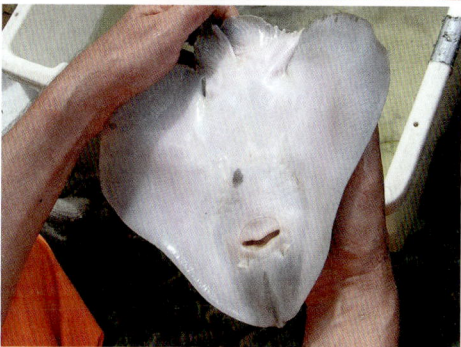

*Winter Skate:*
*(top) upper surface;*
*(bottom) lower surface*

## Winter Skate

### Leucoraja ocellata

**Descr** body is pancake-shaped; tail is long and slender. Colouration of the upper surface is light brown with many small dark spots; snout is blunt and has a translucent appearance; lower surface is white with irregular pale splotches; dorsal surface of winter skate has three or more rows of thorns forming an arrow pattern. **Size** can grow to a maximum length of 110 cm. **Habitat** found only in the Northwest Atlantic. Inhabits the subtidal zone to depths of approximately 100 m.

## Thorny Skate

### Amblyraja radiata

**Descr** Body is pancake-shaped; snout is blunt; row of large thorns along the centre of the back; large thorns scattered on the dorsal surface of the pectoral fins. Colouration is brownish grey on the dorsal surface with dark blotches; under surface is white or sooty white. **Size** may grow to 110 cm in length. **Habitat** found in the western and eastern North Atlantic. Inhabits both hard and soft sea bottoms of the subtidal zone down to the edge of the continental shelf at 200 m depth.

# FAMILY GADIDAE

## Atlantic Cod

*Gadus morhua*

**Descr** body is stout; head and mouth are relatively large; three dorsal fins and two anal fins; tail fin is almost square; barbell near the tip of the lower jaw. Colouration is dark olive-green on the back; lighter olive-green or light-brown on the sides; back and sides are speckled with numerous rounded, reddish-brown spots; lateral line is white; belly is a greyish-white or white. Atlantic cod living year round in bays may have more reddish-brown or golden-brown pigmentation on the sides and belly. **Size** can grow to 180 cm in length and weigh 95 kg. **Habitat** lives in coastal and continental shelf waters on both sides of the North Atlantic Ocean.

## Greenland Cod (Rock Cod)

*Gadus ogac*

**Descr** heavy bodied, tapering to tail; large head and large mouth; three dorsal fins; two anal fins; square tail fin; barbell on the lower jaw. Colouration is yellowish brown to bronze marbling on its sides; lateral line is not distinctly coloured. **Size** maximum recorded length is 70 cm. **Habitat** found in both the northeast and northwest Atlantic Ocean. A marine species adapted to the reduced salinities of nearshore waters, it is commonly found in rocky shallow water of fjords and bays, hence the nickname 'Rock Cod.' Does not grow as large as the Atlantic Cod.

# FAMILY PHYCIDAE

## White Hake

*Urophycis tenuis*

**Descr** soft-bodied, slender fish with a rounded tail; chin has a slender barbell; two dorsal fins; one anal fin; jugular pelvic fins with long, thread-like rays used for tactile sensing of prey on the ocean bottom. Colouration of the back and sides is usually reddish or purple brown; belly is pale grey, yellowish, or white. **Size** may grow up to 135 cm in length and weigh 22 kg. **Habitat** found only in the western Atlantic Ocean.

# FAMILY ZOARCIDAE

## Newfoundland Eelpout
*Lycodes lavalaei*

**Descr** body shape is elongate; head and mouth are large; upper jaw projects over the lower jaw; long dorsal and anal fins are continuous with the tail fin. Colouration is brownish grey with black blotches and irregular vertical bands. **Size** the specimen in the photo, captured in Bonne Bay of western Newfoundland, exceeds the maximum length of 56 cm reported for the species in the scientific literature. **Habitat** inhabits the subtidal zone to depths greater than 500 m.

## Ocean Pout
*Zoarces americanus*

**Descr** body shape is elongate; head is broad and the snout is blunt; eyes are small and located high on the head; large mouth has fleshy lips; tail is pointed; dorsal fin is continuous with the caudal fin and anal fin. Colouration is muddy yellow to reddish brown; belly is white or dull yellow; pectoral fins are reddish orange. **Size** can grow up to a length of 110 cm and weigh 5.4 kg. **Habitat** found in coastal waters in the Northwest Atlantic. Inhabits the subtidal zone down to depths of 150 m.

# FAMILY STICHAEIDAE

## Radiated Shanny (Prickleback)
*Ulvaria subbifurcata*

**Descr** body shape is elongate; a single long dorsal fin with many small spines, hence the nickname 'Prickleback.' Single anal fin has two small spines; tail fin is rounded. Colouration is brown with a yellowish belly; a dark blotch on the dorsal fin and a black bar that runs downward and backward from the eye. **Size** does not grow to more than 18 cm in length. **Habitat** occurs only in the Northwest Atlantic from the Strait of Belle Isle south to the coast of Massachusetts. Lives amongst seaweeds and rocks on hard bottom substrate in subtidal waters.

# FAMILY ANARHICHADIDAE

## Atlantic Wolffish (Striped Wolffish)
*Anarhichas lupus*

**Descr** body shape is elongate; head is blunt; mouth has jaws with canine teeth in the front and moliform teeth in the back; dorsal fin is long and has spines; tail fin is relatively small and rounded; pectoral fins are large and fan-like; pelvic fins are absent. Colouration is dark olive green to purplish brown; dark vertical bars give rise to its nickname 'Striped Wolffish;' underside of the head and belly is dirty white. **Size** can grow to a length of 150 cm and weigh 18 kg. **Habitat** found on both sides of the Atlantic Ocean.

## Spotted Wolffish
*Anarhichas minor*

**Descr** body shape is similar to that of the Atlantic wolffish, but the colouration is different. The spotted wolffish is dull olive green or brown; blackish brown spots on its dorsal fin, anal fin, tail fin, and upper sides; underside of the head and belly is white. **Size** can measure up to 180 cm in length. **Habitat** lives deeper than the Atlantic wolffish, inhabiting waters down to 800 m.

# FAMILY HEMITRIPTERIDAE

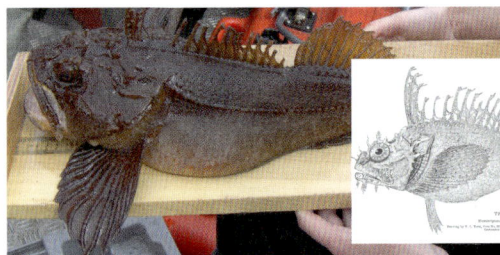

## Sea Raven
*Hemitripterus americanus*

**Descr** moderately elongate, tapering from head to tail; a large head and large mouth; fleshy tabs hanging from the lower jaw; numerous bony knobs around the eyes; prickly skin and short spines on the gill covers; two dorsal fins; first dorsal fin has a ragged outline and the second has a rounded outline; pectoral fins are fanlike; tail fin is rounded. Colouration is reddish brown, marbled with dark brown; belly is yellowish brown. **Size** can grow to 65 cm in length and weigh 3.2 kg. **Habitat** found only in the Northwest Atlantic Ocean. Lives on rocky or hard sand bottoms in coastal and continental shelf waters.

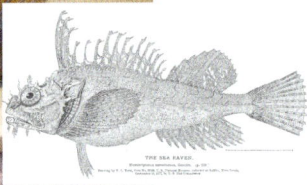

# FAMILY COTTIDAE

## Longhorn Sculpin

*Myoxocephalus octodecemspinosus*

**Descr** body shape is elongate, tapering from the head to a slender tail; head is flattened and has numerous spines and bony protuberances; two long spines near the top of the head give this fish its common name; two dorsal fins and one anal fin; tail fin is rounded. The sculpin uses its fanlike pectoral fins to 'walk' over the sea bottom. Colouration can change to match the environmental background; back is dark olive; sides are pale yellow; body marked with irregular dark crossbars; pectoral fins have dark cross-bands; belly is white. **Size** can grow to 46 cm in length. **Habitat** found only in the western North Atlantic. A common species in coastal waters, especially bays.

## Shorthorn Sculpin

*Myoxocephalus scorpius*

**Descr** body shape is similar to the Longhorn Sculpin. However, the length of the uppermost head spines are much shorter. A longitudinal ridge with three knobs runs along each side of its crown, one knob before the eyes and one knob behind the eyes; blunt spines on its cheeks. Colouration is dark greenish brown on the back and upper sides with dark bars and mottling; belly is yellowish. Males have large, pale spots on the lower sides and belly. **Size** may grow to a maximum length of 90 cm. **Habitat** found on both sides of the North Atlantic Ocean. A common species in coastal waters, especially bays.

# FAMILY CYCLOPTERIDAE

## Lumpfish

*Cyclopterus lumpus*

**Descr** body shape is nearly spherical; skin is leathery and without scales; dorsal fin is encased by a hump; three rows of wart-like tubercles along the sides; pelvic fins form a sucker disc, enabling lumpfish to grip bottom rocks or floating kelp. Colouration can vary from bluish-grey to greenish-brown; belly is usually grey-white, but turns red in breeding males. **Size** females can grow to a length of 60 cm and weigh 9.5 kg. Males are smaller than females of the same age. **Habitat** found along both the western and eastern sides of the North Atlantic Ocean. Lives on the continental shelf down to depths of 300 m.

# FAMILY PLEURONECTIDAE

## Winter Flounder

*Pseudopleuronectes americanus*

**Descr** body shape is laterally compressed and oblong; mouth is small; lower jaw protrudes slightly. During the demersal stage of its life cycle, this flounder lies on its left side. Both eyes are on the right side of the body, the uppermost side when the fish is lying on the sea bottom. The left eye migrates to the right side when the young flounder is still planktonic. Colouration is muddy brown with black mottling on the upper side; underside (blind side) is white with slightly translucent edges tinged with yellow pigment. **Size** can grow up to 65 cm in length and weigh 3.6 kg. **Habitat** found only in the western North Atlantic. Lives on mud bottoms of the subtidal zone down to a depth of about 150 m.

## Yellowtail Flounder

*Limanda ferruginea*

**Descr** laterally compressed, oval-shaped body; mouth is small; tail is rounded. The left eye migrates to the right side when the young flounder is still planktonic. Both eyes look upward when the fish lies on its left side on the sea bottom. Colouration is brownish olive-green on the top (eyed) side and white with a yellow colouring on the underside near the tail; numerous rusty spots on the skin. **Size** can grow to a maximum length of 64 cm. **Habitat** Found on the continental shelf in the Northwest Atlantic from southern Labrador to Chesapeake Bay, Maryland.

# FAMILY SCOPHTHALMIDAE

## Windowpane Flounder

*Scophthalmus aquosus*

**Descr** body shape is laterally compressed and oval. Juveniles are so thin the body is translucent, akin to a 'windowpane.' During the demersal stage, the fish lies on its right side. Both eyes are on the left side; lower jaw protrudes slightly; caudal fin is rounded; dorsal fin, pelvic fin, and anal fin form an almost continuous margin. Colouration of the adult is brownish with dark mottling and white spots on the upper, eyed side; ventral, blind side is white with dark splotches. **Size** can grow to a maximum length of 45 cm. **Habitat** found only in the western North Atlantic. Lives on a sandy sea bottom. Found in the subtidal zone down to a depth of about 50 m.

## PELAGIC SHELF FISHES

Fishes of the continental shelf that live up in the water column are known as 'pelagic' species, to distinguish them from 'demersal' species, which feed and dwell near the sea bottom. Common pelagic fishes of the continental shelf include the Acadian redfish, capelin, American sand lance, Atlantic herring, and Atlantic mackerel.

## FAMILY SCORPAENIDAE

### Acadian Redfish (Beaked Redfish)

*Sebastes fasciatus*

**Descr** deep bodied; head is large; first dorsal fin has spines; gill cover has bony spines; a bony protrusion on the lower jaw gives rise to the nickname, 'beaked redfish'; eyes are large. Coloration is orange to red, sometimes with a brownish-cast. **Size** females grow to about 70 cm in length; males grow to a lesser maximum size of 55 cm. **Habitat** found only in the Northwest Atlantic. Inhabits deepwater channels and slopes of the continental shelf and major deep bays of Newfoundland. Similar in appearance to two other species of redfish: the Golden Redfish (*Sebastes marinus*) and the Deepwater Redfish (*Sebastes mentella*).

## FAMILY AMMODYTIDAE

### American Sand Lance

*Ammodytes americanus*

**Descr** elongate body; snout pointed. Colouration is iridescent blue-green or bronze on the back, gradating to a white belly. **Size** can grow to a length of 25 cm. **Habitat** lives in the Northwest Atlantic, ranging from west Greenland and Labrador south to the coast of Delaware. Large schools often appear in shallow coastal waters.

# FAMILY OSMERIDAE

## Capelin
*Mallotus villosus*

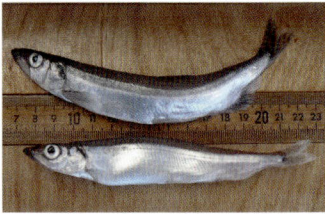

**Descr** body is long and slender; two fins on the back: dorsal fin in the middle and smaller adipose fin just in front of the tail. Colouration of the back is olive-green; sides are silver; belly is silvery-white; skin over the gills is dark. **Size** can grow to a maximum length of 25 cm. **Habitat** circumpolar distribution in the Northern Hemisphere. In summer, schools of capelin migrate inshore to spawn on cobble beaches of Newfoundland and Labrador. Some spawn in the subtidal zone.

# FAMILY CLUPEIDAE

## Atlantic Herring
*Clupea harengus*

**Descr** body shape is deeper than thick; scales are large and loosely attached to the body, so they slough off easily when handled; relatively large mouth; lower jaw projects slightly beyond the upper jaw; tail is deeply forked; single dorsal fin is located midway along the body; saw-tooth keel along its belly. Colouration of the back is steel-blue with green reflections; sides and belly are silvery. **Size** can grow to a maximum length of 45 cm. **Habitat** found in coastal waters shallower than 200 m on both sides of the Atlantic Ocean. Schools commonly observed in the Gulf of St. Lawrence and in coastal waters of the east and south coasts of Newfoundland.

# FAMILY SCOMBRIDAE

## Atlantic Mackerel
*Scomber scombrus*

**Descr** body is streamlined, tapering at snout and tail; distinctive finlets near the tail; scales are small. Colouration of the back is a steel-blue with dark, wavy bands extending down to the midline of the sides; lower sides are silvery with iridescence; belly is whitish. **Size** can grow to a maximum length of 56 cm and weigh 3.4 kg. **Habitat** Inhabits coastal waters in the western and eastern Atlantic Ocean. Schools commonly observed in nearshore waters during the summer.

# MARINE MAMMALS

## ORDER: PINNIPEDIA (SEALS)

Seals (pinnipeds) are classified as either phocids, which do not have external ears (pinnae) and have the front and hind flippers in the same plane as the body, or as oratiids, which have external pinnae and flippers turned under the body, raising it off the ground. Six species, all phocids, occur seasonally in Newfoundland and Labrador waters. Those that give birth ('whelp'), moult, and mate on the spring pack ice are difficult for the casual observer to see.

### Harp Seal

*Pagophilus groenlandica*

**Descr** so-called because of the irregular horseshoe-shaped black band across the silver-grey back of the adult male. **Size** mature males and females are similar in size, at some 1.6 m and 130–150 kg. **Habitat** most common off the northeast coast where they whelp on pack ice during late February–March and produce a single pup with white fur ('whitecoat') averaging 80–85 cm and 10–11 kg at birth.

### Hooded Seal

*Cystophora cristata*

**Descr** characterized by an inflatable bladder on the head of the adult male that when deflated hangs down between the eyes and over the upper lip. The mature adult coat is silvery with dark irregular marks, while the head is without marks and darker than the rest of the body. **Size** mature males average 2.6 m and 300–410 kg whereas females average 2.03 m and 145–300 kg. **Habitat** most common off the northeast coast where they whelp on pack ice in mid March–early April. The single pup averages 1 m and 24 kg at birth, and has a slate blue-grey coat ('blueback') with a pale cream colour on the ventral body surface.

## Grey Seal

*Halichoerus grypus*

**Descr** females have a silver-grey to brown coat with dark patches, while the male coat is darker and often with scarring around the neck. **Size** mature males average 2.5–3.3 m and 170–350 kg and females 1.6–2.0 m and 100–225 kg. **Habitat** most common throughout Newfoundland in July–August as migrants from breeding colonies on Sable Island and in the Gulf of St. Lawrence. Whelping does not occur in Newfoundland as pups are born elsewhere in the northwest Atlantic in late January–early February on inshore rocks, islands, isolated beaches, and pack ice. Pups have a dense, soft silky white fur later replaced by a black-spotted silver coat. They reach 50 kg at weaning.

## Harbour Seal

*Phoca vitulina*

**Descr** the body and flippers are short and the small rounded head gives a dog-like appearance in water. The adult coat varies from brownish black to tan or grey with fine dark spots and a lighter belly. **Size** adult males and females are 1.2–1.6 m and 60–80 kg. **Habitat** most common on the south and west coasts, particularly on rocks, sand bars, and in estuaries. The single pup is born during May–June, weighs 8–12 kg, and has a white coat of a downy fur, which is shed in two weeks.

## Bearded Seal

*Erignathus barbatus*

**Descr** named for their abundant long white vibrissae (whiskers). The adult coat varies from light to dark grey or brown, with the back being darker than the underside. **Size** adult males and females are about 2.1–2.7 m and 200–310 kg. **Habitat** primarily an Arctic species, these solitary animals are occasionally found on the ice off the north coast and Labrador. The single pup is born in late April–May and averages 135 cm and 34 kg. It has a greyish-brown coat with light patches on the face, head, and back.

## Ringed Seal

*Pusa hispida*

**Descr** the adult coat has a grey background with numerous dark spots, particularly on the back, surrounded by light areas forming a ringed pattern. The belly is silver. The vibrissae (whiskers) are profuse and tend to curve down. **Size** adults average 1.5 m and 50–70 kg. **Habitat** although primarily an Arctic species they sometimes occur off the north coast and Labrador. The single pup is born in March–April and averages 60 cm and 4.5 kg. It has a white coat, which is shed in 4–6 weeks for a silver one with dark grey colouring on the back.

# ORDER: CETACEA (WHALES, DOLPHINS, AND PORPOISES)

Living cetaceans are classified as either mysticetes, which sieve plankton through baleen plates in the mouth, or odontocetes, which have teeth and feed primarily on fish and squid. At least twenty species have been reported as permanent residents or migrants in Newfoundland waters. Only those that might be seen from tour boats or terrestrial vantage points are described below. Identification features include the body form when surfacing, the shape of the dorsal and tail fins, and the pattern of the blow or 'spout.'

## MYSTICETES

### Humpback Whale
*Megaptera novaeangliae*

**Descr** dorsally black stocky body with obvious hump. Long pectoral fins, tail fin (fluke) with wavy edges and a pale individually identifiable ventral surface exposed when surfacing and jumping out of the water, or 'breaching'. Broad bushy spout about 3m tall. **Size** adults 12–14 m in length. **Habitat** common in coastal waters during the summer.

### Northern Minke Whale
*Balaenoptera acutorostrata*

**Descr** small whale. Dorsal body black or dark-grey, and ventrally white. A white band on each flipper. When surfacing most of the back, including the dorsal fin and blowholes, appears at once. Sickle-shaped dorsal fin and low (2 m) inconspicuous spout. **Size** averaging 6.9 m length in males and 7.4 m in females. **Habitat** common in coastal waters during the summer.

## Fin Whale

*Balaenoptera physalus*

**Descr** long slender body brownish-grey dorsally and white ventrally. Prominent dorsal fin. Tall (5 m) vertical conical spout. Flat V-shaped head. Asymmetric black-white jaw colouring. Tail rarely seen when surfacing. **Size** adults up to 20 m. **Habitat** Common during early spring to fall in deeper offshore waters.

## Blue Whale

*Balaenoptera musculus*

**Descr** long slender body bluish-grey dorsally and lighter ventrally. Small dorsal fin. Vertical single-column spout 9–12 m. Uniformly grey tail fluke may be raised when diving. **Size** adults up to 30m. **Habitat** most commonly sighted in May–Dec. adjacent to Gulf of St. Lawrence but occasionally in Conception, Placentia, and Trinity Bays. A blue whale skeleton hangs in the atrium of the Core Science Facility, Memorial University, for the general public to view.

## ODONTOCETES

## Beluga Whale

*Delphinapterus leucas*

**Descr** all white with distinctive pro-tuberance ('melon') on the head. Dorsal ridge instead of dorsal fin. Broad short flippers. **Size** adults up to 5 m length. **Habitat** uncommon in inshore and estuarine waters.

## Killer (Orca) Whale

*Orcinus orca*

**Descr** black dorsal surface, white chest and sides, white patch above and behind the eye. Robust body, large (2 m) dorsal fin with dark grey 'saddle patch' behind. **Size** adult females 5–6 m, adult males 9–10 m. **Habitat** usually offshore but occasionally inshore.

## Long-Finned Pilot Whale

*Globicephala melas*

**Descr** locally known as the pothead whale. Dark grey, brown or black, sometimes with light grey patches. Dorsal fin set forward and sweeping backwards. Large bulbous 'melon.' Long, sickle-shaped flippers. Spout more than 1 m and often audible. **Size** adults up to 6 m. **Habitat** usually offshore, but inshore in summer and autumn.

## Atlantic White-Sided Dolphin

*Lagenorhynchus acutus*

**Descr** white to pale yellow patch behind the dorsal fin on each side. Rest of dorsal surface and flippers dark grey to black, white ventrally. **Size** adults up to 2.5 m. **Habitat** common in larger groups offshore.

## Common Dolphin

*Delphinus delphis*

**Descr** dorsally dark, ventrally white, with an hourglass pattern on the sides, light grey, yellow or gold towards the anterior and grey to the posterior. Long thin rostrum ('beak') with a distinct crease between it and the forehead. **Size** adults between 1.9–2.5 m. **Habitat** offshore, but occasionally in inshore waters.

## Harbour Porpoise (Common Porpoise)

*Phocoena phocoena*

**Descr** robust body with the maximum girth anterior to the triangular dorsal fin. Poorly demarcated 'beak.' Dark grey dorsal surface, flippers, dorsal and tail fin. Slightly speckled lighter grey laterally. Whiter ventraly with grey stripes under the throat. **Size** adults up to 1.7 m.

**Habitat** small groups in shallow water and estuaries.

## FOSSILS AND THE PALEONTOLOGICAL GEOHERITAGE OF NEWFOUNDLAND

### INTRODUCTION TO PALEONTOLOGY

We owe much in our modern world to ancient life; besides ourselves. Coal, oil, and gas are the decayed and chemically altered remains of prehistoric organisms; that is why they are called 'fossil fuels.' Paleontology is the branch of geology that deals with the study of ancient life. Paleontology and archeology are sometimes confused. Paleontologists study fossilized organisms, whereas archeologists investigate human remains and artifacts.

There are two types of fossils. Body fossils are partial or complete remains, most commonly shell, skin, bone, or cellular material, including petrified wood, which may, or may not, include original DNA. Most commonly, the organic material is not preserved, but is replaced by one or more minerals; this is particularly true of older fossils.

Trace fossils preserve the activities of these ancient organisms, and include coprolites (fossil dung), burrows, tracks, and trails. For example, dinosaur footprints are trace fossils, as are the tetrapod tracks of the Maritimes and western Newfoundland.

Macrofossils are visible to the naked eye; extremely large macrofossils are termed megafossils. Microfossils require the use of a microscope; extremely small microfossils are termed nannofossils. Fossil constructs are structures created by ancient organisms. Examples of fossil constructs include fossil forests, reefs, hydrothermal vent communities, algal mats, and stromatolite and/or thrombolite mound complexes.

Pseudofossils look like fossils, but actually result from inorganic processes. Common pseudofossils in eastern Newfoundland include crinkly patterns that resemble plant remains; these patterns are actually growths of the mineral pyrolusite.

< *Planispiral Gastropod, western Newfoundland*

Fossils form when an organism dies, is buried, and remains buried. Over time, the enclosing sediments harden to become rock. Normally, only the hard parts of an organism are preserved. When an organism dies, there is usually some time before it gets buried. During that time, the soft parts either rot away or get eaten. Occasionally, as in the Mistaken Point Formation, Avalon Peninsula, and the Burgess Shale of western Canada, a complete ecosystem can be preserved by quick burial including even soft-bodied biota.

*(above left); Fossil tree trunk, Stephenville; (above right) Trilobite tracks Cruziana, Bell Island; (below) An example of pseudofossils, dendrites of the mineral pyrolusite (dark brown), which resemble fossil plants.*

## WHY IT CAN BE DIFFICULT TO IDENTIFY FOSSILS

### COMPACTION OF ORIGINAL SEDIMENTS

Clay muds compact more than lime muds. Consequently, fossils preserved in shale (originally mud) are commonly flattened, their shells cracked and/or broken. Fossils preserved in limestone, on the other hand, often retain their original shape and convexity, i.e., are not flattened at all. In places, flattened and non-flattened individuals of the same species have been mistakenly described as different species.

### DIFFERENT GROWTH STAGES

Certain organisms (e.g., trilobites, graptolites, corals) change their shapes throughout their lifetimes. There are documented examples where the different growth stages of the same fossilized organism have been incorrectly described as separate species.

### INJURIES

There are examples in the paleontological literature where injured trilobites of a particular species have been described as a new species.

### DEFORMATION OF ENCLOSING ROCKS

When rocks are folded and faulted, everything in them, including fossils, can be deformed. Occasionally, deformed and undeformed individuals of the same species have been inaccurately described as different species.

## BIOSTRATIGRAPHY

One of the most important paleontological applications is biostratigraphy (i.e., the relative age dating of rock sequences). Paleontologists and biostratigraphers have long recognized that fossil assemblages occur in a defined order through the sedimentary rock record. These assemblages have been used to define biostratigraphic zones. Zones are typically named for their most common and/or distinctive fossil species. The base of each zone is defined by the first appearance of its characteristic species. The top of a zone is defined by the base of the overlying zone. Two or more zones grouped together form a geologic stage. Stages are linked to form a geologic series. Series combine to define a geologic system or period. The zone is therefore the fundamental building block of the geological time scale. Consequently, discussions of geological history that ignore the timing provided by fossils and fossil zones, do so at their own peril.

Rocks with different ages can strongly resemble each other, particularly when the original sediments were deposited in similar environments. Also, the layers (strata) of one rock formation may be repeated by faulting. Fossils, therefore, provide an elegant way to quickly discriminate between various rock units.

## PALEOECOLOGY

Paleoecology is the study of the lateral distribution of fossil biological communities. In western Newfoundland, particular limestones contain distinct trilobite assemblages; these are called biofacies. Using biofacies analysis, it is possible to identify the environments on the ancient continental shelf in which these trilobites lived (i.e., nearshore, lagoon, reef, offshore, etc.).

## DIFFERENCES IN FOSSILS FROM SEPARATE REGIONS

The Cambrian and Ordovician trilobite faunas of eastern Newfoundland contrast sharply with those from western Newfoundland (and most of North America). This is because the areas existed in two different climatic zones on opposite sides of the Early Paleozoic Iapetus Ocean. While western Newfoundland (and most of North America) was located at or near the equator in relatively warm, shallow water, eastern Newfoundland was in higher (temperate to polar) latitudes and covered by relatively cool, deep water.

Middle and Late Cambrian faunas of eastern Newfoundland (and also New Brunswick, Nova Scotia, Massachusetts) have more in common with those of Norway, Sweden, England, Wales, France, Spain, Germany, and Bohemia (now part of Czech Republic).

(left) Trilobite Bailiaspis, eastern Newfoundland, lived in the temperate to polar region of Iapetus Ocean; (right) Trilobite Olenellus, western Newfoundland, lived near the equator in the Iapetus Ocean

## NEWFOUNDLAND FOSSILS

Newfoundland contains a wealth of paleontology-related geoheritage sites. For instance, eastern Newfoundland has some of the oldest and richest localities of a unique deep water Ediacaran biota on the planet, typified by the fossils of the Mistaken Point Ecological Reserve, Spaniard's Bay, and the eastern Bonavista Peninsula. Furthermore, the type locality of one of the first (if not the first) described (in 1872) Ediacaran fossil, *Aspidella terranovica Billings,* is in downtown St. John's.

The Global Boundary Stratotype Section and Point (GSSP) for the base of the Cambrian Period occurs within the Fortune Head Ecological Reserve on the Burin Peninsula, where it is defined by the First Appearance Datum (FAD) of the trace fossil *Treptichnus pedum*. These earliest Cambrian rocks contain small, shelly fossils, trace fossils, and rare microbial mounds (stromatolites and/or thrombolites); these occur in marine-deposited shale, sandstone, and limestone.

Manuels River is world famous for its Middle Cambrian '*Paradoxides* Beds' studied by Dr. B. F. Howell of Princeton University in the 1910s; unfortunately, his original collections are lost. It was in the Manuels River area where G. F. Matthew's and C. D. Walcott's debate about the relative stratigraphic positions of *Callavia* and *Paradoxides* was settled.

In late Early Cambrian to Ordovician rocks, acritarch microfossils and trilobites are the most common fossils, and these occur in marine-deposited shale and slate, sandstone, and limestone on the Avalon Peninsula (including Bell Island), the Bonavista Peninsula (including Random Island), and the Burin Peninsula. Accompanying these may be less abundant inarticulate brachiopods, graptolites, and hyolithids. Bell Island is world famous for its Early Ordovician trace fossils (tracks, trails, and burrows produced by trilobites and soft-bodied animals).

In central Newfoundland, articulate brachiopods, bivalves, bryozoa, cephalopods, conodont microfossils, corals, crinoids, gastropods, graptolites, ostracodes, trilobites, and trace fossils are variably found in marine-deposited conglomerate, limestone, sandstone, shale, and slate of Ordovician and Silurian age. Fossils are particularly common on New World Island.

*(left) Horn Corals (Silurian), central Newfoundland; (right) Articulate Brachiopod, western Newfoundland*

Western Newfoundland has the greatest variety of fossils in the province. Here, in the 1860s, a substantial number of fossil genera were described for the first time by E. Billings (the Geological Survey of Canada's first paleontologist); the fossils were collected by J. Richardson during field mapping for W. E. Logan's (1863) historic Geology of Canada report. Marine fossils occur on the Port au Port Peninsula and the Great Northern Peninsula in conglomerate, limestone and marble, sandstone, shale, and slate of Cambrian, Ordovician, Silurian, Devonian, and Carboniferous age. These fossils include acritarchs, archaeocyathids, asteroids (sea star), bivalves, articulate and inarticulate brachiopods, bryozoa, cephalopods, chitinozoan and conodont microfossils, conularids, corals, crinoids, gastropods, graptolites, hyolithids, machaeridians, microbial mounds (stromatolites and thrombolites), monoplacophorans, ostracodes, rostroconchs, sponges, trilobites, and trace fossils.

Gros Morne National Park is a UNESCO World Heritage Site. The GSSP for the base of the Ordovician Period is defined at Green Point in the park, based on the FAD of the conodont microfossil *Iapetognathus fluctivagus*.

Plant remains and complete paleoniscid fish, as well as tetrapod tracks, locally occur in Early Carboniferous (Mississippian) terrestrial-

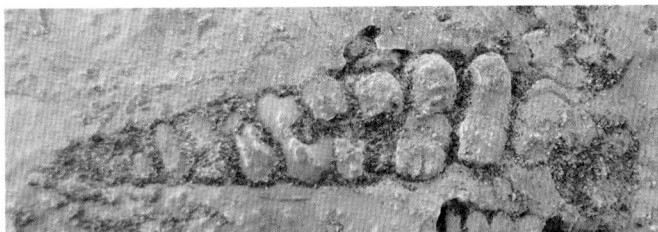

*(top) High-spired Gastropod, western Newfoundland; (bottom left) Coiled Cephalopod, western Newfoundland; (bottom right) Crinoid stem in limestone block, Colonial Building, St. John's*

and freshwater lake-deposited sandstone and shale of the Deer Lake Basin and the Bay St. George Sub-Basin. Blanche Brook, Stephenville, has well-preserved Late Carboniferous (Pennsylvanian) petrified tree trunks and other plant fossils.

Fossils have also been observed from unusual places in Newfoundland. For instance, during offshore oil exploration on the Grand Banks (off eastern Newfoundland), possible dinosaur bone fragments were recovered from core samples. And fossils can even be observed in building stones such as at the Colonial Building in St. John's.

## PROTECTED FOSSILS

Provincially, ownership of all paleontological resources is vested in the Crown. Fossils are protected under two acts.

### THE WILDERNESS AND ECOLOGICAL RESERVES ACT

The Wilderness and Ecological Reserves Act covers fossils within Wilderness and Ecological Reserves. There currently are three fossil-related Ecological Reserves in the province:

- **MISTAKEN POINT** (Avalon Peninsula): A UNESCO World Heritage Site featuring some of the oldest Ediacaran soft-bodied metazoan fossils in the world.

- **FORTUNE HEAD** (Burin Peninsula): The official world-wide reference section (GSSP) for the Precambrian–Cambrian boundary, i.e., the base of the Cambrian System.

- **TABLE POINT** (Great Northern Peninsula): The site contains an unusual Early Ordovician graptolite horizon preserved in dolostone, as well as one of the most diverse and well-preserved assemblages of Middle Ordovician fossils in the world.

### THE HISTORIC RESOURCES ACT

The Historic Resources Act and its regulations. In addition, all fossils of Ediacaran age or older are protected, as are all pre-Quaternary vertebrate fossils, e.g., Carboniferous fish fossils and tetrapod tracks of western Newfoundland.

Fossil collecting is restricted in National and Provincial Parks. Only scientists holding valid permits can collect fossils from these areas.

The island of Newfoundland presents a kaleidoscope of geological rocks and environments that range in age from ca. 1.6 billion years ago, or 1.6 Ga (Giga annum), to modern-day sediments, seascapes, and scenery. The geology of Newfoundland comprises: (1) the bones of the ancient continent of Laurentia, the so-called Canadian Shield; (2) the vestiges of an ancient ocean, the Iapetus, which is now nothing but a phantom; (3) ancient volcanic rocks and deltas that were once connected to what is now the British Isles and North Africa; (4) ancient reefs and mud deposits suffused with fossil remnants of antediluvian organisms; (5) vast bodies of granite that seem almost as seas of crystalline liquid with geometric arrangements of constituent minerals; (6) large bodies of green to brown igneous rock from deep within the Earth that seem to have serpent skins; (7) blankets of rock debris, sand, and erratics from extensive ca. 12,000–20,000-year-old continental glaciers that ripped up and profoundly disguised the ancient bedrock (see Glaciation); and (8) a wide variety of smaller environments including desert-like basins, small igneous rocks with a range of origins, and rocks transformed by the deep crushing pressures of the Earth's relentless internal movement.

Newfoundland represents both the northeastern terminus of the Appalachian Mountain Belt, which extends to the southwest as far as the state of Georgia in the USA and the western edge of the Caledonian Mountain Belt of Europe. The Appalachians were great mountains, perhaps rearing up to the heights of the Himalayas some 450 Ma (million years ago).

The premise for this portion of the field guide is to paint a very broad picture of the rock types present in Newfoundland so that the reader might make a stab at identification when they encounter them on their travels across the island. The review will provide basic information and a series of simple rock identification steps, e.g., colour, grain size, texture, structure, hardness, etc. Geologists typically break rocks open to examine their textures and minerals in detail. You, the reader, won't need to do this, as the rocks in Newfoundland are so superbly exposed in cliffs, road cuts, and beach stones, that the described simple identification techniques will be sufficient for a cursory examination. For more detailed and region-specific geological information, the reader is directed towards two publications: *Newfoundland and Labrador: Traveller's Guide to the Geology*, from the Geological Association of Canada—NL Section edited by S. Colman-Sadd and S. A. Scott, which contains a geological map of the province along with a guide to 127 stops of interest, and (2) Martha Hild's *Geology of Newfoundland Field Guide: Touring Through Time at 48 Scenic Sites*.

A must-see for anybody interested in the geology of Newfoundland is Memorial University's awesome Newfoundland and Labrador Science Centre (MUN) in St. John's; they will tell you the story of Earth.

## ROCK VS. MINERAL

Before one attempts to describe rocks and minerals, their essence must be defined. Minerals are 'naturally occurring, solid inorganic substances that have a definite composition, or range of compositions, and a definite crystal structure.' Over 92% of the minerals at Earth's surface are silicates, meaning that they are composed of some combination of silicon and oxygen along with other elements. The simplest mineral is quartz, which consists solely of silicon and oxygen, and it is the most common mineral in Newfoundland rocks. Economically significant minerals in Newfoundland are less common non-silicates that range from gold, through sulphide minerals (mined for metals), to other minerals such as gypsum, etc.

The precise definition of a rock is that it is 'a coherent aggregate of one or more minerals.' For instance, limestone can be composed solely of the mineral calcite, whereas the rock type granite can be a

*(left) Gold grain in quartz vein, Valentine Lake discovery outcrop; (right) Molybdenite in quartz vein, Ackley City Deposit, Rencontre East*

complex combination of several minerals including quartz, feldspar, mica, etc. There are three broad classes of rocks: sedimentary, igneous, metamorphic.

Within the very broad category of sedimentary rocks, there are two subtypes: 'detrital' (or clastic) and 'chemical.' The dominant subtype is called detrital because it results from the cementation of rock grains (detritus) that were derived from the erosion and weathering of older rocks (i.e., igneous, metamorphic, or sedimentary). Chemical sedimentary rocks formed by precipitation of dissolved elements from water, for instance, limestone forms from the accumulation of shells; animals precipitated the shells from dissolved elements in seawater.

*(left) Detrital sedimentary rock—conglomerate on bottom, sandstone on top, Branch; (right) Chemical sedimentary rock—limestone composed of shells, Port au Port Peninsula*

Igneous rocks are the products from the cooling of magma (i.e., very hot, liquid rock). Igneous rocks are composed of interlocking mineral crystals that grew from the magma liquid as it cooled. Igneous rocks crystallize in three different environments: deep inside the Earth, the so-called 'plutonic' environment, or on the Earth's surface, termed the 'volcanic' environment. The intermediate environment is termed 'hypabyssal' and its igneous rocks have textures midway between those of plutonic and volcanic rocks. Hypabyssal rocks are mainly preserved as dykes, which were the conduits through which volcanic magmas moved to the Earth's surface from their plutonic roots.

*(left) Gabbro (plutonic)—plagioclase feldspar (white) and pyroxene (black), Joanna Lake, Labrador; (right) Granite (plutonic)—quartz (white), K-spar (pink), biotite (black flakes), and xenoliths (large black), Alexander Murray Building (MUN)*

The most significant difference between plutonic and volcanic rocks lies in their grain sizes. Volcanic rocks are fine-grained because they cooled quickly, hence the constituent mineral crystals didn't have a chance to grow. In contrast, because plutonic magmas crystallized at depth in the Earth, they cooled slowly, and the minerals grew into coarse-grained mosaics in which individual minerals can be identified with the naked eye. Hypabyssal dyke rocks can contain both fine and coarse crystals. Some volcanic rocks may contain larger crystals of minerals in a fine-grained matrix, such crystals are termed 'phenocrysts' and the texture 'porphyritic;' the larger crystals may have crystallized deeper in the Earth as the magma flowed to the surface. Likewise, some plutonic magmas contain large crystals conspicuously larger than their matrix; these are termed 'megacrysts' and the texture 'megacrystic.' In some metamorphic rocks, large crystals can overgrow the main mass of the rock; these crystals are called 'porphyroblasts.' The presence of larger mineral crystals set in a finer-grained matrix classifies the rock as being either igneous or metamorphic.

*(left) Phenocrysts (white) in basalt, Notre Dame Bay; (right) Garnet porphyroblasts (red) in metamorphic rock, Labrador*

Plutonic, and to a lesser degree volcanic, igneous rocks can entrain fragments of older, cold rocks as they flow from deeper regions in the Earth. Such fragments of country rock are called 'xenoliths,' and they provide geologists with direct physical evidence of the rocks through which the magmas flowed. The most exotic xenolith-rich igneous rocks are kimberlites, some of which can contain diamonds. Unfortunately, however, there are no known examples of kimberlites in Newfoundland, although there are some in Labrador.

Metamorphic rocks are produced when pre-existing rocks are subjected to sufficient pressures and/or temperatures and /or fluids that they change. Precursor rocks can be igneous, sedimentary, and even metamorphic. The change(s) effected on the rock being metamorphosed can be textural, and/or mineralogical, and/or

*(left) Xenoliths (black) in granite (stripy white), Cape Ray; (right) Granite (pink) plucking pieces of shale host rock (black)—how xenoliths form, Lawn*

chemical. When minerals in a metamorphic rock align themselves in a single, planar, direction they are said to be foliated. In a very broad sense, foliated metamorphic rocks fall into two main classes, 'gneiss' and 'schist.' Gneisses are foliated rocks in which dark platy minerals are segregated from light-coloured minerals producing a layered rock with bands of dark and light minerals. Schists are foliated metamorphic rocks that can be split into irregular plates. In other cases, increased pressure can cause non-platy minerals in pre-existing rocks to recrystallize and grow larger. Because there are no platy minerals present, the resultant metamorphic rock will be granular, e.g., limestone to marble.

Metamorphism ranges up to the point that a rock melts, forming a magma that, when cooled, forms an igneous rock. In areas with very high-grade metamorphism, the parental rock partially melts, yielding a mixture of pre-existing rock and melt; if the magma (liquid) cools before it can move away from the country rock, then a hybrid rock is formed called a 'migmatite'; such rocks are indicative of extreme temperatures and pressures.

*Folded schist (metamorphic rock), Port aux Basques*

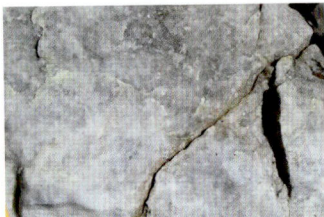

*(top left) Gneiss (metamorphic rock), Taylor Brook, White Bay; (top right) Marble, Taylor Brook, White Bay; (bottom) Migmatite with melted zone (white-pink) in gneiss (metamorphic rock), Taylor Brook, White Bay.*

Metamorphism can also be quite subtle and involve only slight changes in the mineralogy of a rock. If pressure is applied to platy chloritic minerals they can align. For example a basalt can be transformed into a 'greenschist.' Most ancient basalts, such as those in Newfoundland, exhibit at least incipient development of chlorite and/or epidote.

## IDENTIFICATION TECHNIQUES

Geologists refer to an exposed body of rock as an 'outcrop.' There are certainly many outcrops in Newfoundland, so many that the island has been affectionately referred to as the 'rock.' When geologists examine a rock in an outcrop, they look for a variety of physical features in order to discern how the particular rock might extend beneath overlying soil/till, water, or vegetation cover. Piecing the scattered outcrops of a region together, the geologist constructs a geological map, which is a best guess at what rocks may be lurking beneath the surface and how they might be connected to other outcrops.

In attempting to identify a rock, the most important technique would be to look at it. As facile as that sounds, often it is also the most difficult procedure. Geologists spend years learning to classify rocks, and good ones are continually learning. In looking at a rock, one would first note its colour and grain size, and whether the rock you're looking at is exposed as a large cliff, road cut, or plain old outcrop in a field; you would also look for any structures displayed by the entire rock mass. Colour is important as it can yield fundamental information about where the rock may have formed. If a detrital sedimentary rock is red, it would imply that the sediment was

*Red sandstone-conglomerate, Adies Lake, Deer Lake*

deposited in an environment containing free oxygen, which would have essentially rusted any contained iron (i.e., turns red); the red is from the mineral hematite. Such environments would be on land (e.g., river) or near-shore marine. Red conglomerates and sandstones around the Deer Lake region are thought to have been deposited in fault-bounded, on-land, river-fed basins. In some cases, water may have flowed through a rock much later causing iron oxidation and essentially infusing the rock with a red colour.

*Green to black siltstone in road cut, Outer Ring Road, St. John's*

If sediment was deposited in a marine environment, it can range in colour from black to green, as iron would be reduced. Most detrital sedimentary rocks in Newfoundland were deposited in reduced marine environments. Limestones are generally light brown to grey to white, although some on the Avalon Peninsula are red-white. Gypsum and salt deposits, such as those on the west coast, are white. Granites are typically pink to red, but variegated as they can contain red orthoclase, white quartz, grey to white plagioclase feldspar, and black biotite. Basalts and gabbros are generally black to dark green. Serpentinites range in colour from brown to pale and dark green. Metamorphic rocks are generally colour banded with variations of white and black.

The chemical compositions, and hence constituent minerals, of igneous rocks define two discrete end members. Dark-coloured igneous rocks are called mafic; volcanic varieties are basalt, whereas plutonic varieties are classified as gabbro. They are dark because they are composed of dark-coloured, high-temperature, minerals such as olivine, pyroxene, and plagioclase feldspar. In contrast, light-coloured igneous rocks, rhyolites and granites, contain lighter coloured minerals such as quartz and alkali feldspars. This type of magma cools and crystallizes at lower temperatures than mafic magmas and is termed felsic.

Once the colour has been established, the rock outcrop would be examined for structures. Rocks are never exposed where they formed. For example, detrital sedimentary rocks originate as sediment deposited and cemented together in deep ocean basins, deltas, the bottom of lakes or rivers, etc. Plutonic rocks would have crystallized deep inside the Earth's Crust, and metamorphic rocks formed at great depths in the crust. To see these rocks means that they have been moved considerable distances from their place of origin, resulting in the development of secondary structural forms/fabrics.

Two fundamental principles of sedimentary rocks suggest that they were deposited horizontally and that the oldest rocks are always on the bottom (the Law of Superposition). The problem with applying these principles to Newfoundland sedimentary rocks is that they have been so variably jumbled up (folded, turned over, or metamorphosed), that only rarely are they still horizontal, or even subhorizontal. So, when viewing sedimentary rocks in Newfoundland, one should not expect them to necessarily lie flat.

*Tilted layers (bedding) in sedimentary rock, East Coast Trail, Stiles Cove*

*(left) Volcanic breccia from the eruption of a volcano, Whisker Valley; (right) Cross-bedding in sandstone (flow direction R to L), Beamer, Flatrock*

Volcanic igneous rocks were deposited on the Earth's surface generally in horizontal layers as flows, or as gigantic mounds of volcanic material (volcanoes). Volcanic eruptions can produce layers of fine ash, called tuffs, or very coarse-grained volcanic breccias, 'lahars,' which form on the sides of volcanoes. Though volcanic cones no longer exist in Newfoundland due to erosion, their diagnostic volcanic rocks still do.

The simplest type of structure is the repetitive layering of rock termed 'bedding.' Bedding generally indicates that the rock is sedimentary. Detrital sedimentary rocks also exhibit a wide range of structures indicative of their origin as accumulations of loose sediment, including: (1) cross-bedding, which indicates the direction of sediment transport (i.e., which way the transporting current flowed); (2) 'soft sediment deformation' wherein pressure of overlying sediment squeezes lower layers; (3) 'ripple marks,' which indicate that the sediment was deposited in a nearshore to beach area; (4) 'flute' (aka 'load') casts, which indicate which way the current carrying sediment was flowing; and (5) limestone 'concretions' in detrital sedimentary rocks, which indicate the movement of water through a sediment as it is cemented together.

*(top left) Soft sediment deformation in siltstone-sandstone, High Tide Trail, Eastport; (top right) Ripple marks in siltstone, Northern Bay; (botton left) Flute casts (current direction was lower right to upper left), Piccadilly, Port au Port; (bottom right) Limestone concretion in siltstone, Fortune Head*

*(left) Vesicles (gas holes) in dyke, High Tide Trail, Eastport; (right) Amygdules (white) in volcanic rock, Great Colinet Island*

In some cases, volcanic rocks can also be layered and even bedded, but other features would classify them as volcanic. When a magma reaches the Earth's surface, gases can separate from the magma, due to depressurization, leading to the development of gas holes in the cooled rock. Such holes are called 'vesicles,' and the texture 'vesicular;' these are distinctive features of volcanic igneous rocks. In older vesicular volcanic rocks, the vesicles can be filled with minerals precipitated from later fluids that flowed through the rock. The filled vesicles are called 'amygdules' and the resultant texture is 'amygdaloidal.'

*(left) Pillow basalt, Notre Dame Bay; (right) Pillow lava (green) overlain by chert (red) layers, Notre Dame Bay*

When magma erupts underwater, it has great difficulty flowing due to the cooling effect of the surrounding water. The result is that when magma encounters seawater, a thin rind of chilled magma forms on the magma surface, under which the magma would continue to flow, expanding and squishing out from beneath the rind. The consequences of this quick chilling and rind formation are that the resultant rock exhibits what geologists call a 'pillow' texture. The pillows look like stacked ovals. Many of the rocks along the coastline of Notre Dame Bay and inland through Buchans south to Victoria Lake are pillow basalts. The pillow textures indicate that the rocks formed on the ocean floor are analogous to off-shore Iceland. Gas may have filtered out of the cooling pillow, leaving behind concentric layers of vesicles or amygdules. Another common feature of pillow basalt outcrops is the presence of chemical sedimentary rocks composed of silica (quartz), called 'chert,' filling interstices between pillows.

Chert indicates that heated waters (hydrothermal fluids) flowed through the basaltic pillows. If hydrothermal fluid movement was very extensive and lasted for hundreds to thousands of years, metal sulphide minerals may precipitate from the fluid as well. These metals can include copper, lead, zinc, gold, and silver, which can accumulate as massive bodies of sulphide minerals. When preserved, these sulphide mounds can be very important sources of metals.

Many massive sulphide bodies occur in the igneous seafloor rocks of Newfoundland, including the fabulously rich deposit at Buchans, and smaller ones at Tilt Cove, and various other abandoned sites in Notre Dame Bay. These types of deposits have recently been mined at Rambler, near Baie Verte, and Duck Pond, near Buchans. The Rambler Mine is planned to reopen.

In some cases, plutonic rocks can exhibit layering, but the layers are defined by mineral crystals that essentially settled out of a cooling body of magma and collected as layers at the bottom of a magma chamber. Granites and gabbros in general will not exhibit any large-scale structure, unless they are caught up in a large fold. Instead, they will present a texture of interlocking mineral crystals. Dykes of all types, be they granite or basalt, will typically cut through and across other rocks as straight bodies with parallel sides; dykes can be very thin, millimetres to hundreds of metres across and may also be folded, but the sides will still be parallel. If the dyke is horizontal, it is called a 'sill.'

*Mineral layering in plutonic granite, Cape Ray*

*(top left) Basaltic dykes (black) cutting ancient Archean crust, Saglek, Labrador; (top right) Micro granite (pink) dykes and sills, Lawn; (bottom left) Quartz vein (white) cutting siltstone and incorporating fragments, Holyrood; (bottom left) Quartz veins (white) cutting red sandstone, Glenwood*

Metamorphic rocks typically exhibit layered features defined by black to green platy minerals, but elsewhere are defined by wild-looking loops of folded, contorted material.

Not all hydrothermal fluids originate in ocean basins. Some are simply heated waters that circulate through crustal rocks. When these fluids flow through cracks in rock, they can form veins by precipitating minerals in the cracks as they cool. Common vein materials are quartz and calcite. Gold-bearing veins have been found at a variety of sites throughout Newfoundland and a number of these gold deposits are being developed, including the Valentine Lake deposits near Buchans and the New Found Gold deposits near Gander. Hydrothermal fluids can also be derived from granites during cooling and can likewise form veins in host rock. The St. Lawrence fluorspar deposits consist of multi-coloured fluorite veins.

Mega-scale, secondary structure forms include tilting (up to vertical), folding, and faulting on scales that range from hundreds of kms to small scale (mm) fractures/cracks. When geologists examine structures, such as bedded sedimentary rocks, they define the 'strike' and 'dip' of the bedding. The strike is the compass direction relative to true North of a horizontal line along a bedding plane. The dip is the angle from the horizontal of the bedding plane. Other structures with the measurable three-dimensional components of strike and dip include faults, fractures, veins, and schistosity and gneissosity

*Large fold in siltstone-sandstone, Walmart parking lot, Kelsey Drive, St. John's*

in metamorphic rocks. Geologists map out these strikes and dips to define the spatial arrangements of rocks over large regional areas.

Older rocks (sedimentary, igneous, or metamorphic) may be exposed at vertical to near-vertical angles and be overlain by younger sedimentary rocks in which the layers are more horizontal. This is termed an unconformity and these provide profound insights into the nature and great length of geological time. Studies of unconformities by James Hutton, the father of modern geology, led to his conclusions that the Earth has existed for an incredibly long time as have the geological processes that shaped it. An unconformity is essentially a layer where a younger, sedimentary rock, lies on top of an older rock that had been exposed and weathered prior to the younger one being laid down. There are some classic unconformities in Conception

*(top) Strike and dip directions on siltstone, Northern Bay; (bottom left) Fold in mixed shale (black) siltstone (white), Piccadilly, Port au Port; (bottom right) Fold in metamorphosed sedimentary rocks, Ocean View Trail, Pacquet*

*Unconformity; younger sandstone on older eroded rock, Bacon Cove*

Bay at Bacon Cove, where Cambrian sandstone overlies Precambrian volcanic and sedimentary rocks, and at Duffs, near Holyrood, where Cambrian shale rests on Holyrood granite. These features reveal time gaps of millions of years.

The final leg of the identification triad is examination of the rock grain size. If the rock is so fine-grained that individual grains cannot be distinguished, one might have to rely solely on the colour and structure to identify. In a rock with large fragments, the fragments need to be examined as to whether they are transported grains (detritus), mineral crystals, or rock fragments (i.e., xenoliths). Sedimentary rocks are classified on their grain size, so a sedimentary rock with very fine grains (flour-sized) is termed a shale, mudstone, or siltstone; one with sand-sized (pinhead-sized) grains, a sandstone; and large grains, a conglomerate.

*Fossil tree trunk with cell-like chambers, Port au Port*

*(left) Fossil worm burrows (black) in siltstone, Beaver Brook; (right) Bitumen (solid petroleum—black) with calcite (white) in limestone, Deer Lake*

When studying conglomerate layers, geologists typically examine grain size gradation from coarse through finer-grained layers (sandstones, etc.). A conglomerate contains such large fragments, that the transporting agent (e.g., rivers) must have been particularly energetic. When that energy is decreased, the transporting agent can only carry finer-grained particles, hence conglomerate beds are typically overlain by finer-grained sedimentary rocks. If a geologist examines a conglomerate bed and finds that indeed a conglomerate passes upwards into fine-grained layers, they know that the layers of rocks are right-side up; if a fine-grained sedimentary passes upwards into the conglomerate, then the layers are upside down.

Sedimentary rocks may contain fossils as fragments. These can range from shells, to plants, to fossil tracks and burrow holes. Sedimentary rocks in some parts of western Newfoundland (Deer Lake, Port au Port, and Parsons Pond areas), may contain hydrocarbons as liquid petroleum or solid bitumen. The presence of fossils and/or hydrocarbons, definitively identify the rocks as being of sedimentary origin.

One can also easily examine the density and hardness of a rock to aid in identification. Igneous rocks, in particular basalts and gabbros, will feel more dense than sedimentary rocks, the lightest of which would be limestone or gypsum. If a fine-grained rock can be scratched by a knife-blade, it is most likely a sedimentary rock, although the initial stages of metamorphism might make an igneous rock softer than it was originally. Limestones would be softer, and rocks composed of salt and gypsum would be so soft that they can be scratched by a fingernail.

## GEOLOGICAL TIME

The Earth is about 4.55 billion years (Ga) old. Geologists subdivide geological time into two broad ranges distinguished by the presence (or absence) of fossil shells, bones, or crawling tracks. For most of the Earth's history, from about 4.55 Ga to about 541 million years (Ma) ago, there were no macroscopic (i.e., visible to the naked eye) hard-shelled organisms. This vast period is called the Precambrian (i.e., pre-dates the Cambrian Period when significant fossils first appear) and is itself subdivided into the Hadean (4.55 to 3.8 Ga), Archean (3.8 to 2.5 Ga), and Proterozoic (2.5 Ga to 541 Ma) Eons. The time following the Precambrian is called the Phanerozoic Eon (541 Ma to present-day). The Phanerozoic, in turn, is split into the Paleozoic Era (541 to 252 Ma), the Mesozoic Era (252 to 66 Ma), also called the Age of the Dinosaurs, and the Cenozoic Era (66 Ma to present-day), also known as the Age of the Mammals. The Paleozoic Era consists of the Cambrian Period (541 to 485 Ma), the Ordovician Period (485 to 443 Ma), the Silurian Period (443 to 419 Ma), the Devonian Period (419 to 359 Ma), the Carboniferous Period (359 to 299 Ma), and the Permian Period (299 to 254 Ma).

*(top left) Fossils of early complex life forms (Ediacaran), Mistaken Point; (top right) Ediacaran fossil and clay imprint (top), Spaniards Bay; (bottom) GSSP boundary between Precambrian and Cambrian (note ripple marks), Fortune Head*

There are no known Archean rocks in Newfoundland. The oldest rocks are the ca. 1.6 Ga (Proterozoic) gneisses and schists in the interior of the Great Northern Peninsula; most other rocks in Western Newfoundland are Cambrian to Devonian. Rocks on the Avalon and Burin Peninsulas are mainly Late Proterozoic (750 to 541 Ma), but there are Cambrian and Ordovician rocks in the Conception Bay region. Rocks in central Newfoundland range from 600 Ma to the Devonian (ca. 360 Ma). The youngest significant rocks on the island are Carboniferous and occur as flat-lying rocks around Deer Lake, on the Port au Port Peninsula, and in the Anguille Mountains.

Newfoundland rocks played three key roles in the epic saga of early life on the Earth (see Fossils). On the southern Avalon Peninsula, at Mistaken Point, sedimentary rocks contain evidence of the first stirrings of complex multicellular organisms in the time just before the Phanerozoic; the so-called dawn of modern Life. The magnificent Avalon Interpretative Centre at Portugal Cove South tells the story of these sublime fossils and how to visit them. Similar fossils have been discovered in recent years around Spaniard's Bay and Elliston (Bonavista Bay), the latter location is in the UNESCO Discovery Geopark. Hence, the extraordinary story about the beginning of complex life on the Earth is still being teased out of Newfoundland rocks.

In the layers of sedimentary rock at Fortune Head on the Burin Peninsula, the International Union of Geological Sciences (IUGS) has established the exact location of the boundary between the Precambrian and Phanerozoic, i.e., the boundary at the start of modern life. This boundary and the geological section that hosts it is defined as a Global Boundary Stratotype Section and Point (GSSP); see Fossils. For more information one can visit the Fortune Head Interpretation Centre in Fortune. At Green Point in Gros Morne National Park, the IUGS has defined the exact planet-wide boundary (GSSP) between the Cambrian and Ordovician Periods based on the first appearance of a conodont microfossil.

*GSSP boundary between Cambrian and Ordovician Periods, Green Head, Gros Morne National Park*

*Cambrian sponge (archaeocyatha) reef, Pointe Amour*

Cambrian-aged fossil reefs built by extinct sponges are exposed along the seashore at Pointe Amour, southern Labrador. At Flowers Cove, 650 Ma 'thrombolite' fossils, formed by blue-green algae (cyanobacteria), crop out. Cyanobacteria are the longest surviving life on the Earth, they date back to at least 2.8 Ga, and possibly 3.5 Ga.

## BROAD SYNOPSIS OF NEWFOUNDLAND GEOLOGY

Earth is a layered planet with (1) an outermost Crust (5–70 km thick), (2) an intermediate Mantle (2900 km thick), and (3) an inner Core (3500 km thick). The Crust consists of two distinct varieties: (i) continental crust (30–70 km thick) that underlies the continents, and (ii) oceanic crust (5–10 km thick) that underlies the oceans and fundamentally consists of pillow basalt at the surface. Geologically Newfoundland is part of the Earth's Crust, but most uniquely it also contains slivers of ancient Mantle. If one is looking at dark-coloured igneous rocks, they probably represent remnants of ocean crust, whereas granitic igneous rocks would typically represent continental crust.

The Mantle region of the Earth consists of 'ultramafic rocks,' which contain varying ratios of the minerals olivine, pyroxene, and magnetite/chromite. Since ultramafic rocks constitute the intermediate inner layer of the Earth, they are not stable (are 'metastable') at the Earth's surface and hence they readily react with water and the atmosphere to form the secondary mineral serpentine; altered ultramafic rocks are called serpentinites. The mineral serpentine is so named for its cracked and greenish-yellow appearance; it truly does resemble a serpent's skin. Because of their very magnesium-rich composition, ultramafic rocks do not support plant growth and typically have a brownish colour.

The first workers documenting the geology of Newfoundland in the 19th century—J. B. Jukes, Alexander Murray, and James P. Howley—

*Serpentinized ultramafic rock with 'serpent' skin, Winterhouse Brook*

noted the wide variety of rock types and their greatly divergent ages across the island. Later workers realized that there were fundamental differences between the rocks from different parts of the island and that in some places they seemed to have no logical relation to each other. At this same time the theory of plate tectonics was being formulated. In the late 1960s and early 70s, the geology of the island of Newfoundland served as a Rosetta Stone for defining the burgeoning theory of Plate Tectonics, the unifying concept of earth sciences. This theory posits that the Earth's Crust comprises a series of large and small plates that are in constant motion above the hot and plastic Mantle. Newfoundland and Labrador currently sits on the huge North American plate, which extends from the middle of the Atlantic Ocean at the Mid-Atlantic Ridge north to include Greenland and the western half of Iceland, west to the coastlines of western North America, and south to the Caribbean. 'Newfoundland' wasn't always part of this plate.

According to the Plate Tectonic paradigm, plates spread apart from each other along huge chains of cracks in the Crust where fresh magma spews out from the Mantle, ultimately forming sea floor crust and opening an ocean. The Mid-Atlantic Ridge is one of these locations and the North American Plate is continually moving away from the European Plate at an average rate of ca. 2.5 cm a year. The Earth is not increasing in size; therefore, if plates move away from each other in one place, they must collide and crash into each other at other places. This is what is happening on the west coast of North America where the oceanic crust of the Pacific Plate is banging into the North American Plate. These collision zones can have three broad forms, (1) one plate may sink beneath another, (2) the plates may just crumble together in a mass (as the Indian Plate is doing with the Eurasian Plate in the Himalayan Mountains), or, (3) as in the case of the San Andreas Fault of southern California, they may simply move laterally, and drastically, past each other creating earthquake zones. The first two examples are classic Mountain Belts where different portions of Crust and Mantle mingle together. As so aptly expressed by Dr. Martin Feely of Galway University, Ireland, plate tectonics basically indicates that the Earth's Crust is constantly rending and mending.

Geologically the island of Newfoundland comprises three massive crustal blocks separated by large regional faults that transect the island. These blocks are: (1) the Avalon Zone, comprising the Avalon and Burin Peninsulas, eastern Newfoundland to Dover and south to Terrenceville and west to include the Connaigre Peninsula, and small packages along the south coast to La Poile Bay; (2) the Dunnage Zone, which extends from the Avalon Zone west to the west side of the Baie Verte Peninsula southwestwards along the Grand Lake to the Codroy Valley; and (3) the Humber Zone, all that area to the west of the Dunnage Zone. (There is a fourth, small, block of mainly metamorphic rocks called the Gander

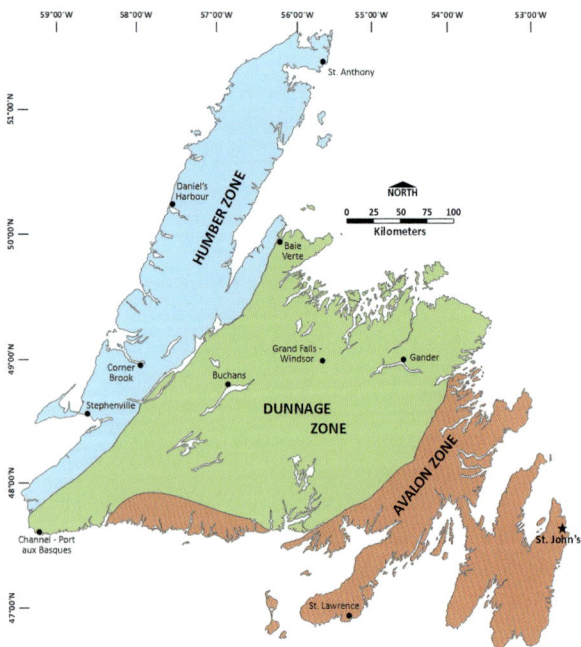

Zone between the Avalon and Dunnage zones, which for simplicity is herein considered as part of the Dunnage Zone). The Avalon and Dunnage Zones are separated by the Dover Fault system and the Humber and Dunnage Zones are separated by the Baie Verte Line–Long Range fault system.

The Avalon Zone broadly comprises Late Precambrian sedimentary and volcanic rocks with granites from near Holyrood, Clarenville down to St. Bernard's, and the northern portions of the Connaigre Peninsula. Most of the sedimentary rocks are black to green and were deposited in deep ocean basins (such as those at Mistaken Point). A subvariety was deposited as distinctive green to black layers called 'turbidites.' These types of rocks formed as repetitive layers in deep marine environments below continental slopes, derived from episodic pulses of sediment shed off the slope. The distinctively red sandstones and conglomerates of Signal Hill and the Southside Hills represent a ca. 600 Ma oxidized deltaic environment.

In Conception Bay, Precambrian sedimentary, volcanic, and plutonic rocks are overlain by Cambrian and Ordovician sedimentary rocks. Along the Manuels River, the Cambrian shales contain classic trilobite fossils. The Ordovician rocks on Bell Island and Kellys Island are exposed as cliffs that shallowly dip northward into Conception Bay. The Bell Island rocks are most famous for their thick layers of iron ore, which were mined from 1895 to 1966. These iron deposits are much younger than the vast 2.0 Ga iron ores of western Labrador and are classified as oolitic because they are composed of small spherical grains of iron oxide. They formed by precipitation of iron from seawater. The geology of the Avalon Zone, and in particular the Cambrian and Ordovician rocks, are superbly explained at the Manuels River Hibernia Interpretation Centre in Conception Bay South. During the summer months, the Bell Island Mines and Museum are open for underground tours.

*(left) Turbidite sedimentary layers; these were deposited off the Precambrian continental slope, Branch; (right) Red sandstones and conglomerates representing Late Phanerozoic deltas once connected to what is now North Africa and the British Isles, Cape Spear*

Although the Avalon Zone contains generally old rocks, some of the youngest rocks on the island are also present in the zone. The St. Lawrence granite, near St. Lawrence on the Burin Peninsula, is a relative youngster at ca. 374 Ma. Fluorite veins were mined at St. Lawrence from 1933 to 1978, 1986 to 1990, and 2018 to 2022; there is much hope that the mine will reopen in 2026. Small ca. 200 Ma dykes and sills of gabbro intrude rocks on the southern Avalon probably related to the opening of the Atlantic Ocean.

Some of the rocks that comprise the Avalon Zone match those in southern Ireland and England, and parts of North Africa. Around 600 Ma, these landmasses constituted a micro-continent called Avalonia, which was separating from the much larger continent Laurentia (proto-North America) along the Iapetus Ocean. About 500 Ma, the ocean spreading stopped and the ocean began to close as Avalonia, started to move towards Laurentia. Eventually the continents collided forming the Appalachian Mountain Belt and the Iapetus Ocean disappeared (ca. 420 Ma). Large-scale plate tectonic processes largely stopped in Newfoundland after the Carboniferous until around 130 Ma when the Atlantic Ocean began to open and separate North America from Europe. The offshore oil-bearing sedimentary basins formed ca. 100 Ma as the ocean opened.

The Dunnage Zone predominantly consists of volcanic and sedimentary rocks deposited in an oceanic environment during both opening and closing of the Iapetus Ocean. For instance, many outcrops along the shorelines of Notre Dame Bay consist of pillow basalts. Large bodies of granite are also very common, most especially along the eastern edge of the zone. These granites formed from the melting of rocks deep in the Crust. The melting was due to enhanced temperatures and pressures induced by plate collisions during formation of the Appalachian Mountain Belt. Since the granite magmas formed from the melting of deep pre-existing crust, they rose through the crust to become masses of plutonic rock that engulfed older rocks. High-grade metamorphic rocks occur near Gander and along the south coast near Port aux Basques.

The Humber Zone is probably the most intricate of all three zones, consisting of a wide range of rock types and geological environments with the greatest spread of ages. The ca. 1.6 Ga gneisses, schists, and foliated granites in the core of the Great Northern Peninsula are ancient crust of the Canadian Shield ('Laurentia'). The coastal plain along the western side of the Great Northern Peninsula is underlain by Late Precambrian to Cambrian–Ordovician limestones and sandstones-shales that were deposited on an ancient shoreline.

The Tablelands and Lewis Hills, and other smaller occurrences of serpentine, represent pieces of ocean crust and upper Mantle from the Dunnage Zone that were pushed unto the Laurentian continental margin during the formation of the Appalachian Mountains and closure of the Iapetus Ocean. These packages of Mantle and ocean crust are called 'ophiolites.'

The massive mountain of rock that constitutes the Tablelands in Gros Morne National Park readily stands out on the landscape of western Newfoundland as a unique zone (deep brown and plantless), so much so that some people suggest that the Tablelands are alien. And alien these rocks really are because they are huge pieces of serpentinized ultramafic rock from the Earth's Mantle; they belong in Hades not on the Earth's surface. The sublime and relatively accessible rocks of the Tablelands are unique on the Earth's surface in being one of the very few places where one can visit the Mantle without doing the impossible and journeying through the Earth's

*(top) Field trip on the serpentinized ultramafic rock that comprises the Tablelands; (bottom) Tablelands Mountain behind Woody Point, view from Norris Point*

Crust, and in fact geologists from all over the world travel to visit this geological mecca. This easy access to the Mantle is one reason that Gros Morne National Park has been designated a UNESCO world heritage site.

Aside from the Tablelands, there are examples of ophiolitic rocks in the Lewis Hills south of Corner Brook, and smaller zones near St. Anthony, along the Baie Verte Peninsula, in the Annieopsquotch Mountains south of Beothuk Lake, in the core of central Newfoundland around Mount Cormack, and through the central portions of Gander Lake.

Since all of these serpentinized ultramafic rock outcrops represent remnants of the Earth's Mantle, their presence along the edges of western and central Newfoundland attests to the tremendous geological forces that moved these rocks from the Mantle to the Earth's surface. Their existence also indicates that the island of Newfoundland was constructed from different zones of the Earth that crashed and stuck together, driven by the relentless propulsion of plate tectonics.

During the Carboniferous, limestones, sandstones, shales, and rare coal were deposited in shallow marine basins around Deer Lake, the Port au Port Peninsula, and the Anguille Mountains; in the case of the Deer Lake Basin, some of the sediments were deposited in river environments on land. These small basins were part of a wide-spread period of relative quiescence during which coal beds were deposited in Cape Breton Island and red sandstones were deposited on Prince Edward Island.

*Gypsum cliffs, Kippens*

The gypsum and salt deposits on the Port au Port Peninsula formed from the evaporation of seawater on arid coastal salt flats (so-called sabhkas); these rocks are white and very soft. Small, thin coal layers, near Grand Lake, in the Codroy Valley, and in the St. George's Bay area formed from the accumulations of plants in ca. 300 Ma swamps. Although small occurrences of 300 Ma fossil wood are present on the Port au Port Peninsula and near Deer Lake, no remains of dinosaurs have yet been found in Newfoundland rocks and may not be as the rocks are probably too old.

The last major event in the geological history of Newfoundland was continental glaciation (see Glaciation). The glaciers stripped the soil away exposing barren rock and sculpting the island topography. The glaciers also carried tremendous quantities of rock debris, which were dropped all over the landscape as ubiquitous till; the bane of gardeners and geologists. The most spectacular member of the till family are large boulders scattered across the landscape, so-called 'erratics.' The Earth, however, is a restless planet, and nothing stays the same for long. For instance, the evidence of recent glaciation in Newfoundland is slowly being covered up and even erratics are being erased.

*Erratic being overgrown by black spruce tree—Eel Brook Trail, Norris Arm*

## TRACKING ANIMALS

Winter is a magical time of year when snow blankets the Newfoundland landscape, making it an excellent opportunity for nature observers. No creature can set foot on the snow cover without leaving its mark, and without summer vegetation, feeding activities are easier to spot.

Although most trees and shrubs have lost their leaves, they can still be identified by their buds and other characteristics. It is useful to identify winter trees and shrubs as many are food sources for animals and sometimes the feeding traces on a plant are sufficient to identify the animal doing the eating. Most of the conifers, however, are evergreen and can be readily identified as at other times of year. Conifer seeds are major food sources for many birds as well as the red squirrel.

The most common animal tracks in the coniferous forest are those of the snowshoe hare (introduced) with the familiar pattern of two larger hind prints slightly ahead of the two smaller forefeet. The red squirrel (also introduced), unlike many of its close relatives, is active winter long. In forested areas where it has left the safety of the trees and scampered over the snow between trees, squirrel tracks, somewhat like miniature versions of the hare, are quite visible.

Moose (introduced) tracks are commonly seen during winter in wooded areas. If the snow is not too deep it is possible to see both the hoof marks, and sometimes also the smaller dewclaws, which the moose uses to splay out its feet for increased surface area in softer snow conditions. In deeper snow, moose tracks are just deep holes in the snow and actual hoof marks are typically unobservable.

In very deep snow conditions, it can be very tiring for moose to move, hence several moose will congregate in a wooded area, where plenty of food is available, and flatten the snow with well-worn

_< Hare and Squirrel tracks_

*(left) Moose browsings; (right) Fox tracks*

tracks. Such well-trodden areas are referred to as 'moose yards,' and it is not uncommon for several dozen moose to congregate in a yard.

Red fox tracks are frequently encountered in winter snow. At first glance their tracks can easily be confused with those of small dogs, except that in firm snow, a hard, shallow, v-shaped ridge on the pad is present, which is absent from dog prints. Typically though, snow conditions do not allow the fox ridge impression to show through and other means must be used to distinguish between dog and fox tracks. The two easiest ways are the straightness of the tracks and registering. Foxes, and coyotes, especially in open areas, tend to walk directly from one point to the next such that their tracks tend to be in straight lines. Dogs, on the other hand, tend to wander here and there, so their tracks are rarely straight. The other way to distinguish fox (and coyote) tracks from those of dogs is to examine whether the animal registered or not. Many wild animals, especially carnivores, tend to place their hind feet in the prints made by the forefeet. When hunting, this ensures that the hind feet do not tread on something that will create a noise (a snapped twig for instance) and scare away potential prey. Foxes and coyotes show registering in their tracks, whereas dogs do not. Dog tracks often leave prints that sometimes overlap, but most often do not, leaving an untidy trail of prints.

Coyote tracks are very similar to those of foxes but do not show the ridge on the hard pad in their prints. Coyote prints are also larger than those of the fox.

The other major mammal carnivore on the island is the Canada lynx, a very wary animal, which tends to stay away from areas frequented by humans, thus their tracks are rarely seen, just like the animals themselves. During winter, fur grows over the pads on the paws of lynx so the individual prints do not have distinct pad marks, the print appearing as a rounded depression in the snow. As with other members of the cat family, the claws are retracted into sheaths when walking, so claw marks do not show in lynx prints. It is easy, therefore, to distinguish fox (and coyote) tracks from those of lynx as members of the dog family have claw marks in their tracks. Since fox, coyote, and lynx all hunt for snowshoe hare in winter, it is always worth examining predator tracks in the vicinity of hare tracks.

The ermine, or short-tailed weasel, is an active predator of both shrews and voles in winter. Its tracks through snow are quite distinctive; pairs of narrow prints, that often, when followed, suddenly disappear! The ermine is not a miniature Houdini but has plunged into the snow in search of prey tunnels. If it detects movement in the snow beneath, it can dive into the snow and enter a vole tunnel; it is slender enough to move through a tunnel in search of a live meal. It will then re-emerge back onto the snow surface. If it has been successful in its hunt, the tracks may even show the drag marks of the head and tail of its prey as it re-emerges and carries it somewhere safe to feast on!

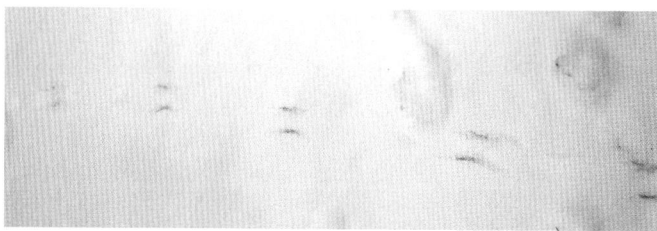

*Ermine tracks*

Mink (introduced) tracks are like those of the ermine but are larger and more likely to be encountered near bodies of water where it can hunt for fish. The river otter, the aquatic cousin of the ermine and mink, is easily distinguished from the others since the former has webbed feet, which show in its tracks. The otter is a very playful and sociable animal and a group of them will often 'play' in the snow by sliding down hills, producing an obvious furrow in the snow. Mink will also do the same on occasions, and both will also slide on their bellies through flat snow, propelling themselves along with their feet. The slides are easily distinguished as otters show the webs in their tracks whereas mink do not.

Since muskrat spend much of their time below the ice in winter, their tracks are rarely seen, but if they do venture out above the ice, their tracks are easily identified by their webbed feet and the tail drag between the footprints.

Meadow vole tracks are also common in winter but are not that obvious because of their small size. When the snow cover is quite shallow their dainty tracks are easily seen, but as the snow deepens, they spend more time in burrows beneath the snow, safe from both predators and the cold winter weather. When the snow melts in the spring, the vole burrows are revealed as extensive runways, particularly in grassy areas where the runways are lined with dead grass.

The diminutive, masked shrew (introduced) cannot move easily through deep snow and so, like the vole, spends much of its time burrowing beneath the snow, often using the same burrows as the voles. Shrew tracks are only found, therefore, at the beginning of winter when there has been a light dusting of snow. Then it is sometimes possible to find tracks looking like little pencil prod marks in the snow. If the snow is a little deeper, it is possible to find furrows produced by the shrew as it literally ploughed its way through the snow. If the furrow suddenly ends without any sign of further tracks, this indicates that the shrew has encountered deeper snow and has tunneled into it.

In addition to prints and tracks in the snow, one can also look for other types of animal evidence including feeding activities, scats, and other signs. Hares feed on buds of low growing shrubs snipping them

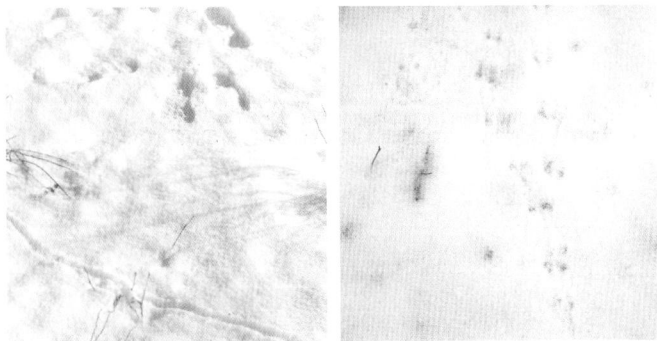

*(left) Shrew tracks; (right) Vole tracks*

off with their sharp teeth. Moose often feed on the same buds, but since they only have lower incisor teeth, they tend to snap the buds off leaving a jagged edge on the branch quite unlike the sharp snip of the hare. Grouse and ptarmigan also snip off buds but usually from less robust branches than hare or moose. Hares will also scrape off the bark from a variety of shrubs and trees and their teeth marks are clearly seen. Voles feed on low-growing shrubs such as blueberry, but the buds they feed on are minute in comparison to hares and moose.

A number of animals deposit their scat (feces) on the snow and those of hare, moose, fox, and grouse are easy to spot and identify. Several mammals will use trees to help sharpen their claws leaving clear claw marks on the tree. The size of the marks and the height above the ground (or snow) will usually reveal the owner (lynx or bear).

Many types of birds frequent the forests in winter and it is much more likely that a winter observer will spot birds rather than mammals. For many birds, the forests contain food sources including conifer seeds, berries, buds, and overwintering insects. Juncos, black-capped and boreal chickadees, and blue and grey jays, are all familiar residents of the winter forests. Areas with plenty of berries, particularly 'dogberries' (mountain ash berries), can attract large flocks of winter-visiting robins, as well as Bohemian and cedar waxwings. Flocks of brightly coloured pine grosbeaks, purple finches, and red crossbills also visit the forests to eat the seeds of fir and spruce.

Bird tracks in the snow are less frequently encountered than the birds themselves, since many of them are tree dwellers and rarely land on the snow. Juncos spend a lot of time feeding on the ground, so their tracks are common. Since these birds hop over the snow, rather than walk, their tracks show pairs of prints side by side. Crow tracks are also common as they forage for any type of food. Since crows walk on the ground rather than hop, their tracks show

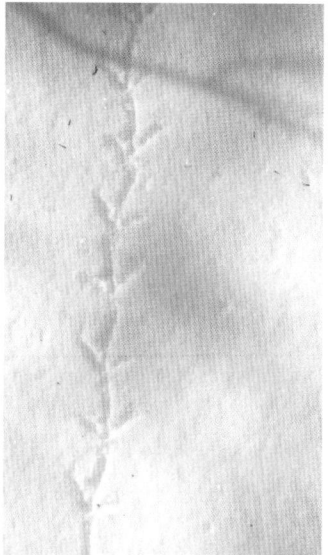

*Grouse tracks*

a walking pattern, one foot ahead of the other and to the side. Crows are lazy walkers, and their tracks show the drag marks of their talons.

Another common bird track in winter belongs to members of the grouse and ptarmigan family. The ruffed grouse feeds on the buds of shrubs projecting up above the snow. The clear, large, typical bird foot pattern of three toes pointing forward and one backward, is particularly distinctive for the grouse. The tracks in the snow extend for many metres in fairly straight lines, with one foot placed directly ahead of the other. The willow ptarmigan has similar feeding preferences but is a resident of more open areas. Ptarmigans are well adapted to a winter life. They take on white winter plumage for camouflage against the snow, and grow feathers over their legs to decrease heat loss and feathers in between the toes to increase the area of the feet.

*Yellow-Legged Gull*

## WINTER GULLS

In the last few years St. John's has become a 'mecca' for bird watchers interested in spotting seabirds not usually encountered anywhere else in North America. These seabirds, gulls to be exact, are winter 'tourists' from the Arctic, and even Europe, that visit Quidi Vidi Lake in the heart of St. John's. Each winter thousands of gulls congregate on the ice covering this lake, and since there is a walking trail all around it, there is no lack of vantage points from which to view the gulls. The other great thing about this venue is its ease of access since it is so close to the city centre. In addition to the gulls, the observer is also often rewarded by the sight of bald eagles as well as other birds of prey.

Some seventeen different species of gulls (including one kittiwake) have been identified at this lake (home to North America's oldest continuous sporting event, the annual St. John's Regatta) with eight winter visitors including three from Europe, four from the Arctic, and even one from Asia. The descriptions that follow are for the seventeen species that have been seen at Quidi Vidi Lake in recent winters. Some of the descriptions for the gulls here may differ from those discussed in the earlier bird section since their winter plumage may be quite different from their summer plumage.

## A QUICK GUIDE TO WINTER GULLS

**Black or very dark grey back:** Lesser black-backed, Great black-backed, Slaty-backed

**Black wing tips:** Black-tailed, Common, Black-headed, Franklin's, Herring, Ring-billed, Yellow-legged, Black-legged kittiwake

**No black colour:** Bonaparte's, Glaucous, Iceland, Ivory, Kumlien's, Thayer's

### Black-Tailed Gull
*Larus crassirostris*

**Descr** medium-sized gull with grey wings and a black tail. Yellow bill has a red and black spot at the tip. Legs are yellow. **Distribution** a vagrant to northeast America from East Asia.

### Bonaparte's Gull
*Chroicocephalus philadelphia*

**Descr** one of the smallest gulls, similar in size to a tern. In winter it is mostly white with a light grey back. The head is white with a black patch behind the eye (similar to the Black-Headed Gull) but the bill is black. The wings are grey with black trailing edges and showing a white triangular area on the leading edge of the wing. **Distribution** its usual range is Alaska, and western and central Canada.

## Black-Headed Gull

*Chroicocephalus ridibundus*

**Descr** while this gull does display a dark brown head in summer, in winter the head is mostly white with a small black patch behind the eye. The back is grey. The legs are bright red and the wing tips and tail are black. The bill is orange with a black tip. **Distribution** its usual range is Iceland and Eurasia.

## Common Gull (Mew Gull)

*Larus canus*

**Descr** a small gull with a white head and grey body, and black wing tips. The bill is thin and greenish-yellow in colour, as are the legs. In winter the head is streaked with brown, and the bill shows a black band around it (as in the Ring-Billed Gull). **Distribution** its usual range is Eurasia and northwest North America.

## Franklin's Gull

*Leucophaeus pipixcan*

**Descr** a small gull with dark grey wings and back. The wing tips are black and there is a white band separating the black tips from the grey of the rest of the wing. In summer the head is black, but in winter the head loses the black and is then whitish with darker streaking on the back of the head. The bill is dark in colour, and the legs are orange. **Distribution** a visitor from the West Coast of North America.

## Glaucous Gull

*Larus hyperboreus*

**Descr** a large white gull, bigger than a Herring Gull, with light grey wings and lacking any black colouration. Has a yellow eye ring. The bill is yellow with a red spot, as in the herring gull. The legs are pinkish. **Distribution** a visitor from the Arctic.

## Great Black-Backed Gull

*Larus marinus*

**Descr** a large very distinctive gull with its black back and wings. The large yellow bill has a red spot, as in the Herring Gull. The legs are pinkish in colour. **Distribution** a year-round resident of the island.

## Herring Gull
*Larus argentatus*

**Descr** our most common gull. The wings and back are light grey, and the wing tips are black. The bill is yellow with a prominent red spot. The legs are pinkish. **Distribution** a year-round resident of the island.

## Iceland Gull
*Larus glaucoides*

**Descr** a white gull with light grey wings, lacking any black colouration. Has a yellow eye and a red eye ring. The yellow bill shows a red spot, as in the Herring Gull. **Distribution** a winter visitor from Greenland.

## Ivory Gull
*Pagophila eburnea*

**Descr** a very small (pigeon-sized) pure white gull. The bill is black with a yellow tip. The legs are black. **Distribution** a visitor from the eastern Arctic.

## Kumlien's Gull
*Larus glaucoides kumlieni*

**Descr** a pale gull very similar to the Iceland Gull but has dark grey markings near the wing tips while the closely related Iceland does not. Is thought to have been derived from the Iceland Gull. **Distribution** an Arctic visitor.

## Lesser Black-Backed Gull
*Larus fuscus*

**Descr** very similar to the Great Black-Backed Gull but smaller (similar in size to the Herring Gull). The yellow bill has a red dot but the legs are yellowish (pinkish in the Great Black-Backed). **Distribution** a visitor from Europe.

## Ring-Billed Gull

*Larus delawarensis*

**Descr** similar to the Herring Gull but smaller. Has a black band around its bill and yellowish or greenish legs. Light grey back and wings. Wing tips are black. **Distribution** a year-round resident of the island.

## Slaty-Backed Gull

*Larus schistisagus*

**Descr** a very large gull with a dark grey back and wings, the latter with a white trailing edge. The bill is yellow with an orange-red spot at the tip. The legs are pink. **Distribution** usually breeds in Alaska but travels widely.

## Thayer's Gull

*Larus glaucoides thayeri*

**Descr** very similar to the Herring Gull in size and colouring. Can be distinguished from the Herring Gull by its brownish eyes (yellow in the Herring Gull) and the red eye ring (yellow in the Herring Gull). The wing tips are dark grey (black in Herring Gull). The legs are pink. **Distribution** an Arctic visitor.

## Yellow-Legged Gull

*Larus michahellis*

**Descr** a large gull formerly regarded as a sub-species of the Caspian Gull. Has grey wings and back, and a black tail. The yellow bill has a red spot near the tip. The legs are yellow. **Distribution** a vagrant to North America from the Mediterranean.

## Black-Legged Kittiwake

*Rissa tridactyla*

**Descr** a small gull (smaller than the Ring-Billed). The wings and back are grey with black wing tips. The bill is yellow but has no markings. The legs are black. **Distribution** a year-round resident of the island.

## ICEBERGS

For most people, icebergs are wonders of nature that they only see in photos or on films such as *Titanic*. For people living in or visiting this province at the right time and place, icebergs are real spectacles of nature as they glide down our coasts or become stranded in shallow bays. There are few other temperate places on the planet where you can see these floating mountains of white ice. Each year we still marvel at them; somehow, icebergs retain their mystery, even if we have seen them time and time again. The town of Twillingate on the northeast coast advertises itself as the 'Iceberg Capital of the World' and is a good place to view icebergs, as are many locations elsewhere on the northeast coast; some icebergs will make it as far south as St. John's. The best viewing time for icebergs is spring and early summer (April, May, and June).

Most of the icebergs travelling past Newfoundland come from about 100 glaciers that calve icebergs in Greenland, while the rest come from the eastern Canadian Arctic islands. Each year, around 40,000 medium to large icebergs calve from Greenland glaciers and about 1% to 2% make it as far south as 48° north latitude (see Sea Ice in Climate). The numbers vary greatly from year to year, and most are seen in spring and early summer.

The icebergs appearing off the island were usually produced the previous year. They then travel north into Baffin Bay before heading south through the Davis Strait, along the Labrador coast, and then along the northeast coast of the island. A few make it south through the Strait of Belle Isle. While most icebergs melt before they can reach warmer climes, icebergs have been seen in Bermuda and Ireland. Since the density of ice is less than that of seawater, about 85% of the iceberg is below the waterline. For more information on these magnificent wonders of nature, please refer to one of the following books: *Icebergs of Newfoundland and Labrador* or *Iceberg Alley: A Journal of Nature's Most Awesome Migration*.

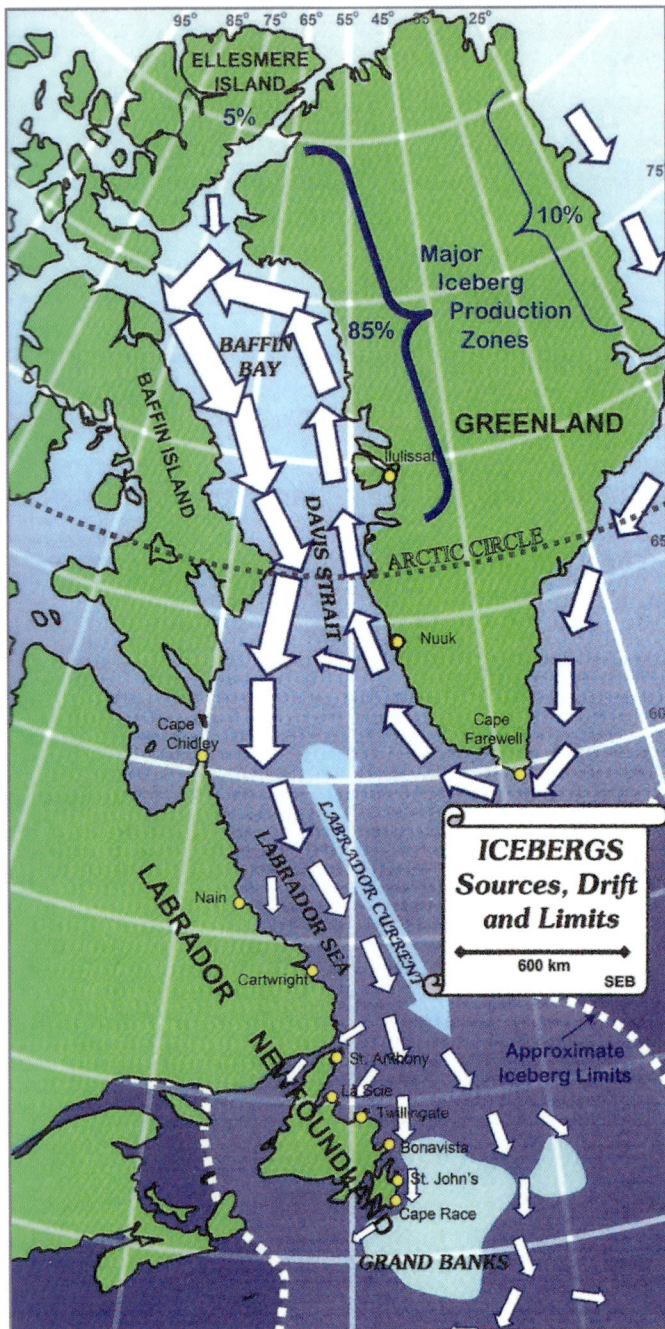

ELLESMERE ISLAND
5%

10%

Major Iceberg Production Zones

85%

BAFFIN BAY

BAFFIN ISLAND

GREENLAND

Ilulissat

DAVIS STRAIT

ARCTIC CIRCLE

Nuuk

Cape Chidley

Cape Farewell

LABRADOR

Nain

LABRADOR SEA

LABRADOR CURRENT

Cartwright

NEWFOUNDLAND

St. Anthony

La Scie

Twillingate

Bonavista

St. John's

Cape Race

GRAND BANKS

**ICEBERGS**
*Sources, Drift and Limits*

600 km

SEB

Approximate Iceberg Limits

The table below explains the terms used for various sizes of iceberg ranging from growlers (small) to very large.

| NAME | HEIGHT (M) | LENGTH (M) | WEIGHT (TONS) |
|---|---|---|---|
| Growler | less than 1 | less than 5 | 1-37 |
| Bergy bit | 1-4 | 5-15 | 38-1000 |
| Small | 5-15 | 15-60 | 1000-65,000 |
| Medium | 16-45 | 60-120 | 65,000-500,000 |
| Large | 46-75 | 120-220 | 500,000-2,900,000 |
| Very Large | over 75 | over 220 | over 2,900,000 |

### A QUICK GUIDE TO ICEBERG SHAPES

Blocky

Pinnacled

Domed

Tabular

Drydocked

Wedged

Icebergs exhibit a variety of shapes but for the most part fit one of six different categories. These are tabular, domed, pinnacled, wedged, drydocked, or blocky. These six types are illustrated in the chart above, and photos of each type are also shown on the following pages.

(top) BLOCKY: A flat-topped iceberg with steep sides; (bottom) DOMED: An iceberg that is smooth, with a rounded top

(top) DRYDOCKED: An iceberg that has eroded and has a U-shaped slot near or at water level, with two or more pinnacles or columns; (bottom) PINNACLED: An iceberg that has a central spire or pyramid and may have additional spires

(top) *TABULAR: A flat-topped iceberg with a width usually more than five times its height;* (bottom) *WEDGED: An iceberg with flat surfaces, steep on one side and gradually sloping to the water on the other side*

**A**way from the major population centres and their human-generated light pollution, the night sky in Newfoundland can be an excellent place to obtain a Northen Hemisphere view of stars and planets. There is a tendency to think that one must have expensive telescopes and other equipment to undertake astronomical observations, but the best instrument to start with is the unaided eye. If you are totally new to observing, get to know the major constellations first; they are the guides to the sky. Just as you would use a map to find your way, a star chart is the same for the sky. You start from a familiar place and then explore more distant areas.

An important tip for successful celestial observations is don't try to observe too much in one night. Pick an area of the sky and get to know it well. Then pick another area nearby and concentrate on that. Trying to observe too much in one night is the best way for the beginner to get totally confused.

## CONSTELLATIONS

The International Astronomical Union has divided the entire sky into eighty-eight distinct constellations. Constellations are essentially patterns defined by the brightest stars visible from the Earth's surface. These patterns and their names reflect cultural interpretations and values. Some can be seen all year round, some in certain seasons, and others are never seen unless you travel to the Southern Hemisphere. What we refer to as constellations are actually 'asterisms', shapes created by virtually connecting bright stars to make patterns. The Big Dipper is an example of an asterism, and we use asterisms to navigate the night sky.

Every star visible from Earth is located within the boundaries of one of the eighty-eight constellations, but not every star is actually part of its host constellation. For example, the asterism Leo consists of a 'backwards question mark' and 'triangle', but the constellation Leo includes many more stars. When a star, planet, or galaxy is said to be in the constellation Leo, it could be anywhere within the defined boundaries of constellation Leo, but not necessarily in the easily identifiable shapes of the asterism Leo.

## PLANETS

Planets move East to West across the sky but aren't fixed like stars in a constellation. The word planet comes from the Greek for 'wanderer'.

While observing a particular constellation on a given night, you might see a star-like object in it that has a different position than a week earlier; this object is probably a planet. The planets look like stars but change position, over time, relative to the background stars. Planets that orbit nearer the Sun than the Earth move faster, and their positional changes are noticeable even to the casual observer. Planets far away from the Sun move very slowly and will often appear in the same constellation for years. To help find the planets, we list the constellations in which the planets appear, although they have no relationship to the constellations.

Once there were nine defined planets, but now there are only eight as Pluto is no longer considered to be one of the regular planets. It can only be seen by a dedicated observer with a large telescope. Mercury, Venus, Mars, Jupiter, and Saturn are easily identified without a telescope or binoculars, but any one planet will not necessarily be visible at any one time of the year, depending on the Earth's position relative to the planet and the Sun. Throughout the year, planets vary greatly in brightness, depending on their distance from Earth and orientation to the Sun. It is interesting to observe Venus pass through its phases as our Moon does. Mercury and Venus are always near the Sun, so observers must be cautious about observing them with optical instruments.

## HOW TO USE A STAR CHART

A star chart is essentially a map of constellations. For this introduction to the night sky in Newfoundland, we will not use full star charts, but rather smaller charts of observable constellations to understand basic celestial distributions. If you become fascinated by the night sky, you may wish to invest in software. We do not endorse any product but, here are some that might be of use: Diffraction Astronomy, Redshift, and Starry Night. Since planets travel so much across the night sky on an annual basis, star charts with their locations become quickly outdated.

From Newfoundland, the Big Dipper constellation is visible year-round, subject to weather, and is the best place to start (Chart 1). Once you find the Big Dipper, you can observe the other major stars in the constellation Ursa Major (UMa), the large bear, of which the Big Dipper is part. Use the pointer stars (Merak and Dubhe) in the dipper to find the Pole Star (Polaris), which is very close to true north from your location. The Pole Star is the brightest star in the Little Dipper (Ursa minor, UMi).

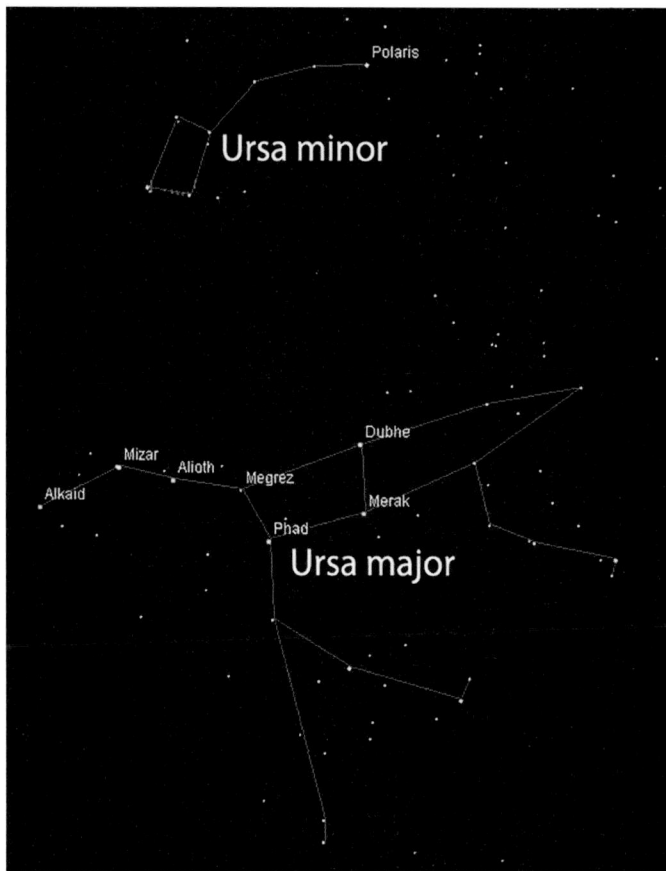

*Chart 1*

Chart 2 shows the locations of many prominent constellations in the northern sky. Starting with UMa (Ursa Major) and UMi (Little Dipper), arrows on the chart point to other constellations on the chart (e.g., from UMa to Polaris and UMi).

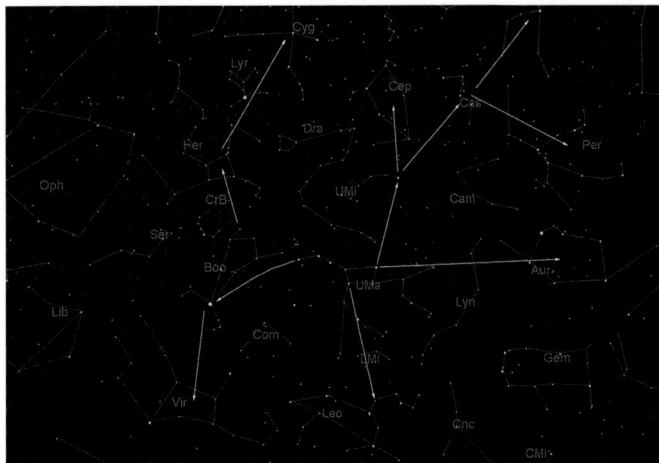

Chart 2

From the Little Dipper, and in particular Polaris, you can find constellation Cassiopeia (Cas), which looks like a letter W (or M).

Now look at the middle star in the handle of the Big Dipper (UMa). If your eyesight is good, you should see that the star labelled Mizar is actually two stars very close together (Chart 3). If you have a pair of binoculars, check to make sure. Follow the handle of the dipper as it curves (you may have to wait for the Big Dipper to be in a convenient position). It seems to point to a bright star. This is Arcturus, the brightest star in the constellation Bootes (Boo). Some say Bootes looks like a big ice-cream cone in the sky.

Once you have found Bootes, follow the imaginary lines (see Chart 2) up to the constellation Hercules (Her) and then on through Lyra (Lyr) to Cygnus (Cyg), the swan. Chart 4, on the opposite page, is a close up of the Her-Lyr-Cyg constellations.

The two stars in the top of the bowl of the Big Dipper point to the constellation Auriga (Aur) whereas the stars in the bowl near the handle attachment point to Leo (Leo).

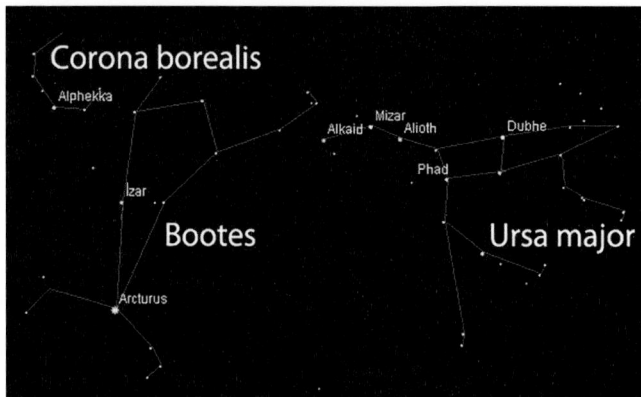

*Chart 3*

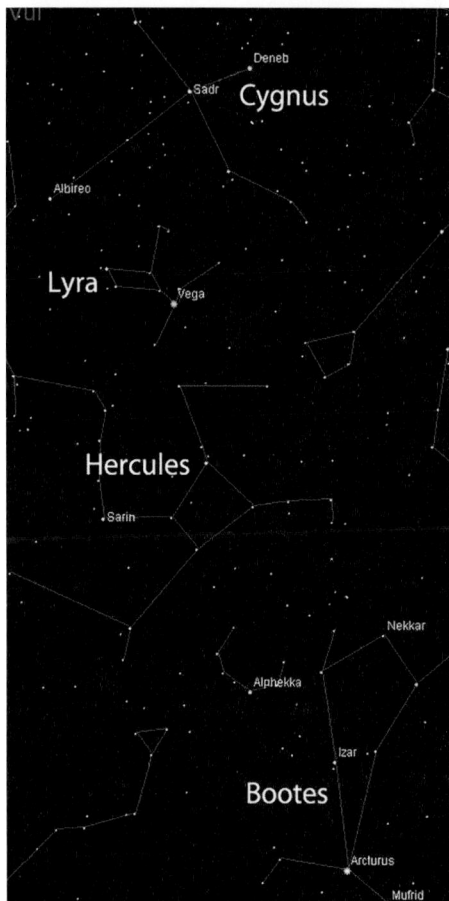

*Chart 4*

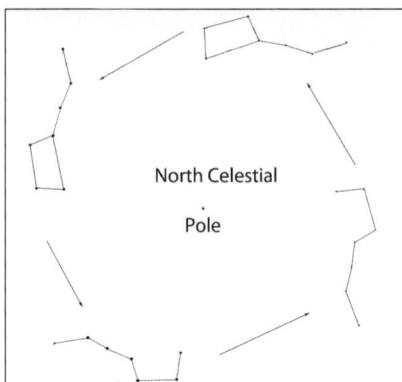

North Celestial
Pole

*Chart 5*

Watch the Big Dipper over a few hours and you will see that it and the whole sky rotates around the North Celestial Pole (Chart 5). The Pole Star, Polaris, is very near this point. Once you know the Big Dipper and the constellations around it, you can view the rotation for other areas of the sky.

In the winter, the constellation Orion (Ori) is easy to find; note charts below with red names are for the winter sky. Locate the three stars that make Orion's belt (Alnitak, Alnilam, and Mintaka). In your imagination, connect the three stars in the belt and project towards the upper right. You will see a bright star, Aldebaran, the brightest star in the constellation Taurus (Tau), the Bull. Keep projecting and you will come across the Pleiades, a beautiful cluster of stars that deserve a lot of observing time when you have binoculars or a telescope (Chart 6).

Now go back to Orion's belt (Chart 7) and project a line to the lower left and find Sirius, the Dog Star, the brightest star in the sky. It is in the constellation Canis Major (CMa).

The bright star in the upper left of Orion (Chart 8) is the supergiant star Betelgeuse. This is the closest star to Earth and it will go supernova sometime in the future; some suggest even in coming decades. To the upper left of Betelgeuse you will find two stars, Castor and Pollux, in the constellation Gemini (Gem).

From the constellation Gemini, it is not difficult to find Leo, the Lion, the front of which looks like a backwards question mark. Once you find Leo, the Big Dipper and other familiar northern constellations are easy to locate.

Chart 6. Note: star names in red indicate the winter sky.

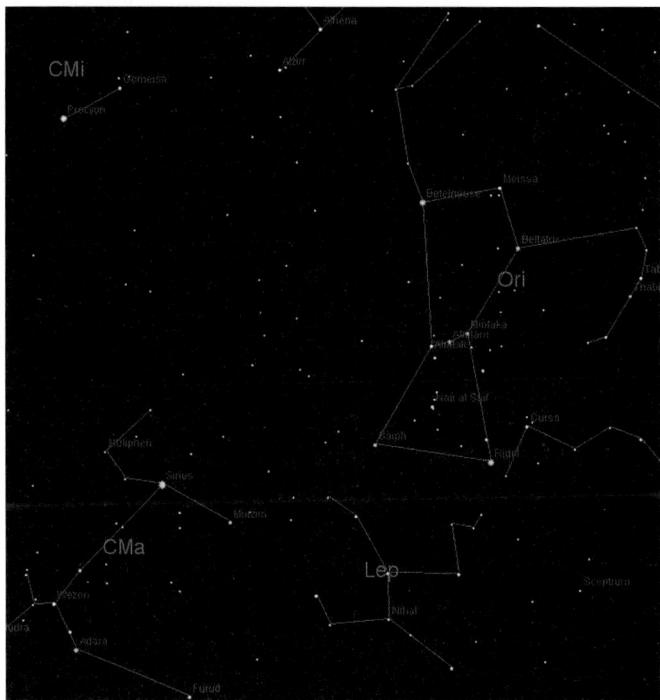

Chart 7

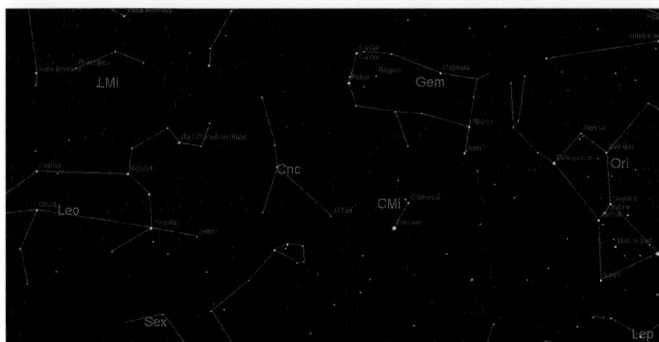

Chart 8

The list below gives you an idea of when to view the major constellations.

## CIRCUMPOLAR CONSTELLATIONS

(These can be seen all year when above the horizon.)

Cepheus (Cep)                    Ursa Major (UMa)
Cassiopeia (Cas)                 Ursa Minor (UMi)
Draco (Dra)

## FALL CONSTELLATIONS

Andromeda (And)                  Pegasus (Peg)
Aquarius (Aqr)                   Perseus (Per)
Aries (Ari)                      Pisces (Psc)
Cetus (Cet)

## WINTER CONSTELLATIONS

Auriga (Aur)                     Gemini (Gem)
Canis Major (CMa)                Monoceros (Mon)
Canis Minor (CMi)                Orion (Ori)
Eridanus (Eri)                   Taurus (Tau)

*Moon over Codroy Valley*

## THE MOON

The Moon moves from West to East, and the Earth rotates in the same direction. Because the Earth rotates faster on its axis, the Moon appears to move from East to West. The Moon moves easterly one moon diameter (0.5 degree) each hour. Use binoculars to watch the Moon when it is near a star, and you will see the easterly motion and possibly see the star as it disappears behind the moon. This is known as an occultation.

### LUNAR ECLIPSES

Lunar eclipses (when the Earth is directly between the Moon and the Sun) can be observed with the naked eye or with binoculars. If a telescope is available, you will have to use a moon filter because the moon will be very bright before and after the eclipse.

### PHOTOGRAPHY

These days, most people have digital cameras and can do their own astrophotography. This can be as simple as pointing a digital camera at the night sky and photographing the constellation, or jury-rigging a digital camera to a pair of binoculars or a telescope and photographing a planet.

Using binoculars, an observer with steady hands can see the four larger moons of Jupiter. However, most of us do not have steady hands. When using binoculars, try leaning against a wall or tree or, better still, attach the binoculars to a tripod. A small bungee cord will work if you do not have a binocular mount.

Photographing the Moon produces some rewarding results. There are many combinations of cameras, lenses, and telescopes you can try. Experimentation is the fun part.

# SITES OF NATURAL INTEREST

The island has a number of national parks, provincial parks, and wilderness and ecological reserves that all contain points of interest to naturalists. It is also home to a number of centres devoted to the plants, wildlife, and geology of the island. Below are listed some of the many sites that would be of most interest to naturalists.

## NATIONAL PARKS

The island has two national parks, Gros Morne on the west coast, and Terra Nova on the east.

**GROS MORNE NATIONAL PARK** is an UNESCO World Heritage Site. It was here that geologists found the evidence that helped to prove the theory of continental drift. The park contains Arctic alpine plants and woodland caribou as well as animals better adapted to Arctic climates such as the rock ptarmigan and Arctic hare.

**TERRA NOVA NATIONAL PARK** is an example of eastern boreal forest and contains a number of fjords, or sounds. It houses marine exhibits and is a great place to see bald eagles, ospreys, and ravens. The park is also home to a small population of the rare pine marten.

*< Tablelands, Gros Morne; (above) Terra Nova National Park*

## PROVINCIAL PARKS

The island has a number of provincial parks, many of which contain interesting plants and animals.

**CATARACTS PROVINCIAL PARK** supports a large number of moss species.

**SANDBANKS PROVINCIAL PARK**, near Burgeo on the south coast, has miles of sandy beaches with a variety of shorebirds.

## WILDERNESS RESERVES

**THE AVALON WILDERNESS RESERVE** has North America's most southerly caribou herd. The northern boundary of the reserve is 50 km south of St. John's. The caribou are often visible in summer from the main roads in the area.

**THE BAY DU NORD WILDERNESS RESERVE**, in south central Newfoundland, is the largest protected area on the island. The reserve includes the wintering area and calving grounds for woodland caribou, as well as supporting many other wildlife species.

Both reserves require an entry permit.

## BOTANICAL & ECOLOGICAL RESERVES

### BURNT CAPE

The Great Northern Peninsula—This is one of the most important botanical sites on the island. The cold climate and calcium-rich soil support a number of northern species. It is home to more than 300 plant species, including thirty rare ones.

### HAWKE HILL

Close to St. John's—The high elevation and cool weather allow Arctic-alpine plants such as *Diapensia* to survive here.

### KING GEORGE IV

Near the Burgeo Highway (Route 480) in west-central Newfoundland—This reserve protects the largest undisturbed river delta system on the island and includes freshwater marshes, rare on the island, but important for waterfowl. It also contains valuable habitat for the La Poile caribou herd of 3400 (est. 2016).

### LITTLE GRAND LAKE (PROVISIONAL)

Thirty km south of Deer Lake—This reserve protects areas of pine marten habitat.

### SANDY COVE

The Great Northern Peninsula—These limestone barrens support Long's Braya, a plant found nowhere else in the world.

### WATTS POINT

Great Northern Peninsula—These calcareous barrens contain a number of rare and endangered plants such as Fernald's Braya.

### WEST BROOK

Close to the TCH, central Newfoundland—This is the site of the largest stand of the province's rarest native conifer, red pine.

*Burnt Cape Ecological Reserve (with rock ptarmigan), Newfoundland*

# SEABIRD RESERVES

### BACCALIEU ISLAND

Off the northern tip of the Avalon Peninsula, near Bay de Verde—This may be the largest seabird colony in the world. It is the site of the largest colony of Leach's storm petrel as well as many other seabirds.

### CAPE ST. MARY'S

South coast of the Avalon Peninsula—This is one of the most spectacular seabird colonies anywhere in the world, including gannets, kittiwakes, and murres. A rock stack just a short distance from viewing areas on the nearby cliffs allows a perfect view of the gannet colony, clearly visible without the aid of binoculars.

### HARE BAY ISLANDS

Near Main Brook, the Great Northern Peninsula—These islands are nesting sites for common eider ducks as well as Arctic terns, double-creasted cormorants, and several species of gulls. This reserve also has rich beds of Early to Middle Ordovician-aged fossil gastropods.

### LAWN BAY

Near Lawn on the Burin Peninsula—Three islands are home to thousands of nesting seabirds including the only colony of Manx shearwaters in North America. The islands also support colonies of Leach's storm petrels, great black-backed gulls, herring gulls, black guillemots, black-legged kittiwakes, and common murres.

### WITLESS BAY

South of St. John's—The islands in this reserve house the largest colony of puffins in North America, and the second largest Leach's storm petrel colony in the world. Several tour boats go close to the islands, an area in which several species of whales can be viewed in summer.

*Northern Gannets* (Morus bassanus) *on nesting cliff at Cape St. Mary's Ecological Reserve, Avalon Peninsula, Newfoundland*

# FOSSIL RESERVES

### FORTUNE HEAD

Burin Peninsula—This site has been designated as the type boundary between the Precambrian Era and the Cambrian Period.

### MISTAKEN POINT

Southern Avalon Peninsula, on the road to Cape Race—This site contains some of the oldest and best preserved complex life forms on Earth. The fossils are of soft-bodied organisms that lived here over 560 million years ago. This reserve was proclaimed as an UNESCO World Heritage Site in 2016.

### TABLE POINT

The Great Northern Peninsula—This site is inhabited by distinctive brachiopods and trilobites from around 460 million years ago at a time when this area lay across the equator.

*(top) Fossil at Mistaken Point Ecological Reserve, Cape Race, Newfoundland; (bottom) High-spired Gastropod cross section, western Newfoundland*

Snowy Owl (Bubo scandiacus), Salmonier Nature Park, Newfoundland

## OTHER SITES OF NATURAL INTEREST

### SALMONIER NATURE PARK

Avalon Peninsula not far from St. John's—This park displays a number of native animals in enclosures representing their natural habitats.

### MEMORIAL UNIVERSITY BOTANICAL GARDEN

St. John's—A nature reserve and botanical garden that features nature trails (with signage), flower gardens, and display areas.

### MUN JOHNSON GEO CENTRE

Signal Hill, St. John's—This centre explains the geology of the province, its rocks, minerals, and fossils, and tells the story of the Earth from its formation over 4.6 billion years ago. Much of the centre is below ground. The main hall displays a very large model of the solar system. The GEO Park outside the centre features a number of trails with interpretive panels describing the geological and botanical features of the park and province.

### MANUELS RIVER HIBERNIA INTERPRETATION CENTRE

Just outside St. John's—Features interactive science exhibits about the biology, geology, palaeontology, and human history of the Manuels River, as well as a café and gift shop. The centre offers a wide variety of programming for the public and for school groups, including tours, workshops, school programs, Girl Guide and Scout programs, and more. There are riverside trails that are great spots for hiking, bird watching, and picnics, offering beautiful scenic views for nature lovers of all ages, and adventure for those who like to explore.

### PETTY HARBOUR MINI AQUARIUM

Petty Harbour just south of St. John's—This small aquarium houses a number of local shallow marine fish and invertebrates in small tanks in which the animals, such as sea stars and hermit crabs, can be touched and handled. This is a great place for kids to become acquainted with local marine fauna.

### THE FLUVARIUM

St. John's—Features a fluvarium level with a spectacular underwater viewing area onto a natural stream, where one can watch brown trout and salmon in their natural habitat. The centre also houses aquaria showcasing the various fish species, such as Atlantic salmon and Arctic char, as well as a number of the amphibians that live in the province.

### THE ROOMS

St. John's—This building is the province's largest public cultural space and houses the Provincial Museum, Art Gallery, and Archives, as well a natural history exhibit displaying a number of provincial animals and plants.

*Viewing trout in Nagle's Hill Brook at the Fluvarium, St. John's, Newfoundland*

## SALMONID INTERPRETATION CENTRE

Grand Falls-Windsor, central Newfoundland—This centre has underwater viewing windows into a salmon ladder, as well as exhibits on the biology and ecology of the Atlantic salmon.

## NEWFOUNDLAND INSECTARIUM

Near Deer Lake, west coast of the island—Houses thousands of different insect and arachnid species. The main exhibit includes both live and preserved insects and is divided into six biogeographical zones showcasing insects from each region. One section is devoted to the insects of the province. The centre also has a glass beehive containing thousands of live honeybees. The butterfly house contains hundreds of live tropical butterflies in a natural setting. The butterflies are free-flying and often land on the visitors! There is also an outdoor walking trail for viewing songbirds, ducks, and aquatic mammals.

## DISCOVERY UNESCO GLOBAL GEOPARK

Bonavista Peninsula—Ten sites scattered around the northern part of the Bonavista Peninsula. Geoparks are sites recognized by UNESCO for their exceptional geological heritage. Rocks dating back more than half a billion years, and some of the best Ediacaran fossils in the world occur in this area. One of the world's oldest complex animal fossils found here, over 560 million years old, *Haootia quadriformis*, is of great importance to our understanding of the origin of animal life.

*Sea arch at Tickle Cove on the Bonavista Peninsula, Discovery UNESCO Global Geopark*

### EDGE OF AVALON INTERPRETIVE CENTRE

Portugal Cove South, southern Avalon Peninsula—Starting point for interpretative tours of the UNESCO World Heritage Site at Mistaken Point. The Centre describes the global significance of the Mistaken Point Ediacaran fauna and the human history of the region.

### FORTUNE HEAD GEOLOGY CENTRE

Fortune, Burin Peninsula—Describes the geological significance of the Global Boundary Stratotype Section and Point (GSSP) between the Precambrian and Phanerozoic at nearby Fortune Head, and also the 1929 Burin Peninsula Tsunami, the most destructive effect from an earthquake in Canadian history.

### BELL ISLAND MINE TOUR AND MUSEUM

Bell Island (ferry from Portugal Cove)—Museum describes the history and geology of the Bell Island Iron Mines, which operated from 1895–1966, one of the longest continuous mining operations in Canadian history. From the museum there are underground tours of the old workings.

*Cliffs on Bell Island, Newfoundland*

## ACKNOWLEDGEMENTS

Dr. Anne-Marie Beckel, then editor at Breakwater, first suggested the idea of a field guide to the Newfoundland natural world that would help the public identify common plants, common animals, and other basic components of the island's nature. Other excellent guidebooks exist, but they are generally focused on specific animal or plant groups.

Clearly an undertaking of this scope and magnitude requires the assistance and input from a great number and range of people without whom the work would not have been possible. It goes without saying that the contributors are owed the greatest appreciation for their outstanding sections. We would especially like to thank Prof. Henry Mann who offered guidance throughout the length of the project. Mr. Joe Brazil, Dr. Norm Catto, Mr. Mac Pitcher, the late Dr. Alan Whittick, Ms. Nathalie Djan-Chékar, Mr. John Maunder, and the late Dr. John Gibson likewise provided much help and advice. Ms. Melanie Knight and staff at the Petty Harbour Mini Aquarium allowed Mike to photograph several specimens there. Mrs. Eileen Collins provided editorial help with the manuscripts. As listed in the photo credits, a large number of individuals made their superb images available.

The staff at Breakwater Books provided encouragement and great assistance through the long, strange trip of this guide's development and publication including Rebecca Rose (President and Publisher), Rebecca Roberts (Marketing), Norma Noseworthy (Office Manager), Jocelyne Thomas (Managing Editor), and Emma Coles (Sales). Through inaugural stages James Langer painstakingly proofed much of the text and Rhonda Molloy provided help with graphic design. Samanda Stroud meticulously completed the final proofreading. Of all the Breakwater people, though, we are most appreciative of Beth Oberholtzer (Design and Production), who kept the enterprise moving along and shared our vision. Thank you all.

## CONTRIBUTORS

**EDWARD ANDREWS** Associate Professor, Environmental Science (Biology), Grenfell Campus, MUN*

**DOUG BOYCE** Project Geologist, Geological Survey Division, Mines Branch, NL Department of Industry, Energy and Technology*

**JOE BRAZIL** Manager of the Endangered Species and Biodiversity Program, Wildlife Division, NL Department of Fisheries, Forestry and Agriculture*—Member NL Wilderness and Ecological Reserves Advisory Council

**DR. STEPHEN BRUNEAU**, P. Eng., Associate Professor, Faculty of Engineering and Applied Science, MUN

**DR. NORM CATTO** Professor, Geography, MUN*

**DR. MICHAEL COLLINS** Professor Emeritus, Biology, and VPA, MUN*

**JIM CORNISH** Teacher, Newfoundland & Labrador English School District*

**DR. TONY DICKINSON** Professor, Biology, and International Centre, MUN*

**DR. GENE HERZBURG** Professor, Biochemistry, MUN*

**LLOYD HOLLETT** Director, Newfoundland Insectarium

**DR. BOB HOOPER** Associate Professor, Biology, MUN*†

**MAC PITCHER** Wildlife Division, NL Department of Fisheries, Forestry and Agriculture*

**DR. PAUL REGULAR** Fisheries and Oceans Canada

**FREDERICK SMITH** Faculty of Science, MUN*

**DR. ALAN WHITTICK** Professor, Biology, MUN*†

**DR. DEREK WILTON** P. Geo., FGC, FRCGS, Honorary Research Professor, Earth Sciences, MUN*—Faculty Researcher CNA

**DR. JOE WROBLEWSKI** Professor, Ocean Sciences, MUN

* Retired

† Deceased

*Harbour Seals, Island Meadows Path, East Coast Trail*

## USEFUL REFERENCES

Andrews, E. 1991. "Frogs and Toads of Western Newfoundland." *The Osprey*, 22 (2): 78–91.

Baxter-Gilbert, J., Lorne King, and Julia L. Riley. 2022. "First report of Eastern Red-backed Salamander (*Plethodon cinereus*) on Newfoundland." *The Canadian Field-Naturalist* 136 (1): 5–9.

Baxter-Gilbert, J. 2012. "Common Garter Snakes (*Thamnophis sirtalis*): Fascinations, Fears and Facts." *The Osprey* 43 (4): 30–31.

Boland, T. 2011. *Trees and Shrubs—Newfoundland and Labrador: Field Guide*. Boulder Publications.

Boland, T. 2017. *Wildflowers and Ferns of Newfoundland*. Boulder Publications.

Bruneau, S. 2004. *Icebergs of Newfoundland and Labrador.* Flanker Press.

Buckle, J. 1971. "A recent introduction of frogs to Newfoundland." *Canadian Field-Naturalist*, 85 (1): 72–74.

Burzynski, M., Henry Mann, and Anne Marceau. 2007. *Exploring the Limestone Barrens of Newfoundland and Labrador*. Gros Morne Co-operating Association.

Chapman, T., Peggy Dixon, Carolyn Parsons, and Hugh Whitney. 2019. *Stouts, Millers, and Forky-Tails: Insects of Newfoundland and Labrador*. Boulder Publications.

Colman-Sadd, S., and Susan Scott. 1994. *Newfoundland and Labrador: Traveller's Guide to the Geology, Guidebook to Stops of Interest*. Newfoundland Department of Mines and Energy.

Conant, R., Joseph T. Collins, Isabelle H. Conant, and Tom R. Johnson. 1998. *A Field Guide to the Reptiles and Amphibians (East and Central North America)*. Houghton-Mifflin Co.

Domm, J. 2006. *Whale Watching on Canada's East Coast*. Formac Publishing Company.

Domm, J. 2012. *Canada's Atlantic Seashore*. Formac Publishing Company.

Gillingham, D., Justin Hodge, Francis Skeard, et al. 2024. "Mi'kmaw knowledge helps uncover a new area of interesting lichen biodiversity on the island of Newfoundland (Ktaqmkuk)." *The Bryologist* 127 (2): 249–268.

Hild, M. H. 2012. *Geology of Newfoundland: Touring through Time at 48 Scenic Sites*. Boulder Publications.

Ledwell, W. 2005. *Whales and Dolphins of Newfoundland & Labrador*. Boulder Publications.

Mactavish, B., Jared Clarke, Jeffrey Wells, Alvin Buckley, and Dave Fifield. 2016. *Checklist (2016) of the Birds of Insular Newfoundland*. Nature Newfoundland and Labrador. https://naturenl.ca/wp-content/uploads/2020/01/NL-checklist-2016.pdf

Maunder, J. 1983. "Amphibians of the Province of Newfoundland." *Canadian Field-Naturalist*, 97 (1): 33–46.

McCloskey, E., and Gregory Kennedy. 2012. *Nature Guide to Atlantic Canada*. Lone Pine Publishing.

Pitcher, M. 2005. "Wood frog (*Rana sylvatica*) well established on Avalon Peninsula." *The Osprey*, 36 (3): 66–67.

Ricciuti, E. 1982. *Fish of the Atlantic*. Hancock House Publishers.

Scott, P., and Dorothy Black. 2006. *Wildflowers of Newfoundland and Labrador*. Boulder Publications.

South, G. R. 1983. *Biogeography and Ecology of the Island of Newfoundland*. Dr. W. Junk Publishers.

Thurston, H. 2011. *The Atlantic Coast—A Natural History*. Greystone Books.

Titford, B., and June Titford. 1995. *A Traveller's Guide to Wild Flowers of Newfoundland, Canada*. Flora Frames.

Voitk, A., and Maria Voitk. 2006. *Orchids on the Rock—The Wild Orchids of Newfoundland*. Gros Morne Co-operating Association.

Voitk, A. 2007. *A Little Illustrated Book of Common Mushrooms of Newfoundland and Labrador*. Gros Morne Co-operating Association.

Warkentin, I., and Sandy Newton. 2009. *Birds of Newfoundland*. Boulder Publications.

Wiersma, Y. F. 2025. "A New Hotspot for Blue Felt Lichen (*Pectenia plumbea*) in Atlantic Canada." *The Northeastern Naturalist* 32(1): 103–113.

Wroblewski, J. 2013. *Marine Wildlife of the Gros Morne National Park Region*. Breakwater Books.

#### SITES OF NATURAL INTEREST

Wilderness and Ecological Reserves: https://www.gov.nl.ca/ecc/natural-areas/wer/

Newfoundland and Labrador Provincial Parks: https://www.parksnl.ca

Gros Morne National Park: https://parks.canada.ca/pn-np/nl/grosmorne

Terra Nova National Park: https://parks.canada.ca/pn-np/nl/terranova

Mistaken Point: https://mistakenpoint.ca/

Salmonier Nature Park: https://www.gov.nl.ca/ffa/wildlife/snp/

MUN Botanical Garden: https://www.mun.ca/botgarden/

MUN Newfoundland and Labrador Science Centre (formerly Johnson Geocentre) : https://www.mun.ca/geocentre/

Manuels River Hibernia Interpretation Centre: https://manuelsriver.ca/visit/

Petty Harbour Mini Aquarium: https://www.miniaqua.org/

The Fluvarium: https://fluvarium.ca/

The Rooms: https://therooms.ca/

Newfoundland Insectarium: https://nlinsectarium.com/

Discovery Geopark: https://discoverygeopark.com/

Fortune Head Geology Centre: https://www.fortunehead.com/

Bell Island Mine Tour and Museum: https://bellislandminetour.com/

#### NIGHT SKY

diffractionlimited.com/product/ecu/

redshift-live.com

store.starrynight.com

# PHOTO AND ILLUSTRATION CREDITS

### COVER

front (FC) Tamarack Bark, Henry Mann
Puffins, Gurpreet Singh/Unsplash
Eastern Tiger Swallowtail, Joe Brazil
Iceberg, Steve Bruneau
*Pholiota squarrosa*, Andrus Voigt
Pine Marten, Joe Brazil
Planispiral Gastropod, Doug Boyce
Lion's Mane, Derek Keats/Wikicommons
Fireweed, Henry Mann

back (BC) Humpback Whale, DFO
Green Comma, Joe Brazil
Showy Lady's Slipper, Henry Mann
*Fucus distichus*, Alan Whittick

page #

### FRONT MATTER

| | |
|---|---|
| 2–3 | Tilting, Beth Oberholtzer |
| 5 | Lupins, Henry Mann |

### INTRODUCTION    Henry Mann, except:

Derek Wilton

| | |
|---|---|
| 11 | Granite boulder |
| 15 | Pitcher Plants |

Gene Herzberg

| | |
|---|---|
| 12 | Great Horned Owl |
| 24 | Downy Woodpecker |
| 30 | Willow Ptarmigan |
| 34 | American Wigeon |

Joe Brazil

| | |
|---|---|
| 12 | Red Fox |
| 24 | Snowshoe Hare |
| 30 | Caribou |

Other

| | |
|---|---|
| 6 | Western Newfoundland, Carol Fung /Unsplash |
| 8 | Map, Rod Churchill |
| 12 | Groove, Norm Catto |
| 14 | Coniferous forest, Michael Collins |
| 18 | Blue Mussels, David Innes |
| 23 | *Craterellus tubaeformis*, Jim Cornish |
| 39–47 | Glaciation images, Norm Catto |

### FUNGI    Andrus Voitk, except:

Maria Voitk

| | |
|---|---|
| 63 | *Fomitopsis ochracea* |
| 65 | *Tyromyces chioneus* |
| 67 | *Suillus ampliporus* var. *cavipes, Suillus grevillei* |

Jim Cornish

| | |
|---|---|
| 51 | *Amanita porphyria, Armillaria solidipes* |
| 52 | *Cortinarius collinitus* |
| 53 | *Coprinopsis atramentaria, Coprinus comatus, Collybia tuberosa* |
| 54 | *Craterellus tubaeformis, Cortinarius armillatus, Cortinarius traganus* |

Jim Cornish (cont'd)

55   *Cortinarius caperatus*
56   *Cortinarius semisanguineus, Hygrocybe conica*
57   *Lactarius helvus*
58   *Lactarius hibbardae, Lactarius thyinos*
59   *Pleurocybella porrigens*
60   *Dacrymyces chrysospermus*
61   *Byssonectria terrestris, Helvella lacunosa*
62   *Clavulina coralloides, Cerrena unicolor, Fomes fomentarius*
63   *Fomitopsis mounceae, Gloeophyllum sepiarium*
64   *Fomitopsis betulina, Panellus stipticus*
65   *Ganoderma applanatum, Lycoperdon perlatum, Apioperdon pyriforme*

## LICHENS    Mac Pitcher

## PLANTS

### Mosses and Liverworts

Mac Pitcher, except:

84   *Andreaea rupestris, Dicranum* sp., *Fontinalis* sp., Alan Whittick
     *buxbaumia* sp., Bernd Haynold/Wikicommons

### Ferns    Henry Mann, except:

92   *Cystopteris fragilis,* Stan Shebs/Wikicommons
     *Phegopteris connectilis,* de:Benutzer:Griensteidl/Wikicommons
93   *Thelypteris noveboracensis,* Krzysztof Ziarnek, Kenraiz
     /Wikicommons
94   *Dryopteris campyloptera,* Michael Collins
95   *Dryopteris carthusiana,* Wasp32/Wikicommons
     *Dryopteris cristata,* Kristian Peters, Fabelfroh/Wikicommons
96   *Dryopteris intermedia,* DEMcGrady/Wikicommons
     *Dryopteris filix-mas,* Valérie75/Wikicommons
99   *Spinulum canadense,* David McCorquodale/Wikicommons

### Conifers, Broad-Leafed Trees, Wildflowers

Henry Mann

## ANIMALS

### Insects    Joe Brazil, except:

Mardon Erbland

159   *Forficula auricularia*
160   *Phileanus* sp., *Chrysopa* sp.
162   *Dermestes lardarius, Adalia bipunctata, Monochamus scutellatus*
163   Limnephilidae Family, *Chrysops* sp.
164   *Musca domestica,* Simuliidae Family
      Elm Sawfly, MamaTeeth/Wikicommons

Other

156   *Lophocampa maculata*, Jeremy deWaard/Wikicommons
157   *Campaea perlata,* Cody Hough/Wikicommons
      *Lambdina fiscellaria*, D. Gordon E. Robertson/Wikicommons
159   Heptageniidae Family, Richard Bartz/Wikicommons
163   *Tipula* sp., Sue Wilton
      *Aedes* sp., Fred Smith

### Amphibians   Joe Brazil, except:

167   Manuels River Trail looking toward Little Bell Island, Derek Wilton

### Reptiles

169   Eastern Garter Snake, Michiel de Wit/Shutterstock

Birds        Gene Herzberg, except:
Dave Fifield
- 174  Long-Tailed Duck
- 180  Thick-Billed Murre
- 186  Northern Goshawk, Merlin
- 187  Spruce Grouse
- 189  Boreal Owl
- 191  Common Raven
- 195  Grey-Cheeked Thrush

Other
- 174  Red-Breasted Merganser, Peter Massas/Wikicommons
- 186  Rough-Legged Hawk, Wild Art/Shutterstock
- 189  Short-Eared Owl, Harold Stiver/Shutterstock
- 193  Bank Swallow, nadezhda F/Shutterstock
       Barn Swallow, Werner Baumgarten/Shutterstock
- 198  Tennessee Warbler, Agami Photo Agency/Shutterstock
- 201  American Tree Sparrow, Mdf/Wikicommons

Mammals      Joe Brazil, except:
Dennis Minty
- 209  Muskrat
- 210  Ermine

Other
- 204  Arctic Fox, Alexey Seafarer/Shutterstock
- 205  Polar Bear, Andrewfel/Shutterstock
- 206  Northern Long-Eared Bat, Zdenek_macat/Shutterstock
       Masked Shrew, Richard Poort/Wikicommons
- 207  Arctic Hare, Steve Sayles/kids.kiddle.com
- 208  Southern Red-Backed Vole, Lev Frid/Shutterstock
       Deer Mouse, Dawn Marsh/Wikicommons
- 209  House Mouse, HWall/Shutterstock
       Newfoundland Beaver, Mac Pitcher
       Norway Rat, Denisa Mikesova/Shutterstock
- 210  Northern River Otter, Gene Herzberg
- 212  Coyote, Mike McGrath
       Canada Lynx, Warren Metcalfe/Shutterstock

## MARINE LIFE
Plants       Alan Whittick, except:
- 218  *Ulva intestinalis,* Teampielgo/Shutterstock
- 219  *Chaetomorpha melagonium*, Gabriele Kothe-Heinrich/Wikicommons
- 226  Bladder Wrack, AlanMorris/Shutterstock
       Knotted Wrack, Dozens/Wikicommons
- 227  Irish Moss, Carlos Rondon/Shutterstock
- 228  *Dumontia contorta,* Carlos Rondon/Shutterstock

Invertebrates Michael Collins, except:
Joe Wroblewski
- 234  Garland Sea Fir
- 238  Scud
- 241  Toad Crab, American Lobster
- 249  Northern Basket Star

Roy Ficken
- 235  Frilled Anemone (left photo)
- 244  Moon Snail
- 246  Common Grey Sea Slug

Other

232   Bread Crumb Sponge, Bengt Littorin/Wikicommons
      Bread Crumb Sponge, detail, Minette Layne-Worthey /Wikicommons
233   Finger Sponge, R L S Photo/Shutterstock
      Boring Sponge, Beernard Picton/iNaturalist
234   Moon Jelly, Alexander Vasenin/Wikicommons
      Lion's Mane, Derek Keats/Wikicommons
235   Frilled Anemone (right photo), Emőke Dénes/Wikicommons
      Northern Red Anemone, R M J Murphy/Wikicommons
236   Clam Worm, Bob Hooper
      Hard Tube Worm, H Helene/Shutterstock
      Twelve-Scaled Worm, gbif.org/Wikicommons
      Lugworm, Auguste Le Roux/Wikicommons
237   Red Lineus (top image), Shoma81/Shutterstock
      Sea Mat, United States Geological Survey/Wikicommons
238   Rockhopper, *Apohyale prevostii*, Hans Hillewaert/Wikicommons
      Beach Flea, Paul A. Carpenter/Shutterstock
239   Planktonic Amphipod, Samuel Jackson Holmes/Wikicommons
240   Rough Barnacle, Maria/Wikicommons
      European Green Crab, Coulanges/Shutterstock:
243   Rough Periwinkle, valda butterworth/Shutterstock
      Smooth Periwinkle, A B S Natural History/Shutterstock
244   Dogwhelk, Martin Fowler/Shutterstock
      Little Chink Shell, Yale Peabody Museum/Wikicommons
245   Tortoiseshell Limpet, H. Zell/Wikicommons
246   Blue Mussel, Dave Innes
247   Horse Mussel, 2DVisualize/Shutterstock
      Baltic Macoma, Shoma81/Shutterstock
      Common Razor Clam, Cweiders/Shutterstock
249   Daisy Brittle Star, lezer/Wikicommons
250   Sand Dollar, Geza Farkas/Shutterstock
      Green Sea Urchin (left), Carolyn Prentice/Wikicommons
      Green Sea Urchin (right), Ryan Hodnett/Wikicommons

Fishes          Joe Wroblewski except:
  Arnault LeBris
      256   Atlantic Salmon parr
            Atlantic Salmon kype
            Juvenile Brook Trout
      257   Rainbow Smelt
      268   Winter Flounder (photo, right)
  Other
      253–254  Drawings, Leah Wroblewski
      255   Atlantic Salmon, Alexander Raths/Shutterstock
      256   Brook Trout, slowmotiongli/Shutterstock (top image)
      257   Arctic Char, FedBul/Shutterstock
            Atlantic Tomcod, P O U L A M O N 2/Wikicommons
      258   Alewife, Smithsonian Environmental Research Center
      259   Ninespine Stickleback, Piet Spaans/Wikicommons
            Rock Gunnel illustration, Krüger/Wikicommons
      260   Fourspine Stickleback, Ryan Melanson
      261   Pipefish, Jack perks/Shutterstock
      264   Atlantic Cod, Xpixel/Shutterstock
      264   Greenland Cod, Michael Bakker Paiva/Wikicommons
            White Hake illustration, Freshwater and Marine Image Bank
      265   Ocean Pout, R L S Photo/Shutterstock

Other (cont'd)

265    Radiated Shanny illustration, National Oceanic and Atmospheric Administration/Wikicommons

266    Atlantic Wolffish, Spotted Wolffish, Jennifer Dawe
Sea Raven illustration, Freshwater and Marine Image Bank

268    Winter Flounder illustration, Freshwater and Marine Image Bank

269    American Sand Lance illustration, Freshwater and Marine Image Bank

270    Atlantic Mackerel, Nosylevy/Shutterstock

Mammals    Jack Lawson except:

214, 275    Atlantic White-Sided Dolphin, Wayne Ledwell

271    Mother and Pup Harp Seals (top left), DFO
Harp Seal White Coat (bottom left), Vladimir Melnik/Shutterstock
Juvenile Hooded Seal (top right), Gary Stenson
Adult Hooded Seal (bottom right), DFO

272    Harbour Seal, Amanda Boyd, US Fish and Wildlife Service/Wikicommons
Bearded Seal, Capt. Bud Chrisman/NOAA

273    Humpback Whale (breach), uncredited photographer/NOAA
Humpback Whale (fluke), Alisha Bube/Shutterstock
Northern Minke Whale, Blo_fotoss/Shutterstock

274    Fin Whale , Aqqa Rosing-Asvid/Wikicommons
Blue Whale, uncredited photographer/NOAA

275    Killer (Orca) Whale, Tory Kalllman/Shutterstock
Long-Finned Pilot Whale, Andrew Sutton/Shutterstock
Common Dolphin, uncredited photographer/NOAA
Harbour Porpoise, Onutancu/Shutterstock

## FOSSILS
Doug Boyce

## ROCKS AND MINERALS
Derek Wilton, except:

300    Mistaken Point Fossils, Martin Feely

304    Map, Rod Churchill

308    Gypsum Cliffs, Kippens, Ray Fennelly

## WINTER
Tracking Animals Michael Collins

Winter Gulls    Gene Herzberg, except:

318    Black-Headed Gull, El Golli Mohamed/Wikicommons

Icebergs    Steve Bruneau

## NIGHT SKY
Fred Smith, except:

328    Starry Night Sky in Newfoundland, Hatt Photography

337    Moon, Henry Mann

## SITES OF NATURAL INTEREST

338    Tablelands, Greg Johnson/Unsplash

339    Terra Nova National Park, Shzphoto/Shutterstock

341    Burnt Cape, Henry Mann

342    Northern Gannets, AndreAnita/Shutterstock:

343    Mistaken Point fossil, Vagabond54/Shutterstock
High-Spired Gastropod, Doug Boyce

344    Snowy Owl, Gilbert S. Grant/Shutterstock

## SITES OF NATURAL INTEREST (cont'd)

343    Fluvarium, JaySo83 /Wikicommons
346    Sea Arch, Ggw /Shutterstock
347    Bell Island, Dennis Minty

## APPENDICES

348    Stiles Cove, Derek Wilton
350    Harbour Seals, Derek Wilton
358    White Pine, Ray Fennelly
372–373  Bay Roberts, Shoreline Walk, Derek Wilton

*White Pine, Gaff Topsail*

# INDEX

## A

*Abies balsamea* . . . . . . . .101
Acadian Redfish . . . . . 269
*Acanthis flammea* . . . . .203
*Accipiter gentilis* . . . . . .186
*Accipiter striatus* . . . . . .186
*Acer rubrum* . . . . . . . . . 109
*Acer spicatum* . . . . . . . . 109
*Acer* spp. . . . . . . . . . . . .104
*Achillea millefolium* . . . .144
Acritarch . . . . . . . . .281, 282
*Actitis macularius* . . . . . .182
*Adalia bipunctata*. . .162, 354
*Adiantum aleuticum* . . . 90
*Aedes* sp. . . . . . . . . .163, 354
*Aegolius funereus* . . . . . .189
*Aeolidia papillosa* . . . . . 246
*Aeshna juncea* . . . . . . . . .158
*Agarum clathratum* .19, 225
*Agelaius phoeniceus* . . . 204
*Aglais milberti* . . . . . . . . .154
*Ahnfeltia plicata* . . . . . .227
*Alaria esculenta* . . . . . . . . . .
. . . . . . . . . . .18, 19, 216, 225
*Alca torda* . . . . . . . . . . .180
*Alces alces* . . . . . . . . . . . .213
Alder . . 28, 32, 64, 104, 154,
. . . . . . . . . .156, 157, 192, 196
Alder Flycatcher . . . . . .192
  see Yellow-Bellied
  Flycatcher
*Alectoria sarmentosa* ssp. .
  *sarmentosa* . . . . . . . . . . 70
Alewife. . . . . . . 255, 258, 356
*Alitta virens* . . . . . . . . . . 236
*Alnus alnobetula*. . . . . . 107
*Alnus incana* . . . . . . . . .107
*Alnus* spp. . . . . . . . . . . . 104
*Alosa pseudoharengus* . .258
Alpine Azalea . . . . . . . . .121
Alpine Bearberry. . . . . 120
Alpine Bilberry . . . . . .120
Alpine Bistort. . . . . . . . .118
Alpine Bloodspot Lichen
. . . . . . . . . . . . . . . . . . . . . .77
Alsike Clover . . . . . . . .148
*Amanita amerivirosa* . . . .50
*Amanita flavoconia* . . . .50
*Amanita fulva* . . . . . . . . . 51
*Amanita muscarua*
  var. *guessowii* . . . . . . . .51
*Amanita porphyria*. . 51, 353

*Amblyraja radiata* . . . . .263
*Amelanchier bartramiana*
. . . . . . . . . . . . . . . . . . . . . .114
American Bittern . . . . .173
American Black Bear . . 211
American Black Duck .172
American Crow. . . . . . .191
American Dune Grass .142
  see Strand Wheat
American Eel . . . . .252, 258
American Golden-Plover
. . . . . . . . . . . . . . . . . . . . .181
American Goldfinch. . .203
American Lobster . . . . . . . .
. . . . . . . . . . . . . . 19, 241, 355
American Marten . . . . . 211
American Mink . . . . . . .210
American Mountain Ash
. . . . . . . . . . . . . . . . . . . . 108
American Pipit. . . . . . .195
American Redstart . . . . . . .
. . . . . . . . . . . 196, 197, 199
American Robin . . . . . .195
American Sand Lance . . . .
. . . . . . . . . . . . . . . 269, 356
American Tree Sparrow
. . . . . . . . . . . . . . . . .201, 355
American Wigeon. . . . . . . .
. . . . . . . . . . . . . . 34, 171, 353
American Yellow Fly Agaric
. . . . . . . . . . . . . . . . . . . . . .51
*Ammodytes americanus* . . .
. . . . . . . . . . . . . . . . . . . . 269
*Anaphalis margaritacea* 144
*Anarhichas lupus* . . . . . 266
*Anarhichas minor*. . . . . 266
*Anas acuta*. . . . . . . . . . . .172
*Anas carolinensis* . . . . . .172
*Anas platyrhynchos* . . . .172
*Anas rubripes*. . . . . . . . . .172
*Anaxyrus americanus*
  *americanus* . . . . . . . . . .168
*Andreaea rupestris* . .84, 354
*Andromeda polifolia*
  var. *latifolia* . . . . . . . . .127
Angel's Wing . . . . . . . . .59
*Angelica lucida* . . . . 137, 152
*Anguilla rostrata*. . . . . . .258
*Anthus rubescens* . . . . . .195
*Apeltes quadracus*. . . . . 260
*Apis mellifera*. . . . . . . . . .165
*Aquarius remigis*. . . . . . .160
*Aralia nudicaulis*. . . . . . .117

Archaeocyatha . . . . . . . .302
Archaeocyathids . . . . . .282
*Arctia parthenos* . . . . . . .157
Arctic Char. . . . . . . . . . . . .
. . . . . . . . . 255, 257, 345, 356
Arctic Fox . . . 204, 205, 355
Arctic Hare . . . . . . . . . . . . .
. . . . . . . . . 205, 207, 339, 355
Arctic Kidney Lichen . . 80
Arctic Raspberry . . . . . .119
Arctic Saucer Lichen . . .81
Arctic Tern . . . . . . .179, 342
*Arctoparmelia centrifug* 76
*Arctostaphylos uva-ursi* .120
*Arctous alpina*. . . . . . . . .120
*Ardenna gravis* . . . . . . . .175
*Ardenna grisea* . . . . . . . .175
*Arenaria interpres* . . . . . .185
*Arethusa bulbosa* . . .26, 125
*Argentina anserina*. . . . .138
*Armeria maritima* . . . . . .123
*Armillaria solidipes*. . 51, 353
Articulate Brachiopod . . . .
  see Brachiopod
Artist's Conk . . . . . . . . . .65
*Ascophyllum nodosum* . . . .
. .223, 225, 226, 230, 234, 355
*Asio flammeus*. . . . . . . . .189
*Asplenium trichomanes-*
  *ramosum*. . . . . . . . . . . . 90
*Asplenium viride* . . . . . . 90
*Asterias rubens* . . . . . . 248
Asteroid (fossil) . . . . . . .282
*Athyrium filix-femina* . . .93
Atlantic Chink Shell. . 244
  see Little Chink Shell
Atlantic Cod. . . . . 262, 264
Atlantic Herring . . . . . . . . .
. . . . . . . . . . . . .262, 269, 270
Atlantic Mackerel . . . . . . . .
. . . . . . . . . . . . .262, 269, 270
Atlantic Puffin . . . . . . . . . .
. . . . . . . . . 16, 180, 342, OFC
Atlantic Salmon . . . . . . .33,
. .254, 255, 256, 345, 346, 356
Atlantic Snailfish. 259, 260
Atlantic Tomcod . . 255, 257
Atlantic White-Sided
  Dolphin 215, 275, 355, 356
Atlantic Wolffish. . . . . . . . .
. . . . . . . . . . . . 262, 266, 357
  see Striped Wolffish
*Aulactinia stella* . . . . . . .235

*Aurelia aurita* . . . . . . . . .234
*Aythya collaris*. . . . . . . . .172
*Aythya marila nearctica* 173

**B**

*Baeomyces rufus*. . . . . . . .77
Bakeapple . . . . . . . . .27, 124
*Balaenoptera acutorostrata*
. . . . . . . . . . . . . . . . . . . . . .273
*Balaenoptera musculus* .274
*Balaenoptera physalus*. .274
*Balanus balanus*. . . . . . 240
Bald Eagle. . . . 185, 317, 339
Balsam Fir. . . . . . . . . . . . . .
. . . . . 15, 21, 22, 73, 101, 157
Balsam Poplar . . . . .22, 105
Baltic Macoma . .247, 356
Banded Cort . . . . . . . . . .54
*Bangia fuscopurpurea* . . . . .
. . . . . . . . . . . . . . . . .227, 231
Bank Swallow . . . . 193, 354
Bank Vole . . . . . . . . . . .205
Barn Swallow. . . . . 193, 355
Barnacle . . 18, 231, 233, 239,
. . . . . . . . . . . 240, 244, 356
   *see* Common Barnacle;
   Northern Rock Barnacle;
   Rough Barnacle
*Bazzania trilobata* . . . . . 88
Beach Flea . . . . . . .238, 356
Beach Pea . . . . . . . . . . . .140
Beaked Redfish . . . . 269
   *see* Acadian Redfish
Bear . . . . . . . . . . . . . . .13, 23,
. . . .29, 205, 211, 213, 315, 355
   *see* American Black Bear;
   Newfoundland Black
   Bear; North America
   Black Bear; Polar Bear
Bearded Seal . . . . .272, 357
Beaver . 13, 33, 205, 209, 355
   *see* Newfoundland
   Beaver
Bebb's Willow . . . .104, 105
Belted Kingfisher . . . . .189
Beluga Whale. . . . . . . .274
*Betula alleghaniensis* . . .106
*Betula cordifolia*. . . . . .106
*Betula papyrifera* . . . . .106
Big Shaggy-Moss. . . . . . 86
Birch Bolete . . . . . . . . . . 66
Birch Polypore. . . . . . . . 64
Bird's-Eye Primrose . . . 131
   *see* Mistassini Primrose
Birdsfoot Trefoil . . . . . .148
Bitter Wart Lichen . . . . .75

Bittersweet. . . . . . . . . . .147
Bivalves . . . . . . . . . . . . . .282
Black and White Warbler
. . . . . . . . . . . . . . . .197, 199
Black Ash . . . . . . . . . . . .110
Black Bear. . . . . . . . . . . . .
. . . . . . . . .13, 23, 29, 205, 213
   *see* American Black Bear;
   Newfoundland Black
   Bear; North American
   Black Bear; Polar Bear
Black Crowberry. . . . . .121
Black Elfin Saddle. . . . .61
Black Guillemot . . . . . . . . .
. . . . . . . . . . . . 179, 180, 342
Black Huckleberry . . . .127
Black Knapweed . . . . . .145
Black Meadowhawk. . .158
Black Medick . . . . . . . .148
Black Morel . . . . . . . . . .61
Black Rock Moss. . . . . . .84
Black Seaside Lichen . . .77
Black Spruce . . . . . . . . . . .
. . . . . . . . 21, 22, 27, 102, 309
Black Vine Weevil . . . . .162
Black-Backed Woodpeck-
er. . . . . . . . . . . . . . . . . . .190
Black-Bellied Plover . . . 181
Black-Capped Chickadee
. . . . . . . . . . . . . . . . 193, 315
Black-footed Reindeer
   Lichen. . . . . . . . . . . . .79
Black-Headed Gull . . . . . . .
. . . . . . . .177, 317, 318, 357
Black-Legged Kittiwake
. . . . . .177, 178, 317, 320, 342
Black-Tailed Gull . . . . . 317
Black-Throated Green
   Warbler . . . . . . . .197, 199
Blackfly. . . . . . . . . . . . . .164
Blackpoll Warbler.197, 199
Blackspotted Stickleback
. . . . . . . . . . . . . . . . .259, 261
Bladder Wrack. 18, 226, 355
Bleeding Mycena . . . . . .59
*Blidingia minima* . . . . . .218
Blood Star. . . . . . . . . . . 249
Blow Fly . . . . . . . . . . . .164
Blue Felt Lichen . . 72, 351
Blue Flag Iris . . . . . .26, 134
Blue Ground Cedar . . . 98
Blue Jay . . . . . . . . . .189, 191
Blue Mussel . . . 18, 19, 246,
. . . . . . . . . . .247, 353, 356
Blue Whale. . . . . . .274, 357
Blue-Bead Lily . . . . . . . .116

   see Corn Lily
Blue-Eyed Grass . . . . . .146
Blue-Headed Vireo. . . . 191
Bog Aster . . . . . . . . .26, 129
Bog Candle. . . . . . . .26, 132
   see Scentbottle
Bog Clubmoss . . . . . . . . 98
Bog Copper . . . . . . . . . . 155
Bog Goldenrod 26, 29, 129
Bog Laurel . . . . . . . .25, 127
Bog Moss . . . 25, 83, 86, 87
Bog Rosemary . . . . .25, 127
Bogbean . . . . . . . . . . . . .131
Bohemian Waxwing . . . . .
. . . . . . . . . . . . . . .196, 315
*Boloria selene* . . . . . . . . . 153
*Bombus* sp. . . . . . . . . . . .165
*Bombycilla cedrorum*. . .196
*Bombycilla garrulus*. . . .196
Bonaparte's Gull . . . . . . 317
*Bonasa umbellus* . . . . . .187
Boreal Bluet . . . . . . . . . .158
Boreal Chickadee . . . . . . . .
. . . . . . . . . . . . . . 24, 193, 315
Boreal Felt Lichen . .72, 73
Boreal Owl. . . . . . .189, 354
Boreal Sea Star . . . . . . 248
   *see* Northern Sea Star
Boring Sponge. . . . 233, 355
*Botaurus lentiginosus* . . 173
*Botrychium lunaria* . . . . 96
*Botrychium virginianum* 96
Bottlebrush Shield Lichen
. . . . . . . . . . . . . . . . . .23, 74
Brachiopod. . .281, 282, 343
   *see* Articulate Brachiopod;
   Inarticulate Brachiopod
Bracken. . . . . . . . . . . . . . 94
*Branta canadensis* . . . . . 171
Braun's Holly Fern . . . 94
Bread Crumb Sponge . . . .
. . . . . . . . . . . . . . . . 233, 355
Brilliant Dung Moss. . . .87
Bristly Black Currant. . 115
British Soldiers Lichen . . .
. . . . . . . . . . . . . . . . . 28, 78
Brook (Mud) Trout. . . . . .
. . . . 13, 33, 254, 255, 256, 356
Broom Moss. . . . . . . . . .84
   *see* Fork-Mosses
Brown Anemone. .235, 246
   *see* Frilled Anemone
Brown Beret Lichen. . . .77
Brown Bootlace Seaweed
. . . . . . . . . . . . . . . . .18, 225
*Bryoria trichodes* . . . . . . 70

Bryozoa . . . . . . . . . .281, 282
Bubo scandiacus . . 189, 344
Bubo virginianus . . . . . .188
Bucephala clangula . . . .174
Bug Mosses . . . . . . . . . . 84
Bumble Bee . . . . . . . . . .165
Bunchberry . . . 23, 112, 123
  see Crackerberry
Bushy Backed Sea Slug . . .
  . . . . . . . . . . . . . . . . . . . . . 246
Buteo lagopus . . . . . . . . .186
Butter and Eggs . . . . . . .146
Butterfish . . . . . . . 20, 259
  see Rock Gunnel
Buxbaumia species . .84, 354
Byssonectria terrestris . . . . .
  . . . . . . . . . . . . . . . . 61, 353

C
Cabbage White . . . . . . . 153
Cakile edentula . . . . . . . .136
Calcarius lapponicus . . .201
Calidris alba . . . . . . . . . .182
Calidris alpina . . . . . . . .184
Calidris canutus . . . . . . .182
Calidris fuscicollis . . . . . .183
Calidris maritima . . . . . .183
Calidris melanotos . . . . .183
Calidris minutilla . . . . . .183
Calidris pusilla . . . . . . . .183
Calliopius laeviusculus . .239
Calliphoridae Family . . .164
Calopogon tuberosus 26, 126
Caltha palustris . . . . . . . 133
Campaea perlata . . . . . . 157
Campanula gieseckeana 123
Camponotus sp. . . . . . . . .165
Canada Goose . . . . . 34, 171
Canada Lynx . . . . . . . . . .23,
  . . 205, 207, 212, 313, 315, 355
Canada Yew . . . . . .101, 103
Canadian Beaver . . . . . . 209
  see Newfoundland Beaver
Canadian Mint . . . . . . . 135
Cancer irroratus . . . . . . 240
Canis latrans . . . . . . . . . .212
Cantharellus enelensis . . .52
Capelin . 20, 262, 269, 270
Capsosiphon fulvescens .218
Carabus nemoralis . . . . .161
Carcinus maenas . . . . . 240
Cardamine pensylvanica .130
Cardamine pratensis . . .130
Cardellina pusilla . . . . . .198
Caribou . . . . . . . . . . . . . . . . .
  . . . . . . . 9, 13, 29, 30, 43, 79,

. .205, 212, 213, 339, 340, 343
  see Newfoundland
  Caribou; Woodland
  Caribou
Carpenter Ant . . . . . . . .165
Carrion Beetle . . . . . . . .161
Caspian Gull . . . . . . . . . .320
Caspian Tern . . . . . . . . .179
Castor canadensis caecator
  . . . . . . . . . . . . . . . . . . . 209
Catharus guttatus . . . . .195
Catharus minimus minimus
  . . . . . . . . . . . . . . . . . . . . .195
Catharus ustulatus . . . . .194
Cedar Waxwing . . . 196, 315
Celastrina argiolus . . . . . 155
Centaurea nigra . . . . . . .145
Cepphus grylle . . . . . . . . .180
Cephalopod . . . . . .281, 282
Ceramium virgatum . . . 229
Cerastium arvense . . . . . 118
Cerrena unicolor . . . . 62, 353
Cetraria islandica . . . . . . 78
Cetraria laevigata . . . . . . 78
Chaenothecopsis vainioana
  . . . . . . . . . . . . . . . . . . . . . 70
Chaetomorpha linum . . 220
Chaetomorpha melagonium
  . . . . . . . . . . . . . . . . . 219, 355
Chaetomorpha sp. .219, 220
Chamaedaphne calyculata
  . . . . . . . . . . . . . . . . . . . . .126
Chamerion angustifolium
  . . . . . . . . . . . . . . . . . . . . . 116
Chamerion latifolium . .122
Charadrius semipalmatus
  . . . . . . . . . . . . . . . . . . . . . .181
Chelone glabra . . . . . . . . 131
Chenopodium album . . . 141
Chitinozoan . . . . . . . . . .282
Chokecherry . . . . 22, 108
Chondrus crispus . . . . . .227
Chorda filum . . . . . . .18, 225
Chordaria flagelliformis . . .
  . . . . . . . . . . . . . . . .222, 223
Chroicocephalus
  philadelphia . . . . . . . . .317
Chroicocephalus ridibundus
  . . . . . . . . . . . . . . . . . 177, 318
Chrysopa sp. . . . . . .160, 354
Chrysops sp. . . . . . . 163, 354
Chuckley Pear . . . . . . . .114
  see Mountain
  Serviceberry
Cichorium intybus . . . . .144
Cicindela sp. . . . . . . . . . .161

Cimbex americana . . . . .164
Cinnamon Fern . . . . 90, 91
Circus cyaneus . . . . . . . .186
Cladonia boryi . . . . . . . . 78
Cladonia cristatella . . . . 78
Cladonia gracilis ssp.
  Gracilis . . . . . . . . . . . . 79
Cladonia maxima . . . . . 79
Cladonia pleurota . . . . . 79
Cladonia rangiferina . . . 79
Cladonia stellaris . . . . . . 79
Cladonia stygia . . . . . . . . 79
Cladonia terrae-novae . . 80
Cladonia verticillata . . . 80
Cladophora albida . . . . .220
Cladophora rupestris .18, 220
Cladophora sericea . . . . 220
Cladophora sp. . . . . . . . .219
Clam . . . . . . . . . . . . 20, 241,
  . . . . 246, 247, 248, 249, 356
  see Common Razor Clam
Clam Worm . . . . . .236, 356
Clangula hyemalis . . . . .174
Clathromorphum
  circumscriptum . 229, 245
Clavulina coralloides 62, 353
Clethrionomys gapperi 208
Clintonia borealis . . . . . .116
Cloudberry . . . . . . . . . . .124
  see Bakeapple
Clover . . . . . . . 147, 148, 153
  see Alsike Clover;
  Hop Clover; Rabbitfoot
  Clover; Red Clover;
  White Clover
Clouded Sulphur . . . . . 153
Club Mushroom Lichen 81
Club-Spur Orchid . . . . . 125
Clupea harengus . . . . . . 270
Coccocarpia palmicola . .72
Coccothraustes vespertinus
  . . . . . . . . . . . . . . . . . . . . .203
Cochlearia groenlandica 136
Cod . . . . 250, 262, 264, 356
  see Atlantic Cod;
  Atlantic Tomcod; Green-
  land Cod; Rock Cod
Coeloglossum viride . . . .122
Coenonympha inornata
  mcisaaci . . . . . . . . . . . . 153
Colander Weed . . . .19, 225
Colaptes auratus . . . . . . .190
Colias philodice . . . . . . . 153
Collybia tuberosa . . . 53, 354
Coltsfoot . . . . . . . . . . . . .145
Columba livia . . . . . . . . .188

*Comarum palustre* . . . . . 133

Common Barnacle . . . . . . .
. . . . . . . . . . . . . 18, 239, 240

Common Bearberry . . . 120

Common Bladderwort . 132

Common Blue . . . . . . 155

Common Butterwort . 134

Common Cattail . . . . . . 136

Common Cord Moss . . 84

Common Crane Fly . . . 163

Common Dolphin 275, 357

Common Drill . . . . . . . 244
  *see* Dogwhelk

Common Eider . . . 173, 342

Common Evening
  Primrose . . . . . . . . . . 146

Common Eyebright . . . 143

Common Freckle Pelt . 80

Common Garter Snake 351

Common Golden Eye . 174

Common Grackle . . . . 204

Common Grey Sea Slug . .
. . . . . . . . . . . . . . . 246, 355

Common Gull . . . . . . . . 318

Common Hempnettle. 147

Common Juniper . . 31, 103

Common Loon . . . . . . . 173

Common Merganser . . 174

Common Murre . . . . . . . . .
. . . . . . . . . . . 179, 180, 342

Common Periwinkle . . . . .
. . . . . . . . . . . . . . . . 19, 243

Common Pipewort . . . 132

Common Polypody . . . 91

Common Porpoise . . . 275

Common Raven . . 191, 354

Common Razor Clam . . . .
. . . . . . . . . . . . 20, 247, 356

Common Redpoll . . . . 203

Common Rock Crab . . . .
. . . . . . . . . . . . . . . . 19, 240

Common Script Lichen 75

Common Speedwell . . . 117

Common Tern . . . . . . . . . .
. . . . . . . . . . 179, 357, 371

Common Toadskin
  Lichen . . . . . . . . . . . . . 76

Common Water Strider
. . . . . . . . . . . . . . . . . 160

Common Yellowthroat . . .
. . . . . . . . . . . . . . 198, 199

Compton Tortoiseshell 154

Concentric Boulder
  Lichen . . . . . . . . . . . . 77

Concentric Ring Lichen 76

Conodont . . . . 281, 282, 301

Conularid . . . . . . . . . . . 282

*Coprinopsis atramentaria*
. . . . . . . . . . . . . . . . 53, 354

*Coprinus comatus* . . 53, 354

*Coptis trifolia* . . . . . . . 124

Coral (fossil) . 279, 281, 282

Coral Lichen . . . . . . . . . 71

Coralina Sea Lavender 140

*Corallina officinalis* . . . . . . .
. . . . . . . . . . . 18, 19, 223, 228

*Corallorhiza trifida* . . . . 118

Corn Lily . . . . . . . . 23, 116

*Cornus canadensis* . . . . 112

*Cornus suecica* . . . . . . . 123

*Corthylio calendula* . . . . 194

*Cortinarius acutus* . . . . . . 52

*Cortinarius armillatus* . . . . .
. . . . . . . . . . . . . . . . 54, 354

*Cortinarius camphoratus* 54

*Cortinarius caperatus* 55, 354

*Cortinarius collinitus* 52, 353

*Cortinarius croceus* . . . . . . .
. . . . . . . . . . . . . 48, 55, 353

*Cortinarius evernius* . . . . . 55

*Cortinarius flexipes* . . . . . 55

*Cortinarius semisanguineus*
. . . . . . . . . . . . . . . . 56, 354

*Cortinarius traganus* 54, 354

*Corvus brachyrhynchos* . 191

*Corvus corax* . . . . . . . . . 191

Coyote . . . . . . . . . . . . 13, 205,
. . . . . . 207, 212, 312, 313, 355

Crab . . . . . . . . . . . . . 19, 151,
. . 238, 240, 241, 345, 355, 356
  *see* Common Rock Crab;
  Decorator Crab;
  European Green Crab;
  Hemit Crab; Toad Crab

Crackerberry . . . . . 112, 123

*Craterellus tubaeformis* . . . .
. . . . . . . . . . . . . . . . 54, 354

Creeping Juniper . . . . . . 103

Creeping Snowberry . . 113

Crested Wood Fern . . . 95

Crinoid . . . . . . . . . . . . . 282

Cruet Collar Moss . . . . . 87

*Cruziana* . . . . . . . . . . . 278

*Ctenucha virginica* . . . . . 156

Cuckoo Flower . . . . . . . 130

Cunner . . . . . . 20, 259, 261

*Cyanea capillata* . . . . . . 234

*Cyanocitta cristata* . . . . . 191

*Cyclopterus lumpus* . . . 267

*Cypripedium acaule* . . . 117

*Cypripedium parviflorum*
  var. *pubescens* . . . . . . 121

*Cypripedium reginae* . . . 133

*Cystoclonium purpureum*
. . . . . . . . . . . . . . . . . . 227

*Cystophora cristata* . . . . 271

*Cystopteris fragilis* . . 92, 354

**D**

*Dacrymyces chrysospermus*
. . . . . . . . . . . . . . . . 60, 353

Dahlia Anemone . . 19, 235
  *see* Northern Red
  Anemone

Daisy Brittle Star . . . . . . . .
. . . . . . . . . . . . 19, 249, 356

*Danaus plexippus* . . . . . . 153

Dark-Eyed Junco . . 24, 200

*Dasiphora fruticosa* . . . . 119

Deadman's Fingers . . . . 233
  *see* Finger Sponge

Death Angel . . . . . . . . . . 50

Decorator Crab . . . . . . . 241
  *see* Toad Crab

Deepwater Redfish . . . 269

Deer Fly . . . . . . . . . . . . . 163

Deer Mouse . 205, 208, 355

Deer Mushroom . . . . . . 60

*Degelia plumbea* . . . . . . . 72

*Delamarea attenuata* . . 222

*Delphinapterus leucas* . . 274

*Delphinus delphis* . . . . . . 275

*Dendrolycopodium*
  *dendroideum* . . . . . . . . 98

*Dendronotus frondosus* 246

*Dermatocarpon luridum* 76

*Dermestes lardarius* . . . . . . .
. . . . . . . . . . . . . . . 162, 354

*Desmarestia aculeata* . . 223

*Desmarestia viridis* . . . . 223

*Devaleraea ramentacea* 228

Dewberry . . . . . . . . . . . 114

*Diapensia lapponica* . . . 119

*Dibaeis baeomyces* . . . . . . 81

*Dicranum species* . . . 84, 354

*Dictyosiphon foeniculaceus*
. . . . . . . . . . . . . . . . . . 223

*Diphasiastrum*
  *complanatum* . . . . . . . 98

*Diphasiastrum tristachyum*
. . . . . . . . . . . . . . . . . . . 98

*Doellingeria umbellata* . 115

Dogberry . . . . . . . . 22, 108
  *see* American Mountain
  Ash

Dogwhelk . 18, 19, 244, 356

Dogwinkle . . . . . . . . . . 244
  *see* Dogwhelk

Dogwood . . . . . 112, 123, 155
Dolphin. . 9, 16, 17, 215, 252,
. . 273, 275, 352, 355, 356, 357
  see Atlantic White-
  Sided Dolphin;
  Common Dolphin
*Dolichousnea longissima* . .
. . . . . . . . . . . . . . . . . . . . . . 71
Double-Crested
  Cormorant . . . . . 176, 342
Downy Woodpecker . . . . .
. . . . . . . . . . . . . . . . . 24, 190
Dragon's Mouth Orchid . .
. . . . . . . . . . . . . . . 25, 26, 125
*Drosera rotundifolia* . . . 124
*Dryas integrifolia* . . . . . . 119
*Dryopteris campyloptera* . . .
. . . . . . . . . . . . . . 94, 95, 354
*Dryopteris carthusiana* . . . .
. . . . . . . . . . . . . . 94, 95, 354
*Dryopteris cristata* . . 95, 354
*Dryopteris filix-mas* . . . . . . .
. . . . . . . . . . . . . 95, 96, 354
*Dryopteris intermedia* . . . . .
. . . . . . . . . . . . . 95, 96, 354
Dulce . . . . . . . . . . . . . . . 232
*Dumontia contorta* . . . . . . .
. . . . . . . . . . . . . . . . 228, 355
Dunlin. . . . . . . . . . . . . . 184
Dwarf Huckleberry . . . 126
*Dynamena pumila* . . . . . 234
*Dytiscus* sp. . . . . . . . . . . . 161

**E**
Early Coralroot . . . . . . . 118
Eastern American Toad
. . . . . . . . . . . . . . . . 166, 168
Eastern Chipmunk. . . . . . .
. . . . . . . . . . . . . . . . 205, 208
Eastern Kingbird. . . . . . . 192
Eastern Tiger Swallowtail
. . . . . . . . . . . . . . . . 152, FC
*Echinarachnius parma* .250
*Ectocarpus fasciculatus* . 221
*Ectocarpus siliculosus* . . 221
Edible Periwinkle . . . . . 243
  see Common Periwinkle
Eel Grass. 20, 216, 217, 239,
. . . . . . . . 240, 257, 259, 261
*Elachista fucicola* . 223, 226
*Elasmostethus cruciatus*160
Elm Sawfly . . . . . . . 164, 354
*Empetrum nigrum* . . . . . 121
*Empidonax alnorum* . . . 192
*Empidonax flaviventris* . 192
*Enallagma boreale* . . . . . 158

*Ensis directus*. . . . . . . . 247
*Epigaea repens* . . . . . . . . 113
*Equisetum arvense* . . . . 100
*Equisetum fluviatile* . . . 100
*Equisetum sylvaticum* . . 100
*Equisetum variegatum* 100
*Eremophilia alpestris* . . .192
*Erignathus barbatus* . . .272
*Eriocaulon aquaticum*. . 132
*Erioderma mollissimum* .72
*Erioderma pedicellatum* . .
. . . . . . . . . . . . . . . . . 73, 88
Ermine 23, 205, 210, 313, 355
  see Short-Tailed Weasel
*Euphagus carolinus* . . . 204
*Euphrasia nemorosa* . . .143
European Earwig . . . . .159
European Green Crab . . . .
. . . . . . . . . . . . . . . 240, 356
European Mountain Ash .
. . . . . . . . . . . . . 22, 104, 108
European Skipper. . . . . 155
European Starling. . . . .195
*Eurybia radula* . . . . . . . 129
Evening Grosbeak 24, 203
Evergreen Wood Fern . 96

**F**
Fairy Flax . . . . . . . . . . . .142
Fairy Puke. . . . . . . . . . . .81
Fairy Ring Mushroom . .58
*Falcipennis canadensis* .187
*Falco columbarius* . . . . .186
False Chanterelle . . . . . .56
False Morel. . . . . . . . . . . .61
Field Chickweed . . . . . .118
Field Horsetail. . . . . . . 100
Field Oxytrope . . . . . . .123
Fin Whale . . . . . 17, 274, 357
Finger Sponge . . . . 233, 355
Finger-Scale Foam Lichen
. . . . . . . . . . . . . . . . . . . . . . 75
Fireweed . . . . 7, 29, 116, FC
Fishbone Beard Lichen . 71
Fishnet Cladonia . . . . . 78
Flat-Topped White Aster
. . . . . . . . . . . . . . . . . . . . . 115
Flatleaf Bladderwort . .134
Flower Fly. . . . . . . . . . . .164
*Fomes fomentarius*. . 62, 353
*Fomitopsis betulina* 64, 354
*Fomitopsis mounceae*63, 353
*Fomitopsis ochracea* 63, 353
*Fontinalis antipyretica* . 84
*Fontinalis* species. . .84, 354
*Forficula auricularia*159, 354

Fork-Mosses. . . . . . . . . 84
Fossil . . . . . . . 7, 9, 277–283,
. . . . 285, 298, 299, 300, 301,
. . . . 302, 305, 309, 342, 343,
. . . . . . . . . 346, 344, 357, 358
  see Acritarchs; Asteroid
  Fossil; *Aspidella
  terranovica Billings;*
  Brachiopod; *Callavia;*
  Cephalopod;
  Chitinozoan;
  Coral Fossil; Conularid;
  Crinoid; Gastropod;
  Graptolite; *Haootia
  quadriformis;
  Iapetognathus
  fluctivagus;*
  Machaeridian; Sponge
  Fossil; Ostracode;
  *Paradoxides;* Tree
  Trunk Fossil;
  *Treptichnus pedum;*
  Trilobite
Four-Spotted Skimmer 158
Fourspine Stickleback . . . .
. . . . . . . . . . . . 259, 260, 356
Fox Sparrow. 24, 199, 201
*Fragaria virginiana* . . . .142
Fragile Fern . . . . . . . . . . 92
Fragrant Water Lily . . .130
Franklin's Gull . . . . 317, 318
*Fratercula arctica* . . . . . .180
*Fraxinus nigra*. . . . . . . . .110
Frayed Ramalina. . . . . . .71
Frilled Anemone. 235, 355
Frizzled Pincushion . . . 88
Froghopper . . . . . . . . . .160
*Frullania asagrayana*. . . 88
*Fucus distichus* . . . . 226, BC
*Fucus edentatus* . . . . . . 226
*Fucus evanescens* . . . . . 226
*Fucus* sp. . . . . 220, 225, 237
*Fucus spiralis*. . . . . . . . . 226
*Fucus vesiculosus* . . . . . 226
*Fulmarus glacialis* . . . . .175
*Funaria hygrometrica* . . 84

**G**
*Gadus morhua* . . . . . . . 264
*Gadus ogac* . . . . . . . . . . 264
*Galeopsis tetrahit* . . . . . .147
Gall of the Earth . . . . . .122
*Gallinago delicata* . . . . .184
*Gammarus* sp . . . . . . . . .238
*Ganoderma applanatum* . .
. . . . . . . . . . . . . . . . . . 65, 353

Garland Sea Fir . . . 234, 355
Gaspereau. . . . . . . . . . . .258
  see Alewife
Gasterosteus aculeatus  260
Gasterosteus wheatlandi261
Gastropod. . . 218, 241, 242,
Gastropod (fossil) 277, 281,
. . . . . . . . . . . 282, 342, 343
  see High-Spired
  Gastropod; Plani-
  spiral Gastropod
Gaultheria hispidula . . . 113
Gavia immer . . . . . . . . . .173
Gaylussacia baccata. . . .127
Gaylussacia bigeloviana 126
Geothlypis philadelphia.198
Geothlypis trichas. . . . . .198
Geum macrophyllum. . . 114
Ghost Pipe . . . . . . . . 23, 113
Giant American Water
  Bug . . . . . . . . . . . . . . .160
Glaucous Gull . . . . . . . . . .
. . . . . . . . 177, 178, 317, 318
Globicephala melas . . . .275
Gloeophyllum sepiarium . . .
. . . . . . . . . . . . . . . . . 63, 353
Golden Redfish . . . . . . 269
Golden Rove Beetle . . . 161
Golden-Crowned Kinglet .
. . . . . . . . . . . . . . . . . . . .194
Goldthread. . . . . . . .23, 124
Gorgonocephalus arcticus. .
. . . . . . . . . . . . . . . . . . . 249
Graphis scripta . . . . . . . .
Graptolite. . . 279, 281, 282
Grassleaf Starwort . . . .143
Grasspink, . . . . . . . 26, 126
Great Black-Backed Gull. .
. . 177, 178, 317, 318, 319, 342
Great Cormorant . . . . .176
Great Horned Owl . . . . . .
. . . . . . . . . . .12, 188, 207, 353
Great Shearwater . . . . .175
Greater Scaup . . . . . . . .173
Greater Water Moss. . . 84
Greater Yellowlegs .27, 184
Green Comma. . . . 154, BC
Green Frog. . . . . . . . . . . .
. . . . . . . . . 27, 166, 168, 169
Green Lacewing . . . . . .160
Green Sea Urchin . . . . . . . .
. . . . . . . . . 19, 250, 250, 356
Green Spleenwort. . . . . 90
Green Woodland Peat
  Moss . . . . . . . . . . . . . . . .87
Green-Pea Mushroom

Lichen. . . . . . . . . . . . . . .81
Green-Winged Teal . . .172
Greenland Cod . . . . . . . . .
. . . . . . . . . . . 262, 264, 356
Greenland Scurvy Grass 136
Grey Jay. . . . . . . 24, 191, 315
Grey Reindeer Lichen . 79
Grey Seal. . . . . . . . .17, 272
Grey Veiled Amanita . . . 51
Grey-Cheeked Thrush. . . .
. . . . . . . . . . . . . . . 195, 354
Ground Beetle . . . . . . . .161
Grove Sandwort . . . . . .136
Grubby . . . . . . . . 259, 262
Gymnocarpium dryopteris
. . . . . . . . . . . . . . . . . . . . .93
Gymnopus dryophilus . . .56
Gyromitra esculenta. . . . .61

H

Habrosyne scripta . . . . .157
Haemorhous purpureus 202
Haircap Mosses. . . . . . . .85
Hairy Woodpecker. . . .190
Halerpestes cymbalaria .138
Haliaetus leucocephalus . . .
. . . . . . . . . . . . . . . . . . . .185
Halichoerus grypus . . . .272
Halichondria panicea . 233
Haliclona oculata. . . . . . 233
Halocynthia pyriformis .251
Halosiphon tomentosa .225
Haootia quadriformis . .346
Harbour Porpoise 275, 357
Harbour Seal . . . . . . . . . . .
. . . . . . . . . .17, 272, 350, 357
Hard Tube Worm . 236, 355
Harebell . . . . . . . . . . . . .123
Harp Seal . . . . . 17, 271, 357
Heal-All. . . . . . . . . . . . .147
Heart Lichen . . . . . . . . . .75
Heartleaf Birch . . . . . . 106
Helvella lacunosa . . 61, 353
Hemaris thysbe . . . . . . .156
Hemitripterus americanus .
. . . . . . . . . . . . . . . . . . 266
Hemlock Looper. . . . . .157
Henricia sanguinolenta 249
Herald Moth . . . . . . . . .156
Hermit Crab . . . . 240, 345
Hermit Thrush . . . . . . .195
Herring Gull .177, 178, 179,
. . . . . 317, 318, 319, 320, 342
High-Spired Gastropod. . .
. . . . . . . . . .277, 282, 343, 357
Hildenbrandia rubra . . 229

Hirundo rustica . . . . . . .193
Homarus americanus . .241
Honckenya peploides. . . 137
Honey Bee . . . . . . .165, 346
Honey Mushroom . . . . . 51
Hooded Ladies'-Tresses. . .
. . . . . . . . . . . . . . . . 26, 143
Hooded Seal. . . . . . 271, 357
Hooker's Iris. . . . . . . . . .140
Hop Clover. . . . . . . . . . .148
Horn Coral. . . . . . . . . . .281
Horned Bladderwort . .128
Horned Lark . . . . . . . . .192
Hornet. . . . . . . . . . . . . .165
  see Paper Wasp
Horntail Sawfly . . . . . . .165
Horse Fart . . . . . . . . . . . .65
Horse Fly . . . . . . . . . . . .163
Horse Mussel. . . . .247, 356
Horsehair Lichen . . . . . 70
House Fly . . . . . . . . . . . .164
House Mouse . . . .209, 355
House Sparrow . . 196, 201
Hummingbird Clearwing
  Moth. . . . . . . . . . . . . .156
Humpback Whale . . . . . .
. . . . . . . 16, 17, 273, 357, BC
Huperzia selago . . . . . . . 99
Hyas coarctatus . . . . . . .241
Hydropunctaria maura. .77
Hydroprogne caspi . . . . .179
Hygrocybe conica . . . 56, 353
Hygrophoropsis
  aurantiaca . . . . . . . . . . .56
Hylocomium splendens . .85
Hyolithid . . . . . . . .281, 282
Hypogymnia hultenii. . . .72
Hypogymnia physodes. . .73

I

Iceberg. . . . . . . . . . . . . . . .
. . . . . . .7, 9, 10, 321–327, FC
Iceland Gull . . . . . . . . . . . .
. . . . . . . . . 177, 178, 317, 319
Iceland Lichen. . . . . . . . 78
Icmadophila ericetorum .81
Idotea baltica . . . . . . . . .239
Inarticulate Brachiopod . .
  see Brachiopod
Interrupted Fern. . . 90, 91
Iris hookeriana . . . . . . . .140
Iris versicolor. . . . . . . . . .134
Irish Moss. . . . .18, 227, 355
Ischnochiton albus . . . . 242
Isothecium myosuroides .85
Ivory Gull 177, 178, 317, 319

**J**

Jellyfish . . . . . . . . . 234, 355
  see Moon Jelly;
  Lion's Mane
*Junco hyemalis* . . . . . . . 200
June Beetle. . . . . . . . . .162
June Bug . . . . . . . . . . . . .162
  see June Beetle
*Juniperus communis* . . .103
*Juniperus horizontalis* .103
*Juniperus* spp. . . . . . . . .101

**K**

Kalm's Lobelia . . . . . . . . 135
*Kalmia angustifolia* . . . .126
*Kalmia polifolia* . . . . . . .127
*Kalmia procumbens*. . . . 121
Kelp Sowbug . . . . . . . . .239
Killer Whale . . . 17, 275, 357
Knotted Wrack 18, 226, 355
Knotty Pearlwort . . . . .137
Kumlien's Gull. . . . 317, 319

**L**

Labrador Tea . . . 25, 32, 126
*Lactarius deceptivus*. . . . .57
*Lactarius glyciosmus* . . . .57
*Lactarius helvus* . . . .57, 354
*Lactarius hibbardae*. . . . . .
 . . . . . . . . . . . . . . . . . .58, 354
*Lactarius lignyotus*. . . . . .57
*Lactarius thyinos* . . .58, 354
*Lacuna vincta* . . . . . . . 244
Ladder Lichen . . . . . . . . 80
Lady Fern . . . . . . . . . . . .93
Lady's Slipper. . . . . . . . . .
 . . . . . . . . . . 23, 117, 121,133
  see Large Yellow Lady's
  Slipper; Pink Lady's
  Slipper; Showy Lady's
  Slipper
*Lagenorhynchus acutus*.275
*Lagopus lagopus*. . . . . . .187
*Lagopus muta*. . . . . . . .188
*Lambdina fiscellaria* . . .157
Lamb's Quarters . . . . . .141
*Lambdina fiscellaria.* . .157
*Laminaria digitata*. . . . .224
*Laminaria* sp. . . . . 232, 237
Lapland Diapensia . . .119
Lapland Longspur. . . . .201
Lapland Rosebay. . . 31, 121
Larch . . 22, 27, 67, 101, 103
  see Tamarack
Larch Sawfly . . . . . . . 206
Larder Beetle . . . . . . . .162

Large Yellow Lady's Slipper
 . . . . . . . . . . . . . . . . . . . 121
Largeleaf Avens. . . . . . . 114
*Larix laricina* . . . . .101, 103
*Larus argentatus* . .178, 319
*Larus canus*. . . . . . . . . .318
*Larus crassirostris*. . . . . .317
*Larus delawarensis*.177, 320
*Larus fuscus*. . . . . . . . . .319
*Larus glaucoides*. . .178, 319
*Larus glaucoides kumlieni* .
 . . . . . . . . . . . . . . . . . . . .319
*Larus glaucoides thayeri*320
*Larus hyperboreus* .178, 318
*Larus marinus*. . . . .178, 318
*Larus michahellis* . . . . .320
*Larus schistisagus*. . . . .320
*Lasallia papulosa* . . . . . 76
*Lathyrus japonicus*. . . . .140
*Lathyrus palustris*. . . . . .140
Least Sandpiper . .182, 183
Leatherback Turtle. . . . 251
Leatherleaf. . . . . . . .25, 126
*Leathesia marina* . . . . . .223
*Leccinum holopus* . . . . . .67
*Leccinum scabrum*. . . . . 66
*Leiothlypis peregrina* . .198
*Lentinus brumalis* . . . . . .64
*Lepidonotus squamatus* . . .
 . . . . . . . . . . . . . . . . . . .236
*Lepiota cristata*. . . . . . . .58
*Lepus americanus*. . . . . 207
*Lepus arcticus bangsii* . . 207
Lesser Black-Backed Gull
 . . . . . . . . . . . . . . . . 317, 319
Lesser Purple Fringed
  Orchid . . . . . . . . . . . . .132
Lesser Yellowlegs . . . . .184
*Lethocerus americanus* .160
Lettered Habrosyne. . . .157
*Leucanthemum vulgare* 145
*Leuconotopicus villosus*.190
*Leucophaeus pipixcan* . .318
*Leucoraja ocellata* . . . . .263
*Leymus mollis*. . . . . . . . .142
*Libellula quadrimaculata* .
 . . . . . . . . . . . . . . . . . . . .158
*Lichenomphalia ericetorum*
 . . . . . . . . . . . . . . . . . . . . .59
*Lichenomphalia umbellifera*
 . . . . . . . . . . . . . . . . . . . . .81
Light Emerald . . . . . . . .157
*Ligusticum scoticum* . . .137
*Limanda ferruginea*. . . 268
*Limecola balthica* . . . . .247
*Limenitis arthemis* . . . .155

*Limnephilidae family*. . . . . .
 . . . . . . . . . . . . . . . . .163, 354
*Limnodromus griseus* . .184
*Limonium carolinianum* . . .
 . . . . . . . . . . . . . . . . . . . .140
*Lineus ruber*. . . . . . . . .237
*Linaria vulgaris*. . . . . . .146
Lincoln's Sparrow 200, 201
*Linnaea borealis*. . . . . . . 116
*Linum catharticum* . . . .142
Lion's Mane . . 234, 355, FC
*Liparis atlantica* . . . . . 260
*Lithobates septentrionalis*
 . . . . . . . . . . . . . . . . . . . .169
*Lithobates sylvatica* . . . .168
*Lithothamnion glaciale*. . . .
 . . . . . . . . . . . 19, 228, 229
Little Brown Bat . 205, 206
Little Chink Shell . . . . . . . .
 . . . . . . . . . . . 19, 244, 356
*Littorina littorea*. . . . . .243
*Littorina obtusata* . . . . .243
*Littorina saxatilis*. . . . . .243
*Littorina* sp. . . . . . . . . . 242
*Lobaria pulmonaria*. . . . .73
*Lobaria scrobiculata* . . . .73
*Lobelia kalmii*. . . . . . . . . 135
Lobster . . . . . . . . . . . 19, 151,
 . . . . . . . . .238, 240, 241, 355
  see American Lobster
Long Beech Fern. . . . . . 92
Long-Finned Pilot Whale .
 . . . . . . . . . . . . . . . . .275, 357
Long-Tailed Duck.174, 354
Longbract Frog Orchid 122
Longhorn Sculpin. . . . . . . .
 . . . . . . . . . 20, 262, 267
*Lonicera villosa*. . . . . . .128
*Lontra canadensis
  canadensis* . . . . . . . . . .210
Lowbush Blueberry . . .120
*Loxia curvirostra* . . . . . 203
Lugworm . . . . . . . . 236, 355
Lumpfish . . . . . . . 262, 267
*Lunatia heros* . . . . . . . . 244
Lungwort . . . . . . . . . . . . .73
Lupin. . . . . 4, 5, 10, 155, 353
*Lycaena epixanthe* . . . . . 155
*Lycodes lavalaei* . . . . . . .265
*Lycoperdon perlatum*. . . . . .
 . . . . . . . . . . . . . . . 65, 353
*Lycopodiella inundata*. . 98
*Lycopodium clavatum*. . 98
*Lycopodium lagopus* . . . 99

Lynx..... 23, 205, 207, 212,
............313, 315, 355
  see Canada Lynx;
  Newfoundland Lynx
Lynx canadensis subsolanus
................212
Lysimachia maritima ..138
Lysimachia terrestris ... 131
Lythrum salicaria...... 133

**M**

Machaeridian ........282
Magnolia Warbler 196, 199
Maianthemum canadense
................116
Maianthemum stellatum
................138
Maianthemum trifolium125
Male Fern............ 96
Mallard........27, 34, 172
Mallotus villosus...... 270
Malva moschata.......146
Maned Nudibranch .. 246
  see Common Grey Sea
  Slug
Marasmius oreades .....58
Marchantia polymorpha 89
Mareca americana.....171
Margarites helicinus....245
Maritime Glasswort...141
Maritime Sunburst
Lichen............... 76
Marsh Blue Violet.. 26, 135
Marsh Cinquefoil.....133
Marsh Marigold .... 133
Marsh Skullcap.......135
Marsh Vetchling......140
Marshberry .........127
Marten ... 13, 24, 205, 207,
............211, 339, 340
  see American Marten;
  Newfoundland Marten;
  Marten Cat; Pine Marten
Marten Cat...........211
Martes Americana atrata
................211
Masked Shrew..........
......23, 205, 206, 314, 355
Matchstick Lichen .... 78
Matricaria discoidea ...144
Matteucia struthiopteris .91
McIsaac's Ringlet .....153
Meadow Vole...........
..........30, 205, 208, 314
Medicago lupulina.....148
Megaceryle alcyon .....189

Megaptera novaeangliae
....................273
Melanoplus sp........159
Melanosiphon intestinalis
....................222
Melospiza georgiana .. 200
Melospiza lincolnii .... 200
Melospiza melodia .... 200
Membranipora
  membranacea .......237
Membranoptera alata ..232
Mentha canadensis ....135
Menyanthes trifoliata .. 131
Mergus merganser .....174
Mergus serrator........174
Merlin...........186, 354
Mertensia maritima....141
Metridium senile...235, 246
Mew Gull ...........318
  see Common Gull
Microgadus tomcod....257
Microtus pennsylvanicus
  terranovae ......... 208
Milbert's Tortoiseshell. 154
Mink Frog... 166, 168, 169
Mistassini Primrose... 131
Mitella nuda ..........117
Mniotilta varia.......197
Modiolus modiolus.... 247
Moehringia lateriflora ..136
Molldow............. 70
  see Witch's Hair
Monarch.............. 153
Moneses uniflora ..... 113
Monk's Hood Lichen...73
Monochamus scutellatus...
..................162, 354
Monoplacophorans ....282
Monostroma grevillei...219
Monotropa uniflora.... 113
Moon Jelly ....234, 355
Moon Snail... 20, 244, 355
Moonwort ........... 96
Moose .9, 21, 23, 30, 61, 101,
...104, 205, 213, 311, 312, 315
Morchella importuna....61
Morus bassanus ...175, 342
Mosquito .. 25, 27, 152, 163
Moss Campion ......118
Mottled Chiton...... 242
Mountain Alder ......107
Mountain Ash . 28, 196, 315
Mountain Cranberry ..120
  see Partridgeberry
Mountain Fly
  Honeysuckle........128

Mountain Maple.. 22, 109
Mountain Serviceberry...
....................22, 114
Mountain Wood Fern . 94
Mourning Cloak......154
Mourning Dove ......188
Mourning Warbler.......
................ 198, 199
Mouse-Tail Moss ......85
Mud Trout ...........256
  see Brook (Mud) Trout
Multiclavula mucida ....81
Multiclavula vernalis....81
Mus musculus ... 209
Musca domestica ..164, 354
Musk Mallow.........146
Muskrat .................
.... 13, 33, 205, 209, 314, 355
Mussel 18, 19, 236, 241, 244,
..... 246, 247, 248, 353, 356
  see Blue Mussel; Horse
  Mussel
Mustela richardsonii ...210
Mycena haematopus ....59
Mycoblastus sanguinarius..
........................75
Myotis lucifugus .... 206
Myotis septentrionalis . 206
Myoxocephalus aenaeus ...
.................... 262
Myoxocephalus
  octodecemspinosus .. 267
Myoxocephalus scorpius267
Myrica gale..........129
Myrionora albidula .... 70
Mytilus edulis ........ 246

**N**

Nabalus trifoliolatus ...122
Nadata gibbosa .......157
Naked Mitrewort ....117
Neogale vison .........210
Nephroma arcticum ... 80
New York Fern ........93
Newfoundland Beaver....
........13, 33, 205, 209, 355
Newfoundland Black Bear
....................211
Newfoundland Caribou ..
..................213, 339
  see Woodland Caribou
Newfoundland
  Chanterelle..........52
Newfoundland Eelpout
.................. 262, 265
Newfoundland Fox ...212

Newfoundland Lynx . . 212
*see* Canada Lynx
Newfoundland Marten 211
Newfoundland Reindeer
Lichen. . . . . . . . . . . . . 80
Newfoundland Wolf 13, 205
*Nicrophorus* sp . . . . . . . . 161
Ninespine Stickleback. . . .
. . . . . 258, 259, 260, 261, 356
North American Black
Bear. . . . . . . . . . . . . . . 211
Northern Basket Star . . . . .
. . . . . . . . . . . . . . . . . 249, 355
Northern Caddisfly . . . 163
Northern Firmoss. . . . . 99
Northern Flicker. . . . . . . .
. . . . . . . . . . . . . . 24, 151, 190
Northern Fulmar . . . . . 175
Northern Gannet . 175, 342
Northern Goldenrod . . 122
Northern Goshawk . . . . .
. . . . . . . . . . . . . . . 186, 354
Northern Harrier . . . . . 186
Northern Holly Fern . . . . .
. . . . . . . . . . . . . . . . 93, 94
Northern Interrupted
Clubmoss. . . . . . . . . . 99
Northern Leopard Frog. . .
. . . . . . . . . . . . . . . . . . . 167
Northern Long-Eared Bat
. . . . . . . . . . . 205, 206, 355
Northern Minke Whale . .
. . . . . . . . . . . . . . . 273, 357
Northern Pintail . . . . . . 172
Northern Pipefish. . . . . . .
. . . . . . . . . . . . 259, 261, 356
Northern Red Anemone. .
. . . . . . . . . . . . . . . 235, 355
Northern River Otter . . 210
Northern Rock Barnacle. .
. . . . . . . . . . . . . . . . . . . 239
*see* Common Barnacle
Northern Running-Pine . .
. . . . . . . . . . . . . . . . . . . 98
Northern Sea Star. 19, 248
Northern Spikemoss . . 99
Northern Waterthrush . . .
. . . . . . . . . . . . . . . 198, 199
Norway Rat . 205, 209, 355
*Nucella lapillus* . . . . . . 244
*Numenius phaeopus* . . . 185
*Nuphar variegata* . . . . . . 130
*Nymphaea odorata* . . . . 130
*Nymphalis antiopa* . . . . 154
*Nymphalis vaualbum* . . 154

**O**

Oak Fern. . . . . . . . . . . . . 93
Ocean Pout . 262, 265, 356
*Ochrolechia frigida* . . . . . 81
*Oclemena nemoralis* . . 129
*Oenothera biennis* . . . . . 146
Old Man's Beard . . . . 23, 71
*Ondatra zibethicus
obscurus* . . . . . . . . . . 209
One-Cone Clubmoss. . 99
One-Flowered
Wintergreen . . . . . 23, 113
One-Sided Wintergreen . .
. . . . . . . . . . . . . . . . . . . 113
*Onoclea sensibilis* . . . . . . 92
*Ontholestes cingulatus* . 161
*Ophioparma ventosa* . . . . 77
*Ophiopholis aculeata*. . 249
Orange Hawkweed . . . 145
Orange Witch's Butter 60
Orca. . . . . . . . . . 17, 275, 357
*see* Killer Whale
*Orcinus orca* . . . . . . . . . 275
*Orthilia secunda* . . . . . . . 113
*Osmerus mordax* . . . . . . 257
*Osmunda cinnamomeum*
. . . . . . . . . . . . . . . . . . . 91
*Osmunda claytoniana* . . 91
*Osmunda regalis* . . . . . . 92
Osprey. . . . . . . 33, 185, 339
Ostracode. . . . . . . 281, 282
Ostrich Feather Moss . 86
Ostrich Fern. . . . . . . 90, 91
*Otiorhynchus sulcatus* . . 162
Owl . . . . . . . . 24, 188, 206
*see* Boreal Owl; Great
Horned Owl; Short-
Eared Owl; Snowy Owl
Oxeye Daisy. . . . . . . . . 145
*Oxytropis campestris* . . . 123
Oyster Leaf. . . . . . . . . . 141

**P**

*Pagophila eburnea* . 178, 319
*Pagophilus groenlandica*271
*Pagurus acadianus* . . . . 240
*Pagurus bernhardus* . . . 240
*Pagurus pubescens* . . . . 240
Painted Lady. . . . . . . . . 155
Pale Beauty . . . . . . . . . . 157
*see* Light Emerald
*Palmaria palmata* . . . . . 232
*Pandion haliaetus* . . . . . 185
*Panellus stipticus* . . . . 64, 354
*Pannaria lurida* ssp.
*Russellii* . . . . . . . . . . . . . 74

Paper Birch . . . . . . . . . . 106
*see* White Birch
Paper Wasp . . . . . . . . . . . 165
*Papilio brevicauda* . . . . . 152
*Papilio glaucus* . . . . . . . . 152
Parasol Moss . . . . . . . . . 87
*see* Brilliant Dung Moss
*Parmelia squarrosa* . . . . 74
Partridge . . . . . . . . 187, 188
*see* Willow Ptarmigan,
Rock Ptarmigan
Partridgeberry . 28, 29, 120
*Passer domesticus* . . . . . 201
*Passerculus sandwichensis*
. . . . . . . . . . . . . . . . . . . 199
*Passerella iliaca*. . . . . . . . 199
Pear-Shaped Puffball . . . 65
Pearly Everlasting . . . . . 144
Pectoral Sandpiper . . . . . .
. . . . . . . . . . . . . . . 182, 183
*Peltigera aphthosa* . . . . . 80
Pennsylvania Bittercress
. . . . . . . . . . . . . . . . . . . 130
*Perisoreus canadensis*. . . 191
*Peromyscus maniculatus*
. . . . . . . . . . . . . . . . . . . 208
*Petalonia fascia* . . . . . . . 222
*Petalonia zosterifolia* . . . 222
*Phalacrocorax auritus* . . 176
*Phalacrocorax carbo* . . . 176
*Phalaropus fulicarius* . . . 176
*Phalaropus lobatus* . . . . 176
*Phegopteris connectilis* . . . .
. . . . . . . . . . . . . . . . 92, 354
*Philaenus* sp. . . . . . . . . . . 160
*Phoca vitulina*. . . . . . . . 272
*Phocoena phocoena* . . . . 275
*Pholiota squarrosa* . . 59, FC
*Pholis gunnellus* . . . . . . . 259
*Phycodrys rubens* . . . . . . 232
*Phyllophaga anxia* . . . . . 162
*Phymatolithon lenormandii*
. . . . . . . . . . . . . . . . . . . 229
*Picea glauca* . . . . . . . . . . 101
*Picea mariana*. . . . . . . . 102
*Picoides arcticus* . . . . . . . 190
*Picoides pubescens* . . . . 190
*Pieris rapae* . . . . . . . . . . 153
Pigeon . . . . . . . 16, 180, 188
*see* Rock Pigeon;
Sea Pigeon
*Pilophorus fibula* . . . . . . 78
*Pilosella aurantiaca* . . . . 145
Pincherry. . . . . . . . . 22, 107
Pincushion . . . . . . . . . . . 88
Pine Grosbeak . . . 202, 315

Pine Marten . . .13, 24, 207,
. . . . . . . . . 211, 339, 340, FC
Pine Siskin. . . . . . . . . . 203
Pineapple Weed. . . . . . .144
*Pinguicula vulgaris.* . . . . .134
*Pinicola enucleator* . . . 202
Pink Earth Lichen. . . . . .81
Pink Lady's Slipper . 23, 117
*Pinus resinosa* . . . . . . . .102
*Pinus* spp. . . . . . . . . . . .101
*Pinus strobus.* . . . . . . . . .102
*Pinus sylvestris* . . . . . . .102
Pitcher Plant. . . . . . . . . . .
. . . . . .9, 15, 25, 128, 163. 353
Planispiral Gastropod . . . .
. . . . . . . . . . . . . . . . .277, FC
Planktonic Amphipod. . . .
. . . . . . . . . . . . . . . 239, 356
*Plantago maritima* . . . .141
*Platanthera blephariglottis*
. . . . . . . . . . . . . . . . . . . .125
*Platanthera clavellata* . .125
*Platanthera dilatata* . . .132
*Platanthera psycodes* . . .132
*Platismatia glauca* . . . . . .74
*Plectrophenax nivalis.* . . 202
*Pleurocybella porrigens* . . .
. . . . . . . . . . . . . . . . .59, 353
*Pleurozium schreberi* . . . .85
Plumboy . . . . . . . . . . . . .114
  see Dewberry
*Pluteus methvenii* . . . . . . 60
*Pluvialis dominica* . . . .181
*Pluvialis squatarola* . . . .181
*Poecile atricapillus* . . . . .193
*Poecile hudsonicus* . . . . .193
*Pogonia ophioglossoides* 125
Polar Bear. . . 204, 205, 355
*Polygonia faunus* . . . . . .154
*Polypodium virginianum* 91
*Polysiphonia flexicaulis* .230
*Polysiphonia* sp. . . 216, 229
*Polysiphonia stricta* . . . .230
*Polystichum braunii*. . . . 94
*Polystichum lonchitis.* . . .93
*Polytrichum* species. . . . .85
*Populus balsamifera.* . . .105
*Populus tremuloides.* . . .104
*Porphyra linearis* . . . . . .231
*Porphyra purpurea* . . . . .231
*Porphyra umbilicalis* . . .231
*Porpidia crustulata* . . . . .77
Porpoise . . . . . . . . . . . . . . .
. . . .16, 17, 252, 273, 261, 264
  see Common Porpoise,
  Harbour Porpoise

Powdered Honeycomb
  Lichen . . . . . . . . . . . . . .72
*Prasiola stipitata* . . . . . .217
Predaceous Diving Beetle
. . . . . . . . . . . . . . . . . . . .161
Prickleback . . . . . . . . . .265
  see Radiated Shanny
Prickly Sowthistle. . . . .139
Prickly Tree-Clubmoss 98
*Primula mistassinica* . . . 131
*Protomonostroma*
  *undulatum* . . . . . . . . .219
*Prunella vulgaris.* . . . . . .147
*Prunus pensylvanica* . . .107
*Prunus* spp. . . . . . . . . . .104
*Prunus virginiana.* . . . . 108
*Pseudocyphellaria crocata* 74
*Pseudocyphellaria perpetua*
. . . . . . . . . . . . . . . . . . . .74
*Pseudopleuronectes*
  *americanus* . . . . . . . . 268
*Pteridium aquilinum* . . . 94
*Ptilium crista-castrensis* 86
*Ptilota serrata* . . . . .230, 232
Puckered Ulota . . . . . . 88
Puffin 16, 180, 342, 353, FC
  see Atlantic Puffin
*Punctaria latifolia* . . . . .222
*Punctaria plantaginea.* .222
Punctured Ribbon Lichen
. . . . . . . . . . . . . . . . . . . .71
*Pungitius pungitius* . . . .259
Purple Finch . . . . . . . . . .
. . . . . . .24, 201, 202, 203, 315
Purple Loosestrife. . . . . 133
Purple Sandpiper. .182, 183
Purple Star. . . . . . . . . . . 248
  see Northern Sea Star
Purple Sunstar . . . . . . . 249
Purple-Stemmed Aster 115
*Pusa hispida* . . . . . . . . . .272
Pussy Willow . . . .104, 105
*Pylaiella littoralis* . . . . . .221

**Q**

*Quiscalus quiscula* . . . . 204

**R**

Rabbitfoot Clover . . . . . 48
*Racomitrium lanuginosum*
. . . . . . . . . . . . . . . . . . 86
Radiated Shanny. . . . . . . .
. . . . . . . . . . . . 262, 265, 356
Rainbow Smelt. . . . . . . . .
. . . . . . . . . . . . 255, 257, 356
*Ralfsia fungiformis.* . . . .221

*Ralfsia verrucosa* . . . . . .221
*Ramalina dilacerata* . . . .71
*Ramalina roesleri* . . . . . . .71
*Ramalina* sp. . . . . . . . . . . .71
*Rana clamitans.* . . . . . . .168
*Rana sylvatica.* . . . . . . . .168
*Rangifer tarandus caribou* .
. . . . . . . . . . . . . . . . . . . .213
Rattlesnake Fern . . . . . . 96
Razorbill. . . . . . . . . . . . 180
Red Admiral . . . . . . . . . .154
Red Belted Conk . . . . . . .63
Red Chiton . . . . . . . . . . 242
Red Clover. . . . . . . . . . . 148
Red Crossbill. . 24, 203, 315
Red Fox. . . . . . . . . . . . . .23,
. . .29, 205, 207, 212, 312, 353
  see Newfoundland Fox
Red Knot . . . . . . . . . . . .182
Red Lineus. . . . . . . 237, 356
Red Maple .22, 27, 104, 109
Red Phalarope . . . . . . . .176
Red Pine . . . .21, 21, 102, 341
Red Sandspurry . . . . . . .143
Red Squirrel . . . . . . . . . . .
. . . . . . 23, 195, 205, 207, 311
Red-Breasted Merganser. .
. . . . . . . . . . . . . . . .174, 354
Red-Breasted Nuthatch194
Red-Crossed Stink Bug 160
Red-Fruited Pixie-Cup
  Lichen . . . . . . . . . . . . . 79
Red-Necked Phalarope .176
Red-Stemmed Feather
  Moss. . . . . . . . . . . . . . . .85
Red-Winged Blackbird 204
*Regulus satrapa* . . . . . . .194
*Rheumaptera hastata* . . 157
*Rhinanthus minor* . . . . .143
*Rhizocarpon concentricum*
. . . . . . . . . . . . . . . . . . . .77
*Rhizocarpon geographicum*
. . . . . . . . . . . . . . . . . . . .77
*Rhizoclonium riparium* .219
*Rhodiola rosea* . . . . . . . .139
*Rhododendron canadense*
. . . . . . . . . . . . . . . . . . . .127
*Rhododendron*
  *groenlandicum.* . . . . . .216
*Rhododendron lapponicum*
. . . . . . . . . . . . . . . . . . . .121
*Rhodomela confervoides*
. . . . . . . . . . . . . . . . . . . .230
Rhodora . 127, 256, 355
*Rhytidiadelphus triquetrus*
. . . . . . . . . . . . . . . . . . . .86

*Ribes glandulosum* . . . . . 115
*Ribes lacustre* . . . . . . . . . 115
Ring-Billed Gull . . . . . . . . . .
. . . . . . . . . 177, 317, 318, 320
Ring-Necked Duck . . . . 172
Ringed Seal . . . . . . . . . . . 272
*Riparia riparia* . . . . . . . . 193
*Rissa tridactyla* . . . . 178, 320
River Beauty . . . . . . . . . . 122
Rock Cod . . . . . . . . . . . . 264
  see Greenland Cod
Rock Gunnel . . 20, 259, 356
Rock Pigeon . . . . . . . . . . 188
Rock Ptarmigan . . . . . . . . .
. . . . . . . . . . . . . 187, 188, 339
Rock Purple . . . . . . . . . . 244
  see Dogwhelk
Rockhopper . . . . . . 238, 356
*Rosa virginiana* . . . . . . . . 114
Rose Pogonia . . . . . . . . . 125
Roseroot . . . . . . . . . . . . . 139
Rostroconch . . . . . . . . . 282
Rough Aster . . . . . . 29, 129
Rough Barnacle . . 240, 356
Rough Periwinkle . . . . . . . .
. . . . . . . . . . . . . 18, 243, 356
Rough-Legged Hawk . . . . .
. . . . . . . . . . . . . . . . 186, 354
Roundleaf Sundew . . . . 124
Royal Fern . . . . . . . . . 90, 92
*Rubus arcticus* . . . . . . . . . 119
*Rubus chamaemorus* . . . 124
*Rubus pubescens* . . . . . . . 114
Ruby-Crowned Kinglet 194
Ruddy Turnstone . . . . . 185
Ruffed Grouse . 24, 187, 316
Running Clubmoss . . . . 98
*Russula montana* . . . . . . 60
*Russula paludosa* . . . . . . 60
Rusty Blackbird . . . . . . 204
Rusty Gilled Polypore . . 63

**S**

*Saccharina latissima* . . . 224
*Saccharina longicruris* . . 224
*Saccorhiza dermatodea* . 224
*Sagina nodosa* . . . . . . . . 137
*Salicornia maritima* . . . . 141
*Salix bebbiana* . . . . . . . . . 105
*Salix discolor* . . . . . . . . . . 105
*Salix* spp. . . . . . . . . . . . . . 104
*Salmo salar* . . . . . . . 254, 255
Salmon . 13, 32, 33, 254, 255,
. . . . . . . . . . . . . 256, 345, 346
  see Atlantic Salmon
Salted Shell Lichen . . . . 72

*Salvelinus alpinus* . . . . . . 257
*Salvelinus fontinalis* . . . . . . .
. . . . . . . . . . . . . . . . 254, 256
Sand Dollar . . 20, 250, 356
Sanderling . . . . . . . . 182, 183
*Sarracenia purpurea* . . . 128
Savannah Sparrow 199, 201
Scalloped Owlet . . . . . . 156
  see Herald Moth
Scentbottle . . . . . . . . . . . 132
*Scoliopteryx libatrix* . . . . 156
*Scomber scombrus* . . . . . . 137
*Scophthalmus aquosus* . . 268
Scotch Lovage . . . . . . . 137
Scotch Pine . . . . . . . . . 102
  see Scots Pine
Scots Pine . . . . . . 101, 102
Scud . . . . . . . 238, 239, 355
*Scutellaria galericulata* . 135
*Scytosiphon lomentaria* . . . .
. . . . . . . . . . . . . . . 222, 223
Sea Blubber . . . . . . . . . . 234
  see Lion's Mane
Sea Lettuce . . . . . . . 18, 219
Sea Mat . . . . . . . . . 237, 356
Sea Milkwort . . . . . . . . 138
Sea Peach . . . . . . . . . . . 251
Sea Pigeon . . . . . . . . . . . 180
  see Black Guillemot
Sea Raven . . . . 262, 266, 356
Sea Rocket . . . . . . . . . . . 136
Sea Slug . . . . . . . . . . . . . 245
Sea Star . . . . . 19, 248, 249
  see Boreal Sea Star;
   Northern Sea Star;
   Purple Sea Star;
Sea Thrift . . . . . . . . . . . . 123
Seabeach Ragwort . . . . 139
Seaside Sandwort . . . 137
Seaside Angelica . 137, 152
Seaside Arrowgrass . . . 142
Seaside Crowfoot . . . . 138
Seaside Goldenrod . . . 139
Seaside Plantain . . . . . . 141
Seasnail . . . . . . . . . . . . . 260
  see Atlantic Snailfish
*Sebastes fasciatus* . . . . . 269
*Sebastes marinus* . . . . . 269
*Sebastes mentella* . . . . . 269
Sedge Darner . . . . . . . . 158
*Seiurus noveboracensis* . 198
*Selaginella selaginoides* . 99
Self-Heal . . . . . . . . . . . 147
  see Heal-all
*Semibalanus balanoides* 239
Semipalmated Plover . . 181

Semipalmated Sandpiper
. . . . . . . . . . . . . . . . 182, 183
*Senecio pseudoarnica* . . . 139
Sensitive Fern . . . . . . . . 92
*Setophaga coronata* . . . . 197
*Setophaga magnolia* . . . . 196
*Setophaga petechia* . . . . 196
*Setophaga ruticilla* . . . . 197
*Setophaga striata* . . . . . 197
*Setophaga virens* . . . . . 197
Shaggy Mane . . . . . . . . . 53
Shaggy Scalycap . . . . . . 59
Sharp Bristly Clubmoss 99
Sharp-Shinned Hawk . . 186
Sheep Laurel . . . . . . . . . . .
. . . . . . . . . 22, 28, 29, 32, 126
Shore Periwinkle . . . . . 243
  see Common Periwinkle
Short-Billed Dowitcher
. . . . . . . . . . . . . . . . . . . . 184
Short-Eared Owl . 189, 354
Short-Horned
  Grasshopper . . . . . . . 159
Short-Tailed Swallowtail
. . . . . . . . . . . . . . . . . . . 152
Short-Tailed Weasel . . . . .
. . . . . . . . . . . 23, 210, 313
  see Ermine
Shorthorn Sculpin . . . . . . .
. . . . . . . . . . . . . . 262, 267
Showy Lady's Slipper . . . . .
. . . . . . . . . . . . . . 133, BC
Showy Mountain Ash . . . . .
. . . . . . . . . . . . . . 22, 108
Shrubby Cinquefoil 31, 119
*Sibbaldia tridentata* . . . . 119
Sideswimmer . . . . . . . . 238
  see Scud
*Silene acaulis* . . . . . . . . . 118
Silver-Bordered Fritillary
. . . . . . . . . . . . . . . . . . . 153
Silver-Spotted Anemone
. . . . . . . . . . . . . . . . . . . 235
Silverweed . . . . . . . . . . . 138
Simuliidae Family . . . . . 164
Siricidae Family . . . . . . 165
*Sisyrinchium montanum*
. . . . . . . . . . . . . . . . . . . 146
*Sitta canadensis* . . . . . . 194
Skunk Currant . . . . . . . 115
Slaty-Backed Gull . 317, 320
Slippery Jack . . . . . . . . . 66
Small Cranberry . . . . . . 127
  see Marshberry
*Smerinthus jamaicensis* . 156
Smooth Cladonia, . . . . 79

Smooth Periwinkle  . . . . . .
. . . . . . . . . . . . . . . . . . 243, 356
Smooth Top Shell . . . . . 245
Snow Bunting  . . . . . . . 202
Snowshoe Hare  23, 24, 205,
. . . 207, 211, 212, 311, 313, 353
Snowy Owl . . 189, 344, 357
*Solanum dulcamara*  . . . 147
*Solaster endeca*  . . . . . . . 249
*Solidago multiradiata*  . . 122
*Solidago sempervirens* . . 139
*Solidago uliginosa* . . . . . 129
*Somateria mollissima* . . . 173
*Sonchus asper* . . . . . . . . . 139
Song Sparrow . . . . 200, 201
Sooty Shearwater  . . . . . 175
*Sorbus americana* . . . . . 108
*Sorbus aucuparia* . . . . . 108
*Sorbus decora* . . . . . . . . 108
*Sorbus* spp. . . . . . . . . . 104
*Sorex cinereus* . . . . . . . . 206
Southern Red-Backed
   Vole . . . . . . . . 205, 208, 355
Spear-Marked Black . . . 157
Speckleberry Lichen . . . . 74
Speckled Alder . . . . . . . 107
*Spergularia rubra* . . . . . . 143
*Sphaerophorus globosus* . 71
*Sphagnum girgensohnii* . 87
*Sphagnum* species  . . . . . . . .
. . . . . . 25, 57, 83, 86, 87, 111
Spinulose Wood Fern  . . 95
*Spinulum annotinum* . . 99
*Spinulum canadense*  . . . . .
. . . . . . . . . . . . . . . . 99, 354
*Spinus pinus* . . . . . . . . . 203
*Spinus tristis* . . . . . . . . . 203
Spiral Wrack . . . . . . . . . 226
*Spiranthes romanzoffiana* .
. . . . . . . . . . . . . . . . . . . 143
*Spirorbis borealis* . . . . . 236
Spittlebug . . . . . . . . . . . 160
   *see* Froghopper
*Spizella arborea* . . . . . . 201
*Splachnum ampullaceum*
. . . . . . . . . . . . . . . . . . . . . 87
*Splachnum rubrum* . . . . . 87
Sponge (fossil) . . . 282, 382
*Spongomorpha aeruginosa*
. . . . . . . . . . . . . . . . . . . 220
*Spongomorpha arcta* . . 220
*Spongomorpha* sp, 219, 220
*Spongonema tomentosum*
. . . . . . . . . . . . . . . . . . . 221
Spotted Sandpiper  . . . . 182
Spotted Tussock Moth 156

Spotted Wolffish . 262, 266
Spruce Grouse  24, 187, 354
St. Lawrence Tiger Moth
. . . . . . . . . . . . . . . . . . . . . 157
Staircase Moss . . . . . . . . 85
Star-Tipped Reindeer
   Lichen . . . . . . . . . . . . . 79
Starfish, *see* Sea Star
Starflower  . . . . . . . . . 23, 112
Starry False Solomon's
   Seal . . . . . . . . . . . . . . . 138
*Stellaria graminea* . . . . . 143
*Stereocaulon
   dactylophyllum* . . . . . . . 75
*Sterna hirundo* . . . . . . . . 179
*Sterna paradisaea* . . . . . . 179
Sticky Tofielda . . . . . . . 132
Strand Wheat . . . . . . . . . 142
Stream Mayfly . . . . . . . . 159
Streamside Stippleback
   Lichen . . . . . . . . . . . . . 76
Striped Iceland Lichen . 78
Striped Wolffish . . 266, 357
   *see* Atlantic Wolffish
*Strongylocentrotus
   droebachiensis* . . . . . . . 250
*Sturnus vulgaris* . . . . . . 195
*Suillus grevillei* . . . . . 67, 353
*Suillus ampliporus* var.
   *cavipes* . . . . . . . . . . . 67, 353
*Suillus clintonianus* . . . . . 67
*Suillus luteus* . . . . . . . . 66
Swainson's Thrush . . . . 194
Swallow . . . . . . . . . . 193, 355
   *see* Bank Swallow; Barn
   Swallow; Tree Swallow
Swamp Candle . . . . . . . . 131
Swamp Horsetail . . . . . 100
Swamp Sparrow . . 200, 201
Swallowtail . . . . . . . . . . 152
   *see* Eastern
   Tiger Swallowtail;
   Short-tailed Swallowtail
Swedish Bunchberry . . 123
Sweet Gale . . . . . . . . . . . . . .
. . . . . . 25, 26, 32, 129, 129
*Sympetrum danae* . . . . . 158
*Symphyotrichum
   puniceum* . . . . . . . . . . 115
*Syngnathus fuscus* . . . . . 261
Syrphidae Family  . . . . . 164

**T**

*Tabanus* sp . . . . . . . . . . . . 163
*Tachycineta bicolor* . . . . . 193
Tall Meadow Rue . . . . . . 114

Tamarack . . . . . . . . . . . . . . .
. . . . . . 22, 27, 31, 103, 157, FC
*Tamias striatus* . . . . . . . 208
*Tamiasciurus hudsonicus*
. . . . . . . . . . . . . . . . . . . 207
*Tautogolabrus adspersus*
. . . . . . . . . . . . . . . . . . . 261
Tawny Grisette . . . . . . . . 51
*Taxus canadensis* . . . . . . 103
*Taxus* sp. . . . . . . . . . . . . 101
Tennessee Warbler . . . . . . .
. . . . . . 196, 198, 199, 355
*Testudinalia testudinalis* . . .
. . . . . . . . . . . . . . . . . . . 245
Textured Lungwort . . . . 73
*Thalictrum pubescens* . . 114
*Thamnophis sirtalis* 169, 351
Thayer's Gull . . . . . 317, 320
The Gypsy . . . . . . . . . . . . 55
*Thelypteris noveboracensis*
. . . . . . . . . . . . . . . . . 93, 354
Thick-Billed Murre . . . . . . .
. . . . . . . . . . . . . 179, 180, 354
Thorny Skate . . . . 262, 263
Three-Toothed
   Cinquefoil . . . . . . . . . . 119
Threeleaf False Solomon's
   Seal . . . . . . . . . . . . . . . 125
Threespine Stickleback
. . . . . . . . . . . . 259, 260, 261
*Thymelicus lineola* . . . . . 155
Tiger Beetle . . . . . . . . . . 161
Tinder Fungus . . . . . . . . 62
Tinker . . . . . . . . . . . . . . 180
   *see* Razorbill
Tippler's Bane . . . . . . . . . 53
*Tipula* sp. . . . . . . . . 163, 354
*Tonicella marmorea* . . . 242
*Tonicella rubra* . . . . . . 242
Tortoiseshell Limpet . . . . .
. . . . . . . . . . 19, 245, 356
Trailing Arbutus . . . . . . 113
Tree Swallow . . . . . . . . . 193
Tree Trunk (fossil) . . . . . . . .
. . . . . . . . . . . . . 278, 283, 298
Trembling Aspen . . . . . . . . .
. . . . . . . . 22, 72, 104, 156, 157
*Triantha glutinosa* . . . . . 132
*Trichaptum abietinum* . 64
*Trientalis borealis* . . . . . . 112
*Trifolium arvense* . . . . . . 148
*Trifolium aureum* . . . . . . 148
*Trifolium hybridum* . . . . 148
*Trifolium pratense* . . . . . 148
*Trifolium repens* . . . . . . 147
*Triglochin maritima* . . . 142

Trilobite........278, 279, ........281, 282, 305, 343
Trilobite *Bailiaspis* ... 280
Trilobite *Olenellus*.... 280
*Tringa flavipes* .......184
*Tringa melanoleuca*....184
*Turdus migratorius* ....195
Turr ............ 179, 180
  see Common Murre;
  Thick-Billed Murre
*Tussilago farfara*.......145
Twelve-Scaled Worm.....
...................236, 355
Twin-Spotted Sphinx
  Moth ..............156
Twinflower ...........116
Two-Spotted Ladybug.. 162
*Typha latifolia* ........136
*Tyrannus tyrannus*.....192
*Tyromyces chioneus* . 65, 353

**U**

*Ulota coarctata* ....... 88
*Ulota phyllantha* ...... 88
*Ulothrix flacca* ...218, 219
*Ulva intestinalis* 18, 218, 355
*Ulva lactuca* .......18, 219
*Ulva linza* ............218
*Ulvaria obscura* .......219
*Ulvaria subbifurcata* ...265
*Uria aalge* ............179
*Uria lomvia*.......... 180
*Urophycis tenuis*...... 264
*Urospora penicilliformis* 217
*Urospora* sp. ..........219
*Urospora wormskioldii* .218
*Urticina felina* ........235
*Ursus americanus
  hamiltoni* .........211
*Usnea filipendula* .......71
*Utricularia cornuta* ....128
*Utricularia intermedia*..134
*Utricularia vulgaris* ....134

**V**

*Vaccinium angustifolium*
....................... 120
*Vaccinium oxycoccos* ...127
*Vaccinium uliginosum*. 120
*Vaccinium vitis-idaea*.. 120
*Vanessa atalanta*.......154
*Vanessa cardui* .........155
Varied Rag Lichen..... 74
Variegated Horsetail... 100
*Veronica officinalis*.....117
*Vertebrata lanosa*. 226, 230

*Vertebrata* sp. ........ 229
*Vespula* sp.............165
*Vexillifera* ............ 70
*Viola cucullata* ........135
*Vireo solitarius* ........191
Virginia Ctenucha.....156
Virginia Rose.........114
Vole Ears............ 72, 73
*Vulpes vulpes deletrix*...212

**W**

Water Mosses ........ 84
Western Maidenhair
  Fern .............. 90
Whale 9, 16, 17, 40, 252, 273, .. 274, 275, 342, 351, 353, 357
  see Beluga Whale;
  Blue Whale; Fin Whale;
  Humpback Whale; Killer
  Whale; Long-Finned
  Pilot Whale; Northern
  Minke Whale; Orca
Whimbrel............185
White Admiral........ 155
White Birch ...........
...... 22, 27, 28, 106, 157
White Cheese Polypore .65
White Chiton........ 242
White Clover.........147
White Dotted Prominent
...................157
White Fringed Orchid....
.................26, 125
White Hake ..... 264, 356
White Mountain Avens119
White Pine .............
.........21, 102, 357, 358
White Spruce...........
.........21, 72, 73, 74, 101
White Turtlehead..... 131
White-Crowned Sparrow.
.............24, 200, 201
White-Rumped
  Sandpiper ......182, 183
White-Spotted Sawyer
  Beetle ...........162
White-Throated Sparrow.
.............24, 200, 201
White-Winged Crossbill..
...................202
Wild Chicory.........144
Wild Lily of the Valley ....
.................23, 116
Wild Sarsaparilla......117
Wild Strawberry.......142
*Wildemania miniata* ...231

Willow Ptarmigan ......
.......... 30, 187, 188, 316
Wilson's Snipe ....... 184
Wilson's Warbler . 198, 199
Windowpane Flounder
.................262, 268
Winged Kelp... 18, 19, 225
Winter Flounder .........
.............262, 268, 356
Winter Polypore ...... 64
Winter Skate..... 262, 263
Witch's Hair .......... 70
Witch's Hat ......... 56
Wolffish. 250, 262, 266, 356
  see Atlantic Wolffish;
  Spotted Wolffish;
  Striped Wolffish
Wood Frog... 166, 168, 351
Woodland Caribou. 213, 339
  see Newfoundland
  Caribou
Woodland Horsetail.. 100
Wooly Fringe-Moss ... 86
Wrinkled Shield Lichen 74

**X**

*Xanthoria parietina* .... 76

**Y**

Yarrow...............144
Yellow Birch.............
............72, 73, 74, 106
Yellow Legs ........ 23, 54
Yellow Map Lichen.....77
Yellow Pond Lily ......130
Yellow Rattle .........143
Yellow Warbler .. 196, 199
Yellow-Bellied Flycatcher .
.....................192
Yellow-Legged Gull 317, 320
Yellow-Rumped Warbler
..................197, 199
Yellowtail Flounder ......
..................262, 268

**Z**

*Zenaida macroura* .... 188
*Zoarces americanus* ... 265
*Zonotrichia albicollis*.. 200
*Zonotrichia leucophrys* ....
..................... 200
*Zostera marina* ....215, 217
.......................

FC = front cover
BC = back cover